BILL BRYSON

The COMPLETE NOTES

Also by Bill Bryson

THE LOST CONTINENT

MOTHER TONGUE

NEITHER HERE NOR THERE

MADE IN AMERICA

A WALK IN THE WOODS

DOWN UNDER

BILL BRYSON
The COMPLETE NOTES

NOTES from a SMALL ISLAND

&

NOTES from a BIG COUNTRY

Doubleday

LONDON · NEW YORK · TORONTO · SYDNEY · AUCKLAND

TRANSWORLD PUBLISHERS
61–63 Uxbridge Road, London W5 5SA
A division of The Random House Group Ltd

RANDOM HOUSE AUSTRALIA (PTY) LTD
20 Alfred Street, Milsons Point, Sydney,
New South Wales 2061, Australia

RANDOM HOUSE NEW ZEALAND LTD
18 Poland Road, Glenfield, Auckland 10, New Zealand

RANDOM HOUSE (PTY) LTD
Endulini, 5a Jubilee Road, Parktown 2193, South Africa

Notes from a Small Island first published 1995 by Doubleday
a division of Transworld Publishers
Copyright © Bill Bryson 1995

Notes from a Big Country first published 1998 by Doubleday
a division of Transworld Publishers
Copyright © Bill Bryson 1998

This omnibus edition published 2000

The articles in *Notes from a Big Country* first appeared in the
Mail on Sunday's *Night & Day* magazine between 6 October 1996
and 17 May 1998.

A catalogue record for this book is available
from the British Library.
ISBN 0385 60131X

Typeset in 11/13pt Sabon by Falcon Oast Graphic Art

Printed in Great Britain
by Mackays of Chatham plc, Chatham, Kent

1 3 5 7 9 10 8 6 4 2

NOTES from a SMALL ISLAND

To Cynthia

I am deeply indebted to the following people for assisting me in various selfless ways during the preparation of this book: Peter and Joan Blacklock, Pam and Allen Kingsland, John and Nicky Price, David Cook and Alan Hume. To all of them, thank you.

PROLOGUE

MY FIRST SIGHT OF ENGLAND WAS ON A FOGGY MARCH NIGHT IN 1973 when I arrived on the midnight ferry from Calais. For twenty minutes, the terminal area was aswarm with activity as cars and lorries poured forth, customs people did their duties, and everyone made for the London road. Then abruptly all was silence and I wandered through sleeping, low-lit streets threaded with fog, just like in a Bulldog Drummond movie. It was rather wonderful having an English town all to myself.

The only mildly dismaying thing was that all the hotels and guesthouses appeared to be shut up for the night. I walked as far as the rail station, thinking I'd catch a train to London, but the station, too, was dark and shuttered. I was standing wondering what to do when I noticed a grey light of television filling an upstairs window of a guesthouse across the road. Hooray, I thought, someone awake, and hastened across, planning humble apologies to the kindly owner for the lateness of my arrival and imagining a cheery conversation which included the line, 'Oh, but I couldn't possibly ask you to feed me at this hour. No, honestly – well, if you're *quite* sure it's no trouble, then perhaps just a roast beef sandwich and a large dill pickle with perhaps some potato salad and a bottle of beer.' The front path was pitch dark and in my eagerness and unfamiliarity with British doorways, I tripped on a step, crashing face-first into the door and sending half a dozen empty milk bottles clattering. Almost immediately the upstairs window opened.

'Who's that?' came a sharp voice.

I stepped back, rubbing my nose, and peered up at a silhouette with hair curlers. 'Hello, I'm looking for a room,' I said.

'We're shut.'

'Oh.' But what about my supper?

'Try the Churchill. On the front.'

'On the front of what?' I asked, but the window was already banging closed.

The Churchill was sumptuous and well lit and appeared ready to receive visitors. Through a window I could see people in suits in a bar, looking elegant and suave, like characters from a Noel Coward play. I hesitated in the shadows, feeling like a street urchin. I was socially and sartorially ill-suited for such an establishment and anyway it was clearly beyond my meagre budget. Only the previous day, I had handed over an exceptionally plump wad of colourful francs to a beady-eyed Picardy hotelier in payment for one night in a lumpy bed and a plate of mysterious *chasseur* containing the bones of assorted small animals, much of which had to be secreted away in a large napkin in order not to appear impolite, and had determined thenceforth to be more cautious with expenditures. So I turned reluctantly from the Churchill's beckoning warmth and trudged off into the darkness.

Further along Marine Parade stood a shelter, open to the elements but roofed, and I decided that this was as good as I was going to get. With my backpack for a pillow, I lay down and drew my jacket tight around me. The bench was slatted and hard and studded with big roundheaded bolts that made reclining in comfort an impossibility – doubtless their intention. I lay for a long time listening to the sea washing over the shingle below, and eventually dropped off to a long, cold night of mumbled dreams in which I found myself being pursued over Arctic ice floes by a beady-eyed Frenchman with a catapult, a bag of bolts and an uncanny aim, who thwacked me repeatedly in the buttocks and legs for stealing a linen napkin full of seepy food and leaving it at the back of a dresser drawer of my hotel room. I awoke with a gasp about three, stiff all over and quivering from cold. The fog had gone. The air was now still and clear, and the sky was bright with stars. A beacon from the lighthouse at the far end of the breakwater swept endlessly over the sea. It was all most fetching, but I was far too cold to appreciate it. I dug shiveringly through my backpack and extracted every potentially warming item I could find – a flannel shirt, two sweaters, an extra pair of jeans. I used some woollen socks as mittens and put a pair of flannel boxer shorts on my head as a kind of desperate headwarmer, then sank heavily back onto the bench and waited patiently for death's sweet kiss. Instead, I fell asleep.

I was awakened again by an abrupt bellow of foghorn, which nearly knocked me from my narrow perch, and sat up feeling wretched but fractionally less cold. The world was bathed in that milky pre-dawn light that seems to come from nowhere. Gulls wheeled and cried over the water. Beyond them, past the stone breakwater, a ferry, vast and well lit, slid regally out to sea. I sat there for some time, a young man with more on his mind than in it. Another booming moan from the ship's foghorn passed over the water, re-exciting the irksome gulls. I took off my sock mittens and looked at my watch. It was 5.55 a.m. I looked at the receding ferry and wondered where anybody would be going at that hour. Where would *I* go at that hour? I picked up my backpack and shuffled off down the prom, to get some circulation going.

Near the Churchill, now itself peacefully sleeping, I came across an old guy walking a little dog. The dog was frantically trying to pee on every vertical surface and in consequence wasn't so much walking as being dragged along on three legs.

The man nodded a good-morning as I drew level. 'Might turn out nice,' he announced, gazing hopefully at a sky that looked like a pile of wet towels. I asked him if there was a restaurant anywhere that might be open. He knew of a place not far away and directed me to it. 'Best transport caff in Kent,' he said.

'Transport calf?' I repeated uncertainly, and retreated a couple of paces as I'd noticed his dog was straining desperately to moisten my leg.

'Very popular with the lorry drivers. They always know the best places, don't they?' He smiled amiably, then lowered his voice a fraction and leaned towards me as if about to share a confidence. 'You might want to take them pants off your head before you go in.'

I clutched my head – 'Oh!' – and removed the forgotten boxer shorts with a blush. I tried to think of a succinct explanation, but the man was scanning the sky again.

'Definitely brightening up,' he decided, and dragged his dog off in search of new uprights. I watched them go, then turned and walked off down the promenade as it began to spit with rain.

The café was outstanding – lively and steamy and deliciously warm. I had a platter of eggs, beans, fried bread, bacon and sausage, with a side plate of bread and marge, and two cups of tea, all for 22p. Afterwards, feeling a new man, I emerged with a toothpick and a burp, and sauntered happily through the streets, watching Dover come to life. It must be said that Dover was not vastly improved by daylight, but I liked it. I liked its small scale and cosy air, and the way everyone said 'Good-morning,' and 'Hello,' and 'Dreadful weather – but it might brighten up,' to everyone else, and the sense that this was just one more in a very long series of fundamentally cheerful, well-ordered, pleasantly uneventful days. No-one in the whole of Dover would have any particular reason to remember 21 March 1973, except for me and a handful of children born that day and possibly one old guy with a dog who had encountered a young fellow with underpants on his head.

I didn't know how early one could decently begin asking for a room in England, so I thought I would leave it till mid-morning. With time on my hands, I made a thorough search for a guesthouse that looked attractive and quiet, but friendly and not too expensive, and at the stroke of ten o'clock presented myself on the doorstep of the one I had carefully selected, taking care not to discompose the milk bottles. It was a small hotel that was really a guesthouse, indeed was really a boarding-house.

I don't remember its name, but I well recall the proprietress, a formidable creature of late middle years called Mrs Smegma, who showed me to a room, then gave me a tour of the facilities and out-lined the many complicated rules for residing there – when breakfast was served, how to turn on the heater for the bath, which hours of the day I would have to vacate the premises and during which brief period a bath was permitted (these seemed, oddly, to coincide), how much notice I should give if I intended to receive a phone call or remain out after 10 p.m., how to flush the loo and use the loo brush, which materials were permitted in the bedroom wastebasket and which had to be carefully conveyed to the outside dustbin, where and how to wipe my feet at each point of entry, how to operate the three-bar fire in my bedroom and when that would be permitted (essentially, during an Ice Age). This was all bewilder-ingly new to me. Where I came from, you got a room in a motel, spent ten hours making a lavish and possibly irredeemable mess of it, and left early the next morning. This was like joining the Army.

'The minimum stay,' Mrs Smegma went on, 'is five nights at one pound a night, including full English breakfast.'

'Five nights?' I said in a small gasp. I'd only intended to stay the one. What on earth was I going to do with myself in Dover for five days?

Mrs Smegma arched an eyebrow. 'Were you hoping to stay longer?'

'No,' I said. 'No. As a matter of—'

'Good, because we have a party of Scottish pensioners coming for the weekend and it would have been awkward. Actually, quite impossible.' She surveyed me critically, as she might a carpet stain, and considered if there was anything else she could do to make my life wretched. There was. 'I'm going out shortly, so may I ask that you vacate your room within quarter of an hour?'

I was confused again. 'I'm sorry, you want me to leave? I've just got here.'

'As per the house rules. You may return at four.' She made to depart but then turned back. 'Oh, and do be so good, would you, as to remove your counterpane each night. We've had some unfortunate occurrences with stains. If you do damage the counterpane, I will have to charge you. You do understand, of course?'

I nodded dumbly. And with that she was gone. I stood there, feeling lost and weary and far from home. I'd spent an hysterically uncomfortable night out of doors. My muscles ached, I was dented all over from sleeping on boltheads, and my skin was lightly oiled with the dirt and grit of two nations. I had sustained myself to this point with the thought that soon I would be immersed in a hot, soothing bath, followed by about fourteen hours of deep, peaceful, wallowing sleep, on plump pillows under a downy comforter.

As I stood there absorbing the realization that my nightmare, far from drawing to a close, was only just beginning, the door opened and Mrs Smegma was striding across the room to the strip light above the sink. She had shown me the correct method for turning it on – 'There's no need to yank it. A gentle tug is sufficient' – and evidently remembered that she had left it burning. She turned it off now with what seemed to me a sharp yank, then gave me and the room a final suspicious once-over, and departed again.

When I was sure she was quite gone, I quietly locked the door, drew shut the curtains and had a pee in the sink. I dug a book from my backpack, then stood for a long minute by the door surveying the tidy, unfamiliar contents of my lonely room.

'And just what the fuck is a counterpane?' I wondered in a small, unhappy voice and quietly took my leave.

What a different place Britain was in the spring of 1973. The pound was worth $2.46. Average weekly take-home pay was £30.11. A packet of crisps was 5p, a soft drink 8p, lipstick 45p, chocolate biscuits 12p, an iron £4.50, an electric kettle £7, a black-and-white TV £60, a colour TV £300, a radio £16, the average meal out £1. A scheduled airline ticket from New York to London cost £87.45 in winter, £124.95 in summer. You could have eight days in Tenerife on a Cook's Golden Wings Holiday for £65 or fifteen days from £93. I know all this because before this trip I looked up the issue of *The Times* for 20 March 1973, the day I arrived in Dover, and it contained a full-page advertisement from the Government outlining how much most of these things cost and how they would be affected by a zippy new tax called VAT, which was to be intro-duced a week or so later. The gist of the advert was that while some things would go up in price with VAT, some things would also go down. (Ha!) I also recollect from my own dwindling cerebral resources that it cost 4p to send a postcard to America by air, 13p for a pint of beer, and 30p for the first Penguin book I ever bought (*Billy Liar*). Decimalization had just passed its second anniversary, but people were still converting in their heads – 'Good lord, that's nearly six shillings!' – and you had to know that a sixpence was really worth 2½p and that a guinea was £1.05.

A surprising number of headlines from that week could as easily appear today: 'French air traffic controllers strike', 'White Paper calls for Ulster power sharing', 'Nuclear research laboratory to be closed', 'Storms disrupt rail services' and that old standby of cricket reports, 'England collapse' (this time against Pakistan). But the most arresting thing about the headlines from that dimly remem-bered week in 1973 was how much industrial unrest there was about: 'Strike threat at British Gas Corporation', '2,000 Civil Servants strike', 'No London edition of *Daily Mirror*', '10,000 laid off after Chrysler men walk out', 'Unions plan crippling action for May Day', '12,000 pupils get day off as teachers strike' – all this from a single week. This was to be the year of the OPEC crisis and the effective toppling of the Heath government (though there wouldn't be a general election until the following February). Before the year was out, there would be petrol rationing and mile-long queues at garages all over the country. Inflation would spiral up to

28 per cent. There would be acute shortages of toilet paper, sugar, electricity and coal, among much else. Half the nation would be on strike and the rest would be on three-day weeks. People would shop for Christmas presents in department stores lit by candles and watch in dismay as their television screens went blank after *News at Ten* by order of the Government. It would be the year of the Sunningdale Agreement, the Summerland disaster on the Isle of Man, the controversy over Sikhs and motorcycle helmets, Martina Navratilova's début at Wimbledon. It was the year that Britain entered the Common Market and – it scarcely seems credible now – went to war with Iceland over cod (albeit in a mercifully wimpy, put-down-those-whitefish-or-we-might-just-shoot-across-your-bow sort of way).

It would be, in short, one of the most extraordinary years in modern British history. Of course, I didn't know this on that drizzly March morning in Dover. I didn't know anything really, which is a strangely wonderful position to be in. Everything that lay before me was new and mysterious and exciting in a way you can't imagine. England was full of words I'd never heard before – streaky bacon, short back and sides, Belisha beacon, serviettes, high tea, ice-cream cornet. I didn't know how to pronounce 'scone' or 'pasty' or 'Towcester' or 'Slough'. I had never heard of Tesco's, Perthshire or Denbighshire, council houses, Morecambe and Wise, railway cuttings, Christmas crackers, bank holidays, seaside rock, milk floats, trunk calls, Scotch eggs, Morris Minors and Poppy Day. For all I knew, when a car had an L-plate on the back of it, it indicated that it was being driven by a leper. I didn't have the faintest idea what GPO, LBW, GLC or OAP stood for. I was positively radiant with ignorance. The simplest transactions were a mystery to me. I saw a man in a newsagent's ask for 'twenty Number Six' and receive cigarettes, and presumed for a long time afterwards that everything was ordered by number in a newsagent's, like in a Chinese takeaway. I sat for half an hour in a pub before I realized that you had to fetch your own order, then tried the same thing in a tea-room and was told to sit down.

The tea-room lady called me love. All the shop ladies called me love and most of the men called me mate. I hadn't been here twelve hours and already they loved me. And everyone ate the way I did. This was truly exciting. For years I'd been the despair of my mother because as a left-hander I politely declined to eat the American way – grasping the fork in your left hand to steady the food while cutting, then transferring it to your right hand to lift the food to your mouth. It all seemed ridiculously cumbersome, and here suddenly was a whole country that ate the way I did. And they drove on the left! This was paradise. Before the day was half over, I knew that this was where I wanted to be.

I spent a long day wandering aimlessly and happily along residential streets and shopping streets, eavesdropping on conversations at bus-stops and street corners, looking with interest in the windows of greengrocers and butchers and fishmongers, reading fly-posters and planning applications, quietly absorbing. I climbed up to the castle to admire the view and watch the shuttling ferries, had a respectful look at the white cliffs and Old Town Gaol, and in the late afternoon on an impulse went to a movie, attracted by the prospect of warmth and by a poster depicting an array of scantily clad young ladies in seductive mood.

'Circle or stalls?' said the ticket lady.

'No, *Suburban Wife-Swap*,' I answered in a confused and furtive voice.

Inside, another new world opened for me. I saw my first cinema adverts, my first trailers presented in a British accent, my first British Board of Film Censors certificate ('This movie has been passed as suitable for Adults by Lord Harlech, who enjoyed it very much'), and discovered, to my small delight, that smoking was permitted in British cinemas and to hell with the fire risks. The film itself provided a rich fund of social and lexical information, as well as the welcome opportunity to rest my steaming feet and see a lot of attractive young women disporting in the altogether. Among the many terms new to me were 'dirty weekend', 'loo', 'complete pillock', 'au pair', 'semi-detached house', 'shirt-lifter' and 'swift shag against the cooker', all of which have proved variously useful since. During the interval – another exciting new development for me – I had my first Kia-Ora, purchased from a monumentally bored young lady who had the remarkable ability to pull fifteen selected items from her illuminated tray and make change without ever removing her gaze from an imaginary spot in the middle distance. Afterwards I dined at a small Italian restaurant recommended by Pearl and Dean and returned contentedly to the guesthouse as night stole over Dover. It was altogether a thoroughly satisfying and illuminating day.

I'd intended to turn in early, but on the way to my room I noticed a door marked RESIDENTS' LOUNGE and put my head in. It was a large parlour, with easy chairs and a settee, all with starched anti-macassars; a bookcase with a modest selection of jigsaw puzzles and paperback books; an occasional table with some well-thumbed magazines; and a large colour television. I switched on the TV and looked through the magazines while I waited for it to warm up. They were all women's magazines, but they weren't like the magazines my mother and sister read. The articles in my mother's and sister's magazines were always about sex and personal gratification. They had titles like 'Eat Your Way to Multiple Orgasms', 'Office Sex – How to Get It', 'Tahiti: The Hot New Place for Sex' and 'Those Shrinking Rainforests – Are They Any Good for Sex?' The British magazines addressed more modest aspirations. They had titles like 'Knit Your Own Twinset', 'Money-Saving Button Offer', 'Make This Super Knitted Soap-Saver' and 'Summer's Here – It's Time for Mayonnaise!'

The programme that unfolded on the television was called *Jason King*. If you're of a certain age and lacked a social life on Friday evenings in the early Seventies, you may recall that it involved a ridiculous rake in a poofy kaftan whom women unaccountably appeared to find alluring. I couldn't decide whether to take hope from this or be depressed by it. The most remarkable thing about the programme was that, though I saw it only once more than twenty years ago, I have never lost the desire to work the fellow over with a baseball bat studded with nails.

Towards the end of the programme another resident came in, carrying a bowl of steaming water and a towel. He said, 'Oh!' in surprise when he saw me and took a seat by the window. He was thin and red-faced and filled the room with a smell of liniment. He looked like someone with unhealthy sexual ambitions, the sort of person your PE teacher warned that you would turn into if you masturbated too extravagantly (someone, in short, like your PE teacher). I couldn't be sure, but I would almost have sworn that I had seen him buying a packet of fruit gums at *Suburban Wife-Swap* that afternoon. He looked stealthily at me, possibly thinking something along the same lines, then covered his head with the towel and lowered his face to the bowl, where it remained for much of the rest of the evening.

A few minutes later a bald-headed, middle-aged guy – a shoe salesman, I would have guessed – came in, said, 'Hullo!' to me and 'Evening, Richard,' to the towelled head and took a seat beside me. Shortly after that we were joined by an older man with a walking-stick, a dicky leg and a gruff manner. He looked darkly at us all, nodded the most tinily precise of acknowledgements, and fell heavily into his seat, where he spent the next twenty minutes manoeuvring his leg this way and that, as if positioning a heavy piece of furniture. I gathered that these people were all long-term residents.

A sitcom came on called *My Neighbour is a Darkie*. I suppose that wasn't its actual title, but that was the gist of it – that there was something richly comic in the notion of having black people living next door. It was full of lines like 'Good lord, Gran, there's a coloured chappie in your cupboard!' and 'Well, I couldn't see him in the *dark*, could I?' It was hopelessly moronic. The bald-headed guy beside me laughed until he was wiping tears from his eyes, and from under the towel there came occasional snorts of amusement, but the colonel, I noticed, never laughed. He simply stared at me, as if trying to remember what dark event from his past I was associated with. Every time I looked over, his eyes were fixed on me. It was unnerving.

A starburst briefly filled the screen, indicating an interval of adverts, which the bald-headed man used to quiz me in a friendly but confusingly disconnected way as to who I was and how I had fallen into their lives. He was delighted to find that I was American. 'I've always wanted to see America,' he said. 'Tell me, do you have Woolworth's there?'

'Well, actually, Woolworth's is American.'

'You don't say!' he said. 'Did you hear that, Colonel? Woolworth's is American.' The colonel seemed unmoved by this intelligence. 'And what about cornflakes?'

'I beg your pardon?'

'Do you have cornflakes in America?'

'Well, actually, they're American, too.'

'Never!'

I smiled weakly, and begged my legs to stand me up and take me out of there, but my lower body seemed oddly inert.

'Fancy! So what brings you to Britain then if you have cornflakes already?'

I looked at him to see if the question was serious, then embarked reluctantly and falteringly on a brief résumé of my life to that point, but after a moment I realized that the programme had restarted and he wasn't even pretending to listen, so I tailed off, and instead spent the whole of part two absorbing the heat of the colonel's glare.

When the programme finished, I was about to hoist myself from the chair and bid this happy trio a warm adieu when the door opened and Mrs Smegma came in with a tray of tea things and a plate of biscuits of the sort that I believe are called teatime variety, and everyone stirred friskily to life, rubbing their hands keenly and saying, 'Ooh, lovely.' To this day, I remain impressed by the ability of Britons of all ages and social backgrounds to get genuinely excited by the prospect of a hot beverage.

'And how was *World of Birds* tonight, Colonel?' asked Mrs Smegma as she handed the colonel a cup of tea and a biscuit.

'Couldn't say,' said the colonel archly. 'The television –' he smacked me in the side of the head with a meaningful look '– was tuned to the other side.' Mrs Smegma gave me a sharp look, too, in sympathy. I think they were sleeping together.

'*World of Birds* is the colonel's favourite,' she said to me in a tone that went some distance past hate, and handed me a cup of tea with a hard whitish biscuit.

I mewed some pitiful apology.

'It was puffins tonight,' blurted the red-faced fellow, looking very pleased with himself.

Mrs Smegma stared at him for a moment as if surprised to find that he had the power of speech. 'Puffins!' she said and gave me a still more withering expression that asked how anyone could be so lacking in fundamental human decency. 'The colonel adores puffins. Don't you, Arthur?' She was definitely sleeping with him.

'I do rather,' said the colonel, biting unhappily into a chocolate bourbon.

In shame, I sipped my tea and nibbled at my biscuit. I had never had tea with milk in it before or a biscuit of such rocklike cheer-lessness. It tasted like something you would give a budgie to strengthen its beak. After a minute the bald-headed guy leaned close to me and in a confiding whisper said, 'You mustn't mind the colonel. He hasn't been the same since he lost his leg.'

'Well, I hope for his sake he soon finds it,' I replied, hazarding a little sarcasm. The bald-headed guy guffawed at this and for one terrifying moment I thought he was going to share my little quip with the colonel and Mrs Smegma, but instead he thrust a meaty hand at me and introduced himself. I don't remember his name now, but it was one of those names that only English people have – Colin Crapspray or Bertram Pantyshield or something similarly improbable. I gave a crooked smile, thinking he must be pulling my leg, and said, 'You're kidding.'

'Not at all,' he replied coldly. 'Why, do you find it amusing?'

'It's just that it's kind of . . . unusual.'

'Well, *you* may think so,' he said and turned his attention to the colonel and Mrs Smegma, and I realized that I was now, and would doubtless forever remain, friendless in Dover.

Over the next two days, Mrs Smegma persecuted me mercilessly, while the others, I suspected, scouted evidence for her. She reproached me for not turning the light off in my room when I went out, for not putting the lid down in the toilet when I'd finished, for taking the colonel's hot water – I'd no idea he had his own until he started rattling the doorknob and making aggrieved noises in the corridor – for ordering the full English breakfast two days running and then leaving the fried tomato both times. 'I see you've left the fried tomato again,' she said on the second occasion. I didn't know quite what to say to this as it was incontestably true, so I simply furrowed my brow and joined her in staring at the offending item. I had actually been wondering for two days what it was. 'May I request,' she said in a voice heavy with pain and years of irritation, 'that in future if you don't require a fried tomato with your breakfast that you would be good enough to tell me.'

Abashed, I watched her go. 'I thought it was a blood clot!' I wanted to yell after her, but of course I said nothing and merely skulked from the room to the triumphant beams of my fellow residents.

After that, I stayed out of the house as much as I could. I went to the library and looked up 'counterpane' in a dictionary so that I might at least escape censure on that score. (I was astonished to find out what it was; for three days I'd been fiddling with the window.) Within the house, I tried to remain silent and inconspicuous. I even turned over quietly in my creaking bed. But no matter how hard I tried, I seemed fated to annoy. On the third afternoon as I crept in Mrs Smegma confronted me in the hallway with an empty cigarette packet, and demanded to know if it was I who had thrust it in the privet hedge. I began to understand why innocent people sign extravagant confessions in police stations. That evening, I forgot to turn off the water heater after a quick and stealthy bath and compounded the error by leaving strands of hair in the plughole. The next morning came the final humiliation. Mrs

Smegma marched me wordlessly to the toilet and showed me a little turd that had not flushed away. We agreed that I should leave after breakfast.

I caught a fast train to London, and had not been back to Dover since.

CHAPTER ONE

THERE ARE CERTAIN IDIOSYNCRATIC NOTIONS THAT YOU QUIETLY COME to accept when you live for a long time in Britain. One is that British summers used to be longer and sunnier. Another is that the England football team shouldn't have any trouble with Norway. A third is the idea that Britain is a big place. This last is easily the most intractable.

If you mention in the pub that you intend to drive from, say, Surrey to Cornwall, a distance that most Americans would happily go to get a taco, your companions will puff their cheeks, look knowingly at each other, and blow out air as if to say, 'Well, now *that's* a bit of a tall order,' and then they'll launch into a lively and protracted discussion of whether it's better to take the A30 to Stockbridge and then the A303 to Ilchester or the A361 to Glastonbury via Shepton Mallet. Within minutes the conversation will plunge off into a level of detail that leaves you, as a foreigner, swivelling your head in quiet wonderment.

'You know that layby outside Warminster, the one with the grit box with the broken handle?' one of them will say. '*You* know, just past the turnoff for Little Puking but before the B6029 mini-roundabout. By the dead sycamore.'

At this point, you find you are the only person in the group not nodding vigorously.

'Well, about a quarter of a mile past there, not the first left turning, but the second one, there's a lane between two hedgerows – they're mostly hawthorn but with a little hazel mixed in. Well, if you follow that road past the reservoir and under the railway bridge, and take a sharp right at the Buggered Ploughman –'

'Nice little pub,' somebody will interject – usually, for some reason, a guy in a bulky cardigan. 'They do a decent pint of Old Toejam.'

'– and follow the dirt track through the army firing range and round the back of the cement works, it drops down onto the B3689 Ram's Dropping bypass. It saves a good three or four minutes and cuts out the rail crossing at Great Shagging.'

'Unless, of course, you're coming from Crewkerne,' someone else will add eagerly. 'Now, if you're coming from Crewkerne. . .'

Give two or more men in a pub the names of any two places in Britain and they can happily fill hours. Wherever it is you want to go, the consensus is generally that it's just about possible as long as you scrupulously avoid Okehampton, the Hanger Lane gyratory system, central Oxford and the Severn Bridge westbound between the hours of 3 p.m. on Fridays and 10 a.m. on Mondays, except bank holidays when you shouldn't go anywhere at all. 'Me, I don't even walk to the corner shop on bank holidays,' some little guy on the margins will chirp up proudly, as if by staying at home in Staines he has for years cannily avoided a notorious bottleneck at Scotch Corner.

Eventually, when the intricacies of B-roads, contraflow blackspots and good places to get a bacon sandwich have been discussed so thoroughly that your ears have begun to seep blood, one member of the party will turn to you and idly ask over a sip of beer when you were thinking of setting off. When this happens, you must never answer truthfully and say, in that kind of dopey way of yours, 'Oh, I don't know, about ten, I suppose,' because they'll all be off again.

'Ten o'clock?' one of them will say and try to back his head off his shoulders. 'As in ten o'clock *a*.m.?' He'll make a face like someone who's taken a cricket ball in the scrotum but doesn't want to appear wimpy because his girlfriend is watching. 'Well, it's entirely up to you, *of course*, but personally if *I* was planning to be in Cornwall by three o'clock tomorrow, I'd have left yesterday.'

'*Yesterday?*' someone else will say, chortling softly at this misplaced optimism. 'I think you're forgetting, Colin, that it's half-term in North Wiltshire and West Somerset this week. It'll be murder between Swindon and Warminster. No, you want to have left a week last Tuesday.'

'And there's the Great West Steam Rally at Little Dribbling this weekend,' somebody from across the room will add, strolling over to join you because it's always pleasant to bring bad motoring news. 'There'll be 375,000 cars all converging on the Little Chef roundabout at Upton Dupton. We once spent eleven days in a tail-back there, and that was just to get out of the car park. No, you want to have left when you were still in your mother's womb, or preferably while you were spermatozoa, and even then you won't find a parking space beyond Bodmin.'

Once, when I was younger, I took all these alarming warnings to heart. I went home, reset the alarm clock, roused the family at four, to protests and general consternation, and had everyone bundled into the car and on the road by five. As a result, we were in Newquay in time for breakfast and had to wait around for seven hours before the holiday park would let us have one of their wretched chalets. And the worst of it was that I'd only agreed to go there because I thought the town was called Nookie and I wanted to stock up on postcards.

The fact is that the British have a totally private sense of distance. This is most visibly seen in the shared pretence that Britain is a lonely island in the middle of an empty green sea. Oh, yes, I know you are all aware, in an abstract sort of way, that there is a sub-stantial landmass called Europe near by and that from time to time it is necessary to go over there to give old Jerry a drubbing or have a holiday on the Med, but it's not near by in any meaningful sense in the way that, say, Disney World is. If your concept of world geography was shaped entirely by what you read in the papers and saw on television, you would have no choice but to conclude that America must be about where Ireland is, that France and Germany lie roughly alongside the Azores, that Australia occupies a hot zone somewhere in the region of the Middle East, and that pretty much all the other sovereign states are either mythical (viz., Burundi, El Salvador, Mongolia and Bhutan) or can only be reached by space-ship. Consider how much news space in Britain is devoted to marginal American figures like Oliver North, Lorena Bobbitt, and O.J. Simpson – a man who played a sport that most Britons don't understand and then made commercials for rental cars and that was it – and compare that with *all* the news reported in any year from Scandinavia, Austria, Switzerland, Greece, Portugal and Spain. It's crazy really. If there's a political crisis in Italy or a nuclear spill in Karlsruhe, it gets maybe eight inches on an inside page. But if some woman in Shitkicker, West Virginia, cuts off her husband's dick and flings it out the window in a fit of pique, it's second lead on the *9 O'clock News* and *The Sunday Times* is mobilizing the 'Insight' team. You figure it.

I can remember, after I had been living about a year in Bournemouth and bought my first car, fiddling with the car radio and being astounded at how many of the stations it picked up were in French, then looking at a map and being even more astounded to realize that I was closer to Cherbourg than I was to London. I mentioned this at work the next day and most of my colleagues refused to believe it. Even when I showed them on a map, they frowned doubtfully and said things like, 'Well, yes, it may be closer in a strict *physical* sense,' as if I were splitting hairs and that really a whole new concept of distance was required once you waded into the English Channel – and of course to that extent they were right. Even now, I am frequently dumbfounded to realize that you can get on an airplane in London and in less time than it takes to get the foil lid off the little container of UHT milk and its contents distributed all over yourself and the man next to you (and it's amazing, isn't it, how much milk one of those little tubs holds?), you're in Paris or Brussels and everyone looks like Yves Montand or Jeanne Moreau.

I mention this because I was experiencing much the same sort of sense of wonderment as I stood on a dirty beach at Calais, on an unusually bright, clear autumn afternoon, staring at an outcrop on the horizon that was clearly and sunnily the White Cliffs of Dover. I knew, in a theoretical sort of way, that England was only a spit over 20 miles off, but I couldn't quite believe that I could stand on a foreign beach and actually *see* it. I was so astonished, in fact, that I sought confirmation from a man trudging past in reflective mood.

'*Excusez-moi, monsieur,*' I enquired in my best French. '*C'est Angleterre* over there?'

He looked up from his thoughts to where I was pointing, gave a deeply gloomy nod as if to say, 'Alas, yes,' and trudged on.

'Well, fancy,' I murmured and went to see the town.

Calais is an interesting place that exists solely for the purpose of giving English people in shell suits somewhere to go for the day. Because it was heavily bombed in the war, it fell into the hands of post-war town planners and in consequence looks like something left over from a 1957 *Exposition du Cément*. An alarming number of structures in the centre, particularly around the cheerless Place d'Armes, seem to have been modelled on supermarket packaging, primarily packets of Jacob's Cream Crackers. A few structures are even built across roads – always a sign of 1950s planners smitten with the novel possibilities of concrete. One of the main buildings in the centre, it almost goes without saying, is a Holiday Inn/ cornflakes box.

But I didn't mind. The sun was shining in a kindly Indian summer way and this was France and I was in that happy frame of mind that always comes with the start of a long trip and the giddy prospect of spending weeks and weeks doing nothing much and calling it work. My wife and I had recently taken the decision to move back to the States for a bit, to give the kids the chance of experiencing life in another country and my wife the chance to shop until 10 p.m. seven nights a week. I had recently read that 3.7 million Americans, according to a Gallup poll, believed that they had been abducted by aliens at one time or another, so it was clear that my people needed me. But I had insisted on having one last look at Britain – a kind of valedictory tour round the green and kindly island that had so long been my home. I had come to Calais because I wanted to re-enter England as I'd first seen it, from the sea. Tomorrow I would catch an early ferry and begin the serious business of investigating Britain, examining the nation's public face and private parts, as it were, but today I was carefree and un-attached. I had nothing to do but please myself.

I was disappointed to note that nobody on the streets of Calais looked like Yves Montand or Jeanne Moreau or even the delightful Philippe Noiret. This was because they were all Britons dressed in sportswear. They all looked as if they should have whistles around their necks and be carrying footballs. Instead, they were lugging heavy carrier-bags of clinking bottles and noisome cheeses and wondering why they had bought the cheese and what they were going to do with themselves until it was time to catch the four o'clock ferry home. You could hear them bickering in small, unhappy voices as they passed. 'Sixty francs for a packet of bloody goat's cheese? Well, she won't thank you for *that*.' They all looked as if they ached for a nice cup of tea and some real food. It occurred to me that you could make a small fortune with a hamburger stand. You could call it Burgers of Calais.

It must be said that apart from shopping and bickering quietly there isn't a great deal to do in Calais. There's the famous Rodin statue outside the Hotel de Ville and a single museum, the Musée des Beaux-Arts et de la Dentelle ('The Museum of Beautiful Art and of the Teeth', if my French hasn't abandoned me), but the museum was closed and the Hotel de Ville was a long slog – and anyway the Rodin statue is on every postcard. I ended up, like everyone else, nosing around the souvenir shops, of which Calais has a certain amplitude.

For reasons that I have never understood, the French have a particular genius when it comes to tacky religious keepsakes, and in a gloomy shop on a corner of the Place d'Armes, I found one I liked: a plastic model of the Virgin Mary standing with beckoning arms in a kind of grotto fashioned from seashells, miniature starfish, lacy sprigs of dried seaweed and a polished lobster claw. Glued to the back of the Madonna's head was a halo made from a plastic curtain ring, and on the lobster claw the model's gifted creator had painted an oddly festive-looking '*Calais!*' in neat script. I hesitated because it cost a lot of money, but when the lady of the shop showed me that it also plugged in and lit up like a funfair ride at Margate, the only question in my mind was whether one would be enough.

'*C'est très jolie*,' she said in a kind of astonished hush when she realized that I was prepared to pay real money for it, and bustled off to get it wrapped and paid for before I came to my senses and cried, 'Say, where am I? And what, pray, is *this* tacky piece of Franco-merde I see before me?'

'*C'est très jolie*,' she kept repeating soothingly, as if afraid of disturbing my wakeful slumber. I think it may have been some time since she had sold a Virgin-Mary-with-Seashells Occasional Light. In any case, as the shop door shut behind me, I distinctly heard a whoop of joy.

Afterwards, to celebrate, I called in for a coffee at a popular café on the rue de Gaston Papin et Autres Dignitaires Obscures. Indoors, Calais seemed much more agreeably Gallic. People greeted each other with two-cheeked kisses and wreathed themselves in blue smoke from Gauloises and Gitanes. An elegant woman in black across the room looked uncannily like Jeanne Moreau having a quick fag and a Pernod before playing a funeral scene in a movie called *La Vie Drearieuse*. I wrote a postcard home and enjoyed my coffee, then passed the hours before dusk waving in a friendly but futile way at the bustling waiter in the hope of coaxing him back to my table to settle my modest account.

I dined cheaply and astonishingly well at a little place across the road – there is this to be said for the French: they can make chips – drank two bottles of Stella Artois in a café, where I was served by a Philippe Noiret lookalike in a slaughterhouse apron, and retired early to my modest hotel room, where I played with my seashell Madonna for a bit, then got into bed and passed the night listening to cars crashing in the street below.

In the morning, I breakfasted early, settled my bill with Gérard Depardieu – now there was a surprise – and stepped out to another promising day. Clutching an inadequate little map that came with my ferry ticket, I set off in search of the ferry terminus. On the map it looked to be quite near by, practically in the town centre, but in reality it was a good two miles away at the far end of a bewildering wasteland of oil refineries, derelict factories, and acres of waste ground strewn with old girders and piles of jagged concrete. I found myself squeezing through holes in chainlink fences and picking my way between rusting railway carriages with broken windows. I don't know how other people get to the ferry at Calais, but I had the distinct feeling that no-one had ever done it this way before. And all the while I walked I was uncomfortably aware – actually in a whimpering panic – that departure time was drawing nigh and that the ferry terminus, though always visible, never seemed to get any closer.

Eventually, after dodging across a dual carriageway and clambering up an embankment, I arrived breathless and late and looking like someone who'd just survived a mining disaster, and was hustled aboard a shuttle bus by an officious woman with a serious case of dysmenorrhoea. On the way, I took stock of my possessions and discovered with quiet dismay that my beloved and costly Madonna had lost her halo and was shedding seashells.

I boarded the ship perspiring freely and with a certain disquiet. I'm not a good sailor, I freely admit. I get sick on pedalos. Nor was I helped by the fact that this was one of those Ro-Ro ferries (short for roll on, roll over) and that I was entrusting my life to a company that had a significantly less than flawless record when it came to remembering to shut the bow doors, the nautical equivalent of forgetting to take off your shoes before getting into the bath.

The boat was chock-a-block with people, all of them English. I spent the first quarter of an hour wandering around wondering how they had got there without getting filthy, inserted myself briefly into the shell-suited mayhem that was the duty-free shop and as quickly found my way out again, strolled around the cafeteria with a tray looking at the food and then put the tray back (there was a queue for this), searched for a seat among hordes of dementedly lively children, and finally found my way out onto the breezy deck where 274 people with blue lips and dancing hair were trying to convince themselves that because the sun was shining they couldn't possibly be cold. The wind whipped our anoraks with a sound like gunshot, scooted small children along the deck and, to everyone's private gratification, tipped a styrofoam cup of tea onto a fat lady's lap.

Before long, the White Cliffs of Dover rose from the sea and began creeping towards us and in no time at all, it seemed, we were sailing into Dover Harbour and clumsily nuzzling up to the dock. As a disembodied voice instructed foot passengers to assemble at the starboard egress point on Deck ZX-2 by the Sunshine Lounge – as if that meant anything to anybody – we all embarked on long, befuddled, highly individual explorations of the ship: up and down stairways, through the cafeteria and club-class lounge, in and out of storerooms, through a kitchen full of toiling lascars, back through the cafeteria from another angle, and finally – without knowing quite how – out into the welcoming, watery sunshine of England.

I was eager to see Dover again after all these years. I strode into the centre along Marine Parade and with a small cry of pleasure spied the shelter I'd slept in those many years ago. It was covered in about eleven more layers of bile-green paint but otherwise unchanged. The view out to sea was likewise unchanged, though the water was bluer and more glittery than when I'd last seen it. But everything else looked different. Where I recalled there being a row of elegant Georgian terraces there was now a vast and unbecoming brick apartment block. Townwall Street, the main through road to the west, was wider and more menacing with traffic than I remembered, and there was now a subway to the town centre, which itself was unrecognizable.

The main shopping street had been pedestrianized and the Market Square had been turned into a kind of piazza with show-off paving and the usual array of cast-iron trimmings. The whole town centre seemed uncomfortably squeezed by busy, wide relief roads of which I had no recollection and there was now a big tourist edifice called the White Cliffs Experience, where, I presume from the name, you can discover what it feels like to be 800-million-year-old chalk. I didn't recognize anything. The trouble with English towns is that they are so indistinguishable one from another. They all have a Boots and W.H. Smith and Marks & Spencer. You could be anywhere really.

I plodded distractedly through the streets, unhappy that a place so central to my memories was so unfamiliar. Then, on my third grumbling pass through the town centre, on a lane I would swear I had never walked before, I came across the cinema, still recognizable as the home of *Suburban Wife-Swap* despite a heavy patina of arty refurbishment, and everything suddenly became clear. Now that I had a fixed point of reference, I knew precisely where I was. I strode purposefully 500 yards north and then west – now I could almost have done it blindfolded – and found myself square in front of Mrs Smegma's establishment. It was still a hotel and looked substantially unchanged, as far as I could remember, except for the addition of some hardstanding in the front garden and a plastic sign announcing colour TVs and *en suite* bathrooms. I thought about knocking at the door, but there didn't seem much point. The dragonlike Mrs Smegma must be long since gone – retired or dead or perhaps resident in one of the many nursing homes that crowd the south coast. She couldn't possibly have coped with the modern age of British guesthouses, with their *en suite* bathrooms and coffee-making facilities and people having pizzas delivered to their rooms.

If she is in a nursing home, which would certainly be my first choice, I do hope the staff have the compassion and good sense to scold her frequently for dribbling on the toilet seat, leaving her breakfast unfinished and generally being helpless and tiresome. It would do so much to make her feel at home.

Cheered by this thought, I strolled up the Folkestone Road to the rail station and bought a ticket for the next train to London.

CHAPTER TWO

GOODNESS ME, BUT ISN'T LONDON BIG? IT SEEMS TO START ABOUT twenty minutes after you leave Dover and just goes on and on, mile after mile of endless grey suburbs with their wandering ranks of terraced houses and stuccoed semis that always look more or less identical from a train, as if they've been squeezed out of a very large version of one of those machines they use to make sausages. How, I always wonder, do all the millions of occupants find their way back to the right boxes each night in such a complex and anonymous sprawl?

I'm sure I couldn't. London remains a vast and exhilarating mystery to me. I lived and worked in or around it for eight years, watched London news on television, read the evening papers, ranged extensively through its streets to attend weddings and retirement parties or go on hare-brained quests for bargains in far-flung breakers' yards, and still I find that there are great fragments of it that I have not just never visited but never heard of. It constantly amazes me to read the *Evening Standard* or chat with an acquaintance and encounter some reference to a district that has managed to elude my ken for twenty-one years. 'We've just bought a little place in Fag End, near Tungsten Heath,' somebody will say and I'll think, I've never even *heard* of that. How can this possibly be?

I had stuck a *London A–Z* in my rucksack and came across it now while searching unsuccessfully for half a Mars bar I was sure was in there. Plucking it out, I idly leafed through its busy pages, as ever amazed and quietly excited to find it peppered with districts,

villages, sometimes small swallowed cities whose names, I would
swear, had not been there the last time I looked – Dudden Hill,
Plashet, Snaresbrook, Fulwell Cross, Elthorne Heights, Higham
Hill, Lessness Heath, Beacontree Heath, Bell Green, Vale of Health.
And the thing is, I know that the next time I look there will be
other, different names. It is as deep a mystery to me as the lost
tablets of Titianca or the continuing appeal to millions of Noel
Edmonds.

I have the greatest admiration for the A–Z and the way it scrupulously fixes and identifies every cricket ground and sewage works,
every forgotten cemetery and wandering suburban close, and packs
the densest names on to the tiniest, obscurest spaces. I flipped to the
index and, for want of anything better to do, absorbed myself
there. I calculated that there are 45,687 street names in London
(give or take), including 21 Gloucester Roads (as well as a generous
slew of Gloucester Crescents, Squares, Avenues and Closes), 32
Mayfields, 35 Cavendishes, 66 Orchards, 74 Victorias, 111 Station
Roads or similar, 159 Churches, 25 Avenue Roads, 35 The
Avenues, and other multiples without number. There are, however,
surprisingly few really interesting sounding places. There are a few
streets that sound like medical complaints (Glyceina Avenue,
Shingles Lane, Burnfoot Avenue), a few that sound like names on
an anatomical chart (Thyrapia and Pendula Roads), a few that
sound vaguely unsavoury (Cold Blow Lane, Droop Street, Gutter
Lane, Dicey Avenue), and a few that are pleasingly ridiculous
(Coldbath Square, Glimpsing Green, Hamshades Close, Cactus
Walk, Nutter Lane, The Butts), but there is very little that could be
called truly arresting. I read once that in Elizabethan times there
was a Gropecunt Lane somewhere in the City, but evidently no
longer. I spent half an hour amusing myself in this way, pleased to
be entering a metropolis of such dazzling and unknowable complexity, and had the bonus pleasure, when I returned the book to
the bag, of finding the half-eaten Mars bar, its leading edge covered
in a small festival of lint, which didn't do a great deal for the
flavour but did add some useful bulk.

Victoria Station was swarming with the usual complement of
lost-looking tourists, lurking touts and passed-out drunks. I can't
remember the last time I saw anyone at Victoria who looked like he
was there to catch a train. On my way out, three separate people
enquired whether I had any spare change – 'No, but thank you for
asking!' – which wouldn't have happened twenty years ago. Then,

not only were panhandlers something of a novelty but they always had a good story about having lost their wallet and desperately needing £2 to get to Maidstone to donate bone marrow to their kid sister or something, but now they just flatly ask for money, which is quicker but less interesting.

I took a cab to Hazlitt's Hotel on Frith Street. I like Hazlitt's because it's intentionally obscure – it doesn't even have a sign out front – which puts you in a rare position of strength with your cab driver. Let me say right now that London cab drivers are, without question, the finest in the world. They're trustworthy, safe, generally friendly, always polite. They keep their vehicles spotless inside and out, and they will put themselves to the most extra-ordinary inconvenience to drop you at the front entrance of your destination. There are really only two odd things about them. One is that they cannot drive more than 200 feet in a straight line. I've never understood this, but no matter where you are or what the driving conditions, every 200 feet a little bell goes off in their heads and they abruptly lunge down a side-street. And when you get to your hotel or railway station or wherever it is you are going, they like to drive you all the way around it at least once so that you can see it from all angles before alighting.

The other distinctive thing about them, and the reason I like to go to Hazlitt's, is that they cannot bear to admit that they don't know the location of something they feel they ought to know, like a hotel. They would sooner entrust their teenaged daughters to Alan Clark for a weekend than concede even fractional ignorance of The Knowledge, which I think is rather sweet. So what they do instead is probe. They drive for a bit, then glance at you in the mirror and in an over-casual voice say, 'Hazlitt's – that's the one on Curzon Street, innit, guv? Opposite the Blue Lion?' But the instant they see a knowing smile of demurral forming on your lips, they hastily say, 'No, hang on a minute, I'm thinking of the Hazelbury. Yeah, the Hazelbury. You want *Hazlitt's*, right?' He'll drive on a bit in a fairly random direction. 'That's this side of Shepherd's Bush, innit?' he'll suggest speculatively.

When you tell him that it's on Frith Street, he says, 'Yeah, that's the one. Course it is. I know it – modern place, lots of glass.'

'Actually, it's an eighteenth-century brick building.'

'Course it is. I know it.' And he immediately executes a dramatic U-turn, causing a passing cyclist to steer into a lamppost (but that's all right because he has on cycle clips and one of those geeky slipstream helmets that all but invite you to knock him over). 'Yeah, you had me thinking of the Hazelbury,' the driver adds, chuckling as if to say it's a lucky thing he sorted that one out for you, and then lunges down a little side-street off the Strand called Running Sore Lane or Sphincter Passage, which, like so much else in London, you had never noticed was there before.

Hazlitt's is a nice hotel, but the thing I like about it is that it doesn't act like a hotel. It's been there for years, and the staff are friendly – always a novelty in a big city hotel – but they do manage to give the *slight* impression that they haven't been doing this for very long. Tell them that you have a reservation and want to check in and they get a kind of panicked look and begin a perplexed search through drawers for registration cards and room keys. It's really quite charming. And the delightful girls who clean the rooms – which, let me say, are always spotless and exceedingly comfortable – seldom seem to have what might be called a total command of English, so that when you ask them for a bar of soap or something, you see that they are watching your mouth closely and then, pretty generally, they return after a bit with a hopeful look bearing a pot plant or a commode or something that is manifestly not soap. It's a wonderful place. I wouldn't go anywhere else.

It's called Hazlitt's because it was the home of the essayist, and all the bedrooms are named after his chums or women he shagged there or something. I confess that my mental note card for the old boy is a trifle sketchy. It reads:

> Hazlitt (sp?), William (?), English (poss. Scottish?) essayist.
> Lived: before 1900. Most famous work: don't know. Quips,
> epigrams, bons mots: don't know. Other useful inform-
> ation: his house is now a hotel.

As always, I resolved to read up on Hazlitt some time to correct this gap in my knowledge and, as always, immediately forgot it. Instead, I dropped my rucksack on the bed, extracted a small note-book and a pen, and hit the streets in a spirit of enquiry and boyish keenness.

I do find London exciting. Much as I hate to agree with that tedious old git Samuel Johnson, and despite the pompous imbecility of his famous remark about when a man is tired of London he is tired of life (an observation exceeded in fatuousness only by 'Let a smile be your umbrella'), I can't dispute it. After seven years of living in the country in the sort of place where a dead cow draws a crowd, London can seem a bit dazzling.

I can never understand why Londoners fail to see that they live in the most wonderful city in the world. It is far more beautiful and interesting than Paris, if you ask me, and more lively than anywhere but New York – and even New York can't touch it in lots of important ways. It has more history, finer parks, a livelier and more varied press, better theatres, more numerous orchestras and museums, leafier squares, safer streets, and more courteous inhabitants than any other large city in the world.

And it has more congenial small things – incidental civilities you might call them – than any other city I know: cheery red pillar boxes, drivers who actually stop for you on pedestrian crossings, lovely forgotten churches with wonderful names like St Andrew by the Wardrobe and St Giles Cripplegate, sudden pockets of quiet like Lincoln's Inn and Red Lion Square, interesting statues of obscure Victorians in togas, pubs, black cabs, double-decker buses, helpful policemen, polite notices, people who will stop to help you when you fall down or drop your shopping, benches everywhere. What other great city would trouble to put blue plaques on houses to let you know what famous person once lived there or warn you to look left or right before stepping off the kerb? I'll tell you. None.

Take away Heathrow Airport, the weather and any building that Richard Seifert ever laid a bony finger to, and it would be nearly perfect. Oh, and while we're at it we might also stop the staff at the British Museum from cluttering the forecourt with their cars and instead make it into a kind of garden, and also get rid of those horrible crush barriers outside Buckingham Palace because they look so straggly and cheap – not at all in keeping with the dignity of her poor besieged Majesty within. And, of course, put the Natural History Museum back to the way it was before they started dicking around with it (in particular they must restore the display case showing insects infesting household products from the 1950s), and remove the entrance charges from all museums at once, and make Lord Palumbo put the Mappin and Webb building back, and bring back Lyons Corner Houses but this time with food you'd like to eat, and maybe the odd Kardomah for old times' sake, and finally, but most crucially, make the board of directors of British Telecom go out and personally track down every last red phone box that they sold off to be used as shower stalls and garden sheds in far-flung corners of the globe, make them put them all back and then sack them – no, kill them. Then truly will London be glorious again.

This was the first time in years I'd been in London without having anything in particular to do and I felt a small thrill at finding myself abroad and unrequired in such a great, teeming urban organism. I had an amble through Soho and Leicester Square, spent a little time in the bookshops on Charing Cross Road rearranging books to my advantage, wandered aimlessly through Bloomsbury and finally over to Gray's Inn Road to the old Times building, now the offices of a company I had never heard of, and felt a pang of nostalgia such as can only be known by those who remember the days of hot metal and noisy composing rooms and the quiet joy of being paid a very good wage for a twenty-five-hour week.

When I started at *The Times* in 1981, just after the famous year-long shutdown, overmanning and slack output were prodigious to say the least. On the Company News desk where I worked as a sub-editor, the five-man team would wander in about two-thirty and spend most of the afternoon reading the evening papers and drinking tea while waiting for the reporters to surmount the daily challenge of finding their way back to their desks after a three-hour lunch involving several bottles of jolly decent Châteauneuf du Pape; compose their expenses; complete hunched and whispered phone calls to their brokers with regard to a little tip they'd picked up over the crème brûlée; and finally produce a page or so of copy before retiring parched to the Blue Lion across the road. At about half-past five, we would engage in a little light subbing for an hour or so, then slip our arms into our coats and go home. It seemed very agreeably unlike work. At the end of the first month, one of my colleagues showed me how to record imaginary expenditures on an expense account sheet and take it up to the third floor, where it could be exchanged at a little window for about £100 in cash – more money, literally, than I had ever held before. We got six weeks' holiday, three weeks' paternity leave and a month's sabbatical every four years. What a wonderful world Fleet Street then was and how thrilled I was to be part of it.

Alas, nothing that good can ever last. A few months later, Rupert Murdoch took over *The Times* and within days the building was full of mysterious tanned Australians in white short-sleeved shirts, who lurked in the background with clipboards and looked like they were measuring people for coffins. There is a story, which I suspect may actually be true, that one of these functionaries wandered into a room on the fourth floor full of people who hadn't done anything in years and, when they proved unable to account convincingly for themselves, sacked them at a stroke, except for one fortunate fellow who had popped out to the betting shop. When he returned, it was to an empty room and he spent the next two years sitting alone wondering vaguely what had become of his colleagues.

In our department the drive for efficiency was less traumatic. The desk I worked on was subsumed into a larger Business News desk, which meant I had to work nights and something more closely approximating eight-hour days, and we also had our expenses cruelly lopped. But the worst of it was that I was brought into regular contact with Vince of the wire room.

Vince was notorious. He would easily have been the world's most terrifying human had he but been human. I don't know quite what he was, other than it was five foot six inches of wiry malevolence in a grubby T-shirt. Reliable rumour had it that he was not born, but had burst full-formed from his mother's belly and then skittered off to the sewers. Among Vince's few simple and generally neglected tasks was the nightly delivery to us of the Wall Street report. Each night I would have to go and try to coax it from him. He was generally to be found in the humming, unattended mayhem of the wire room, lounging in a leather chair liberated from an executive office upstairs, with his blood-tipped Doc Martens plonked on the desk before him beside, and sometimes actually in, a large open box of pizza.

Every night I would knock hesitantly at the open door, and politely ask if he had seen the Wall Street report, pointing out that it was now quarter-past eleven and we should have had it at half-past ten. Perhaps he could look for it among the reams of unwatched paper tumbling out of his many machines?

'I don't know wevver you noticed,' Vince would say, 'but I'm eating pizza.'

Everybody had a different approach with Vince. Some tried to get threatening. Some tried bribery. Some tried warm friendship. I begged.

'Please, Vince, can't you just get it for me, please. It won't take a sec and it would make my life so much easier.'

'Fuck off.'

'Please, Vince. I have a wife and family, and they're threatening to sack me because the Wall Street report is always late.'

'Fuck off.'

'Well, then, how about if you just tell me where it is and I get it myself.'

'You can't touch nuffink in here, you know that.' The wire room was the domain of a union mysteriously named NATSOPA. One of the ways NATSOPA maintained its vice-like grip on the lower echelons of the newspaper industry was by keeping technological secrets to itself, like how to tear paper off a machine. Vince, as I recall, had gone on a six-week course to Eastbourne. It left him exhausted. Journalists weren't even allowed over the threshold.

Eventually, when my entreaties had declined into a kind of helpless bleating, Vince would sigh heavily, jam a wedge of pizza in his mouth and come over to the door. He would stick his face right in mine for a full half-minute. This was always the most unnerving part. His breath smelled primeval. His eyes were shiny and ratlike. 'You're fucking *annoying* me,' he would say in a low growl, flecking my face with bits of wet pizza, and then he would either get the Wall Street report or he would retire to his desk in a dark mood. There was never any telling which.

Once, on a particularly difficult night, I reported Vince's insubordination to David Hopkinson, the night editor, who was himself a formidable figure when he chose to be. Harrumphing, he went off to sort things out and actually went in the wire room – an impressive flouting of the rules of demarcation. When he emerged a few minutes later, looking flushed and wiping bits of pizza from his chin, he seemed a different man altogether. In a quiet voice he informed me that Vince would bring along the Wall Street report shortly but that perhaps it was best not to disturb him further just at present. Eventually I discovered that the simplest thing to do was get the closing prices out of the first edition of the *FT*.

To say that Fleet Street in the early 1980s was out of control barely hints at the scale of matters. The National Graphical Association, the printers' union, decided how many people were needed on each paper (hundreds and hundreds) and how many were to be laid off during a recession (none), and billed the management accordingly. Managements didn't have the power to hire and fire their own print workers, indeed generally didn't even know how many print workers they employed. I have before me a headline from December 1985 saying: 'Auditors find 300 extra printing staff at *Telegraph*'. That is to say, the *Telegraph* was paying salaries to 300 people who didn't actually work there. Printers were paid under a piece-rate system so byzantine that every composing room on Fleet Street had a piece-rate book the size of a telephone directory. On top of plump salaries, printers received special bonus payments – sometimes calculated to the eighth decimal point of a penny – for handling type of irregular sizes, for dealing with heavily edited copy, for setting words in a language other than English, for the white space at the ends of lines. If work was done out of house – for instance, advertising copy that was set outside the building – they were compensated for not doing it. At the end of each week, a senior NGA man would tot all these extras up, add a little something for a handy category called 'extra trouble occasioned', and pass the bill to the management. In consequence, many senior printers, with skills no more advanced than you would expect to find in any back-street print shop, enjoyed incomes in the top 2 per cent of British earnings. It was crazy.

Well, I don't need to tell you how it turned out. On 24 January 1986, *The Times* abruptly sacked 5,250 members of the most truculent unions – or deemed them to have dismissed themselves. On the evening of that day, the editorial staff were called into an upstairs conference room where Charlie Wilson, the editor, climbed onto a desk and announced the changes. Wilson was a terrifying Scotsman and a Murdoch man through and through. He said to us: 'We're sending ye tae Wapping, ye soft, English nancies, and if ye wairk very, very hard and if ye doonae git on ma tits, then mebbe I'll not cut off yer knackers and put them in ma Christmas pudding. D'ye have any problems with tha'?' Or words to that effect.

As 400 skittish journalists tumbled from the room, jabbering excitedly and trying to come to terms with the realization that they were about to be immersed in the biggest drama of their working lives, I stood alone and basking in the glow of a single joyous thought: I would never have to work with Vince again.

CHAPTER THREE

I HADN'T BEEN BACK TO WAPPING SINCE I'D LEFT THERE IN THE SUMMER
of 1986 and was eager to see it again. I had arranged to meet an
old friend and colleague, so I went now to Chancery Lane and
caught an Underground train. I do like the Underground. There's
something surreal about plunging into the bowels of the earth to
catch a train. It's a little world of its own down there, with its own
strange winds and weather systems, its own eerie noises and oily
smells. Even when you've descended so far into the earth that
you've lost your bearings utterly and wouldn't be in the least
surprised to pass a troop of blackened miners coming off shift,
there's always the rumble and tremble of a train passing somewhere
on an unknown line even further below. And it all happens in such
orderly quiet: all these thousands of people passing on stairs and
escalators, stepping on and off crowded trains, sliding off into the
darkness with wobbling heads, and never speaking, like characters
from *Night of the Living Dead*.

As I stood on the platform beneath another, fairly recent London
civility – namely an electronic board announcing that the next train
to Hainault would be arriving in 4 mins – I turned my attention to
the greatest of all civilities: the London Underground Map. What a
piece of perfection it is, created in 1931 by a forgotten hero named
Harry Beck, an out-of-work draughtsman who realized that when
you are underground it doesn't matter where you are. Beck saw –
and what an intuitive stroke this was – that as long as the stations
were presented in their right sequence with their interchanges
clearly delineated, he could freely distort scale, indeed abandon it

altogether. He gave his map the orderly precision of an electrical wiring system, and in so doing created an entirely new, *imaginary* London that has very little to do with the disorderly geography of the city above.

Here's an amusing trick you can play on people from Newfoundland or Lincolnshire. Take them to Bank Station and tell them to make their way to Mansion House. Using Beck's map – which even people from Newfoundland can understand in a moment – they will gamely take a Central Line train to Liverpool Street, change to a Circle Line train heading east and travel five more stops. When eventually they get to Mansion House they will emerge to find they have arrived at a point 200 feet further down the same street, and that you have had a nice breakfast and done a little shopping since you last saw them. Now take them to Great Portland Street and tell them to meet you at Regent's Park (that's right, same thing again!), and then to Temple Station with instructions to rendezvous at Aldwych. What fun you can have! And when you get tired of them, tell them to meet you at Brompton Road Station. It closed in 1947, so you'll never have to see them again.

The best part of Underground travel is that you never actually see the places above you. You have to imagine them. In other cities station names are unimaginative and mundane: Lexington Avenue, Potsdammerplatz, Third Street South. But in London the names sound sylvan and beckoning: Stamford Brook, Turnham Green, Bromley-by-Bow, Maida Vale, Drayton Park. That isn't a city up there, it's a Jane Austen novel. It's easy to imagine that you are shuttling about under a semi-mythic city from some golden, pre-industrial age. Swiss Cottage ceases to be a busy road junction and becomes instead a gingerbread dwelling in the midst of the great oak forest known as St John's Wood. Chalk Farm is an open space of fields where cheerful peasants in brown smocks cut and gather crops of chalk. Blackfriars is full of cowled and chanting monks, Oxford Circus has its big top, Barking is a dangerous place overrun with packs of wild dogs, Theydon Bois is a community of industrious Huguenot weavers, White City is a walled and turreted elysium built of the most dazzling ivory, and Holland Park is full of windmills.

The problem with losing yourself in these little reveries is that when you surface things are apt to be disappointing. I came up now at Tower Hill and there wasn't a tower and there wasn't a hill.

There isn't even any longer a Royal Mint (which I always preferred to imagine as a very large chocolate wrapped in green foil) as it has been moved somewhere else and replaced with a building with lots of smoked glass. Much of what once stood in this noisy corner of London has been swept away and replaced with big buildings with lots of smoked glass. It was only eight years since I'd last been here, but were it not for the fixed reference points of London Bridge and the Tower I'd scarcely have recognized the neighbourhood.

I walked along the painfully noisy street called The Highway, quietly agog at all the new development. It was like being in the midst of an ugly-building competition. For the better part of a decade, architects had been arriving in the area and saying, 'You think *that's* bad? Wait'll you see what *I* can do.' And there, towering proudly above all the clunky new offices, was the ugliest piece of bulk in London, the News International complex, looking like the central air-conditioning unit for the planet.

When I last saw it, in 1986, it stood forlornly amid acres of empty warehouses and puddly wasteground. The Highway, as I recalled it, was a comparatively sedate throughway. Now heavy lorries pounded along it, making the pavements tremble and giving the air an unhealthy bluish tinge. The News International compound was still surrounded with sinister fencing and electronic gates, but there was a new maximum-security reception centre that looked like something you'd expect to find at a plutonium depot at Sellafield. Goodness knows what terrorist contingency they have allowed for, but it must be something ambitious. I'd never seen a more unbreachable-looking complex.

I presented myself at the security window and waited outside while my colleague was summoned. The most eerie thing about the scene now was how serene it was. The memory seared into my skull was of crowds of demonstrators and police on horses and angry pickets who one minute would be screaming at you with wild eyes and big teeth and the next would say, 'Oh, hi, Bill, didn't recognize you,' and then exchange fags and talk about what a dreadful business this all was. And it was a dreadful business, for among the 5,000 sacked workers were hundreds and hundreds of decent, mild-mannered librarians, clerks, secretaries and messengers whose only sin was to have joined a union. To their eternal credit, most bore those of us still in work no personal grudges, though I confess the thought of Vince stepping from the crowd with a machete always hastened my steps through the gate.

For about 500 yards along the northern side of the compound, abutting Pennington Street, stands a low, windowless, brick building, an old storehouse left over from the days when the East End was a bustling port and distribution point for the City. Gutted and kitted out with hi-tech trappings, this rather unlikely building became, and remains, the offices of *The Times* and *Sunday Times*. Inside, throughout that long winter of 1986, while we fumblingly found our way through a new computerized technology, we could hear chants and turmoil, the muffled clops of passing police horses, the roar and shrieks of a baton charge, but because the building was windowless, we couldn't see anything. It was very odd. We would watch it on the *9 O'clock News*, then step outside and there it would be in three dimensions – the most bitter and violent industrial dispute yet seen on the streets of London – happening just outside the front gate. It was a deeply bizarre experience.

To keep morale up, the company each night brought round boxes of sandwiches and beer, which seemed a cheery gesture until you realized that the largesse was carefully worked out to provide each member of staff with one damp ham sandwich and a six-ounce can of warm Heineken. We were also presented with glossy brochures showing the company's plans for the site once the dispute was over. No two people seem to remember the same things from this brochure. I clearly recall architect's drawings of a large indoor swimming-pool, with unusually sleek and healthy-looking journalists diving off a low board or lounging with feet dangling in the water. Others remember squash courts and exercise rooms. One guy I know recollects a ten-pin bowling alley. Nearly everybody recalls a large modern bar such as you might find in the first-class lounge of a well-appointed airport.

Even from beyond the security perimeter, I could see several new buildings inside, and I couldn't wait to find out exactly what facilities the staff had been blessed with. It was the first question I asked my old colleague – whose name I dare not confide here lest he find himself abruptly transferred to classified advertising telesales – when he came to collect me at the gate. 'Oh, I remember the swimming-pool,' he said. 'We never heard anything more about that once the dispute was over. But give them their due, they've increased our hours. They now let us work an extra day every fortnight without additional pay.'

'Their way of showing they think highly of you all?'

'They wouldn't ask us to do more work if they didn't like the way we did it, would they?'

Quite.

We strolled along the main thoroughfare of the plant between the old brick storehouse and the monumental printworks. People passed like extras in a Hollywood movie – a workman with a long plank of wood, two women in smart business suits, a guy with a hardhat and a clipboard, a deliveryman cradling a large pot plant. We passed through a door into *The Times* editorial suite and I gasped quietly. It is always a small shock to go back to a place where you worked years before and see the same faces toiling at the same desks – a combination of sudden familiarity, as if you've never been away at all, and profound, heartfelt gratitude because you have. I saw my old friend Mickey Clark, now a media star, and found Graham Searjeant in his little cave made of newspapers and press releases, some of them dating back to the days when Mr Morris was still making motorcars, and encountered many other friends and former colleagues. We did all the usual things – compared stomachs and bald patches and made lists of the missing and dead. It was quite splendid really. Afterwards, I was taken to lunch in the canteen. At the old Times building on Gray's Inn Road the canteen had been in a basement room that had the charm and ambience of a submarine and the food had been slopped out by humourless drones who always brought to mind moles in aprons, but this was bright and spacious, with a wide choice of tempting dishes served by chirpy cockney girls in bright, clean uniforms. The dining area itself was unchanged except for the view. Where formerly had sprawled a muddy swamp crisscrossed with neglected water channels full of bedsteads and shopping trolleys, there now stood row upon row of designer houses and jaunty blocks of flats of the kind you always find around redeveloped waterfronts in Britain, the sort of buildings where all the balconies and exterior trim are made from lengths of tubular metal painted red.

It occurred to me that though I had worked at this site for seven months, I had never seen Wapping and was, of a sudden, keen to have a look at it. When I had finished my pudding and bid fond farewells to my ex-colleagues, I hastened out through the security gates, intentionally failing to turn in my security pass in the hope that nuclear attack sirens would sound and men in chemical warfare suits would begin a sprinting search of the compound for me, and then, with nervous backward glances, I redoubled my pace up

Pennington Street as it occurred to me that at News International this was not actually outside the bounds of possibility.

I had never strolled through Wapping because during the dispute it was unsafe to. The pubs and cafés of the district teemed with disgruntled printers and visiting delegations of sympathizers – Scottish miners were particularly feared for some reason – who would happily have torn a wimpy journalist's limbs from his sockets to use as torches for that night's procession. One journalist who encountered some former printers in a pub some way from Wapping had a glass smashed in his face and, as I recall, nearly died, or at the very least failed to enjoy the rest of his evening.

So unsafe was it, particularly after dark, that the police often wouldn't let us out until the small hours, particularly on nights of big demos. Because we never knew when we would be set free, we had to form our cars into a line and then sit for hour upon hour in the freezing cold. Some time between 11 p.m. and 1.30 a.m., when a significant portion of the braying throngs had been beaten back or dragged off to jail or had just wandered home, the gates would be thrown open and a great fleet of News International trucks would roar down a ramp and out onto The Highway, where they would be met by a barrage of bricks and crush barriers from whatever was left of the mob. The rest of us, meanwhile, were instructed to make haste in convoy through the back lanes of Wapping and to disperse when we were a safe distance from the plant. This worked well enough for several nights, but one evening we were sent on our way just as the pubs were shutting. As we were proceeding down some darkened, narrow street, suddenly people were stepping out of the shadows and into the road, kicking doors and heaving whatever came to hand. Ahead of me there were startling explosions of glass and intemperate shouting. To my deep and lasting astonishment someone about six cars ahead of me – a fussy little man from the foreign desk, who even now I would happily drag over rough ground behind a Land-Rover – got out to look at the damage to his car, as if he thought he might have run over a nail, bringing those of us behind to a halt. I remember watching in sputtering dismay as he tried to press back into position a flapping piece of trim, then turning my head to find at my window an enraged face – a white guy with dancing dreadlocks and an army surplus jacket – and everything took on a strange dreamlike quality. How odd, I thought, that a total stranger was about to pull me from my car and beat me mushy for the benefit of printworkers he had never met, who would mostly despise him as an unkempt hippie, would certainly never let him into their own union, and who had enjoyed decades of obscenely inflated earnings without once showing collective support for any other union, including, on occasion, provincial branches of their own NGA. Simultaneously it occurred to me that I was about to squander my small life for the benefit of a man who had, without apparent hesitation, given up his own nationality out of economic self-interest, who didn't know who I was, would as lightly have discarded me if a machine could be found to do my job, and whose idea of maximum magnanimity was to hand out a six-ounce can of beer and a limp sandwich. I could imagine the company writing to my wife: 'Dear Mrs Bryson: In appreciation of your husband's recent tragic death at the hands of a terrifying mob, we would like you to have this sandwich and can of lager. PS – Could you please return his parking pass?'

And all the time this was going on, while a large wild man with dreadlocks was trying to wrench open my door with a view to carrying me off wriggling into the darkness, some halfwit from the foreign desk fifty yards ahead was walking slowly around his Peugeot, assessing it deliberatively like someone about to buy a second-hand car, and occasionally pausing to look with puzzlement at the bricks and blows raining down on the cars behind him, as if it were some kind of freak weather occurrence. Eventually, he got back in his car, checked the rearview mirror, made sure his newspaper was still on the seat beside him, put on his indicator, checked the mirror again and pulled off, and my life was saved.

Four days later, the company stopped bringing round free sandwiches and beer.

It was thus very refreshing to walk without fear for my life through the dozing streets of Wapping. I have never bought into that quaint conceit about London being essentially a cluster of villages – where else have you seen villages with flyovers, gasometers, reeling derelicts and a view of the Post Office Tower? – but to my delight and surprise Wapping did, in fact, rather feel like one. Its shops were small and varied and the streets had cozy names: Cinnamon Street, Waterman Way, Vinegar Street, Milk Yard. The council estates were snug and cheery looking, and the looming warehouses had almost all been smartly renovated as flats. I instinctively quivered at the sight of yet more glossy red trim and the thought of these once-proud workplaces filled with braying twits named Selena and Jasper, but it must be said that they have clearly brought some prosperity to the neighbourhood and doubt-less saved the old warehouses from far sadder fates.

Near Wapping Old Stairs, I had a look at the river and tried to imagine, without the tiniest measure of success, what these old neighbourhoods must have looked like in the eighteenth and nine-teenth centuries when they teemed with workers and the wharves were piled high with barrels of the spices and condiments that gave the surrounding streets their names. As recently as 1960, over 100,000 people worked on the docks or drew their livings from it, and Docklands was still one of the busiest ports in the world. By 1981, every London dock was closed. The view of the river from Wapping now was as tranquil and undisturbed as a Constable land-scape. I watched the river for perhaps thirty minutes and saw just one boat go by. Then I turned and began the long trek back to Hazlitt's.

CHAPTER FOUR

I SPENT A COUPLE MORE DAYS IN LONDON DOING NOTHING MUCH. I DID a little research in a newspaper library, spent most of one afternoon trying to find my way through the complex network of pedestrian subways at Marble Arch, did a little shopping, saw some friends.

Everyone I saw said, 'Gosh, you're brave!' when I revealed that I was planning to travel around Britain by public transport, but it never occurred to me to go any other way. You are so lucky in this country to have a relatively good public transport system (relative, that is, to what it will be when the Tories finish with it) and I think we should all try harder to enjoy it while it's still there. Besides, driving in Britain is such a dreary experience these days. There are far too many cars on the road, nearly double what there were when I first came here, and in those days people didn't actually drive their cars. They just parked them in the driveway and buffed them up once every week or so. About twice a year they would 'get the car out' – those were the words they used, like that in itself was a big operation – and pootle off to visit relatives in East Grinstead or have a trip to some place like Hayling Island or Eastbourne, and that was about it, apart from the buffing.

Now everyone drives everywhere for everything, which I don't understand because there isn't a single feature of driving in Britain that has even the tiniest measure of enjoyment in it. Just consider the average multi-storey car park. You drive around for ages, and then spend a small eternity shunting into a space that is exactly two inches wider than the average car. Then, because you are parked next to a pillar, you have to climb over the seats and end up squeezing butt-first out of the passenger door, in the process transferring all the dirt from the side of your car to the back of your smart new jacket from Marks & Spencer. Then you go hunting for some distant pay-and-display machine, which doesn't make change or accept any coin introduced since 1976, and wait on an old guy who likes to read all the instructions on the machine before committing himself and then tries to insert his money through the ticket slot and maintenance keyhole.

Eventually you acquire a ticket and trek back to your car where your wife greets you with a 'Where have you *been*?' Ignoring her, you squeeze past the pillar, collecting a matching set of dust for the front of your jacket, discover that you can't reach the windscreen as the door only opens three inches, so you just sort of throw the ticket at the dashboard (it flutters to the floor but your wife doesn't notice so you say, 'Fuck it,' and lock the door), and squeeze back out where your wife sees what a scruff you've turned into after she spent all that time dressing you and beats the dust from you with paddled hands while saying, 'Honestly, I can't take you *anywhere*.'

And that's just the beginning. Arguing quietly, you have to find your way out of this dank hellhole via an unmarked door leading to a curious chamber that seems to be a composite of dungeon and urinal, or else wait two hours for the world's most abused and unreliable-looking lift, which will only take two people and already has two people in it – a man whose wife is beating dust from his new Marks & Spencer jacket and berating him in clucking tones.

And the remarkable thing is that everything about this process is intentionally – mark this, intentionally – designed to flood your life with unhappiness. From the tiny parking bays that can only be got into by manoeuvring your car through a forty-six-point turn (why can't the spaces be angled, for crying out loud?) to the careful placing of pillars where they will cause maximum obstruction, to the ramps that are so dark and narrow and badly angled that you always bump the kerb, to the remote, wilfully unhelpful ticket machines (you can't tell me that a machine that can recognize and reject any foreign coin ever produced couldn't make change if it wanted to) – *all* of this is designed to make this the most dispiriting experience of your adult life. Did you know – this is a little-known fact but absolute truth – that when they dedicate a new multi-storey car park the Lord Mayor and his wife have a ceremonial pee in the stairwell? It's true.

And that's just one tiny part of the driving experience. There are all the other manifold annoyances of motoring, like National Express drivers who pull out in front of you on motorways, eight-mile-long contraflow systems erected so that some guys on a crane can change a lightbulb, traffic lights on busy roundabouts that never let you advance more than twenty feet at a time, motorway service areas where you have to pay £4.20 for a minipot of coffee and a jacket potato with a sneeze of cheddar in it and there's no point in going to the shop because the men's magazines are all sealed in plastic and you don't need any Waylon Jennings Highway Hits tapes, morons with caravans who pull out of side-roads just as you approach, some guy in a Morris Minor going 11 mph through the Lake District and collecting a three-mile following because, apparently, he's always wanted to lead a parade, and other challenges to your patience and sanity nearly beyond endurance. Motorized vehicles are ugly and dirty and they bring out the worst in people. They clutter every kerbside, turn ancient market squares into disorderly jumbles of metal, spawn petrol stations, second-hand car lots, Kwik-Fit centres and other dispiriting blights. They are horrible and awful and I wanted nothing to do with them on this trip. And besides, my wife wouldn't let me have the car.

Thus it was that I found myself late on a grey Saturday afternoon, on an exceptionally long and empty train bound for Windsor. I sat high on the seat in an empty carriage, and in fading daylight watched as the train slid past office blocks and out into the forests of council flats and snaking terrace houses of Vauxhall and Clapham. At Twickenham, I discovered why the train was so long and so empty. The platform was jammed solid with men and boys in warm clothes and scarves carrying glossy programmes and little bags with tea flasks peeping out: obviously a rugby crowd from the Twickenham grounds. They boarded with patience and without pushing, and said sorry when they bumped or inadvertently impinged on someone else's space. I admired this instinctive consideration for others, and was struck by what a regular thing that is in Britain and how little it is noticed. Nearly everyone rode all the way to Windsor – I presume there must be some sort of parking arrangement there; Windsor can't provide that many rugby fans – and formed a patient crush at the ticket barrier. An Asian man collected tickets in fast motion and said thank you to every person who passed. He didn't have time to examine the tickets – you could have handed him a cornflakes boxtop – but he did manage to find a vigorous salute for all, and they in turn thanked *him* for relieving them of their tickets and letting them pass. It was a little miracle of orderliness and goodwill. Anywhere else there'd have been someone on a box barking at people to form a line and not push.

The streets of Windsor were shiny with rain and unseasonally dark and wintry, but they were still filled with throngs of tourists. I got a room in the Castle Hotel on the High Street, one of those peculiarly higgledy-piggledy hotels in which you have to embark on an epic trek through a succession of wandering corridors and firedoors. I had to go up one flight of stairs and, some distance further on, down another in order to reach the distant wing of which my room was the very last. But it was a nice room and, I presumed, handy for Reading if I decided to exit through the window.

I dumped my pack and hastened back the way I came, keen to see a little of Windsor before the shops shut. I knew Windsor well because we used to shop there when we lived in Virginia Water down the road, and I strode with a proprietorial air, noting which shops had altered or changed hands over the years, which is to say most of them. Beside the handsome town hall stood Market Cross House, a building so perilously leaning that you can't help wonder if it was built that way to attract Japanese visitors with cameras. It was now a sandwich bar, but, like most of the other shops on the pretty jumble of cobbled streets around it, it has been about a million things, usually tourist-connected. The last time I was here most of them were selling egg-cups with legs; now they seemed to specialize in twee little cottages and castles. Only Woods of Windsor, a company that manages to get more commercial mileage out of lavender than I would ever have thought possible, is still there selling soaps and toilet water. On Peascod Street, Marks & Spencer had expanded, Hammick's and Laura Ashley had moved locations, and the Golden Egg and Wimpy were, not surprisingly, long gone (though I confess a certain fondness for the old-style Wimpys with their odd sense of what constituted American food, as if they had compiled their recipes from a garbled telex). But I was pleased to note that Daniel's, the most interesting department store in Britain, was still there.

Daniel's is the most extraordinary place. It has all the features you expect of a provincial department store – low ceilings, tiny obscure departments, frayed carpets held down with strips of electrician's tape, a sense that this space was once occupied by about eleven different shops and dwellings all with slightly different elevations – but it has the oddest assortment of things on sale: knicker elastic and collar snaps, buttons and pinking shears, six pieces of Portmeirion china, racks of clothing for very old people, a modest few rolls of carpet with the sort of patterns you get when you rub your eyes too hard, chests of drawers with a handle missing, wardrobes on which one of the doors quietly swings open fifteen seconds after you experimentally shut it. Daniel's always puts me in mind of what Britain might have been like under Communism.

It has long seemed to me unfortunate – and I'm taking the global view here – that such an important experiment in social organization was left to the Russians when the British would have managed it so much better. All those things that are necessary to the successful implementation of a rigorous socialist system are, after all, second nature to the British. For a start, they like going without. They are great at pulling together, particularly in the face of adversity, for a perceived common good. They will queue patiently for indefinite periods and accept with rare fortitude the imposition of rationing, bland diets and sudden inconvenient shortages of staple goods, as anyone who has ever looked for bread at a supermarket on a Saturday afternoon will know. They are comfortable with faceless bureaucracies and, as Mrs Thatcher proved, tolerant of dictatorships. They will wait uncomplainingly for years for an operation or the delivery of a household appliance. They have a natural gift for making excellent jokes about authority without seriously challenging it, and they derive universal satisfaction from the sight of the rich and powerful brought low. Most of those above the age of twenty-five already dress like East Germans. The conditions, in a word, are right.

Please understand I'm not saying that Britain would have been a happier, better place under Communism, merely that the British would have done it properly. They would have taken it in their stride, with good heart, and without excessive cheating. In point of fact, until about 1970 it wouldn't have made the slightest discernible difference to most people's lives, and might at least have spared us Robert Maxwell.

I rose early the next day and attended to my morning hygiene in a state of small excitation because I had a big day ahead of me. I was going to walk across Windsor Great Park. It is the most splendid park I know. It stretches over forty enchanted square miles and incorporates into its ancient fabric every manner of sylvan charm: deep primeval woodlands, bosky dells, wandering footpaths and bridleways, formal and informal gardens and a long, deeply fetching lake. Scattered picturesquely about are farms, woodland cottages, forgotten statues, a whole village occupied by estate workers and things that the Queen has brought back from trips abroad and couldn't think of anywhere else to put – obelisks and totem poles and other curious expressions of gratitude from distant outposts of the Commonwealth.

The news had not yet come out that there was oil under the park and that it all soon might turn into a new Sullom Voe (but don't be alarmed; the local authority will make them screen the derricks with shrubs), so I didn't realize that I ought to drink things in carefully in case the next time I came this way it looked like an Oklahoma oilfield. At this time, Windsor Great Park continued to enjoy a merciful obscurity, which I find mystifying in an open space so glorious on the very edge of London. Only once could I remember any reference to the park in the newspapers, a couple of years before when Prince Philip had taken a curious disliking to an avenue of ancient trees and had instructed Her Majesty's Tree-Choppers to remove them from the landscape.

I expect their branches had imperilled the progress through the park of his horses and plus-four, or whatever it is you call those creaking contraptions he so likes to roam around in. You often see him and other members of the royal family in the park, speeding past in assorted vehicles on their way to polo matches or church services in the Queen Mother's private compound, the Royal Lodge. Indeed, because the public aren't allowed to drive on the park roads, a significant portion of the little traffic that passes is generated by royals. Once, on Boxing Day when I was ambling along in a paternal fashion beside an offspring on a shiny new tricycle, I became aware with a kind of sixth sense that we were holding up the progress of a car and turned to find that it was being driven by Princess Diana. As I hastened myself and my child out of the way, she gave me a smile that melted my heart, and since that time I have never said a word against the dear sweet girl, however pressed by those who think that she is a bit off her head because she spends £28,000 a year on leotards and makes occasional crank phone calls to hunky military men. (And who among us hasn't? is my unanswerable reply.)

I strode along the aptly named Long Walk from the base of

Windsor Castle to the equestrian statue of George III, known to
locals as the Copper Horse, at the summit of Snow Hill, where I
rested at the base and soaked up one of the most comely views in
England: the majestic sprawl of Windsor Castle 3 miles away at
the end of the Long Walk, with the town at its feet and, beyond,
Eton, the misty Thames Valley and low Chiltern Hills. Deer grazed
in picturesque herds in a clearing below and early-morning strollers
began to dot the long avenue framed by my splayed feet. I
watched planes taking off from Heathrow and found on the
horizon the faint but recognizable shapes of Battersea Power
Station and the Post Office Tower. I can remember being very
excited to discover that I could see London from way out here. It
is, I believe, the only spot this far out where you can see it. Henry
VIII rode to this summit to hear the cannons announce the
execution of Anne Boleyn, though now all I could hear were
the drones of airliners banking to land, and the startling yap of a
large shaggy dog that appeared suddenly at my elbow, its owners
following up a side hill, and offered me a large saliva specimen,
which I declined.

I struck off through the park, past the grounds of the Royal
Lodge, the pink Georgian house where the Queen and Princess
Margaret spent their girlhoods, and through the surrounding
woods and fields to my favourite corner of the park, Smith's Lawn.
It must be the finest lawn in Britain, flat and flawlessly green and
built on an heroic scale. There's almost never a soul up there,
except when there's a polo match on. It took me the better part of
an hour to cross it, though I went some distance out of my way to
investigate a forlorn statue on the periphery, which turned out to be
of Prince Albert, and another hour to find my way through the
Valley Gardens and on to Virginia Water Lake, steaming softly
in the cool morning air. It's a lovely piece of work, the lake, created
by the Duke of Cumberland as a somewhat odd way of celebrating
all those Scots he'd left inert or twitching on the battlefield of
Culloden, and it is intensely picturesque and romantic in that
way that only created landscapes can be, with sudden vistas
perfectly framed by trees and a long decorative stone bridge. At the
far end there is even a cluster of fake Roman ruins, opposite
Fort Belvedere, the country home where Edward VIII made
his famous abdication broadcast so that he could be free to go
fishing with Goebbels and marry that sour-faced Simpson woman,
who, with the best will in the world and bearing in mind my

patriotic obligations to a fellow American, has always struck me as a frankly unlikely choice of shag.

I only mention this because the nation seemed to be embarking on a similar monarchical crisis at this time. I must say, I can't begin to understand the attitudes of the British nation towards the royal family. For years – may I be candid here for a moment? – I thought they were insupportably boring and only marginally more attractive than Wallis Simpson, but everybody in England adored them. Then when, by a small miracle, they finally started doing arresting and erratic things and making the *News of the World* on merit – when, in a word, they finally became *interesting* – the whole nation was suddenly saying, 'Shocking. Let's get rid of them.' Only that week, I had watched with open mouth an edition of *Question Time* in which one of the questions seriously discussed by the panel had been whether the nation should dispense with Prince Charles and leapfrog to little Prince William. Putting aside for the moment the question of the wisdom of investing a lot of faith in the un-matured genetic output of Charles and Diana, which I would charitably describe as touching, it seemed to me to miss the whole point. If you are going to have a system of hereditary privilege, then surely you have to take what comes your way no matter how ponderous the poor fellow may be or how curious his taste in mistresses.

My own views on the matter are neatly encapsulated in a song of my own composition called 'I'm the Eldest Son of the Eldest Son of the Eldest Son of the Eldest Son of the Guy Who Fucked Nell Gwynne', which I should be happy to send under separate cover upon receipt of £3.50 + 50p post and packaging.

In the meantime, you will have to imagine me humming this cheery ditty as I stepped smartly through the roar of traffic along the A30 and made my way down Christchurch Road to the sedate and leafy village of Virginia Water.

CHAPTER FIVE

MY FIRST SIGHT OF VIRGINIA WATER WAS ON AN UNUSUALLY SULTRY afternoon at the very end of August 1973, some five months after my arrival in Dover. I had spent the summer travelling around in the company of one Stephen Katz, who had joined me in Paris in April and whom I had gratefully seen off from Istanbul some ten days before. I was tired and road-weary, but very glad to be back in England. I stepped from a London train and was captivated instantly. The village of Virginia Water looked tidy and beckoning. It was full of lazy late-afternoon shadows and an impossible green lushness such as could only be appreciated by someone freshly arrived from an arid clime. Beyond the station rose the Gothic tower of Holloway Sanatorium, a monumental heap of bricks and gables in parklike grounds just beyond the station.

Two girls I knew from my home town worked as student nurses at the sanatorium and had offered me sleeping space on their floor and the opportunity to ring their bath with five months of accumulated muck. My intention was to catch a flight home from Heathrow the next day; I was due to resume my listless university studies in two weeks. But over many beers in a cheery pub called the Rose and Crown, it was intimated to me that the hospital was always looking for menial staff and that I, as a native speaker of English, was a shoo-in. The next day, with a muzzy head and without benefit of reflection, I found myself filling in forms and being told to present myself to the charge nurse on Tuke Ward at 7 a.m. the following morning. A kindly little man with the intelligence of a child was summoned to take me to stores to collect a weighty set

of keys and a teetering mountain of neatly folded hospital clothing
– two grey suits, shirts, a tie, several white lab coats (what did they
have in mind for me?) – and to deliver me to Male Hostel B across
the road, where a crone with white hair showed me to a spartan
room and, in a manner reminiscent of my old friend Mrs Smegma,
issued a volley of instructions concerning the weekly exchange of
soiled sheets for clean, the hours of hot water, the operation of the
radiator, and other matters much too numerous and swiftly
presented to take in, though I was rather proud to catch a passing
reference to counterpanes. Been there, I thought.

I composed a letter to my parents telling them not to wait supper;
passed a happy few hours trying on my new clothes and posing
before the mirror; arranged my modest selection of paperback
books on the window-sill; popped out to the post office and had a
look around the village; dined at a little place called the Tudor
Rose; then called in at a pub called the Trottesworth, where I found
the ambience so agreeable and the alternative forms of amusement
so non-existent that I drank, I confess, an intemperate amount of
beer; and returned to my new quarters by way of several shrubs and
one memorably unyielding lamppost.

In the morning I awoke fifteen minutes late and found my way
blearily to the hospital. Amid the mêlée of a shift change, I asked
the way to Tuke Ward and arrived, hair askew and weaving slightly,
ten minutes late. The charge nurse, a friendly fellow of early middle
years, welcomed me warmly, told me where I'd find tea and biscuits
and cleared off. I scarcely ever saw him after that. Tuke Ward was
inhabited by long-stay male patients in a state of arrested insanity
who, mercifully, seemed to look entirely after themselves. They
fetched their own breakfasts from a trolley, shaved themselves,
made their own beds after a fashion and, while I was momentarily
engaged in a futile search for antacids in the staff loo, quietly
departed. I emerged to find, to my confusion and alarm, that I was
the only person left on the ward. I wandered puzzled through the
day room, kitchen and dormitories, and opened the ward door to
find an empty corridor with a door to the world standing open at
its far end. At that moment the phone in the ward office rang.

'Who's that?' barked a voice.

I summoned enough power of speech to identify myself and
peered out the office window, expecting to see the thirty-three
patients of Tuke Ward dashing from tree to tree in a desperate bid
for freedom.

'Smithson here,' said the voice. Smithson was the head nursing officer, an intimidating figure with mutton chops and a barrel chest. He'd been pointed out to me the day before. 'You're the new boy, are you?'

'Yes, sir.'

'Jolly there?'

I blinked, confused, and thought what odd turns of phrase the English had. 'Well, actually it's very quiet.'

'No, John Jolly, the charge nurse – is he there?'

'Oh. He's gone.'

'Did he say when he'd be back?'

'No, sir.'

'Everything under control?'

'Well actually' – I cleared my throat – 'it appears that the patients have escaped, sir.'

'They've what?'

'Escaped, sir. I just went to the bathroom and when I came out—'

'They're supposed to be off the ward, son. They'll be on gardening detail or at occupational therapy. They leave every morning.'

'Oh, thank Christ for that.'

'I beg your pardon?'

'Thank goodness for that, sir.'

'Yes, quite.' He rang off.

I spent the rest of the morning wandering alone around the ward, looking in drawers and wardrobes and under beds, exploring store cupboards, trying to figure out how to make tea from loose leaves and a sieve, and, when my constitution proved up to it, having a private world skidding championship along the well-polished corridor that ran between the patients' rooms, complete with whispered and respectful commentary. When it got to be one-thirty and no-one had told me to go to lunch, I dismissed myself and went to the canteen, where I sat alone with a plate of beans, chips and a mysterious item later identified to me as a Spam fritter, and noticed that Mr Smithson and some of his colleagues, at a table across the room, were having a discussion of considerable mirth and, for some reason, casting merry looks in my direction.

When I returned to the ward, I discovered that several of the patients had returned in my absence. Most of them were slumped in chairs in the day room, sleeping off the exertions of a morning spent leaning on a rake or counting Rawlplugs into boxes, except for one dapper and well-spoken fellow in tweeds who was

watching a test match on the television. He invited me to join him
and, upon discovering that I was an American, enthusiastically
explained to me this most bewildering of sports. I took him to be a
member of staff, possibly the mysterious Mr Jolly's afternoon
replacement, possibly a visiting psychiatrist, until he turned to me,
in the midst of a detailed explication of the intricacies of spin bowling, and said suddenly and conversationally: 'I have atomic balls,
you know.'

'Excuse me?' I replied, my mind still on the other type of balls.

'Porton Down. 1947. Government experiments. All very hush-
hush. You mustn't tell a soul.'

'Ah . . . no, of course.'

'I'm wanted by the Russians.'

'Oh . . . ah?'

'That's why I'm here. Incognito.' He tapped his nose significantly
and cast an appraising glance at the dozing figures around us. 'Not
a bad place really. Full of madmen, of course. Positively teeming
with lunatics, poor souls. But they do a lovely jam roly-poly on
Wednesdays. Now this is Geoff Boycott coming up. Lovely touch.
He'll have no trouble with Benson's delivery, just you see.'

Most of the patients on Tuke Ward were like that when you got
to know them – superficially lucid, but, underneath, crazy as an
overheated dog. It is an interesting experience to become
acquainted with a country through the eyes of the insane, and, if I
may say so, a particularly useful grounding for life in Britain.

And so my first permanent days in Britain passed. At night I went
to the pub and by day I presided over a mostly empty ward. Each
afternoon about four o'clock a Spanish lady in a pink coverall
would appear with a clattering tea trolley and the patients would
stir to life to get a cup of tea and a slice of yellow cake, and from
time to time the elusive Mr Jolly dropped by to dispense medicines
or re-order biscuits, but otherwise things were very quiet. I
developed a passable understanding of cricket and my skidding
came on a treat.

The hospital, I came to discover, was its own little universe,
virtually complete unto itself. It had its own joinery shop and
electricians, plumbers and painters, its own coach and coach driver.
It had a snooker room, a badminton court and swimming-pool, a
tuck shop and a chapel, a cricket pitch and social club, a podiatrist
and hairdresser, kitchens, sewing room and laundry. Once a week
they showed movies in a kind of ballroom. It even had its own

mortuary. The patients did all the gardening that didn't involve sharp tools and kept the grounds immaculate. It was a bit like a country club for crazy people. I liked it very much.

One day, during one of Mr Jolly's periodic visits – I never did discover what he did during his absences – I was despatched to a neighbouring ward called Florence Nightingale to borrow a bottle of thorazine to keep the patients docile. Flo, as it was known to the staff, was a strange and gloomy place, full of much more seriously demented people who wandered about or rocked ceaselessly in high-backed chairs. While the sister went off with jangling keys to sort out the thorazine I stared at the jabbering masses and gave thanks that I had given up hard drugs. At the far end of the room, there moved a pretty young nurse of clear and radiant goodness, caring for these helpless wrecks with boundless reserves of energy and compassion – guiding them to a chair, brightening their day with chatter, wiping dribble from their chins – and I thought: This is *just* the sort of person I need.

We were married sixteen months later in the local church, which I passed now as I made my way down Christchurch Road, shuffling along through papery leaves, under a tunnel of lofty boughs, humming the last eight bars of 'Nell Gwynne'. The big houses along Christchurch Road were unchanged, except for the addition on each of a security box and floodlights of the sort that come on for no reason late at night.

Virginia Water is an interesting place. It was built mostly in the Twenties and Thirties, with two small parades of shops and, surrounding them, a dense network of private roads winding through and around the famous Wentworth Golf Course. Scattered among the trees are rambling houses, often occupied by celebrities and built in a style that might be called Ostentatious English Vernacular or perhaps Game Stab at Lutyens, with busy rooflines crowded with gables and fussy chimneypots, spacious and multiple verandas, odd-sized windows, at least one emphatic chimney breast and acres of trailing roses over a trim little porch. It felt, when I first saw it, rather like walking into the pages of a 1937 *House and Garden*.

But what lent Virginia Water a particular charm back then, and I mean this quite seriously, was that it was full of wandering lunatics. Because most of the patients had been resident at the sanatorium for years, and often decades, no matter how addled their thoughts or hesitant their gait, no matter how much they mumbled and muttered, adopted sudden postures of submission or demonstrated any of a hundred other indications of someone comfortably out to lunch, most of them could be trusted to wander down to the village and find their way back again. Each day you could count on finding a refreshing sprinkling of lunatics buying fags or sweets, having a cup of tea or just quietly remonstrating with thin air. The result was one of the most extraordinary communities in England, one in which wealthy people and lunatics mingled on equal terms. The shopkeepers and locals were quite wonderful about it, and didn't act as if anything was odd because a man with wild hair wearing a pyjama jacket was standing in a corner of the baker's declaiming to a spot on the wall or sitting at a corner table of the Tudor Rose with swivelling eyes and the makings of a smile, dropping sugar cubes into his minestrone. It was, and I'm still serious, a thoroughly heartwarming sight.

Among the five hundred or so patients at the sanatorium was a remarkable idiot savant named Harry. Harry had the mind of a small, preoccupied child, but you could name any date, present or future, and he would instantly tell you what day of the week it was. We used to test him with a perpetual calendar and he was never wrong. You could ask him the date of the third Saturday of December 1935 or the second Wednesday of July 2017 and he would tell you faster than any computer could. Even more extraordinary, though it merely seemed tiresome at the time, was that several times a day he would approach members of the staff and ask them in a strange, bleating voice if the hospital was going to close in 1980. According to his copious medical notes, he had been obsessed with this question since his arrival as a young man in about 1950. The thing is, Holloway was a big, important institution, and there were never any plans to close it. Indeed there were none right up until the stormy night in early 1980 when Harry was put to bed in a state of uncharacteristic agitation – he had been asking his question with increasing persistence for several weeks – and a bolt of lightning struck a back gable, causing a devastating fire that swept through the attics and several of the wards, rendering the entire structure suddenly uninhabitable.

It would make an even better story if poor Harry had been strapped to his bed and perished in the blaze. Unfortunately for purposes of exciting narrative all the patients were safely evacuated into the stormy night, though I like to imagine Harry with his lips contorted in a rapturous smile as he stood on the lawn, a blanket round his shoulders, his face lit by dancing flames, and watched the conflagration that he had so patiently awaited for thirty years.

The inmates were transferred to a special wing of a general hospital down the road at Chertsey, where they were soon deprived of their liberty on account of their unfortunate inclination to cause havoc in the wards and alarm the sane. In the meantime, the sanatorium had quietly mouldered away, its windows boarded or broken, its grand entrance from Stroude Road blocked by a heavy-duty metal gate topped with razor wire. I lived in Virginia Water for five years in the early Eighties when I was working in London and occasionally stopped to peer over the wall at the neglected grounds and general desolation. A series of development companies had taken it over with ambitious plans to turn the site into an office park or conference centre or compound of executive homes. They had set up some Portakabins and stern signs warning that the site was patrolled by guard dogs, which, if the illustration was to be believed, were barely under control, but nothing more positive than this was ever done. For well over a decade this fine old hospital, probably one of the dozen finest Victorian structures still standing, had just sat, crumbling and forlorn, and I had expected it to be much the same – indeed, was rehearsing an obsequious request to the watchman to be allowed to go up the drive for a quick peek since the building itself couldn't much be seen from the road.

So imagine my surprise when I crested a gentle slope and found a spanking new entrance knocked into the perimeter wall, a big sign welcoming me to Virginia Park and, flanking a previously unknown vista of the sanatorium building, a generous clutch of smart new executive homes behind. With mouth agape, I stumbled up a freshly asphalted road lined with houses so new that there were still stickers on the windows and the yards were seas of mud. One of the houses had been done up as a show home and, as it was a Sunday, it was busy with people having a look. Inside, I found a glossy brochure full of architects' drawings of happy, slender people strolling around among handsome houses, listening to a chamber orchestra in the room where I formerly watched movies in the company of twitching lunatics, or swimming in an indoor pool sunk into the floor of the great Gothic hall where I had once played badminton and falteringly asked the young nurse from Florence Nightingale for a date, with a distant view, if she could possibly spare the time, of marrying me. According to the rather sumptuous accompanying prose, residents of Virginia Park could choose between several dozen detached executive homes, a scattering of townhouses and flats, or one of twenty-three grand apartments carved out of the restored san, now mysteriously renamed Crosland House. The map of the site was dotted with strange names – Connolly Mews, Chapel Square, The Piazza – that owed little to its previous existence. How much more appropriate, I thought, if they had given them names like Lobotomy Square and Electroconvulsive Court. Prices started at £350,000.

I went back outside to see what I could get for my £350,000. The answer was a smallish but ornate home on a modest plot with an interesting view of a nineteenth-century mental hospital. I can't say that it was what I had always dreamed of. All the houses were built of red brick, with old-fashioned chimney pots, gingerbread trim and other small nods to the Victorian age. One model, rather mundanely known as House Type D, even had a decorative tower. The result was that they looked as if they had somehow been pupped by the sanatorium. You could almost imagine them, given sufficient time, growing into sanatoria themselves. Insofar as such a thing can work at all, it worked surprisingly well. The new houses didn't jar against the backdrop of the old sanatorium and at least – something that surely wouldn't have happened a dozen years ago – that great old heap of a building, with all its happy memories for me and generations of the interestingly insane, had been saved. I doffed my hat to the developers and took my leave.

I had intended to stroll up to my old house, but it was a mile off and my feet were sore. Instead, I headed down Stroude Road, past the site of the old hospital social club, now replaced by a dwelling of considerable ugliness, and the scattered buildings that had once been hostels for nursing and domestic staff, and bet myself £100 that the next time I passed this way they would be gone and replaced by big houses with double garages.

I walked the two miles to Egham, and called at the house of a delightful lady named Mrs Billen who is, among her many other selfless kindnesses, my mother-in-law. While she bustled off to the kitchen in that charming flutter with which all English ladies of a certain age receive sudden guests, I warmed my toes by the fire and reflected (for such was my state of mind these days) that this was the first English house I had ever been in, other than as a paying guest. My wife had brought me here as her young swain one Sunday afternoon many years before and we had sat, she and I and her family, tightly squeezed into this snug and well-heated lounge watching *Bullseye* and *The Generation Game* and other televisual offerings that seemed to me interestingly lacking in advanced entertainment value. This was a new experience for me. I hadn't seen my own family in what might be called a social setting since about 1958, apart from a few awkward hours at Christmases, so there was a certain cosy novelty in finding myself in the midst of so much familial warmth. It is something that I still very much admire in the British, though I confess a certain passing exultation when I learned that they were taking *Bullseye* off the air.

My mother-in-law – Mum – appeared with a tray of food such as made me wonder for a moment if she had mistaken me for a party of lumberjacks. As I greedily tucked into a delicious, steaming heap that brought to mind the Cairngorms re-created in comestible form, and afterwards sat slumped with coffee and a happily distended stomach, we chattered away about this and that – the children, our impending move to the States, my work, her recent widowhood. Late in the evening – late, that is, for a couple of old-timers like us – she went into bustling mode again and after making a great deal of industrious-sounding noises from every quarter of the house, announced that the guest room was ready. I found a neatly turned-down bed complete with hot-water bottle and, after the most cursory of ablutions, crawled gratefully into it, wondering why it is that the beds in the houses of grandparents and in-laws are always so deliciously comfortable. I was asleep in moments.

CHAPTER SIX

AND SO TO BOURNEMOUTH. I ARRIVED AT FIVE-THIRTY IN THE EVENING in a driving rain. Night had fallen heavily and the streets were full of swishing cars, their headlights sweeping through bullets of shiny rain. I'd lived in Bournemouth for two years and thought I knew it reasonably well, but the area around the station had been extensively rebuilt, with new roads and office blocks and one of those befuddling networks of pedestrian subways that compel you to surface every few minutes like a gopher to see where you are.

By the time I reached the East Cliff, a neighbourhood of medium-sized hotels perched high above a black sea, I was soaked through and muttering. The one thing to be said for Bournemouth is that you are certainly spoiled for choice with hotels. Among the many gleaming palaces of comfort that lined every street for blocks around, I selected an establishment on a side-street for no reason other than that I rather liked its sign: neat capitals in pink neon glowing beckoningly through the slicing rain. I stepped inside, shedding water, and could see at a glance it was a good choice – clean, nicely old-fashioned, attractively priced at £26 B & B according to a notice on the wall, and with the kind of smothering warmth that makes your glasses steam and brings on sneezing fits. I decanted several ounces of water from my sleeve and asked for a single room for two nights.

'Is it raining out?' the reception girl asked brightly as I filled in the registration card between sneezes and pauses to wipe water from my face with the back of my arm.

'No, my ship sank and I had to swim the last seven miles.'

'Oh, yes?' she went on in a manner that made me suspect she was not attending my words closely. 'And will you be dining with us tonight, Mr –' she glanced at my water-smeared card '– Mr Brylcreem?' I considered the alternative – a long slog through stair-rods of rain – and felt inclined to stay in. Besides, between her cheerily bean-sized brain and my smeared scrawl, there was every chance they would charge the meal to another room. I said I'd eat in, accepted a key and drippingly found my way to my room.

Among the many hundreds of things that have come a long way in Britain since 1973, and if you stop to think about it for even a moment you'll see that the list is impressively long, few have come further than the average English hostelry. Nowadays you get a colour TV, coffee-making tray with a little packet of modestly tasty biscuits, a private bath with fluffy towels, a little basket of cotton-wool balls in rainbow colours, and an array of sachets or little plastic bottles of shampoo, bath gel and moisturizing lotion. My room even had an adequate bedside light and two soft pillows. I was very happy. I ran a deep bath, emptied into it all the gels and moisturizing creams (don't be alarmed; I've studied this closely and can assure you that they are all the same substance), and, as a fiesta of airy bubbles began their slow ascent towards a position some three feet above the top of the bath, returned to the room and slipped easily into the self-absorbed habits of the lone traveller, unpacking my rucksack with deliberative care, draping wet clothes over the radiator, laying out clean ones on the bed with as much fastidiousness as if I were about to go to my first high-school prom, arranging a travel clock and reading material with exacting precision on the bedside table, adjusting the lighting to a level of considered cosiness, and finally retiring, in perky spirits and with a good book, for a long wallow in the sort of luxuriant foam seldom seen outside of Joan Collins movies.

Afterwards, freshly attired and smelling bewitchingly of attar of roses, I presented myself in the spacious and empty dining salon and was shown to a table where the array of accoutrements – a wineglass containing a red paper napkin shaped into a floret, stainless-steel salt and pepper shakers resting in a little stainless-steel boat, a dish containing wheels of butter carefully shaped like cogs, a small-necked vase bearing a sprig of artificial lilies – instantly informed me that the food would be mediocre but presented with a certain well-practised flourish. I covered my eyes, counted to four and extended my right hand knowing it would alight on a basket of bread rolls proffered by a hovering waiter – a mastery of timing that impressed him considerably, if I may say so, and left him in no doubt that he was dealing with a traveller who knew his way around creamy green soups, vegetables served with nested spoons and circlets of toughened rawhide parading under the name *medallions of pork*.

Three other diners arrived – a rotund mother and father and an even larger teenaged son – whom the waiter thoughtfully seated in a place where I could watch them without having to crane my neck or reposition my chair. It is always interesting to watch people eat, but nothing provides more interest than the sight of a tableful of fat people tucking into their chow. It is a curious thing but even the greediest and most rapacious fat people – and the trio before me could clearly have won championships for rapacity – never look as if they are enjoying themselves. It is as if they are merely fulfilling some kind of long-standing obligation to maintain their bulk. When there is food before them they lower their heads and hoover it up, and in between times they sit with crossed arms staring uneasily at the room and acting as if they have never been introduced to the people sitting with them. But roll up a sweet trolley and everything changes. They begin to make rapturous cooing noises and suddenly their little corner of the room is full of happy conversation. Thus it was tonight. Such was the speed with which my dining partners consumed the provends set before them that they beat me by half a course and, to my frank horror, between them consumed the last of the profiteroles and Black Forest gâteau from the sweet trolley. The boy, I noticed, had a double heap of both, the greedy fat pig.

I was left to choose between a watery dribble of trifle, a meringue confection that I knew would explode like a party popper as soon as I touched a spoon to it, or any of about a dozen modest cuplets of butterscotch pudding, each with a desultory nubbin of crusty yellow cream on top. In dim spirits, I chose a butterscotch pudding, and as the tubby trio waddled past my table, their chins glistening with chocolate, I answered their polite, well-fed smiles with a flinty hard look that told them not to try anything like that with me ever again. I think they got the message. The next morning at breakfast they took a table well out of my line of vision and gave me a wide berth at the juice trolley.

Bournemouth is a very fine place in a lot of ways. For one thing it has the sea, which will be handy if global warming ever reaches its full potential, though I can't see much use for it at present, and there are the sinuous parks, collectively known as the Pleasure Gardens, that neatly divide the two halves of the town centre and provide shoppers with a tranquil green place to rest on their long slog from one side of the centre to the other – though, of course, if it weren't for the parks there wouldn't be the long slog. Such is life.

The parks used to be described on maps as the Upper Pleasure Gardens and Lower Pleasure Gardens, but some councillor or other force for good realized the profound and unhealthy implications of placing Lower and Pleasure in such immediate proximity and successfully lobbied to have Lower removed from the title, so now you have the Upper Pleasure Gardens and the mere Pleasure Gardens, and lexical perverts have been banished to the beaches where they must find such gratification as they can by rubbing themselves on the groynes. Anyway, that's the kind of place Bournemouth is – genteel to a fault and proud of it.

Knowing already of the town's carefully nurtured reputation for gentility, I moved there in 1977 with the idea that this was going to be a kind of English answer to Bad Ems or Baden-Baden – manicured parks, palm courts with orchestras, swank hotels where men in white gloves kept the brass gleaming, bosomy elderly ladies in mink coats walking those little dogs you ache to kick (not out of cruelty, you understand, but from a simple, honest desire to see how far you can make them fly). Sadly, I have to report that almost none of this awaited me. The parks were very fine, but instead of opulent casinos and handsome kursaals, they offered a small band-stand occupied on occasional Sundays by brass bands of mixed talent dressed like bus conductors, and small wooden erections – if you will excuse the term in the context of the Lower Pleasure Gardens – bedecked with coloured glass pots with a candle inside, which I was assured were sometimes lit on calm summer evenings and thus were transformed into glowing depictions of butterflies, fairies and other magical visions guaranteed to provide hours of healthy nocturnal enjoyment. I couldn't say because I never saw them lit, and in any case, a shortage of funds and the un-conscionable tendency of youths to yank the pots from their frames and smash them at each other's feet for purposes of amusement meant that the structures were soon dismantled and taken away.

I strolled through the (Lower) Pleasure Gardens and on to the tourist information centre on Westover Road to see what alternative entertainments were on offer, and couldn't find out on account of you now had to pay for every piece of printed information that wasn't nailed to the wall. I laughed in their faces, of course.

At first glance, the town centre looked largely unchanged, but in fact progress and the borough council had been at work everywhere. Christchurch Road, the main thoroughfare through the centre, had been extensively pedestrianized and decorated with a curious glass and tubular steel edifice that looked like a bus shelter for giants. Two of the shopping arcades had been nicely tarted up and there was now a McDonald's, a Waterstone's and a Dillons, as well as one or two other establishments less directly connected to my personal requirements. Mostly, however, things had been subtracted. Beale's department store had closed its excellent book department, Dingle's had intemperately got rid of its food hall, and Bealeson's, yet another department store, had gone altogether. The International Store had likewise vanished, as had, more distressingly, an elegant little bakery, taking the world's best sugar doughnuts with it, alas, alas. On the plus side, there wasn't a scrap of litter to be found, whereas in my day Christchurch Road was an open-air litter bin.

Around the corner from the old vanished bakery on Richmond Hill were the splendid, vaguely art deco offices of the *Bournemouth Evening Echo*, where I worked for two years as a sub-editor in a room borrowed from a Dickens novel – untidy stacks of paper, gloomy lighting, two rows of hunched figures sitting at desks, and all of it bathed in a portentous, exhausting silence, the only noises the fretful scratchings of pencils and a soft but echoing *tunk* sound each time the minute hand on the wall clock clicked forward a notch. From across the road, I peered up at my old office windows now and shivered slightly.

After our marriage, my wife and I had gone back to the States for two years while I finished college, so my job at the *Echo* was not only my first real job in Britain, but my first real grown-up job, and throughout the two years I worked there I never ceased to feel like a fourteen-year-old masquerading as an adult, doubtless because nearly all my fellow sub-editors were old enough to be my father, except for a couple of cadaverous figures at the far end who were old enough to be their fathers.

I sat next to a pair of kindly and learned men named Jack Straight and Austin Brooks, who spent two years patiently explaining to me the meaning of *sub judice* and the important distinction in English law between taking a car and stealing a car. For my own safety, I was mostly entrusted with the job of editing the Townswomen's Guild and Women's Institute reports. We received stacks and stacks of these daily, all seemingly written in the same florid hand and all saying the same numbing things: 'A most fascinating demonstration was given by Mr Arthur Smoat of Pokesdown on the Art of Making Animal Shadows', 'Mrs Evelyn Stubbs honoured the assembled guests with a most fascinating and amusing talk on her recent hysterectomy', 'Mrs Throop was unable to give her planned talk on dog management because of her recent tragic mauling by her mastiff, Prince, but Mrs Smethwick gamely stepped into the breach with an hilarious account of her experiences as a freelance funeral organist.' Every one of them went on and on with page after page of votes of thanks, appeals for funds, long-winded accounts of successful jumble sales and coffee mornings, and detailed lists of who had supplied which refreshments and how delightful they all were. I have never experienced longer days.

The windows, I recall, could only be opened by means of a long pole. About ten minutes after we arrived each morning, one sub-editor so old he could barely hold a pencil would begin scraping his chair about in an effort to get some clearance from his desk. It would take him about an hour to get out of his chair and another hour to shuffle the few feet to the window and finagle it open with the pole and another hour to lean the pole against the wall and shuffle back to his desk. The *instant* he was reseated, the man who sat opposite him would bob up, stride over, shut the window with the pole and return to his seat with a challenging look on his face, at which point the old boy would silently and stoically begin the chair-scraping process all over again. This went on every day for two years through all seasons.

I never saw either one of them do a lick of work. The older fellow couldn't, of course, because he spent all but a few moments each day travelling to or from the window. The other guy mostly sat sucking on an unlit pipe and staring at me with a kind of smirk. Every time our gazes locked he would ask me some mystifying question to do with America. 'Tell me,' he would say, 'is it true that Mickey Rooney never consummated his marriage with Ava Gardner, as I've read?' or 'I've often wondered, and perhaps you can tell me, why is it that the nua-nua bird of Hawaii subsists only on pink-shelled molluscs when white-shelled molluscs are more numerous and of equal nutritive value, or so I've read.'

I would look at him, my mind fogged with Townswomen's Guild and Women's Institute reports, and say, 'What?'

'You *have* heard of the nua-nua bird, I take it?'

'Er, no.'

He would cock an eye. 'Really? How extraordinary.' And then he'd suck his pipe.

It was altogether a strange place. The editor was a recluse who had his meals brought to his chamber by his secretary and seldom ventured out. I only saw him twice in all the time I was there, once when he interviewed me, a meeting that lasted three minutes and seemed to cause him considerable discomfort, and once when he opened the door that connected his room to ours, an event so unusual that we all looked up. Even the old boy paused in his endless shuffle to the window. The editor stared at us in a kind of frozen astonishment, clearly dumbfounded to find a roomful of sub-editors on the other side of one of his office doors, looked for a moment as if he might speak, then wordlessly retreated, shutting the door behind him. It was the last I ever saw of him. Six weeks later, I took a job in London.

Something else that had changed in Bournemouth was that all the little coffee bars had gone. There used to be one every three or four doors, with their gasping espresso machines and sticky tables. I don't know where holidaymakers go for coffee nowadays – yes I do: the Costa del Sol – but I had to walk nearly all the way to the Triangle, a distant point where local buses go to rest between engagements, before I was able to have a modest and refreshing cup.

Afterwards, fancying a bit of an outing, I caught a bus to Christchurch with a view to walking back. I got a seat at the top front of a yellow double-decker. There is something awfully exhilarating about riding on the top of a double-decker. You can see into upstairs windows and peer down on the tops of people's heads at bus-stops (and when they come up the stairs a moment later you can look at them with a knowing look that says: 'I've just seen the top of your head') and there's the frisson of excitement that comes with careering round a corner or roundabout on the brink of catastrophe. You get an entirely fresh perspective on the world. Towns generally look more handsome from the top deck of a bus, but nowhere more so than Bournemouth. At street level, it's essentially like any other English town – lots of building society offices and chain stores, all with big plate-glass windows – but upstairs you suddenly realize that you are in one of Britain's great Victorian communities. Bournemouth didn't even exist before about 1850 – it was just a couple of farms between Christchurch and Poole – and then it positively boomed, throwing up piers and promenades and miles of ornate brick offices and plump, stately homes, most of them with elaborate corner towers and other busy embellishments that are generally now evident only to bus riders and window cleaners.

What a shame it is that so little of this Victorian glory actually reaches the ground. But then, of course, if you took out all that plate glass and made the ground floors of the buildings look as if they belonged to the floors above, we might not be able to see right into every Sketchley's and Boots and Leeds Permanent Building Society and what a sad loss that would be. Imagine passing a Sketchley's and not being able to see racks of garments in plastic bags and an assortment of battered carpet shampooers and a lady at the counter idly cleaning her teeth with a paperclip, and think how dreary life would be. Why, it's unthinkable.

I rode the bus to the end of the line, the car park of a big new Sainsbury's at the New Forest end of Christchurch, and found my way through a network of pedestrian flyovers to the Highcliffe road. About a half-mile further on, down a little side-road, stood Highcliffe Castle, formerly the home of Gordon Selfridge, the department store magnate, and now a ruin.

Selfridge was an interesting fellow who provides a salutary moral lesson for us all. An American, he devoted his productive years to building Selfridges into Europe's finest shopping emporium, in the process turning Oxford Street into London's main shopping venue. He led a life of stern rectitude, early bedtimes and tireless work. He drank lots of milk and never fooled around. But in 1918 his wife died and the sudden release from marital bounds rather went to his head. He took up with a pair of Hungarian–American cuties known in music-hall circles as the Dolly Sisters, and fell into rakish ways. With a Dolly on each arm, he took to roaming the casinos of Europe, gambling and losing lavishly. He dined out every night, invested foolish sums in racehorses and motorcars, bought Highcliffe Castle and laid plans to build a 250-room estate at Hengistbury Head near by. In ten years he raced through $8 million, lost control of Selfridges, lost his castle and London home, his racehorses and his Rolls-Royces, and eventually ended up living alone in a small flat in Putney and travelling by bus. He died penniless and virtually forgotten on 8 May 1947. But of course he had had the inestimable pleasure of bonking twin sisters, which is the main thing.

Today Highcliffe's stately Gothic shell stands crowded by bungalows, an incongruous sight, except at the back where the grounds run down to the sea through a public car park. I'd like to have known how the house had come to be in such a parlous and neglected state, but there was no-one around its brooding eminence and there were no cars in the car park. I followed some rickety wooden steps down to the beach. The rain had stopped in the night, but the sky was threatening and there was a stiff breeze that made my hair and clothes boogie and had the sea in a frenzy of froth. I couldn't hear anything but the pounding of waves. Leaning steeply into the wind, I trudged along the beach in the posture of someone shouldering a car up a hill, passing in front of a long crescent of beach huts, all of identical design but painted in varying bright hues. Most were shut up for the winter, but about three-quarters of the way along one stood open, rather in the manner of a magician's box, with a little porch on which sat a man and a woman in garden chairs, huddled in arctic clothing with lap blankets, buffeted by wind that seemed constantly to threaten to tip them over backwards. The man was trying to read a newspaper, but the wind kept wrapping it around his face.

They both looked very happy – or if not happy exactly, at least highly contented, as if this were the Seychelles and they were drinking gin fizzes under nodding palms rather than sitting half-perished in a stiff English gale. They were contented because they owned a little piece of prized beach-front property for which there was no doubt a long waiting-list and – here was the true secret of their happiness – any time they wanted they could retire to the hut and be fractionally less cold. They could make a cup of tea and, if they were feeling particularly rakish, have a chocolate digestive biscuit. Afterwards, they could spend a happy half-hour packing their things away and closing up hatches. And this was all they required in the world to bring themselves to a state of near rapture.

One of the charms of the British is that they have so little idea of their own virtues, and nowhere is this more true than with their happiness. You will laugh to hear me say it, but they are the happiest people on earth. Honestly. Watch any two Britons in conversation and see how long it is before they smile or laugh over some joke or pleasantry. It won't be more than a few seconds. I once shared a railway compartment between Dunkirk and Brussels with two French-speaking businessmen who were obviously old friends or colleagues. They talked genially the whole journey, but not once in two hours did I see either of them raise a flicker of a smile. You could imagine the same thing with Germans or Swiss or Spaniards or even Italians, but with Britons – never.

And the British are so easy to please. It is the most extraordinary thing. They actually like their pleasures small. That is why, I suppose, so many of their treats – teacakes, scones, crumpets, rock cakes, Rich Tea biscuits, fruit Shrewsburys – are so cautiously flavourful. They are the only people in the world who think of jam and currants as thrilling constituents of a pudding or cake. Offer them something genuinely tempting – a slice of gâteau or a choice of chocolates from a box – and they will nearly always hesitate and begin to worry that it's unwarranted and excessive, as if any pleasure beyond a very modest threshold is vaguely unseemly.

'Oh, I shouldn't really,' they say.

'Oh, go on,' you prod encouragingly.

'Well, just a small one then,' they say and dartingly take a small one, and then get a look as if they have just done something *terribly* devilish. All this is completely alien to the American mind. To an American the whole purpose of living, the one constant confirmation of continued existence, is to cram as much sensual pleasure as possible into one's mouth more or less continuously. Gratification, instant and lavish, is a birthright. You might as well say 'Oh, I shouldn't really' if someone tells you to take a deep breath.

I used to be puzzled by the curious British attitude to pleasure, and that tireless, dogged optimism of theirs that allowed them to attach an upbeat turn of phrase to the direst inadequacies – 'well, it makes a change', 'mustn't grumble', 'you could do worse', 'it's not much, but it's cheap and cheerful', 'it was quite nice *really*' – but gradually I came round to their way of thinking and my life has never been happier. I remember finding myself sitting in damp clothes in a cold café on a dreary seaside promenade and being presented with a cup of tea and a teacake and going 'Ooh, lovely!', and I knew then that the process had started. Before long I came to regard all kinds of activities – asking for more toast in a hotel, buying wool-rich socks at Marks & Spencer, getting two pairs of trousers when I only really needed one – as something daring, very nearly illicit. My life became immensely richer.

I exchanged smiles now with the happy couple at their hut, and trudged on along the beach to Mudeford, a hamlet standing on a spit of sandy land between the sea and the reedy sprawl of Christchurch Harbour, with a handsome view across to the Priory. Mudeford was once a refuge of smugglers, but today it is little more than a small, rather tatty parade of shops and a Volvo garage surrounded by houses, all with jaunty nautical names: Saltings, Hove To, Sick Over the Side.

I walked through it and on into Christchurch by way of a long, messy street lined with garages, dusty-looking shops and half-dead pubs, thence on to Bournemouth through Tuckton, Southbourne and Boscombe. Time had not done many favours to most of these places. Christchurch's and Southbourne's shopping precincts both appeared to be locked in a slow, untidy spiral of decline, and at Tuckton Bridge a once-lovely pub on the banks of the River Stour had had its lawns sacrificed to make room for a large car park. Now it was something called a Brewers Fayre, an offshoot of the Whitbread organization. It was awful but clearly and depressingly popular. Only Boscombe seemed to have picked itself up a little. Once, the main road through it had been ugly enough to make you gasp, full of blown litter, tacky shops and cruelly unsympathetic supermarkets and department stores crammed into Victorian frontages. Now the street had been smartly pedestrianized along part of its length, the Royal Arcade was being done up with style and care and the whole was generously scattered with antique shops, which were considerably more interesting to look at than the previous range of tanning salons and bedding centres. At the far end, a shop called the Boscombe Antique Market had a big sign in the window that said 'We Buy Anything!', which seemed an unusually generous offer, so I went inside, gobbed on the counter and barked, 'How much for that then?' I didn't, of course – it was shut – but I'd have liked to.

It was a long haul from Highcliffe to Bournemouth, ten miles or so altogether, and well into my daily happy hour by the time I reached East Overcliff Drive and the last leg to town. I paused to lean on a white fence rail and take in the view. The wind had died and in the pale evening light Poole Bay, as the sea at Bournemouth is called, was entrancing: a long, majestic curve of crumbly cliffs and wide golden beaches stretching from below the Isle of Wight to the purply Purbeck Hills. Before me the lights of Bournemouth and Poole twinkled invitingly in the gathering dusk. Far below, the town's two piers looked cheerful and dashing, and far out at sea the lights of passing ships bobbed and blinked in the dusky light. The world, or at least this little corner of it, seemed a good and peaceful place, and I was immensely glad to be there.

Throughout this trip, I would have moments of quiet panic at the thought of ever leaving this snug and homey little isle. It was a melancholy business really, this trip of mine – a bit like wandering through a much-loved home for a last time. The fact is, I liked it here. I liked it very much. It only took a friendly gesture from a shopkeeper, or a seat by the fire in a country pub, or a view like this to set me thinking that I was making a serious, deeply misguided mistake.

Which is why, if you were one of those clifftop strollers in Bournemouth that mild evening, you may have seen a middle-aged American wandering past in a self-absorbed manner and muttering in the tone of a mantra: 'Think of Cecil Parkinson's hair. Think of VAT at 17.5 per cent. Think of loading your car to overflowing with rubbish on a Saturday and driving to the tip only to find that it is shut. Think of hosepipe bans after ten months of rain. Think of the strange, unshakeable fondness of BBC1 for *Cagney and Lacey* repeats. Think of . . .'

CHAPTER SEVEN

I WENT TO SALISBURY ON A BIG RED DOUBLE-DECKER BUS THAT SWAYED down winding country roads and clattered through overhanging branches in a most exciting way. I like Salisbury very much. It's just the right size for a town – big enough for cinemas and bookshops, small enough to feel friendly and livable.

I picked my way through a busy market in the square and tried to imagine what the British see in these things. They always look so depressingly tawdry, with their upended crates and trodden lettuce leaves and grubby plastic awnings held together with clips. In French markets you pick among wicker baskets of glossy olives and cherries and little wheels of goat's cheese, all neatly arrayed. In Britain you buy tea towels and ironing-board covers from plastic beer crates. British markets never fail to put me in a gloomy and critical frame of mind.

Walking through the busy shopping streets now, I found it was the unattractive things that jumped out at me – Burger Kings and Prontaprints and Superdrugs and all the other manifold Enemies of the High Street, all of them with windows cluttered with announcements of special offers and all of them shoehorned into buildings without even the most fleeting nod to their character or age. In the centre of town, on a corner that ought to have been a visual pleasure, there stood a small building occupied by a Lunn Poly travel agency. Upstairs the structure was half-timbered and quietly glorious; downstairs, between outsized sheets of plate glass covered with handwritten notices of cheap flights to Tenerife and Malaga, the façade had been tiled – *tiled* – with a mosaic of little multi-toned squares that looked as if they had been salvaged from a King's Cross toilet. It was just awful. I stood before it and tried to imagine what combination of architects, corporate designers and town planners could have allowed this to be done to a fine timber-framed seventeenth-century building, and could not. And the thing was that it was really not a great deal worse than many other frontages along the street.

It sometimes occurs to me that the British have more heritage than is good for them. In a country where there is so astonishingly much of everything, it is easy to look on it as a kind of inexhaustible resource. Consider the numbers: 445,000 listed buildings, 12,000 medieval churches, 1,500,000 acres of common land, 120,000 miles of footpaths and public rights of way, 600,000 known sites of archaeological interest (98 per cent of them with no legal pro-tection). Do you know that in my Yorkshire village alone there are more seventeenth-century buildings than in the whole of North America? And that's just one obscure hamlet with a population comfortably under one hundred. Multiply that by all the other villages and hamlets in Britain and you see that the stockpile of ancient dwellings, barns, churches, pinfolds, walls, bridges and other structures is immense almost beyond counting. There is so much of it everywhere that it's easy to believe that you can take away chunks of it – a half-timbered frontage here, some Georgian windows there, a few hundred yards of ancient hedge or drystone wall – and that there will still be plenty left. In fact, the country is being nibbled to death.

It astounds me how casual are the planning regulations in such a sensitive environment. Did you know that even in conservation areas a houseowner may remove all the original doors and windows, cover the roof with hacienda-style tiles and the façade with artificial stone cladding, take down the garden wall, crazy pave the lawn and add a plywood porch, and still be deemed, in the eyes of the law, to be maintaining the carefully preserved tone of the neighbourhood? Just about the only thing he can't do, in fact, is tear the house down – but even that is a largely hypothetical legal nicety. In 1992, a development company in Reading tore down five listed buildings in a conservation area, was taken to court and fined all of £675.

Despite a certain stirring of consciousness in recent years, house-holders throughout the country can still do pretty much anything they want with their homes, farmers can still throw up mammoth tin sheds and grub up hedges, British Telecom can whip away red phone boxes and replace them with shower stalls, petrol companies can erect huge flat canopies on every forecourt, and retailers can impose their plasticky corporate styles on the most architecturally sensitive of structures, and there's nothing you can do about it. Actually, there is one little thing you can do: withhold your custom. I am proud to tell you that I haven't gone in a Boots in years and won't until they restore the frontages of their principal outlets in Cambridge, Cheltenham, York and such others as I might care to add to the list from time to time, and I would willingly get drenched to the bone if I could find a single petrol station within twenty miles of my home that didn't have a flying canopy.

Salisbury, I must point out in fairness, is actually much better at looking after itself than most other towns. Indeed, it is the very handsomeness of the place generally that makes the odd desecrations so difficult to bear. Moreover, it appears, little by little, to be getting better. The local authorities had recently insisted that a cinema owner preserve the half-timbered façade on a sixteenth-century building in the town centre and I noticed two places where developers appeared to be actually taking apart buildings that had been despoiled during the dark ages of the Sixties and Seventies and restoring them with diligence and care. One of the developers' boards boasted that it did this sort of thing more or less always. May it prosper for ever.

I would probably forgive Salisbury anything as long as they never mess with the Cathedral Close. There is no doubt in my mind that Salisbury Cathedral is the single most beautiful structure in England and the close around it the most beautiful space. Every stone, every wall, every shrub is just right. It is as if every person who has touched it for 700 years has only improved it. I could live on a bench in the grounds. I sat on one now and gazed happily for a half-hour at this exquisite composition of cathedral, lawns and solemn houses. I'd have stayed longer except that it began to drizzle, so I got up to have a look around. I went first to the Salisbury Museum in the hope that there would be a kindly person behind the counter who would let me leave my rucksack while I looked at the museum and cathedral. (There was, bless him.) The Salisbury Museum is outstanding and I urge you to go there at once. I hadn't intended to linger, but it was packed with diverting Roman oddments and old pictures and little scale models of Old Sarum and the like, for which I am always a sucker.

I was particularly interested in the Stonehenge Gallery because I was going there on the morrow, so I read all the instructive labels attentively. I know this goes without saying, but it really was the most incredible accomplishment. It took 500 men just to pull each sarsen, plus 100 more to dash around positioning the rollers. Just think about it for a minute. Can you imagine trying to talk 600 people into helping you drag a fifty-ton stone eighteen miles across the countryside, muscle it into an upright position and then saying, 'Right, lads! Another twenty like that, plus some lintels and maybe a couple of dozen nice bluestones from Wales, and we can *party*!' Whoever was the person behind Stonehenge was one dickens of a motivator, I'll tell you that.

From the museum, I wandered across the broad lawn to the cathedral. In the tragic event that you have never been there, I warn you now that Salisbury has long been the most money-keen of English cathedrals. I used to be pretty generally unsympathetic about ecclesiastical structures hectoring visitors for funds, but then I met the vicar of the University Church of St Mary the Virgin in Oxford – the most-visited parish church in England – and learned that its 300,000 annual visitors between them deposit a miserly £8,000 in the collection boxes, since which time I have mellowed considerably. I mean to say, these are glorious structures and deserve our grateful support. But Salisbury, I must say, takes things a good step beyond what I would call discreet solicitation.

First, you have to pass a cinema-style ticket booth where you are encouraged to pay a 'voluntary' admission charge of £2.50, then once inside you are repeatedly assaulted with further calls on your pocket. You are asked to pay to hear a recorded message or make a brass rubbing, to show your support for the Salisbury Cathedral Girl Choristers and the Friends of Salisbury Cathedral, and to help restore something called the Eisenhower flag, a seriously faded and tattered Stars and Stripes that once hung in Eisenhower's command post at Wilton House near by. (I left 10p and a note saying: 'But why did you let it get in such a state in the first place?') Altogether, I counted nine separate types of contributions box between the admission booth and the gift shop – ten if you include the one for votive candles. On top of that, you could hardly move through the nave without bumping into an upright display introducing the cathedral staff (there were smiling photographs of each of them, as if this were a Burger King) or discussing the Church's voluntary work overseas or glass cases with cutaway models showing how the cathedral was constructed – diverting, I grant you, but surely more appropriate to the museum across the close. It was a mess. How long, I wonder, till you climb into an electric cart and are whirred through the 'Salisbury Cathedral Experience' complete with animatronic stonemasons and monks like Friar Tuck? I give it five years.

Afterwards, I collected my rucksack from the kindly man at the Salisbury Museum and trudged off to the central tourist office, where I presented the young man behind the counter with a complicated prospective itinerary through Wiltshire and Dorset, from Stonehenge to Avebury and on to Lacock, Stourhead Gardens and possibly Sherborne, and asked him if he could tell me which buses I needed to catch that would let me see them all in three days. He looked at me as if I were wildly eccentric and said: 'Have you by any chance travelled by bus in Britain before?' I assured him that I had, in 1973. 'Well, I think you'll find that things have changed a bit.'

He fetched me a slender leaflet giving the bus times between Salisbury and points west and helped me locate the modest section dealing with journeys to Stonehenge. I had hoped to catch an early-morning bus to Stonehenge with a view to proceeding on to Avebury for the afternoon, but this, I instantly apprehended, was an impossibility. The first bus to Stonehenge didn't leave until almost eleven in the morning. I gave a snort of disbelief.

'I believe you'll find the local taxi services will take you to Stonehenge, wait for you there, and bring you back for about twenty pounds. A lot of our American visitors find this very satisfactory.'

I explained to him that though I was technically an American, I had lived in Britain long enough to be careful with my money, and, though I had not yet reached the point where I extracted coins one at a time from a little plastic squeeze pouch, I would not willingly part with £20 for any good or service that I couldn't take home with me and get years of faithful use out of afterwards. I retired to a nearby coffee shop with a sheaf of bus timetables and, extracting from my rucksack a weighty Great Britain Railway Passenger Timetable purchased specially for this trip, began a lengthy cross-study of the various modes of public travel available through Wessex.

I was mildly astounded to discover that many substantial communities had no rail services at all – Marlborough, Devizes and

Amesbury to name but three. None of the bus timetables appeared
to interconnect in any meaningful way. Buses to places like Lacock
were woefully infrequent and generally made the return journey
more or less immediately, leaving you the choice of staying for fourteen minutes or seven hours. It was all most discouraging.

Frowning darkly, I went off to the offices of the local newspaper
to find the desk of one Peter Blacklock, an old friend from *The
Times* now working in Salisbury, who had once carelessly
mentioned that he and his wife Joan would be delighted to put me
up if I was ever passing through Salisbury. I had dropped him a line
a few days before telling him that I would call at his office at 4.30
on whatever day it was, but the note must never have reached him
because when I arrived at 4.29 he was just easing himself out of a
back window. I'm joking, of course! He was waiting for me with
twinkling eyes and gave every impression that he and the saintly
Joan couldn't wait for me to eat their food, drink their liquor, muss
the guest bed and help them pass the night with a robust seven-hour
version of my famous Nasal Symphony. They were kindness itself.

In the morning, I walked with Peter into town while he pointed
out local landmarks – the spot where *As You Like It* was first performed, a bridge used by Trollope in the *Barchester Chronicles* –
and parted outside the newspaper offices. With two hours to kill, I
pootled about aimlessly, peering in shops and drinking cups of
coffee, before finally calling at the bus station, where a crowd
of people were already waiting for the 10.55 to Stonehenge. The
bus didn't arrive until after eleven and then it took nearly twenty
minutes for the driver to dispense tickets since there were many
tourists from foreign lands and few of them seemed able, poor
souls, to grasp the idea that they needed to hand over money and
acquire a little slip of paper before they could take a seat. I paid
£3.95 for a return ticket on the bus, then a further £2.80 for
admission at Stonehenge itself. 'Can I interest you in a guidebook
at two pounds sixty-five?' the ticket lady asked me and received in
reply a hollow laugh.

Things had changed at Stonehenge since I was last there in the
early Seventies. They've built a smart new gift shop and coffee bar,
though there is still no interpretation centre, which is entirely
understandable. This is, after all, merely the most important prehistoric monument in Europe and one of the dozen most visited
tourist attractions in England, so clearly there is no point in spending foolish sums making it interesting and instructive. The big

change is that you can no longer go right up to the stones and scratch 'I LOVE DENISE' or whatever on them, as you formerly were able. Now you are held back by a discreet rope a considerable distance from the mighty henge. This had actually effected a significant improvement. It means that the brooding stones aren't lost among crowds of daytrippers, but left in an undisturbed and singular glory.

Impressive as Stonehenge is, there comes a moment somewhere about eleven minutes after your arrival when you realize you've seen pretty well as much as you care to, and you spend another forty minutes walking around the perimeter rope looking at it out of a combination of politeness, embarrassment at being the first from your bus to leave and a keen desire to extract £2.80 worth of exposure from the experience. Eventually I wandered back to the gift shop and looked at the books and souvenirs, had a cup of coffee in a styrofoam cup, then wandered back to the bus-stop to wait for the 13.10 to Salisbury, and divided my time between wondering why they couldn't provide benches and where on earth I might go next.

CHAPTER EIGHT

AMONG THE MANY THOUSANDS OF THINGS THAT I HAVE NEVER BEEN able to understand, one in particular stands out. That is the question of who was the first person who stood by a pile of sand and said, 'You know, I bet if we took some of this and mixed it with a little potash and heated it, we could make a material that would be solid and yet transparent. We could call it glass.' Call me obtuse, but you could stand me on a beach till the end of time and never would it occur to me to try to make it into windows.

Much as I admire sand's miraculous ability to be transformed into useful objects like glass and concrete, I am not a great fan of it in its natural state. To me, it is primarily a hostile barrier that stands between a car park and water. It blows in your face, gets in your sandwiches, swallows vital objects like car keys and coins. In hot countries, it burns your feet and makes you go 'Ooh! Ah!' and hop to the water in a fashion that people with better bodies find amusing. When you are wet, it adheres to you like stucco, and cannot be shifted with a fireman's hose. But – and here's the strange thing – the moment you step on a beach towel, climb into a car or walk across a recently vacuumed carpet it all falls off.

For days afterwards, you tip astounding, mysteriously undiminishing piles of it onto the floor every time you take off your shoes, and spray the vicinity with quantities more when you peel off your socks. Sand stays with you for longer than many contagious diseases. And dogs use it as a lavatory. No, you may keep sand as far as I am concerned.

But I am prepared to make an exception for Studland Beach,

where I found myself now, having had a nifty brainstorm the previous day on the Salisbury bus. I had dredged my memory banks and remembered a small promise I'd made to myself many years before: that one day I would walk the Dorset coast path, and now here I was on this sunny autumnal morn, fresh off the Sandbanks ferry, clutching a knobby walking-stick that I had treated myself to in a moment of impetuosity in Poole, and making my way around the regal sweep of this most fetching of beaches.

It was a glorious day to be abroad. The sea was blue and covered with dancing spangles, the sky was full of drifting clouds white as bedsheets, and the houses and hotels of Sandbanks behind me looked radiant, almost Mediterranean, in the clear air. I turned with a light heart and made my way along the moist, packed sand at the water's edge towards the village of Studland and beckoning green hills beyond.

The Studland peninsula is well known as the only place where you can see all seven British reptiles – the grass snake, smooth snake, adder, slow worm, common lizard, sand lizard and Michael Portillo. For much of its length, the beach is reserved for naturists, which always adds a measure of interest to any walk along it, though today, in fact, there wasn't a soul to be seen along its three fetching miles; nothing before me but virgin sand and behind only my own footprints.

Studland village is a pretty little place scattered among trees, with a Norman church and some fine views over the bay. I followed the path round the edge of the village and up the hill towards Handfast Point. Halfway along, I met a couple out walking two large black dogs of uncertain genetic background. The dogs were romping playfully in the tall grass, but, as always happens, at the first sight of me their muscles tautened, their eyes turned a glowing red, their incisors grew a sudden inch and they were transformed into beasts of prey. In a trice they were at me, barking savagely and squabbling over sinew and nipping at my dancing ankles with horrible yellowy teeth.

'Would you please get your fucking animals off me!' I cried in a voice that sounded uncannily like that of Minnie Mouse.

The owner loped up and began attaching leads. He had on some stupidly jaunty flat cap like Abbott and Costello would wear in a golfing sketch. 'It's your stick,' he said accusingly. 'They don't like sticks.'

'What, they only attack cripples?'

'They just don't like sticks.'

'Well, then maybe your stupid wife should walk ahead with a sign saying: "Look Out! Stick-Crazy Dogs Coming."' I was, you may gather, a trifle upset.

'Look here, sunshine, there's no need to get *personal*.'

'Your dogs attacked me for no reason. You shouldn't have dogs if you can't control them. And don't you call me sunshine, *bub*.'

We stood glowering at each other. For one moment, it looked as if we might actually grapple and end up rolling around in the mud in an unseemly fashion. I restrained a wild impulse to reach out and flip his cap from his head. But then one of the dogs went for my ankles again and I retreated a few steps up the hill. I stood on the hillside, shaking my stick at them like some wild-haired lunatic. 'And your hat's stupid, too!' I shouted as they huffed off down the hill. That done, I smoothed down my jacket, composed my features and proceeded on my way. Well, honestly.

Handfast Point is a grassy cliff that ends in a sudden drop of perhaps 200 feet to seriously frothy seas. It takes a special blend of nerve and foolishness to creep up to the edge and have a look. Just beyond it stand two stranded pinnacles of limestone known as Old Harry and Old Harry's Wife, all that remains of a land bridge that once connected Dorset to the Isle of Wight, eighteen miles away across the bay and just visible through a cloak of salty mists.

Beyond the headland, the path climbed steeply to Ballard Down, a taxing slog for an old puffed-out flubba-wubba like me, but worth it for the view, which was sensational – like being on top of the world. For miles around, the Dorset hills rolled and billowed, like a shaken-out blanket settling on to a bed. Country lanes wandered among plump hedgerows and the hillsides were prettily dotted with woodlands, farmsteads and creamy flecks of sheep. In the distance the sea, bright and vast and silvery blue, stretched away to a mountain of tumbling cumulus. At my feet far below, Swanage huddled against a rocky headland on the edge of a horse-shoe bay, and behind me lay Studland, the marshy flats of Poole Harbour and Brownsea Island, and beyond that a hazy infinity of meticulously worked farmland. It was beautiful beyond words, one of those rare moments when life seems perfect. As I stood there, spellbound and quite alone, a bank of cloud drifted in front of the sun, and through it there poured magnificent spears of shimmery light, like escalators to heaven. One of them fell at my feet and for one moment I would almost swear I heard celestial music, an arpeggio of harps, and a voice speak to me: 'I've just sent those dogs into a nest of adders. Have a nice day.'

I went over to a stone bench that had been thoughtfully conveyed to this lofty summit for the benefit of weary chaps like me – it really is extraordinary how often you encounter some little kindly gesture like this in Britain – and took out my Ordnance Survey 1:25,000 map of Purbeck. As a rule, I am not terribly comfortable with any map that doesn't have a You-Are-Here arrow on it somewhere, but the Ordnance Survey maps are in a league of their own. Coming from a country where mapmakers tend to exclude any landscape feature smaller than, say, Pike's Peak, I am constantly impressed by the richness of detail on the OS 1:25,000 series. They include every wrinkle and divot on the landscape, every barn, milestone, wind pump and tumulus. They distinguish between sand pits and gravel pits and between power lines strung from pylons and power lines strung from poles. This one even included the stone seat on which I sat now. It astounds me to be able to look at a map and know to the square metre where my buttocks are deployed.

In my idle perusal, I noticed that a mile or so to the west there stood a historic obelisk. Wondering why anyone would erect a monument in such a remote and challenging spot, I struck off along the crest of the hill to have a look. It was the longest mile I can remember walking. I passed through grassy fields, through flocks of skittish sheep, over stiles and through gates, without any sign of my goal drawing nearer, but I doggedly pressed on because – well, because if you are stupid you do. Eventually, I arrived at a modest, wholly unremarkable granite obelisk. The weathered inscription revealed that in 1887 the Dorset Water Board had run a pipe past this point. Well, yippee, I thought. Pursing my lips and referring once more to my map, I noticed that just a bit further on was something called the Giant's Grave, and I thought: Well, that sounds interesting.

So I plodded off to see it. That's the trouble, you see. There's always some intriguing landmark just over the next contour line. You could spend your life moving from stone circle to Roman settlement (remains of) to ruined abbey and never see but a fraction of them even in a small area, particularly if, like me, you seldom actually find them. I never found the Giant's Grave. I think I was close, but I can't be sure. The one notable drawback of these OS maps is that sometimes perhaps they give you too much detail.

With so many possible landscape features to choose among, it's easy to convince yourself that you are pretty much wherever you want to be. You see a grove of trees and you stroke your chin and think, Well, now, let's see, that must be Hanging Snot Wood, which means that *that* odd-looking hillock is almost certainly Jumping Dwarf Long Barrow, in which case that place on the far hill must be Desperation Farm. And so you strike off confidently until you come up against some obviously unexpected landscape feature like Portsmouth and realize that you have gone somewhat astray.

Thus it was that I spent a quiet, sweatily perplexed afternoon tramping through a large, forgotten, but very green and pretty corner of Dorset, looking for an inland route to Swanage. The more I plunged on, the less defined did the footpaths become. By mid-afternoon, I found myself increasingly crawling under barbed wire, fording streams with my pack on my head, wrenching my leg from bear traps, falling down, and longing to be elsewhere. Occasionally, I would pause to rest and try to identify some small point of congruence between my map and the surrounding landscape. Eventually I would rise, peel a cowpat from my seat, purse my lips and strike off in an entirely new direction. By such means did I find myself, late in the afternoon and somewhat to my surprise, arriving footsore, travel-soiled and decorated about the extremities with interesting rivulets of dried blood, in Corfe Castle.

To celebrate my good fortune at finding myself anywhere at all, I went to the best hotel in town, an Elizabethan manor on the main street called Mortons House. It looked a thoroughly agreeable place and my spirits swelled. Moreover, they could accommodate me.

'Come far?' asked the girl at the desk as I filled in the registration card. The first rule of walking is, of course, to lie through your teeth.

'Brockenhurst,' I said, nodding gravely.

'Goodness, that's a long way!'

I sniffed in a frankly manful way. 'Yeah, well, I've got a good map.'

'And where are you off to tomorrow?'

'Cardiff.'

'Gosh! On foot?'

'Never go any other way.' I hoisted my pack, picked up my room key and gave her a man-of-the-world wink that would, I fancy, have made her swoon had I been but twenty years younger, considerably better looking and not had a large dab of cowshit on the end of my nose.

I spent a few minutes turning a large white towel black, then hurried out to see the village before everything shut. Corfe is a popular and pretty place, a cluster of stone cottages dominated by the lofty, jagged walls of its famous and much-photographed castle – everyone's favourite ruin after Princess Margaret. I treated myself to a pot of tea and a cake at the busy and cheerful little National Trust Tea Room, then hastened next door to the castle entrance. Admission was £2.90 – which I thought a bit steep for a heap of rubble – and the place was closing in ten minutes, but I bought a ticket anyway because I didn't know when I might pass this way again. The castle was pretty thoroughly dismantled by anti-royalists during the Civil War and then the townspeople helped themselves to most of what was left, so there isn't a great deal to look at but some ragged fragments of wall, but the views across the surrounding valley were exceedingly becoming, with the fading sunlight throwing long shadows on the hillsides and a hint of evening mist creeping in among the hollows.

I had a long, hot bath at the hotel and then, feeling happily knackered, decided to content myself with such pleasures as Mortons House could provide. I had a couple of drinks in the bar, then was summoned to the dining room. There were eight other diners, all white-haired, well dressed and nearly silent. Why are the English so quiet in hotel dining rooms? There wasn't a sound in the room but for the quiet scrapings of cutlery and murmured two-second conversations like:

'Supposed to be fine again tomorrow.'

'Oh? That's good.'

'Mmm.'

And then silence.

Or:

'Soup's nice.'

'Yes.'

And then silence.

Given the nature of the hotel I'd expected the menu to feature items like brown Windsor soup and roast beef and Yorkshire pudding, but of course things have moved on in the hotel trade. The menu now was richly endowed with ten-guinea words that you wouldn't have seen on a menu ten years ago – 'noisettes', 'tartare', 'duxelle', 'coulis', 'timbale' – and written in a curious inflated language with eccentric capitalizations. I had, and I quote, 'Fanned Galia Melon and Cumbrian Air Dried Ham served with a Mixed leaf Salad' followed by 'Fillet Steak served with a crushed Black Peppercorn Sauce flamed in Brandy and finished with Cream', which together were nearly as pleasurable to read as to eat.

I was greatly taken with this new way of talking and derived considerable pleasure from speaking it to the waiter. I asked him for a lustre of water freshly drawn from the house tap and presented *au nature* in a cylinder of glass, and when he came round with the bread rolls I entreated him to present me a tonged rondel of blanched wheat oven baked and masked in a poppy-seed coating. I was just getting warmed up to this and about to ask for a fanned lap coverlet, freshly laundered and scented with a delicate hint of Omo, to replace the one that had slipped from my lap and now lay recumbent on the horizontal walking surface anterior to my feet when he handed me a card that said 'Sweets Menu' and I realized that we were back in the no-nonsense world of English.

It's a funny thing about English diners. They'll let you dazzle them with piddly duxelles of this and fussy little noisettes of that, but don't fuck with their puddings, which is my thinking exactly. All the dessert entries were for gooey dishes with good English names. I had sticky toffee pudding and it was splendid. As I finished, the waiter invited me to withdraw to the lounge where a caisson of fresh-roasted coffee, complemented by the chef's own selection of mint wafers, awaited. I dressed the tabletop with a small circlet of copper specie crafted at the Royal Mint and, suppressing a small eruction of gastro-intestinal air, effected my egress.

Because I had strayed from the coast path, my first order of business the next morning was to find my way back to it. I left Corfe and lumbered gaspingly up a ferociously steep hill to the nearby village of Kingston. It was another glorious day and the views from Kingston over Corfe and its castle – suddenly distant and miniature – were memorable.

I picked up a mercifully level footpath and followed it for two miles through woods and fields along the crest of a hanging valley to rejoin the coast path at a lonely and dramatic eminence called Houns-tout Cliff. The view once again was stunning: whaleback hills and radiant white cliffs, dotted with small coves and hidden beaches washed by a blue and infinite sea. I could see all the way to Lulworth, my destination for the day, some ten miles and many daunting whalebacks to the west.

I followed the path up steep hills and down. It was only ten in the morning, but already it was unseasonably warm. Most of the Dorset coast hills are no more than a few hundred feet high, but they are steep and numerous and I was soon sweaty, shagged out and thirsty. I took off my pack and discovered with a groan that I had left my fancy new water bottle, bought in Poole and diligently filled that morning, back at the hotel. There's nothing like having nothing to drink to bring on a towering thirst. I plodded on, hoping against hope that there would be a pub or café in Kimmeridge, but as I approached from a high path above its lovely bay I could see that it was too small to be likely to offer anything. Taking out my binoculars I surveyed the village from afar and discovered that there was a Portakabin of some type by the car park. A little tea-room on wheels, perhaps. I hastened along the path, past a sadly neglected folly called the Clavel Tower, and down a steep path to the beach. Such was the distance involved that it took the better part of an hour. Crossing my fingers, I picked my way over the beach and went up to the Portakabin. It was a National Trust recruitment point and it was closed.

I made an anguished face. I had a throat like sandpaper. I was miles from anywhere and there was no-one around. At that moment, by a kind of miracle, an ice-cream van came trundling down the hill playing a twinkly tune and set up at the edge of the car park. I waited an impatient ten minutes while the young man in charge unhurriedly opened up various hatches and set out things. The instant the window slid open I asked him what he had to drink. He rooted around and announced that he had six small bottles of Panda Cola. I bought them all and retired to the shady side of the van, where I feverishly removed the plastic lid from one and poured its life-saving contents down my gullet.

Now I don't want you to think for a moment that Panda Cola is in any way inferior to Coke, Pepsi, Dr Pepper, Seven-Up, Sprite, or any of the other many flavoured drinks that unaccountably enjoy a larger patronage, or that serving a soft drink warm strikes me as remotely eccentric, but there was something curiously unsatisfying about the drinks I had just acquired. I drank one after another until my stomach was taut and sloshing, but I couldn't say that I actually felt refreshed. Sighing, I put the two remaining bottles in my ruck-sack, in case I had a syrup crisis later on, and continued on my way.

A couple of miles beyond Kimmeridge, at the far side of a monumentally steep hill, stands the little lost village of Tyneham, or what's left of it. In 1943, the Army ordered Tyneham's inhabitants to leave for a bit as they wanted to practise lobbing shells into the surrounding hillsides. The villagers were solemnly promised that once Hitler was licked they could all come back. Fifty-one years later they were still waiting. Forgive my disrespectful tone, but this seems to me disgraceful, not simply because it's a terrible inconvenience to the inhabitants (especially those that might have forgotten to cancel their milk), but also for poor sods like me who have to hope that the footpath through the firing range is open, which it is but occasionally. In fact, on this day it was open – I had prudently checked before setting off – so I was able to wander up and over the steep hill out of Kimmeridge and have a look round the clutch of roofless houses that is about all that remains of Tyneham. When I was last there in the late 1970s, Tyneham was forlorn, overgrown and practically unknown. Now it's become something of a tourist attraction. The county council has put up a big car park and the school and church have been restored as small museums, with photographs showing what it was like in Tyneham in the old days, which seems kind of a shame. I liked it much better when it was a proper ghost town.

I know the Army needs some place for gunnery practice, but surely they could find some new and less visually sensitive location to blow up – Keighley, say. The odd thing was that I couldn't see any sign of devastation on the hillsides. Big red numbered signs were scattered strategically about, but they were uniformly unblemished, as was the landscape around them. Perhaps the Army shoots Nerf balls or something. Who can say? Certainly not I because my diminishing physical resources were entirely consumed by the challenge of hauling myself up a killer slope that led to the summit of Rings Hill, high above Worbarrow Bay. The view was sensational – I could see all the way back to Poole Harbour – but what commanded my attention was the cruel discovery that the path immediately plunged back down to sea level before starting back up an even more formidable flanking hill. I fortified myself with a Panda Cola and plunged on.

The neighbouring eminence, called Bindon Hill, was a whopper. It not only rose straight up to the lower reaches of the troposphere but then presented a lofty up-and-down ridge that ran on more or less for ever. By the time the straggly village of West Lulworth hove into view and I began a long, stumbling descent, my legs seemed able to bend in several new directions and I could feel blisters bubbling up between my toes. I arrived in Lulworth in the delirious stagger of someone wandering in off the desert in an adventure movie, sweat-streaked, mumbling and frothing little nose rings of Panda Cola.

But at least I had surmounted the most challenging part of the walk and now I was back in civilization, in one of the most delightful small seaside resorts in England. Things could only get better.

CHAPTER NINE

ONCE MANY YEARS AGO, IN ANTICIPATION OF THE CHILDREN WE WOULD one day have, a relative of my wife's gave us a box of Ladybird Books from the 1950s and '60s. They all had titles like *Out in the Sun* and *Sunny Days at the Seaside*, and contained meticulously drafted, richly coloured illustrations of a prosperous, contented, litter-free Britain in which the sun always shone, shopkeepers smiled, and children in freshly pressed clothes derived happiness and pleasure from innocent pastimes – riding a bus to the shops, floating a model boat on a park pond, chatting to a kindly policeman.

My favourite was a book called *Adventure on the Island*. There was, in fact, precious little adventure in the book – the high point, I recall, was finding a starfish suckered to a rock – but I loved it because of the illustrations (by the gifted and much-missed J. H. Wingfield), which portrayed an island of rocky coves and long views that was recognizably British, but with a Mediterranean climate and a tidy absence of pay-and-display car parks, bingo parlours and the tackier sort of amusement arcades. Here commercial activity was limited to the odd cake shop and tea-room.

I was strangely influenced by this book and for some years agreed to take our family holidays at the British seaside on the assumption that one day we would find this magic place where summer days were forever sunny, the water as warm as a sitz-bath and commercial blight unknown.

When at last we began to accumulate children, it turned out that they didn't like these books at all because the characters in them never did anything more lively than visit a pet shop or watch a fisherman paint his boat. I tried to explain that this was sound preparation for life in Britain, but they wouldn't have it and instead, to my dismay, attached their affections to a pair of irksome little clots called Topsy and Tim.

I mention this here because of all the little seaside places we went to over the years, Lulworth seemed the closest to this idealized image I had in my head. It was small and cheerful and had a nice old-fashioned feel. Its little shops sold seaside-type things that harked back to a more innocent age – wooden sailboats, toy nets on poles, colourful beachballs held in long string bags – and its few restaurants were always full of happy trippers enjoying a cream tea. The intensely pretty, almost circular cove at the village's feet was strewn with rocks and boulders for children to clamber over and dotted with shallow pools in which to search for miniature crabs. It was altogether a delightful spot.

So imagine my surprise, when I emerged fresh-scrubbed from my hotel in search of drink and a hearty, well-earned dinner, to discover that Lulworth wasn't anything like I remembered. Its central feature was a vast and unsightly car park, which I had quite forgotten, and the shops, pubs and guesthouses along the street to the cove were dusty and looked hard up. I went in a large pub and almost immediately regretted it. It had that sickly, stale smell of slopped beer and was full of flashing fruit machines. I was almost the only customer in the place, but nearly every table was covered with empty pint glasses and ashtrays overflowing with fag ends, crisp packets and other disorderly detritus. My glass was sticky and the lager was warm. I drank up and tried another pub near by, which was marginally less grubby but scarcely more congenial, with battered décor and loud music of the Kylie Minogue Shout Loud and Wiggle Your Little Tits school of musical entertainment. It's small wonder (and I speak as an enthusiast) that so many pubs are losing their trade.

Discouraged, I repaired to a nearby restaurant, a place where my wife and I used to have crab salads and fancy ourselves genteel. Things had changed here, too. The menu had plunged downmarket to the scampi, chips and peas level, and the food was heartily mediocre. But the truly memorable thing was the service. I have never seen such resplendent ineptitude in a restaurant. The place was packed, and it soon became evident that not one party was happy. Almost every dish that appeared from the kitchen had something on it that hadn't been ordered or lacked something that had.

Some people sat foodless for ages while others at their table were presented all their courses more or less at once. I ordered a prawn cocktail, waited thirty minutes for it and then discovered that several of the prawns were still frozen. I sent it back and never saw it again. Forty minutes later a waitress appeared with a plate of plaice, chips and peas and couldn't find a taker so I had it, although I'd ordered haddock. When I finished, I calculated my bill from the menu, left the right money, minus a small reckoning for the frozen prawns, and departed.

Then I went back to my hotel, a place of deep and depressing cheerlessness, with nylon sheets and cold radiators, went to bed and read by the light of a 7-watt bulb and made a small, heartfelt vow never to return to Lulworth so long as I might live.

In the morning I awoke to find rain falling over the hills in great blown sheets. I breakfasted, settled the bill and spent a protracted period struggling into waterproofs in the front hallway. It's a funny thing. I dress myself most days without incident, but give me a pair of waterproof trousers to put on and it's as if I've never stood unaided. I spent twenty minutes crashing into walls and furniture, falling into pot plants and, in one particularly notable outburst, hopping on one leg for some fifteen feet before wrapping my neck around a newel post.

When at last I was fully kitted out, I caught a glimpse of myself in a full-length wall mirror and realized I looked uncannily like a large blue condom. Thus attired and accompanied with each step by an irritating rustle of nylon, I picked up my rucksack and walking-stick and took to the hills. I proceeded up Hambury Tout, past Durdle Door and the steep-sided valley engagingly called Scratchy Bottom, and on up a steep, muddy, zigzagging path to a lonely, fog-shrouded eminence called Swyre Head. The weather was appalling and the rain maddening.

Indulge me for a moment, if you will. Drum on the top of your head with the fingers of both hands and see how long it takes before either it gets seriously on your nerves or everyone in the vicinity is staring at you. In either case, you will find that you are happy to stop it. Now imagine those drumming fingers are raindrops endlessly beating on your hood and that there's nothing you can do about it, and moreover that your glasses are two circles of steamy uselessness, that you are slipping around on a rain-slickened path a single misstep from a long fall to a rocky beach –

a fall that would reduce you to little more than a smear on a piece of rock, like jam on bread. I imagined the headline – 'American writer dies in fall; was leaving country anyway' – and plodded on, squinting Magoo-like, with feelings of foreboding.

It is twelve miles from Lulworth to Weymouth. In *Kingdom by the Sea*, Paul Theroux gives the impression that you can walk it in an easy lope and still have time for a cream tea and to slag off the locals, but I trust he had better weather than I. It took me most of the day. The walking beyond Swyre Head was mostly along mercifully flat, if lofty, cliffs high above a cadaverous grey sea, but the footing was treacherous and the going slow. At Ringstead Bay the hills abruptly ended in a final steep descent to the beach. I rode an ooze of flowing mud down the hill to the bay, pausing only long enough to belly into boulders and carry out a few tree resiliency tests. At the bottom I pulled out my map and, making calipers of my fingers, worked out that I had only covered about five miles. It had taken most of the morning. Frowning at my lack of progress, I shoved the map into a pocket and moodily trudged on.

The rest of the day was a dreary, wet tramp along low hills above a pounding surf. The rain eased off and turned into an insidious drizzle – that special English kind of drizzle that hangs in the air and saps the spirit. About one o'clock Weymouth materialized from the mists, far off across a long curve of bay, and I gave a small cry of joy. But its seeming nearness was a cruel deception. It took me almost two hours to reach the town's outskirts, and another hour to walk along the front to the centre, by which time I was tired and limping. I got a room in a small hotel and spent a long time lying on the bed, booted and still condomed, before I could summon the strength to change into something less obviously mirth-making, have a light wash and hit the town.

I liked Weymouth a good deal more than I'd expected to. It has two claims to fame. In 1348 it was the place where the Black Death was introduced into England and in 1789 it became the world's first seaside resort when that tedious lunatic George III started a fashion for sea-bathing there. Today the town tries to maintain an air of Georgian elegance and generally nearly succeeds, though like most seaside resorts it had about it a whiff of terminal decline, at least as far as tourism goes. The Gloucester Hotel, where George and his retinue stayed (it was a private house then), had recently closed and now Weymouth didn't have a single decent large hotel, a sad omission in an old seaside town. But I'm happy to report that it does have many good pubs and one outstanding restaurant, Perry's, all of them in the harbour-front district, a tarted-up neighbourhood with fishing smacks bobbing on the water and a jaunty nautical air that makes you half expect to see Popeye and Bluto come loping round the corner. Perry's was crowded and cheerful and a joy to the spirits after Lulworth. I had local mussels from Poole – after three days of hard walking it came as a shock to realize that Poole was still local – and a highly creditable sea bass, and afterwards retired to the kind of dark and low-ceilinged pub where you feel as if you ought to be wearing a bulky Aran sweater and a captain's cap. I enjoyed myself very much and drank so much my feet stopped aching.

To the west of Weymouth stands the fifty-mile-long arc of Lyme Bay. Since the landscape just west of Weymouth is not particularly, or even fractionally, memorable, I took a taxi to Abbotsbury, and began my walk midway along Chesil Beach. I don't know what Chesil Beach is like towards the Weymouth end, but along this stretch it consisted of great drifts of small, kidney-shaped pebbles worn to a uniform smoothness by eons of wave action. They are nearly impossible to walk on since you sink to your ankle-tops with each step. The coast path is on firmer ground immediately behind the beach, but leaves you unable to see over the stony dunes. Instead, you just hear the sea, crashing into the shore on the other side and sending endless successions of pebbles clattering along the water's edge. It was the most boring walk I've ever had. My blisters soon began to throb. I can stand most kinds of pain, even watching Jeremy Beadle, but I do find blisters particularly disagreeable. By the time I reached West Bay, early in the afternoon, I was ready for a good sit-down and something to eat.

West Bay is an odd little place, spread out in a higgledy-piggledy fashion across a duney landscape. It had something of the air of a gold-rush town, as if it had sprung up hurriedly, and it looked poor and grey and spray-battered. I hunted around for some place to eat and happened on a nondescript-looking establishment called the Riverside Café. I opened the door and found myself in the most extraordinary setting. The place was heaving. The air was thick with shrill London-style chatter and all the customers looked as if they had just stepped out of a Ralph Lauren advertisement. They all had jumpers slung casually round their shoulders and sunglasses perched on their heads. It was as if a little piece of Fulham or

Chelsea had been magically wafted to this God-forsaken corner of
the Dorset coast.

Certainly I had never seen this kind of tempo outside a restaurant
in London. Waiters and waitresses dashed everywhere trying to
fulfil what appeared to be an inexhaustible demand to keep the
customers fed and, above all, supplied with wine. It was quite
extraordinary. As I stood there, trying to maintain my bearings,
Keith Floyd, the food johnny, wobbled past. I was impressed.

It all rather went to my head. I'm not usually much of one for
lunch, but the food smelled so wonderful and the ambience was so
extraordinary that I found myself ordering like a trencherman. I
had a starter of scallop and lobster terrine, an exquisite fillet of sea
bass with green beans and a mountain of chips, two glasses of wine,
and rounded it off with coffee and a generous slab of cheesecake.
The proprietor, a jolly nice man named Arthur Watson, wandered
among the tables and even called on me. He told me that until ten
years before the place had once been just a normal café doing roast
lunches and burger and chips, and little by little they had begun
introducing fresh fish and fancier foods and found there was a
clamour for it. Now it was packed out every mealtime and had just
been named the *Good Food Guide*'s restaurant of the year for
Dorset, but they still did burgers and they still did chips with everything, and I thought that was just wonderful.

It was gone three when I emerged from the Riverside with a light
head and heavy everything else. Taking a seat on a bench, I pulled
out my map and realized with a snort of dismay that I was still ten
miles from Lyme Regis, with the 626 feet of Golden Cap, the
highest hill on the south coast, standing between me and it. My
blisters throbbed, my legs ached, my stomach was grotesquely
distended and a light rain was beginning to fall.

As I sat there, a bus pulled up. I got up and put my head in the
open door. 'Going west?' I said to the driver. He nodded.
Impulsively, I lumbered aboard, bought a ticket and took a seat
towards the back. The trick of successful walking, I always say, is
knowing when to stop.

CHAPTER TEN

I SPENT THE NIGHT IN LYME REGIS AND PASSED THE FOLLOWING morning poking about in the town before catching a bus to Axminster and a train on to Exeter, a process that consumed considerably more time than I had expected. Daylight was fading by the time I stepped from Exeter St David's into a light but annoying rain.

I wandered through the city examining hotels from the street, but they all seemed a bit grand for me, and eventually ended up at the central tourist office, feeling mildly lost and far from home. I wasn't quite sure what I was doing here. I looked through racks of leaflets for shire-horse centres, petting zoos, falconry centres, miniature pony centres, model railways, butterfly farms, and something called – I jest not – Twiggy Winkie's Farm and Hedgehog Hospital, none of which seemed to address my leisure requirements. Nearly all the leaflets were depressingly illiterate, particularly with regard to punctuation – I sometimes think that if I see one more tourist leaflet that says 'Englands Best' or 'Britains Largest' I will go and torch the place – and they all seemed so pathetically modest in what they had to offer. Nearly all of them padded out their lists of featured attractions with things like 'Free Car Park', 'Gift Shop and Tea-Room' and the inevitable 'Adventure Playground' (and then were witless enough to show you in the photograph that it was just a climbing-frame and a couple of plastic animals on springs). Who goes to these places? I couldn't say, I'm sure.

There was a notice on the counter saying that the office booked rooms, so I asked the helpful lady if she would secure me lodgings.

She interviewed me candidly with regard to how much I was prepared to pay, which I always find embarrassing and frankly
un-English, and by a process of attrition we established that I fell
into a category that could be called cheap but demanding. It
happened that the Royal Clarence was doing a special deal with
rooms at £25 a night if you promised not to steal the towels, and I
leapt at that because I'd passed it on the way in and it looked
awfully nice, a big white Georgian place on the cathedral square.
And so it proved to be. The room was newly decorated and big
enough for hotel-room Olympics – wastebin basketball, furniture
steeplechase, jumping on to the bed by means of a swing on the
bathroom door and a well-timed leap, and other perennial
favourites of the lone traveller. I had a short but vigorous workout,
showered, changed and hit the streets famished.

Exeter is not an easy place to love. It was extensively bombed
during the war, which gave the city fathers a wonderful opportunity, enthusiastically seized, to rebuild most of it in concrete. It
was only a little after six in the evening, but the city centre was
practically dead. I wandered around beneath gloomy street lights,
looking in shop windows and reading those strange posters – bills,
as they are known in the trade – that you always find for provincial
newspapers. I have an odd fascination with these because they are
always either wholly unfathomable to non-locals ('Letter Box
Rapist Strikes Again', 'Beulah Flies Home') or so boring that you
can't imagine how anyone could possibly have thought they would
boost sales ('Council Storm Over Bins Contract', 'Phone Box
Vandals Strike Again'). My favourite – this is a real one, which I
saw many years ago in Hemel Hempstead – was 'Woman, 81, Dies'.

Perhaps I took all the wrong streets, but there seemed to be no
restaurants anywhere in central Exeter. I was only looking for
something modest that didn't have 'Fayre', 'Vegan' or 'Copper
Kettle' in the title, but all that happened was I kept wandering
down restaurantless streets and coming up against monstrous relief
roads with massive roundabouts and complicated pedestrian crossings that clearly weren't designed to be negotiated on foot by
anyone with less than six hours to spare. Finally, I happened on a
hilly street with a few modest eateries and plunged randomly into
a Chinese restaurant. I can't say why exactly, but Chinese
restaurants make me oddly uneasy, particularly when I am dining
alone. I always feel that the waitress is saying: 'One beef satay and
fried rice for the imperialist dog at table five.' And I find chopsticks

frankly distressing. Am I alone in thinking it odd that a people ingenious enough to invent paper, gunpowder, kites and any number
of other useful objects, and who have a noble history extending
back 3,000 years, haven't yet worked out that a pair of knitting
needles is no way to capture food? I spent a perplexed hour
stabbing at rice, dribbling sauce across the tablecloth and lifting
finely poised pieces of meat to my mouth only to discover that they
had mysteriously vanished and weren't to be found anywhere. By
the time I finished, the table looked as if it had been at the centre
of a violent argument. I paid my bill in shame and slunk out the
door and back to the hotel where I watched a little TV and snacked
on the copious leftovers that I found in sweater folds and trouser
turnups.

In the morning, I rose early and went out for a look round the
town. Exeter was locked in a foggy gloom that didn't do anything
for its appearance, though the cathedral square was very handsome
and the cathedral, I was impressed to find, was open even at eight
in the morning. I sat for some time at the back and listened to the
morning choir practice, which was quite wonderful. Then I wandered down to the old quay area to see what I might find there. It
had been artily renovated with shops and museums, but all of them
were closed at this time of day – or perhaps this time of year – and
there wasn't a soul about.

By the time I returned to the High Street, the shops were opening. I hadn't had breakfast because it wasn't included in my special
room rate, so I was feeling immoderately peckish and began a hunt
for cafés, but again Exeter seemed strangely lacking. In the end, I
went into Marks & Spencer to buy a sandwich.

Although the store had only just opened, the food hall was busy
and there were long queues at the tills. I took a place in a line
behind eight other shoppers. They were all women and they all did
the same mystifying thing: they acted surprised when it came time
to pay. This is something that has been puzzling me for years.
Women will stand there watching their items being rung up, and
then when the till lady says, 'That's four-twenty, love,' or whatever,
they suddenly look as if they've never done this sort of thing before.
They go 'Oh!' and start rooting in a flustered fashion in their handbag for their purse or chequebook, as if no-one had told them that
this might happen.

Men, for all their many shortcomings, like washing large pieces
of oily machinery in the kitchen sink or forgetting that a painted

door stays wet for more than thirty seconds, are generally pretty good when it comes to paying. They spend their time in line doing a wallet inventory and sorting through their coins. When the till person announces the bill, they *immediately* hand over an approximately correct amount of money, keep their hand extended for the change however long it takes or foolish they may begin to look if there is, say, a problem with the till roll, and then – mark this – pocket their change *as they walk away* instead of deciding that now is the time to search for the car keys and reorganize six months' worth of receipts.

And while we're on this rather daring sexist interlude, why is it that women never push toothpaste tubes up from the bottom and always try to get somebody else to change a lightbulb? How are they able to smell and hear things that are so clearly beyond the range of human acuity, and how do they know from another room that you are about to dip a finger into the icing of a freshly made cake? Why, above all, do they find it so unsettling if you spend more than four minutes a day on the toilet? This last is another long-standing mystery to me. A woman of my close acquaintance and I regularly have surreal conversations that run something like this:

'What are you doing in there?' (This said in an edgy tone.)

'I'm descaling the kettle. What do you think I'm doing in here?'

'You've been in there half an hour. Are you reading?'

'No.'

'You're reading, aren't you? I can hear the pages.'

'Honestly, I'm not.' That is to say, I *was* reading until a minute ago but now, of course, I'm talking to you, dear.

'Have you covered up the keyhole? I can't see anything.'

'Please tell me that you're not down on your hands and knees trying to look through the keyhole at your husband having a bowel movement in his own bathroom. Please.'

'You come out of there now. You've been in there for nearly three-quarters of an hour just *reading*.'

As she retreats, you sit there thinking, Did all that really just happen or have I wandered into a Dada exhibition? And then, shaking your head, you return to your magazine.

Still, it must be said that women are great with children, vomit and painted doors – three months after a painted door has dried they will still be touching it as if suspecting it might turn on them – which makes up for a lot, so I smiled benignly at the parade of

flustered ladies ahead of me until it was my turn to demonstrate to
the ones following how to do this sort of thing properly, but frankly
I don't think they took it in.

I ate my sandwich on the street, then returned to the hotel,
gathered up my things, settled the bill, stepped back outdoors and
thought: Now what? I wandered back to the rail station and had a
look at the flickering television screens. I thought about catching
a train to Plymouth or Penzance but the next one wasn't for a
couple of hours. There was, however, a train to Barnstaple leaving
shortly. It occurred to me that I could go there and then make my
way by bus along the north Devon coast to Taunton or Minehead.
I could stop *en route* at Lynton and Lynmouth, and possibly
Porlock and Dunster. It seemed a capital idea.

I asked the man in the ticket window for a single to Barnstaple.
He told me a single was £8.80, but he could do me a return for
£4.40.

'You wouldn't care to explain the logic of that to me, would
you?' I asked.

'I would if I could, sir,' he responded with commendable
frankness.

I took my pack and ticket to the requisite platform, where I sat
on a bench and passed the time watching the station pigeons. They
really are the most amazingly panicky and dopey creatures. I
couldn't imagine an emptier, less satisfying life. Here are instructions for being a pigeon: 1. Walk around aimlessly for a while,
pecking at cigarette butts and other inappropriate items. 2. Take
fright at someone walking along the platform and fly off to a girder.
3. Have a shit. 4. Repeat.

The platform televisions weren't working and I couldn't understand the announcements – it took me ages to work out that
'Eczema' was actually Exmouth – so every time a train came in, I
had to get up and make enquiries. For reasons that elude rational
explanation, British Rail always puts the destinations on the front
of the train, which would be awfully handy if passengers were waiting on the tracks, but not perhaps ideal for those boarding it from
the side. Most of the other passengers evidently couldn't hear the
announcements because when the Barnstaple train eventually came
in, half a dozen of us formed a patient queue beside a BR employee
and asked him if this was the Barnstaple train.

For the benefit of foreign readers, I should explain that there is a
certain ritual involved in this. Even though you have heard the

conductor tell the person ahead of you that this is the Barnstaple train, you still have to say, 'Excuse me, is this the Barnstaple train?' When he acknowledges that the large linear object three feet to your right is indeed the Barnstaple train, you have to point to it and say, '*This* one?' Then when you board the train you must additionally ask the carriage generally, 'Excuse me, is this the Barnstaple train?' to which most people will say that they think it is, except for one man with a lot of parcels who will get a panicked look and hurriedly gather up his things and get off.

You should always take his seat since you will generally find that he has left behind a folded newspaper and an uneaten bar of chocolate, and possibly a nice pair of sheepskin gloves.

Thus it was that I found myself sliding out of Exeter St David's Station while a man laden with parcels trotted along beside my window mouthing sentiments I couldn't decipher through the thick glass, and taking stock of my new possessions – a *Daily Mirror* and a Kit Kat, but unfortunately no gloves. We rattled out through the Exeter suburbs and into the lush Devon countryside. I was on what was called the Tarka Line – something to do with that story about an otter, which evidently was written somewhere in the vicinity. The countryside round about was gorgeous and extravagantly green. You could be excused for thinking that the principal industry of Britain is the manufacture of chlorophyll. We chuntered along between wooded hills, scattered farms, churches with square towers that made them look like leftover pieces from a very large chess set. I soon settled into that happy delirium that the motion of a train always induces in me, and only half noted the names of the little villages we passed through – Pinhead, West Stuttering, Bakelite, Ham Hocks, Sheepshanks.

It took over an hour and a half to cover the thirty-eight miles to Barnstaple, where I alighted and headed into town across a long bridge over the swift-flowing River Taw. I wandered around for a half an hour through narrow shopping streets and a large, cheerless covered market thinly arrayed with people selling handicraft items, and felt content that there was no need to linger here. Barnstaple used to be a major rail interchange, with three stations, but now there is just the one with its infrequent pootling services to Exeter, and a bus station overlooking the river. I went into the bus station and found two women sitting in an office beyond an open door, talking together in that quaint 'Oi be drinkin zoider' accent of this part of the world.

I asked them about buses to Minehead, about thirty miles to the east along the coast. They looked at me as if I'd asked for connections to Tierra del Fuego.

'Oh, you won't be gittin to Moinhead this toim of year, you won't be,' said one.

'No buses to Moinhead arter firrrrst of Octobaaarrrr,' chimed in the second one.

'What about Lynton and Lynmouth?'

They snorted at my naïvety. This was England. This was 1994.

'Porlock?'

Snort.

'Dunster?'

Snort.

The best they could suggest was that I take a bus to Bideford and see if I could catch another bus on from there. 'They may be runnin the Scarrrrrlet Loin out of Bideforrrrrd, they may be, oi they may, they may – but can't be sartin.'

'Will there be more people like you there?' I wanted to say but didn't. The only other option they could suggest was a bus to Westward Ho! but there didn't seem much point since I couldn't go anywhere else from there and anyway I couldn't face spending the night in an ejaculation, as it were. I thanked them and departed.

I stood outside in a froth of uncertainty and tried to think what to do next. All my carefully laid plans were coming unravelled. I retired to the curiously named Royal and Fortescue Hotel, where I ordered a tuna sandwich and a cup of coffee from a mute and charmless waitress, and rooted in my pack for my timetable, where I discovered that I had twenty-three minutes to eat my sandwich, drink my coffee, and waddle the mile back to the railway station to catch a train to Exeter, where I could start again.

I swallowed my sandwich nearly whole when it came, gulped two sips of coffee, threw some money on the table and fled for the station, terrified that I would miss the train and have to spend the night in Barnstaple. I just made it. When I got to Exeter, I marched straight up to the TV screens, determined to take the first train to anywhere.

Thus it was that I found myself in the hands of fate and bound for Weston-super-Mare.

CHAPTER ELEVEN

THE WAY I SEE IT, THERE ARE THREE REASONS NEVER TO BE UNHAPPY.

First, you were born. This in itself is a remarkable achievement. Did you know that each time your father ejaculated (and frankly he did it quite a lot) he produced roughly 25 million spermatozoa – enough to repopulate Britain every two days or so? For you to have been born, not only did you have to be among the few batches of sperm that had even a theoretical chance of prospering – in itself quite a long shot – but you then had to win a race against 24,999,999 or so other wriggling contenders, all rushing to swim the English Channel of your mother's vagina in order to be the first ashore at the fertile egg of Boulogne, as it were. Being born was easily the most remarkable achievement of your whole life. And think: you could just as easily have been a flatworm.

Second, you are alive. For the tiniest moment in the span of eternity you have the miraculous privilege to exist. For endless eons you were not. Soon you will cease to be once more. That you are able to sit here right now in this one never-to-be-repeated moment, reading this book, eating bon-bons, dreaming about hot sex with that scrumptious person from accounts, speculatively sniffing your armpits, doing whatever you are doing – just *existing* – is really wondrous beyond belief.

Third, you have plenty to eat, you live in a time of peace and 'Tie a Yellow Ribbon Round the Old Oak Tree' will never be number one again.

If you bear these things in mind, you will never be truly unhappy – though in fairness I must point out that if you find yourself alone in Weston-super-Mare on a rainy Tuesday evening you may come close.

It was only a little after six when I stepped from the Exeter train and ventured into the town, but already the whole of Weston appeared to be indoors beyond drawn curtains. The streets were empty, dark and full of slanting rain. I walked from the station through a concrete shopping precinct and out on to the front where a black unseen sea made restless whooshing noises. Most of the hotels along the front were dark and empty, and the few that were open didn't look particularly enticing. I walked a mile or so to a cluster of three brightly lit establishments at the far end of the promenade and randomly selected a place called the Birchfield. It was fairly basic, but clean and reasonably priced. You could do worse, and I have.

I gave myself a cursory grooming and wandered back into town in search of dinner and diversion. I had an odd sense that I had been here before, which patently I had not. My only acquaintance with Weston was that John Cleese had once told me (I'm not really dropping names; I was interviewing him for a newspaper article; he is a jolly nice fellow, by the way) that he and his parents lived in a flat in Weston, and that when they moved out Jeffrey Archer and his parents moved in, which I thought was kind of remarkable – the idea of these two boys in short trousers saying hello and then one of them going on to greatness. What made Weston feel familiar was, of course, that it was just like everywhere else. It had Boots and Marks & Spencer and Dixons and W.H. Smith and all the rest of it. I realized with a kind of dull ache that there wasn't a single thing here that I hadn't seen a million times already.

I went into a pub called the Britannia Inn, which was unfriendly without being actually hostile, and had a couple of lonely pints, then ate at a Chinese restaurant, not because I craved Chinese but because it was the only place I could find open. I was the only customer. As I quietly scattered rice and sweet and sour sauce across the tablecloth, there were some rumbles of thunder and, a moment later, the heavens opened – and I mean opened. I have seldom seen it rain so hard in England. The rain spattered the street like a shower of ball-bearings and within minutes the restaurant window was wholly obscured with water, as if someone were running a hose over it. Because I was a long walk from my hotel, I spun out the meal, hoping the weather would ease off, but it didn't, and eventually I had no choice but to step out into the rainy night.

I stood beneath a shop awning next door and wondered what to do. Rain battered madly on the awning and rushed in torrents through the gutters. All along the road it poured over the sides of overstretched gutters and fell to the pavement in an endless clatter. With my eyes closed it sounded like I was in the midst of some vast, insane tap-dancing competition. Pulling my jacket above my head, I waded out into the deluge, then sprinted across the street and impulsively took refuge in the first bright, open thing I came to – an amusement arcade. Wiping my glasses with a bandanna, I took my bearings. The arcade was a large room full of brightly pulsating machines, some of them playing electronic tunes or making un-bidden *kerboom* noises, but apart from an overseer sitting at a counter with a drooping fag and a magazine, there was no-one in the place so it looked eerily as if the machines were playing themselves.

With the exception of penny falls and those crane things that give you three microseconds to try to snatch a stuffed animal and in which the controls don't actually correspond to the movements of the grabber bucket, I don't understand arcade games at all. Generally I can't even figure out where to insert the money or, once inserted, how to make the game start. If by some miracle I manage to surmount these two obstacles, I invariably fail to recognize that the game has come to life and that I am wasting precious seconds feeling in remote coin-return slots and searching for a button that says 'Start'. Then I have thirty confused seconds of being immersed in some frantic mayhem without having the faintest idea what's going on, while my children shout, 'You've just blown up Princess Leila, you stupid shit!' and then it says 'Game Over'.

This is more or less what happened to me now. For no reason that I can possibly attach a rational explanation to, I put 50p in a game called Killer Kickboxer or Kick His Fucking Brains Out or something like that, and spent about a minute punching a red button and waggling a joystick while my character – a muscular blond fellow – kicked at drapes and threw magic discs into thin air while a series of equally muscular but unscrupulous Orientals assaulted him with kidney chops and flung him to the carpet.

I had a strange hour in which I wandered in a kind of trance feeding money into machines and playing games I couldn't follow. I drove racing cars into bales of hay and obliterated friendly troops with lasers and unwittingly helped zombie mutants do unspeakable things to a child. Eventually I ran out of money and stepped out into the night. I had just a moment to note that the rain had eased a little and that the street was flooded, evidently from a clogged drain, when a red Fiesta sped through the puddle at great speed and unusually close to the kerb, transferring nearly all the water from the puddle and on to me.

To say that I was drenched barely hints at my condition. I was as soaked as if I had fallen into the sea. As I stood there spluttering and gasping, the car slowed, three close-cropped heads popped out the windows, shouted some happy greeting along the lines of 'Nyaa-nyaa, nyaa-nyaa!' and sped off. Glumly, I walked back along the prom, squelching with each step and shivering with cold. I don't wish to reduce this cheery chronicle to pathos, but I had only recently recovered from a fairly serious bout of pneumonia. I won't say that I nearly died, but I was ill enough to watch *This Morning with Richard and Judy*, and I certainly didn't want to be in that condition again. To add to my indignity, the Fiesta came past on a victory lap and its pleasure-starved occupants slowed to offer me another triumphal 'Nyaa-nyaa' before speeding off into the night with a screech and a brief, uncontrolled fishtail slide that un-fortunately failed to bury them in a lamppost.

By the time I reached my distant hotel, I was feeling thoroughly chilled and wretched. So imagine my consternation, if you will, when I discovered that the reception area was in semi-darkness and the door was locked. I looked at my watch. It was only nine o'clock, for Christ sake. What kind of town was this? There were two doorbells, and I tried them both but without response. I tried my room key in the door and of course it didn't work. I tried the bells again, leaning on them both for many minutes and growing increasingly angry. When this elicited no satisfaction, I banged on the glass door with the flat of my hand, then with a fist and finally with a stout boot and a touch of frenzy. I believe I may also have filled the quiet streets with shouting.

Eventually the proprietor appeared at the top of some basement stairs, looking surprised. 'I'm so sorry, sir,' he said mildly as he unlocked the door and let me in. 'Have you been out there long?'

Well, I blush to think at how I ranted at the poor man. I used immoderate language. I sounded like Graham Taylor before they led him off and took away his warm-up suit. I accused him and his fellow townspeople of appalling shortages of intelligence and charm. I told him that I had just passed the dreariest evening of my life in this God-forsaken hell-hole of a resort, that I had been soaked to the skin by a carful of young men who between them were ten IQ points short of a moron, that I had walked a mile in wet clothes, and had now spent nearly half an hour shivering in the cold because I had been locked out of my own hotel at nine o'clock in the fucking evening.

'May I remind you,' I went on in a shrill voice, 'that two hours ago you said goodbye to me, watched me go out the door and disappear down the street. Did you think I wasn't coming back? That I would sleep in a park and return for my things in the morning? Or is it merely that you are a total imbecile? Please tell me because I would very much like to know.'

The proprietor flinchingly soaked up my abuse and responded with fluttering hands and a flood of apologies. He offered me a tray of tea and sandwiches, to dry and press my wet clothes, to escort me to my room and turn on my radiator personally. He did everything but fall to my feet and beg me to run him through with a sabre. He positively implored me to let him bring me something warming on a tray.

'I don't want anything but to go to my room and count the minutes until I get out of this fucking dump!' I shouted, perhaps a trifle theatrically but to good effect, and stalked up the stairs to the first floor where I plodded about heatedly in the corridor for some minutes and realized that I didn't have the faintest idea which was my room. There was no number on the key.

I returned to the reception area, now once more in semi-darkness, and put my head by the basement door. 'Excuse me,' I said in a small voice, 'could you please tell me what room I'm in?'

'Number twenty-seven, sir,' came a voice from the darkness.

I stood for some time without moving. 'Thank you,' I said.

'It's quite all right, sir,' came the voice. 'Have a good night.'

I frowned and cleared my throat. 'Thank you,' I said again and retired to my room, where the night passed without further incident.

In the morning, I presented myself in the sunny dining room and, as I had feared, the proprietor was waiting to receive me. Now that I was dry and warm and well rested I felt terrible about my outburst of the night before.

'Good-morning, sir!' he said brightly as if nothing had happened, and showed me to a window table with a nice view of the sea. 'Sleep all right, did you?'

I was taken aback by his friendliness. 'Uh, yes. Yes, I did as a matter of fact.'

'Good! Splendid! Juice and cereal on the trolley. Please help your-self. Can I get you the full English breakfast, sir?'

I found this unmerited *bonhomie* unbearable. I tucked my chin into my chest and in a furtive grumble said: 'Look here, I'm very sorry for what I said last night. I was in a bit of a temper.'

'It's quite all right, sir.'

'No really, I'm, um, very sorry. Bit ashamed, in fact.'

'Consider it forgotten, sir. So – full English breakfast, is it?'

'Yes, please.'

'Very good, sir!'

I've never had such good or friendly service anywhere, or felt more like a worm. He brought my food promptly, chattering away about the weather and what a glorious day it promised to be. I couldn't understand why he was so forgiving. Only gradually did it occur to me what a strange sight I must have presented – a middle-aged man with a rucksack, visiting a place like Weston out of season for no evident reason, fetching up at their hotel and bellow-ing and stomping about over a trifling inconvenience. He must have thought I was mad, an escaped lunatic perhaps, and that this was the safest way to approach me. Either that, or he was just an extremely nice person. In either case, I salute him now.

Weston was surprisingly lovely in morning sunshine. Out in the bay an island called Flat Holm basked in the clear, clean air and beyond it rose the green hills of Wales, twelve miles or so across the water. Even the hotels that I had disdained the night before didn't look half bad.

I walked to the station and took a train to Chepstow and a bus on to Monmouth. The Wye Valley was as beautiful as I remem-bered it from years before – dark woods, winding river, lonely white farmhouses high up on steep slopes – but the villages between were rather astonishingly charmless and seemed to consist mostly of petrol stations, pubs with big car parks and gift shops. I watched out for Tintern Abbey, made famous, of course, by the well-known Wordsworth poem, 'I Can Be Boring Outside the Lake District Too', and was disappointed to find that it didn't stand out in the country as I recalled but on the edge of an unmemorable village.

Monmouth, however, seemed to be a fine, handsome town with a sloping High Street and an imposing town hall. In front of it stood a statue of Charles Stewart Rolls, son of Lord and Lady Llangattock, 'pioneer of ballooning, motoring and aviation, who died in a crash at Bournemouth in July 1910', according to the inscription. He was shown holding a model of an early bi-plane, which made him look rather like King Kong swatting away attacking craft. There was no indication of what his local connection might be. The Monmouth Bookshop on Church Street had a book of mine in the window, and so of course gets a mention here.

I had it in mind to do another little walk while the weather was fine, so I didn't linger. I bought a pasty in a baker's and ate it as I found my way to the Wye. I picked up a riverside path by the town's handsome stone bridge and followed it north along the Welsh bank. For the first forty minutes, I was accompanied by the ceaseless roar of traffic on the A40, but at a place called Goldsmith's Wood the river bent sharply away from the road and I was suddenly in another, infinitely more tranquil world. Birds fussed and twittered in the trees above and small, unseen creatures plinked into the water at my approach. The river, sparkling and languid and framed by hills of autumn-coloured trees, was very beautiful and I had it all to myself. A mile or two further on, I paused to study the map and noticed a spot on a nearby hill called King Arthur's Cave. I couldn't pass that up, so I lumbered up the hill and poked around among likely spots. After about an hour of clambering over boulders and fallen trees, I found it, to my mild astonishment. It wasn't much – just a shallow chamber hewn by nature from a limestone cliff-face – but I had a pleasing sense of being its first visitor in years. At any rate, there were none of the usual signs of visitation – graffiti and abandoned beer cans – which may make it unique in Britain, if not the world.

Because time was getting on, I decided to take a shortcut through the hilly woods, but I neglected to note that I was at the uppermost of a very tight band of contour lines. In consequence, I found myself a moment later descending a more or less perpendicular hill in an entirely involuntary fashion, bounding through the woods with great leaps and outflung arms in a manner oddly reminiscent of George Chakiris in *West Side Story*, except of course that this was Wales and George Chakiris didn't shit himself with terror, before eventually, after several bouncing somersaults and an epochal eighty-yard slide on my stomach, ending up on the very lip of a giddy precipice, with a goggle-eyed view of the glittery Wye a hundred feet below. I cast my gaze back along my suddenly motionless body to find that my left foot had fortuitously snagged on a sapling. Had the sapling not been there I would not be here.

Muttering, 'Thank you, Lord, I owe you one,' I hauled myself to my feet, dusted twigs and leaf-mould from my front, and clambered laboriously back up the hill to the path I had so intemperately forsaken. By the time I reached the riverbank another hour had gone. It took another hour or so to hike on to Symonds Yat, a spacious wooded bluff at the top of a formidable hill, with long views in many directions. It was exceedingly fetching – a hang-glider's vista over the meandering river and an Arcadian landscape of fields and woodland stretching off to the distant Black Mountains.

'Not bad,' I said, 'not bad at all,' and wondered if there was anywhere near by where I could get a cup of tea and possibly change my pants.

CHAPTER TWELVE

THERE ARE CERTAIN THINGS THAT YOU HAVE TO BE BRITISH OR AT LEAST older than me, or possibly both, to appreciate: Sooty, Tony Hancock, *Bill and Ben the Flowerpot Men*, Marmite, skiffle music, that *Morecambe and Wise* segment in which Angela Rippon shows off her legs by dancing, Gracie Fields singing 'Sally', George Formby doing anything, *Dixon of Dock Green*, HP sauce, salt cellars with a single large hole, travelling funfairs, making sandwiches from bread you've sliced yourself, really milky tea, allotments, the belief that household wiring is an interesting topic for conversation, steam trains, toast made under a gas grill, thinking that going to choose wallpaper with your mate constitutes a reasonably good day out, wine made out of something other than grapes, unheated bedrooms and bathrooms, seaside rock, erecting windbreaks on a beach (why, pray, are you *there* if you need a windbreak?) and taking an interest in by-elections. There may be one or two others that don't occur to me at the moment.

I'm not saying that these things are bad or boring or misguided, merely that their full value and appeal yet eludes me. Into this category, I would also tentatively insert Oxford.

I have the greatest respect for the university and its 800 years of tireless intellectual toil, but I must confess that I'm not entirely clear what it's *for*, now that Britain no longer needs colonial administrators who can quip in Latin. I mean to say, you see all these dons and scholars striding past, absorbed in deep discussions about the Leibniz–Clarke controversy or post-Kantian aesthetics and you think: Most impressive, but perhaps a tad indulgent in a country where there are 3 million unemployed and the last great invention was cat's-eyes? Only the night before there had been an item on *News at Ten* in which Trevor McDonald had been radiant with joy to announce that the Samsung Corporation was building a new factory in Tyneside which would provide jobs for 800 people who were willing to wear orange boilersuits and do t'ai chi for a half-hour every morning. Now call me an unreconstructed philistine, but it seems to me – and I offer this observation in a spirit of friend-ship – that when a nation's industrial prowess has plunged so low that it is reliant on Korean firms for its future economic security, then perhaps it is time to re-address one's educational priorities and maybe give a little thought to what's going to put some food on the table in about 2010.

I remember once years ago watching a special international edition of *University Challenge* between a team of British scholars and a team of American scholars. The British team won so handily that they and Bamber Gascoigne and the studio audience were deeply, palpably embarrassed. It really was the most dazzling dis-play of intellectual superiority. The final score was something like 12,000 to 2. But here's the thing. I am certain beyond the tiniest measure of doubt that if you tracked down the competitors to see what has become of them since, you would find that every one of the Americans is pulling down $350,000 a year trading bonds or running corporations while the British are studying the tonal qualities of sixteenth-century choral music in Lower Silesia and wearing jumpers with holes in them.

But don't worry. Oxford has been pre-eminent since the Middle Ages, and I am sure that it will remain so long after it has become the University of Oxford (Sony UK) Ltd. The university, it must be said, has become infinitely more commercial-minded. At the time of my visit, it was just finishing a successful, five-year, £340-million fund-raising campaign, which was most impressive, and it had learned the value of corporate sponsorship. If you look through the prospectus you'll find it littered with references to things like The All-New Shredded Wheat (No Added Sugar or Salt) Chair of Eastern Philosophy and the Harris Carpets Why-Pay-More Thousands of Rolls in Stock at Everyday Low Prices School of Business Management.

This business of corporate sponsorship is something that seems to have crept into British life generally in recent years without being much remarked upon. Nowadays you have the Canon League, the

Coca-Cola Cup, the Ever-Ready Derby, the Embassy World Snooker Championships. The day can't be far off when we get things like the Kellogg's Pop Tart Queen Mother, the Mitsubishi Corporation Proudly Presents Regents Park, and Samsung City (formerly Newcastle).

But I digress. My gripe with Oxford has nothing to do with fund-raising or how it educates its scholars. My gripe with Oxford is that so much of it is so ugly. Come with me down Merton Street and I will show you what I mean. Note, as we stroll past the backs of Christ Church, the studied calm of Corpus Christi, the soft golden glow of Merton, that we are immersed in an architectural treasure house, one of the densest assemblages of historic buildings in the world, and that Merton Street presents us with an unquestionably becoming prospect of gabled buildings, elaborate wrought-iron gates and fine seventeenth- and eighteenth-century townhouses. Several of the houses have been mildly disfigured by the careless addition of electrical wires to their façades (something that other less intellectually distracted nations would put inside) but never mind. They are easily overlooked. But what is this inescapable intrusion at the bottom? Is it an electrical substation? A halfway house designed by the inmates? No, it is the Merton College Warden's Quarters, a little dash of mindless Sixties excrescence foisted on an otherwise largely flawless street.

Now come with me while we backtrack to Kybald Street, a forgotten lane lost amid a warren of picturesque little byways between Merton Street and the High. At its eastern extremity Kybald Street ends in a pocket-sized square that positively cries out for a small fountain and maybe some benches. But what we find instead is a messy jumble of double- and triple-parked cars. Now on to Oriel Square: an even messier jumble of abandoned vehicles. Then on up Cornmarket (avert your gaze; this is *truly* hideous), past Broad Street and St Giles (still more automotive messiness) and finally let us stop, exhausted and dispirited, outside the unconscionable concrete eyesore that is the University Offices on the absurdly named Wellington Square. No, let's not. Let's pass back down Cornmarket, through the horrible, low-ceilinged, ill-lit drabness of the Clarendon Shopping Centre, out on to Queen Street, past the equally unadorable Westgate Shopping Centre and central library with its heartless, staring windows and come to rest at the outsized pustule that is the head office of Oxfordshire County Council. We could go on through St Ebbes, past the brutalist compound of the magistrates' courts, along the bleak sweep of Oxpens Road, with its tyre and exhaust centres and pathetically under-landscaped ice rink and car parks, and out onto the busy squalor of Park End Street, but I think we can safely stop here at the County Council, and save our weary legs.

Now none of this would bother me a great deal except that everyone, but everyone, you talk to in Oxford thinks that it is one of the most beautiful cities in the world, with all that that implies in terms of careful preservation and general liveability. Now I know that Oxford has moments of unutterable beauty. Christ Church Meadow, Radcliffe Square, the college quads, Catte Street and Turl Street, Queens Lane and much of the High Street, the botanic garden, Port Meadow, University Parks, Clarendon House, the whole of north Oxford – all very fine. It has the best collection of bookshops in the world, some of the most splendid pubs and the most wonderful museums of any city of its size. It has a terrific indoor market. It has the Sheldonian Theatre. It has the Bodleian Library. It has a scattering of prospects that melt the heart.

But there is also so much that is so wrong. How did it happen? This is a serious question. What sort of mad seizure was it that gripped the city's planners, architects and college authorities in the 1960s and 1970s? Did you know that it was once seriously proposed to tear down Jericho, a district of fine artisans' homes, and to run a bypass right across Christ Church Meadow? These ideas weren't just misguided, they were criminally insane. And yet on a lesser scale they were repeated over and over throughout the city. Just look at the Merton College Warden's Quarters – which is not by any means the worst building in the city. What a remarkable series of improbabilities were necessary to its construction. First, some architect had to design it, had to wander through a city steeped in 800 years of architectural tradition, and with great care conceive of a structure that looked like a toaster with windows. Then a committee of finely educated minds at Merton had to show the most extraordinary indifference to their responsibilities to posterity and say to themselves, 'You know, we've been putting up handsome buildings since 1264; let's have an ugly one for a change.' Then the planning authorities had to say, 'Well, why not? Plenty worse in Basildon.' Then the whole of the city – students, dons, shopkeepers, office workers, members of the Oxford Preservation Trust – had to acquiesce and not kick up a fuss. Multiply this by, say, 200 or 300 or 400 and you have modern

Oxford. And you tell me that it is one of the most beautiful, well-preserved cities in the world? I'm afraid not. It is a beautiful city that has been treated with gross indifference and lamentable incompetence for far too long, and every living person in Oxford should feel a little bit ashamed.

Goodness me! What an outburst! Let's lighten up and go look at some good things. The Ashmolean, for instance. What a wonderful institution, the oldest public museum on Planet Earth and certainly one of the finest. How is it that it is always so empty? I spent a long morning there politely examining the antiquities, and had the place all to myself but for a party of schoolchildren who could occasionally be sighted racing between rooms pursued by a harried-looking teacher, then strolled over to the Pitt-Rivers and University museums, which are also very agreeable in their quaint, welcome-to-the-1870s sort of way. I trawled through Blackwell's and Dillon's, poked about at Balliol and Christ Church, ambled through University Parks and Christ Church Meadow, ranged out through Jericho and the stolid, handsome mansions of north Oxford.

Perhaps I'm too hard on poor old Oxford. I mean, it is basically a wonderful place, with its smoky pubs and bookshops and scholarly air, as long as you fix your gaze on the good things and never go anywhere near Cornmarket or George Street. I particularly like it at night when the traffic dies away enough that you don't need an oxygen mask and the High Street fills up with those mysteriously popular doner kebab vans, which tempt me not (how can anyone eat something that looks so uncannily as if it has been carved from a dead man's leg?) but do have a kind of seductive Hopperish glow about them. I like the darkness of the back lanes that wander between high walls, where you half expect to be skewered and dismembered by Jack the Ripper or possibly a doner kebab wholesaler. I like wandering up St Giles to immerse myself in the busy conviviality of Brown's Restaurant – a wonderful, friendly place where, perhaps uniquely in Britain, you can get an excellent Caesar salad and a bacon cheeseburger without having to sit among pounding music and a lot of ersatz Route 66 signs. Above all, I like to drink in the pubs, where you can sit with a book and not be looked on as a social miscreant, and be among laughing, lively young people and lose yourself in reveries of what it was like when you too had energy and a flat stomach and thought of sex as something more than a welcome chance for a lie-down.

*

I'd impetuously said I would stay for three nights when I booked
into my hotel, and by mid-morning of the third day I was beginning
to feel a little restless, so I decided to have a walk to Sutton
Courtenay for no reason other than that George Orwell is buried
there and it seemed about the right distance. I walked out of the city
by way of a water meadow to North Hinksey and onwards towards
Boar's Hill through an area called, with curious indecisiveness,
Chilswell Valley or Happy Valley. It had rained in the night and the
heavy clay soil stuck to my boots and made the going arduous.
Soon I had an accumulation of mud that doubled the size of my
feet. A bit further on the path had been covered with loose
chippings, presumably to make the going easier, but in fact the
chippings stuck to my muddy boots so that it looked as if I were
walking around with two very large currant buns on my feet. At the
top of Boar's Hill I stopped to savour the view – it's the one that led
Matthew Arnold to spout that overwrought nonsense about
'dreaming spires', and it has been cruelly despoiled by those marching electricity pylons which Oxfordshire has in greater abundance
than any county I know – and to scrape the mud from my boots
with a stick.

Boar's Hill has some appealing big houses but I don't think I
could happily settle there. I noted three driveways with signs saying
'No Turning'. Now tell me, just how petty do you have to be, how
ludicrously possessive of your little piece of turf, to put up a sign
like that? What harm can there possibly be in some lost or mis-
directed person turning a car round in the edge of your driveway?
I always make a point of turning round in such driveways, whether
I need to or not, and I urge you to join me in this practice. It is
always a good idea to toot your horn two or three times to make
sure that the owner sees you. Also, while I think of it, can I ask you
to tear up your junk mail, particularly when that mail invites
you to take on more debt, and return it to the sender in the post-
paid envelope? It would make a far more effective gesture if there
were thousands of us doing it.

I reached Abingdon by way of a back lane from Sunningwell.
Abingdon had one of the best-kept council estates I think I've ever
seen – huge sweeps of lawn and neat houses – and a handsome
town hall built on stilts as if somebody was expecting a forty-day
flood, but that's as much as I'm prepared to say for Abingdon. It
has the most appalling shopping precinct, which I later learned
had been created by sweeping away a raft of medieval houses, and

NOTES from a SMALL ISLAND

a kind of dogged commitment to ugliness around its fringes.

Sutton Courtenay seemed considerably further on than I recalled it from the map, but it was a pleasant walk with frequent views of the Thames. It is a charming place, with some fine homes, three agreeable-looking pubs, and a little green with a war memorial, beside which stands the churchyard where not only George Orwell lies, but also H.H. Asquith. Call me a perennial Iowa farmboy, but I never fail to be impressed by how densely packed with worthies is this little island. How remarkable it is that in a single village churchyard you find the graves of two men of global stature. We in Iowa would be proud of either one of them – indeed, we would be proud of Trigger the Wonder Horse or the guy who invented traffic cones or pretty much anyone at all.

I walked into the graveyard and found Orwell's grave. It had three straggly rose bushes growing out of it and some artificial flowers in a glass jar, before a simple stone with a curiously terse inscription:

Here Lies Eric Arthur Blair
Born June 25th 1903
Died January 21st 1950

Not much sentiment there, what? Near by was the grave of Herbert Henry Asquith. It was one of those tea-caddy tombs, and it was sinking into the ground in an alarming manner. His inscription too was mysteriously to the point. It said simply:

Earl of Oxford and Asquith
Prime Minister of England
April 1908 to December 1916
Born 12 September 1852
Died 15 February 1928

Notice anything odd there? I bet you did if you are Scottish or Welsh. The whole place was a bit strange. I mean to say, here was a cemetery containing the grave of a famous author that was made as anonymous as if he had been buried a pauper, and another of a man whose descendants had apparently forgotten exactly what he was Prime Minister of and which looked seriously in danger of being swallowed by the earth. Next to Asquith lay one Ruben Loveridge 'who fell asleep 29th April 1950' and near by was a grave shared by two men: 'Samuel Lewis 1881–1930' and 'Alan Slater 1924–1993'. What an intriguing little community this was – a place where men are entombed together and they bury you if you fall asleep.

On second thought, I think we Iowans would be content to let you keep Orwell and Asquith as long as we could have the guy who was buried alive.

CHAPTER THIRTEEN

I SUSPENDED MY PRINCIPLES AND HIRED A CAR FOR THREE DAYS. WELL, I had to. I wanted to see the Cotswolds and it doesn't take long to work out that you can't see the Cotswolds unless you have your own motive power. As long ago as 1933, J.B. Priestley was noting in *English Journey* that even then, in those golden pre-Beeching days, there was just one line through the Cotswolds. Now there isn't even that, except for one that runs uselessly along the edges.

So I hired a car in Oxford and set off with that giddying sense of unbounded possibility that comes when I find myself in charge of two tons of unfamiliar metal. My experience with hire cars is that generally they won't let you leave a city until they have had a chance to say goodbye to most of it. Mine took me on a long tour through Botley and Hinkley, on a nostalgic swing past the Rover works at Cowley and out through Blackbird Leys before conveying me twice around a roundabout and flinging me, like a spacecraft in planetary orbit, back towards town. I was powerless to do anything about this, largely because my attention was preoccupied with trying to turn off the back windscreen wiper, which seemed to have a mind of its own, and figuring out how to remove an opaque cloud of foamy washing fluid from the front windscreen, which shot out in great obscuring streams irrespective of which switch I pushed or stalk I waggled.

At least it gave me a chance to see the little-known but intriguing Potato Marketing Board building at Cowley, into whose car park I pulled to turn around when I realized I was utterly lost. The building was a substantial 1960s edifice, four storeys high and large enough, I would have guessed, to accommodate 400 or 500 workers. I got out to wipe the windscreen with some pages torn from an owner's manual I found in the glove box, but was soon staring at the arresting grandeur of the Potato Marketing Board HQ. The scale of it was quite astounding. How many people does it take to market potatoes, for goodness' sake? There must be doors in there marked 'Department of King Edwards' and 'Unusual Toppings Division', people in white shirts sitting around long tables while some guy with a flip chart is telling them about exciting plans for the autumn campaign for Pentland Squires. What a strange circumscribed universe they must live in. Imagine devoting the whole of your working life to edible tubers, losing sleep because somebody else was made No. 2 in Crisps and Reconstituteds or because the Maris Piper graph is in a tailspin. Imagine their cocktail parties. It doesn't bear thinking about.

I returned to the car and spent some time experimenting with the controls and thinking how much I hated these things. Some people are made for cars and some people aren't. It's as simple as that. I hate driving cars and I hate thinking about cars and I hate talking about cars. I especially hate it when you get a new car and go in the pub because somebody will always start quizzing you about it, which I dread because I don't even understand the questions.

'So you've got a new car, huh?' they'll say. 'How's it drive?'

You see, I'm lost already. 'Well, like a *car*. Why, have you never been in one?'

And then they start peppering you with questions. 'What sort of mileage you get? How many litres? What's the torque? Got twin overhead cams or double-barrelled alternator-cum-carburettor with a full pike and a double-twist dismount?' I can't for the life of me understand why anyone would want to know all this shit about a machine. You don't take that kind of interest in anything else. I always want to say: 'Hey, I hear you've got a new refrigerator. How many gallons of freon does that baby hold? What's its BTU rating? How's it *cool*?'

This car had the usual array of switches and toggles, each illustrated with a symbol designed to confound. Really now, what is one to make of a switch labelled |Ø|? How can anyone be expected to work out that a rectangle that looks like a television set with poor reception indicates the rear window heater? In the middle of this dashboard were two circular dials of equal size. One clearly indicated speed, but the other totally mystified me. It had two pointers on it, one of which advanced very slowly and the other of which didn't appear to move at all. I looked at it for ages before it finally dawned on me – this is true – that it was a clock.

By the time I found my way to Woodstock, ten miles north of Oxford, I was quite exhausted and very happy to bump to a halt against a kerb and abandon the thing for a few hours. I must say I like Woodstock very much. I'm told that it can be something of a nightmare in summer, but I've only seen it out of season and it has always been splendid. Its Georgian houses have a confident, almost regal air, its pubs are numerous and snug, its shops interesting and varied and their frontages uniformly unspoiled. There isn't a piece of brass in town that doesn't gleam. The Post Office had an old-fashioned black-and-silver sign, far more elegant and classy than that red-and-yellow logo they use now, and even Barclays Bank had somehow managed to resist the urge to cover the front of its building with lots of aqua-blue plastic.

The High Street was busy with shunting Volvos and tweedy shoppers with raffia baskets slung over their arms. I ambled along the shops, pausing now and again to peer in windows, and past the proud Georgian houses before coming abruptly to the entrance to Blenheim Palace and Park. Beneath an imposing ornamental arch there was a ticket booth and a sign saying that admission for an adult was £6.90, though closer inspection revealed that this included entrance to the palace tour, butterfly house, miniature train, adventure playground and a whole cornucopia of other cultural diversions. Lower down, the sign noted that admission to the grounds alone was 90p. I may be easily fooled, but nobody takes 90p from me without good reason. I had a trusty Ordnance Survey map and could see that this was a public right of way, so I strode through the gate with a sneer and my hand on my wallet, and the man in the ticket booth wisely decided not to tamper with me.

The transformation when you pass through the gate is both immediate and stunning. On one side you are in a busy village, and on the other you are suddenly thrust into a rural Arcadia of the sort that seems incomplete without a couple of Gainsborough figures ambling by. Before me spread 2,000 acres of carefully composed landscape – stout chestnuts and graceful sycamores, billiard-table lawns, an ornamental lake bisected by an imposing bridge, and in the centre of it all the monumental baroque pile of Blenheim Palace. It was very fine.

I followed the curving road through the grounds, past the palace

and busy visitors' car park, and on around the periphery of the
Pleasure Gardens. I would come back to check this out, but at
the moment I was headed across the park and to an exit on the
other side on the Bladon road. Bladon is a nondescript little place
trembling under the weight of passing goods traffic, but in its centre
is the churchyard where Winston Churchill lies buried. It had begun
to rain and as it was a bit of a hike up a busy road, I began to wonder
if this was worth the effort, but when I reached it I was glad I had.
The churchyard was lovely and secluded and Churchill's grave so
modest that it took some finding among the tumbling gravestones. I
was the only visitor. Churchill and Clemmie shared a simple and
seemingly forgotten plot, which I found both surprisingly touching
and impressive. Coming as I do from a country where even the most
obscure and worthless of presidents get a huge memorial library
when they pop their clogs – even Herbert Hoover, way out in Iowa,
has a place that looks like the headquarters of the World Trade
Organization – it was remarkable to think that Britain's greatest
twentieth-century statesman was commemorated with nothing more
than a modest statue in Parliament Square and this simple grave. I
was impressed by this commendable show of restraint.

I retraced my steps to Blenheim and had a nose around the
Pleasure Gardens and other outdoor attractions. 'Pleasure Gardens'
apparently was short for 'It's a Pleasure to Take Your Money', since
it seemed largely dedicated to helping visitors to part with further
sums in a gift shop and tea-room or by buying garden gates,
benches and other such items produced by the Blenheim estate
sawmill. Dozens of people poked around happily, seemingly undisturbed by the thought that they had paid £6.90 for the privilege
of looking at the sort of items they could see for free at any decent
garden centre. As I left the gardens and walked back towards the
palace, I took the opportunity to study the miniature steam train. It
ran over a decidedly modest length of track across one corner of the
grounds. The sight of fifty English people crouched on a little train
in a cold grey drizzle waiting to be taken 200 yards and thinking
they were having fun is one that I shall not forget in a hurry.

I followed a paved path to the front of the palace and over
Vanbrugh's grand bridge to the mighty, absurdly egocentric column
that the first Duke of Marlborough erected at the top of a hill overlooking the palace and lake. It really is the most extraordinary
edifice, not only because it is lofty and impressive, but because it
dominates the view from at least a hundred palace windows. What

kind of person, I wondered, would erect a 100-foot-high column to himself in his own grounds? How striking was the contrast with the simple grave of dear old Winnie.

Maybe I'm a bit simple, but it has always seemed to me that the scale of Blenheim Palace and the scale of Marlborough's achievement are curiously disproportionate. I can understand how in a moment of mad rejoicing a grateful nation might have awarded him, say, a two-week timeshare for life in the Canaries and maybe a set of cutlery or a Teasmade, but I can't for the life of me comprehend how a scattering of triumphs in obscure places like Oudenard and Malplaquet could be deemed to have entitled the conniving old fart to one of the great houses of Europe and a dukedom. More extraordinary still to my mind is the thought that nearly 300 years later the duke's heirs can litter the grounds with miniature trains and bouncing castles, charge admission and enjoy unearned positions of rank and privilege simply because a distant grandsire happened to have a passing talent for winning battles. It seems a most eccentric arrangement to me.

I remember once reading that the tenth Duke of Marlborough, on a visit to one of his daughter's homes, announced in consternation from the top of the stairs that his toothbrush wasn't foaming properly. It turned out that his valet had always put toothpaste on his brush for him, and as a consequence the duke was unaware that dental implements didn't foam up spontaneously. I rest my case.

As I was standing there taking in the view and reflecting on the curious practice of primogeniture, some well-groomed young woman on a bay horse bounded past very near to where I was standing. I've no idea who she was, but she looked rich and privileged. I gave her a little smile, such as one habitually gives strangers in an open place, and she stared flatly back at me as if I was not important enough to smile at. So I shot her. Then I returned to the car and drove on.

I spent two days driving through the Cotswolds and didn't like it at all – not because the Cotswolds were unlovely but because the car was. You are so sealed off from the world in a moving vehicle, and the pace is all wrong. I had grown used to moving about at walking speed or at least at British Rail speed, which is often, of course, much the same thing. So it was with relief, after a day spent dashing about through various Chippings and Slaughters and Tweeness-upon-the-Waters, that I abandoned the car in a car park in Broadway and took to my feet.

The last time I had seen Broadway, on an August afternoon some years before, it had been a nightmare of sclerotic traffic and flocks of shuffling daytrippers, but now, out of season, it seemed quiet and forgotten, its High Street nearly empty. It's an almost absurdly pretty place with its steeply pitched roofs, mullioned windows, prolific gables and trim little gardens. There is something about that golden Cotswold stone, the way it absorbs sunlight and then feeds it back so that even on the dullest days villages like Broadway seem to be basking in a perennial glow. This day, in fact, was sunny and gorgeous, with just a tang of autumn crispness in the air which gave the world a marvellous clean, fresh-laundered feel. Halfway along the High Street I found a signpost for the Cotswold Way and plunged off down a track between old buildings. I followed the path across a sunny meadow and up the long slope towards Broadway Tower, an outsized folly high above the village. The view from the top over the broad Vale of Evesham was, as always from such points, sensational – gently undulating trapezoids of farmland rolling off to a haze of distant wooded hills. Britain still has more landscape that looks like an illustration from a children's story book than any other country I know – a remarkable achievement in such a densely crowded and industrially minded little island. And yet I couldn't help feeling that the view may have been more bucolic and rewarding ten or perhaps twenty years ago.

It is easy to forget, in a landscape so timeless and fetching, so companionably rooted to an ancient past, how easily it is lost. The panorama before me incorporated electricity pylons, scattered housing estates and the distant sunny glints of cash and carry ware-houses. Far worse, the dense, carefully knitted network of hedgerows was showing distinct signs of becoming frayed and dis-jointed, like the pattern on a candlewick bedspread that has been picked off by idle fingers. Here and there fragments of overgrown hedge stood stranded and forlorn in the midst of otherwise featureless fields.

Did you know that between 1945 and 1985 England lost 96,000 miles of hedgerows – enough to girdle the earth four times? So muddled has been government policy towards the countryside that for a period of twenty-four years farmers could actually get one grant to plant hedgerows and another to grub them up. Between 1984 and 1990, despite the withdrawal of government money to plough up hedgerows, a further 53,000 miles were lost. You often hear it said (and I know because I once spent three days at a symposium on hedgerows; the things I do to keep my children in Reeboks) that hedgerows are, in fact, a transitory feature of the landscape, a relic of the enclosure movements, and that trying to save them merely thwarts the natural evolution of the countryside. Indeed, increasingly you hear the view that conservation of all types is fussy, retrograde and an impediment to progress. I have before me as I write a quote from Lord Palumbo arguing that the whole vague notion of heritage 'carries the baggage of nostalgia for a non-existent golden age which, had it existed, might well have been the death of invention', which is so fatuous it breaks my heart.

Quite apart from the consideration that if you followed that argument to its logical conclusion you would tear down Stonehenge and the Tower of London, in point of fact many hedgerows have been there for a very, very long time. In Cambridgeshire, I know of a particularly lovely hedge, called Judith's Hedge, that is older than Salisbury Cathedral, older than York Minster, older indeed than all but a handful of buildings in Britain, and yet no statute stands between it and its destruction. If the road needed widening or the owners decided they preferred the property to be bounded by fence-posts and barbed wire, it would be the work of but a couple of hours to bulldoze away 900 years of living history. That's insane. At least half the hedgerows in Britain predate the enclosure movements and perhaps as many as a fifth date back to Anglo-Saxon times. Anyway, the reason for saving them isn't because they have been there for ever and ever, but because they clearly and un-equivocally enhance the landscape. They are a central part of what makes England England. Without them, it would just be Indiana with steeples.

It gets me a little wild sometimes. You have in this country the most comely, the most parklike, the most flawlessly composed countryside the world has ever known, a product of centuries of tireless, instinctive improvement, and you are half a generation from destroying most of it for ever. We're not talking here about 'nostalgia for a non-existent golden age'. We're talking about some-thing that is green and living and incomparably beautiful. So if one more person says to me, 'Hedgerows aren't really an ancient feature of the landscape, you know,' I shall very likely punch him in the hooter. I'm a great believer in Voltaire's famous maxim, 'Sir, I may not agree with what you say, but I shall defend to the death your right to be a complete asshole,' but there comes a time when a line must be drawn.

*

I struck off down a wooded back lane to Snowshill, three miles away. The leaves were golden and rustly and the sky vast and blue and empty but for an occasional slow-moving wedge of migrating birds. It was a wonderful day to be abroad – the kind of day that has you puffing your chest and singing 'Zippity Doo Dah' in the voice of Paul Robeson. Snowshill drowsed in the sunshine, a cluster of stone cottages gathered round a sloping green. I bought an entrance ticket to Snowshill Manor, now in the hands of the National Trust but from 1919 to 1956 the home of an eccentric character named Charles Wade, who devoted his life to accumulating a vast and unfocused assortment of stuff, some of it very good, some of it little more than junk – clavichords, microscopes, Flemish tapestries, snuff and tobacco boxes, maps and sextants, samurai armour, penny-farthing bicycles, you name it – until he had filled his house so full that there was no room left for him. He spent his last years living happily in an outbuilding, which, like the house, has been preserved as it was on the day he died. I enjoyed it very much, and afterwards, as the sun sank in the west and the world filled with long shadows and a vague, entrancing smell of woodsmoke, I hiked back to my car a happy man.

I spent the night in Cirencester and the next day, after a pleasant look around the little Corinium Museum with its outstanding but curiously little-known collection of Roman mosaics, coins and other artefacts, drove on to Winchcombe to see the real thing *in situ*. On a hill above Winchcombe, you see, there is a little-visited site so singular and wonderful that I hesitate even to mention it. Most of the relatively few visitors who intrude upon this tranquil corner of the Cotswolds generally content themselves with a look around Sudeley Castle or a hike to the remote hump of the famous Belas Knap long barrow. But I headed straight for a grassy hillside path called the Salt Way, so named because in medieval times salt was conveyed along it. It was an enchanting walk through open countryside, with long views across sharply defined valleys that seemed never to have seen a car or heard the sound of a chainsaw.

At a place called Cole's Hill the path plunged abruptly into a seriously overgrown wood, dark and primeval in feel and all but impenetrable with brambles. Somewhere in here, I knew, was my goal – a site listed on the map as 'Roman villa (remains of)'. For perhaps half an hour, I hacked through the growth with my stick before I came upon the foundations of an old wall. It looked like nothing much – the remains of an old pigsty perhaps – but a few feet further on, all but obscured by wild ivy, were more low walls, a whole series of them, on both sides of the path. The path itself was paved with flagstones underneath a carpet of wet leaves, and I knew that I was in the villa. In one of the relict chambers, the floor had been carefully covered with plastic fertilizer bags weighted with stones at each corner. This is what I had come to see. I had been told about this by a friend but had never really believed it. For underneath those bags was a virtually complete Roman mosaic, about five feet square, exquisitely patterned and flawlessly preserved but for a tiny bit of fracturing around the edges.

I cannot tell you how odd it felt to be standing in a forgotten wood in what had once been, in an inconceivably distant past, the home of a Roman family, looking at a mosaic laid at least 1,600 years ago when this was an open sunny space, long before this ancient wood grew up around it. It is one thing to see these things in museums, quite another to come upon one on the spot where it was laid. I have no idea why it hadn't been gathered up and taken away to some place like the Corinium Museum. I presume it is a terrible oversight, but I am so grateful to have had the chance to see it. I sat for a long time on a stone, riveted with wonder and admiration. I don't know what seized me more, the thought that people in togas had once stood on this floor chatting in vernacular Latin or that it was still here, flawless and undisturbed, amid this tangle of growth.

This may sound awfully stupid, but for the first time it dawned on me in a kind of profound way that all those Roman antiquities I had gazed at over the years weren't created with a view to ending up one day in museums. Because the mosaic was still in its original setting, because it hadn't been roped off and placed inside a modern building, it was still clearly and radiantly a *floor* and not merely some diverting artefact. This was something meant to be walked on and used, something that had unquestionably felt the shuffle of Roman sandals. It had a strange kind of spell about it that left me quietly agog.

After a long time, I got up and carefully put back all the fertilizer bags and reweighted them with stones. I picked up my stick, surveyed my work to make sure all was in order, then turned and began the long process of hacking my way back to that strange and careless place that is the twentieth century.

CHAPTER FOURTEEN

I WENT TO MILTON KEYNES, FEELING THAT I OUGHT TO AT LEAST HAVE a look at a new town. Milton Keynes takes some getting to from Oxford, which is a little odd because it's only just up the road. I selected it as my destination on the basis of a quick look at a road map, assuming that I would, at worst, have to take a train to Bicester or some such place and then another from there. In fact, I had to go all the way back to London, catch an Underground train to Euston and then finally a train to Milton Keynes – an overall journey of perhaps 120 miles in order to travel between two towns about thirty miles apart.

It was costly and time-consuming and left me feeling a tiny bit fractious, not least because the train from Euston was crowded and I ended up sitting facing a bleating woman and her ten-year-old son, who kept knocking my shins with his dangling legs and irritating me by staring at me with piggy eyes while picking his nose and eating the bogies. He appeared to regard his nose as a kind of mid-faced snack dispenser. I tried to absorb myself in a book, but I found my gaze repeatedly rising against my wishes to find him staring at me with a smug look and a busy finger. It was quite repellent and I was very pleased, when the train finally pulled into Milton Keynes, to get my rucksack down from the overhead rack and drag it across his head as I departed.

I didn't hate Milton Keynes immediately, which I suppose is as much as you could hope for the place. You step out of the station and into a big open square lined on three sides with buildings of reflective glass, and have an instant sense of spaciousness such as you almost never get in English towns. The town itself stood on the slope of a small hill a good half-mile away beyond a network of pedestrian tunnels and over a large open space shared by car parks and those strange new-town trees that never seem to grow. I had the distinct feeling that the next time I passed this expanse of grass and asphalt it would be covered with brick office buildings with coppery windows.

Though I have spent much time wandering through new towns trying to imagine what their creators could possibly have been thinking, I had never been to Milton Keynes. In many ways, it was much superior to any new town I had seen before. The underpasses were faced with polished granite and were largely free of graffiti and the permanent murky puddles that seem to be a design feature of Basingstoke and Bracknell.

The town itself was a strange amalgam of styles. The grassless, shady strips along the centres of the main boulevards gave them a vaguely French air. The landscaped light industrial parks around the fringes looked German. The grid plan and numbered street names recalled America. The buildings were of the featureless sort you find around any international airport. In short, it looked any-thing but English.

The oddest thing was that there were no shops and no-one about. I walked for some distance through the central core of the town, up one avenue and down another and through the shadowy streets that connected them. Every car park was full and there were signs of life behind the gaping office windows, but almost no passing traffic and never more than one or two other pedestrians along the endless vistas of road. I knew there was a vast shopping mall in the town somewhere because I had read about it in Mark Lawson's *The Battle for Room Service*, but I couldn't for the life of me find it, and I couldn't even find anyone to ask. The annoying thing was that nearly all the buildings looked like they might be shopping malls. I kept spotting likely looking contenders and going up to investigate only to discover that it was the headquarters for an insurance company or something.

I ended up wandering some distance out into a residential area – a kind of endless Bovisville of neat yellow-brick homes, winding streets, and pedestrian walkways lined with never-grow trees – but there was still no-one about. From a hilltop I spied a sprawl of blue roofs about three-quarters of a mile off and thought that might be the shopping mall and headed off for it. The pedestrian walkways, which had seemed rather agreeable to me at first, began to become irritating. They wandered lazily through submerged cuttings, nicely landscaped but with a feeling of being in no hurry to get you anywhere. Clearly they had been laid out by people who had thought of it as a two-dimensional exercise. They followed circuitous, seemingly purposeless routes that must have looked pleasing on paper, but gave no consideration to the idea that people, faced with a long walk between houses and shops, would mostly like to get there in a reasonably direct way. Worse still was the sense of being lost in a semi-subterranean world cut off from visible landmarks. I found myself frequently scrambling up banks just to see where I was, only to discover that it was nowhere near where I wanted to be.

Eventually, at the end of one of these muttered scrambles, I found that I was beside a busy dual carriageway exactly opposite the blue-roofed sprawl I had begun searching for an hour earlier. I could see signs for Texas Homecare and a McDonald's and other such places. But when I returned to the footway I couldn't begin to work out how to get over there. The paths forked off in a variety of directions, disappearing round landscaped bends, none of which proved remotely rewarding when looked into. In the end I followed one sloping path back up to street level, where at least I could see where I was, and walked along it all the way back to the train station, which now seemed so absurdly remote from the residential areas that clearly only a total idiot could possibly have thought that Milton Keynes would be a paradise for walkers. It was no wonder that I hadn't passed a single pedestrian all morning.

I reached the station far more tired than the distance walked would warrant and gasping for a cup of coffee. Outside the station there was a map of the town, which I hadn't noticed on the way in, and I studied it now, dying to know where the shopping mall was. It turned out that I had been about a hundred feet from it on my initial reconnoitre of the town centre, but had failed to recognize it.

Sighing, and feeling an unaccountable determination to see this place, I headed back through the pedestrian subways, over the open ground and back through the lifeless core of office buildings, reflecting as I went what an extraordinary piece of work it was for a planner, confronted with a blank sheet of paper and a near infinity of possibilities for erecting a model community, to decide to put the shopping centre a mile from the railway station.

It seems almost impossible to believe, but the shopping centre was even worse designed than the town around it. Indeed, it must be a source of mirth wherever shopping-mall designers gather. It was absolutely enormous – more than a million square feet – and it contained every chain store that there has ever been or will ever be. But it was dark and determinedly unlovely and built along two straight, featureless parallel avenues that must run for half a mile. Unless in my delirium I overlooked them, and I think not, there was no food court, no central gathering place, nowhere much to sit, no design feature to encourage you to warm to this place to even the most fractional degree. It was like being in the world's largest bus station. The toilets were few and hard to find, and in consequence were as crowded with users as if it were half-time at a football match. I had always thought of the Metro Centre at Gateshead as my worst nightmare made whole, but it is a place of infinite charm and endless delight compared with the mall at Milton Keynes.

I had a cup of coffee in the grubbiest McDonald's I ever hope to visit and, clearing a space among the accumulated litter left by earlier users of my table, sat with my railway timetable and accompanying route map and felt a stab of despair at the discovery that the options before me were to go back to London or onward to Rugby, Coventry or Birmingham. I had no desire to do any of these. It seemed like days rather than mere hours since I had dropped off my hire car in Oxford and set off for the station with the simple-minded plan of travelling from Oxford to Cambridge by way of a lunchtime break at Milton Keynes.

Time was leaking away. I had, in some remote, half-forgotten life, sat at a kitchen table in a house in the Yorkshire Dales and worked out that I could comfortably cover the whole country in six or, at the outside, seven weeks. And that included airy plans to go practically everywhere – to the Channel Islands, Lundy, Shetland, Fair Isle, virtually all the cities. I had read John Hillaby's *Journey Through Britain* and he had *walked* from Land's End to John O'Groats in eight weeks. Surely with the assistance of a fleet modern public transport system I could see most of Britain in six or seven weeks. But now here I was, having used up nearly half my allotted time, and I hadn't even penetrated as far as the Midlands.

So, in a dim frame of mind, I gathered up my things, walked to the station and caught a train back to London where, in effect, I would have to start all over again. I couldn't think where to go, so I did what I often do. As the train marched through the rolling, autumn-bare farmlands of Buckinghamshire, I spread out a map and lost myself in the names. This is, to me, one of the deep and abiding pleasures of life in Britain.

I wonder if other people notice how much comparative pleasure there is in drinking in a pub called The Eagle and Child or Lamb and Flag rather than, say, Joe's Bar. Personally, I find endless satisfaction in it. I love to listen to the football results and the lulling rollcall of team names – Sheffield Wednesday, West Bromwich Albion, Partick Thistle, Queen of the South; what glory there is in those names – and I find strange comfort in the exotic and mystifying litany of the shipping forecasts. I have no idea what they mean – 'Viking rising five, backing four; Dogger blowing strong, steady as she goes; Minches gale force twelve, jeez Louise' – but they exert a powerful soothing effect on me. I genuinely believe that one of the reasons Britain is such a steady and gracious place is the calming influence of the football results and shipping forecasts.

There is almost no area of British life that isn't touched with a kind of genius for names. Just look at the names of the prisons. You could sit me down with a limitless supply of blank paper and a pen and command me to come up with a more cherishably ridiculous name for a prison and in a lifetime I couldn't improve on Wormwood Scrubs or Strangeways. Even the common names of wildflowers – stitchwort, lady's bedstraw, blue fleabane, feverfew – have an inescapable enchantment about them.

But nowhere, of course, are the British more gifted than with place names. There are some 30,000 place names in Britain, a good half of them, I would guess, notable or arresting in some way. There are villages without number whose very names summon forth an image of lazy summer afternoons and butterflies darting in meadows: Winterbourne Abbas, Weston Lullingfields, Theddlethorpe All Saints, Little Missenden. There are villages that seem to hide some ancient and possibly dark secret: Husbands Bosworth, Rime Intrinseca, Whiteladies Aston. There are villages that sound like toilet cleansers (Potto, Sanahole, Durno) and villages that sound like skin complaints (Scabcleuch, Whiterashes, Scurlage, Sockburn). In a brief trawl through any gazetteer you can find fertilizers (Hastigrow), shoe deodorizers (Powfoot), breath fresheners (Minto), dog food (Whelpo) and even a Scottish spot remover (Sootywells). You can find villages that have an attitude problem (Seething, Mockbeggar, Wrangle) and villages of strange phenomena (Meathop, Wigtwizzle, Blubberhouses). And there are villages almost without number that are just endearingly inane –

Prittlewell, Little Rollright, Chew Magna, Titsey, Woodstock Slop, Lickey End, Stragglethorpe, Yonder Bognie, Nether Wallop and the unbeatable Thornton-le-Beans. (Bury me there!) You have only to cast a glance across a map or lose yourself in an index to see that you are in a place of infinite possibility.

Some parts of the country seem to specialize in certain themes. Kent has a peculiar fondness for foodstuffs: Ham, Sandwich. Dorset goes in for characters in a Barbara Cartland novel: Bradford Peverell, Compton Valence, Langton Herring, Wootton Fitzpaine. Lincolnshire likes you to think it's a little off its head: Thimbleby Langton, Tumby Woodside, Snarford, Fishtoft Drove, Sots Hole and the truly arresting Spitall in the Street.

It's notable how often these places cluster together. In one compact area south of Cambridge, for instance, you can find Blo Norton, Rickinghall Inferior, Hellions Bumpstead, Ugley and (a personal favourite) Shellow Bowells. I had an impulse to go there now, to sniff out Shellow Bowells, as it were, and find what makes Norton Blo and Rickinghall Inferior. But as I glanced over the map my eye caught a line across the landscape called the Devil's Dyke. I had never heard of it, but it sounded awfully promising. I decided on an impulse to go there.

Thus it was that I found myself late the next morning wandering a back lane outside the Cambridgeshire hamlet of Reach looking for the dike's start. It was a rotten day. A steamroom fog filled the air and visibility was next to nothing. The dike rose up suddenly, almost alarmingly, out of the soupy greyness, and I clambered up to its top. It is a strange and brooding eminence, particularly in thick fog and out of season. Built during the darkest of the Dark Ages some 1,300 years ago, the Devil's Dyke is an earthen embankment that rises up to sixty feet above the surrounding landscape and runs in a straight line for 7½ miles between Reach and Ditton Green. Disappointingly, no-one knows why it is called the Devil's Dyke. The name isn't recorded before the sixteenth century. Standing as it does in the midst of flat fenlands, it has a kind of menacing, palpably ancient air, but also a feeling of monumental folly. It required an immense commitment of labour to construct, but it didn't take a whole lot of military genius to realize that all an invading army had to do was go around it, which is what all of them did, and within no time at all the Devil's Dyke had ceased to have any use at all except to show people in the fen country what it felt like to be sixty feet high.

Still, it offers an agreeable, easy stroll along its grassy summit, and on this bleak morning I had it all to myself. Not until I reached the approximate midway point did I begin to see other people, mostly exercising their dogs on the broad sward of Newmarket Heath and looking ghostly in the unearthly fog. The dike runs right through the grounds of Newmarket Racecourse, which I thought rather jolly though I couldn't see a damn thing, and thence on through prosperous-looking horse country. Gradually the fog began to thin and between the skeletal trees I glimpsed a succession of large stud farms, each with a white-fenced paddock, a big house and a sprawl of ornate stable blocks with cupolas and weather-vanes that made them look uncannily like a modern Asda or Tesco's. Pleasant as it was to have an easy, flat ramble along such a well-defined route, it was also a trifle dull. I walked for a couple of hours without passing anyone and then abruptly the dike ended in a field outside Ditton Green, and I was left standing there with an unsettling sense of anticlimax. It was only a little after two in the afternoon and I was nowhere near tired. I knew that Ditton had no railway station, but I had presumed I could catch a bus to Cambridge, and indeed I discovered in the local bus shelter that I could – if I waited two days. So I trudged four miles to Newmarket down a busy road, had an idle look around there, then caught a train to Cambridge.

One of the sustaining pleasures of a long tramp in the country, particularly out of season, is the thought that eventually you will find a room in a snug hostelry, have a series of drinks before a blazing fire and then dine on hearty viands to which the day's exercise and fresh air have clearly entitled you. But I arrived in Cambridge feeling fresh and untaxed and entitled to nothing. Worse still, presuming that the walk would be more challenging than it was and that I might arrive late, I had booked a room in the University Arms Hotel in the expectation that it would have the requisite blazing fire, the hearty viands and something of the air of a senior common room. In fact, as I discovered to my quiet dismay, it was an overpriced modern block and my gloomy room was lamentably at odds with its description in my guidebook.

I had a listless look round the city. Now Cambridge, I know, is a very fine city and a great place for names – Christ's Pieces alone takes some beating – but I couldn't make myself warm to it this day. The central market was a tatty mess, there seemed a discouraging surfeit of concrete structures around the centre, and by late afternoon everything was drenched in a cheerless drizzle. I ended up nosing around in second-hand bookshops. I was looking for nothing in particular, but in one I came across an illustrated history of Selfridges Department Store and I took it eagerly from the shelf, hoping for an explanation of how Highcliffe Castle had fallen into dereliction and, better still, for prurient anecdotes involving Selfridge and the libidinous Dolly Sisters.

Alas, this appeared to be a sanitized version of the Selfridge story. I found only a single passing mention of the Dollys, which implied that they were just a couple of innocent waifs in whom Selfridge took an avuncular interest. Of Selfridge's precipitate decline from rectitude there was scarcely a mention and of Highcliffe Castle nothing at all. So I put the book back and, realizing that somehow everything I did this day would be touched with disappointment, I went and had a pint of beer in an empty pub, a mediocre dinner in an Indian restaurant, a lonely walk in the rain, and finally retired to my room, where I discovered that there was nothing at all of note on television, and realized that I had left my walking-stick in Newmarket.

I retired with a book only to discover that the bedside lightbulb was gone – not burned out but gone – and passed the remaining hours of the evening lying inert on the bed and watching a *Cagney and Lacey* rerun, partly out of a curious interest to detect what it is about this ancient programme that so besots the controller of BBC1 (only possible answer: Sharon Gless's chest) and partly because of its guaranteed narcotic effect. I fell asleep with my glasses on and awoke at some indeterminate hour to find the TV screen a frantic, noisy blizzard. I got up to switch it off, tripped heavily over some unyielding object and managed the interesting trick of turning off the TV with my head. Curious to know how I had managed this, in case I decided to make it a party piece, I discovered that the offending object was my stick, which was not in Newmarket after all, but on the floor, lodged between a chair and a bed leg.

Well, that's one good thing, I thought and, gracing my nostrils with two walrus tusks of tissue to stanch a sudden flow of blood, climbed wearily back into bed.

CHAPTER FIFTEEN

I WENT TO RETFORD. I CAN'T EXPLAIN IT. THROUGH MY MORNING ablutions, the gentle removal of the tissues from my swollen nostrils, through breakfast and checking out of the hotel and the long walk to the station, it was my solemn and dutiful intention to go to Norwich and thence to Lincoln. But for some reason, as soon as I entered the station and spied a British Rail map on the wall, I had a strange, sudden hankering to go somewhere entirely new, and Retford jumped out at me.

For the past seven years, I had passed through Retford every time I took a train between Leeds and London. It was one of the main stops on the east coast line, but I had never seen anyone get on or anyone get off there. On my British Rail route map, Retford was accorded capital letters, giving it equal typographical standing with Liverpool, Leicester, Nottingham, Glasgow and all the other substantial communities of Britain, and yet I knew nothing about it. In fact, I don't believe I had even heard of it before I saw its lonely station for the first time from the train. More than that, I had never met anyone who had been there or knew anything about it. My *AA Book of British Towns* included lavish and kindly descriptions of every obscure community you could think to name – Kirriemuir, Knutsford, Prestonpans, Swadlincote, Bridge of Allan, Duns, Forfar, Wigtown – but of Retford it maintained a stern and mysterious silence. Clearly, it was time to check this place out.

So I caught a train to Peterborough and then another on the main line north. I hadn't slept particularly well on account of an unsettling dream involving Cagney and Lacey and the discovery that I hadn't filed a US tax return since 1975 (they threatened to turn me over to that guy who takes his shirt off in the opening credits, so you can imagine the state of my bedclothes when I awoke with a gasp about dawn), and I was looking forward to one of those quiet, soothing journeys of the kind that British Rail are always promising – the ones where your shoes turn into slippers and Leon Redbone sings you to sleep.

So it was with some dismay that I discovered that the seat behind me was occupied by Vodaphone Man. These people are getting to be a real nuisance, aren't they? This one was particularly irritating because his voice was loud and self-satisfied and littered with moronspeak, and his calls were so clearly pointless:

'Hello, Clive here. I'm on the 10.07 and should be at HQ by 1300 hours as expected. I'm going to need a rush debrief on the Pentland Squire scenario. What say? No, I'm out of the loop on Maris Pipers. Listen, can you think of *any* reason why anyone would employ a total anus like me? What's that? Because I'm the sort of person who's happy as a pig in shit just because he's got a mobile phone? Hey, *interesting* concept.' Then a few moments of silence and: 'Hello, love. I'm on the 10.07. Should be home by five. Yes, just like every other night. No reason to tell you at all except that I've got this phone and I'm a complete fuckwit. I'll call again from Doncaster for no reason.' Then: 'Clive here. Yeah, I'm still on the 10.07 but we had a points failure at Grantham, so I'm looking now at an ETA of 13.02 rather than the forecast 1300 hours. If Phil calls, will you tell him that I'm still a complete fuckwit? Brill.' And so it went all morning.

Thus it was with some relief that I found myself, alone among the many passengers, alighting in Retford, an occurrence so unusual that it brought station employees to the windows, and walking into town through a clinging mist of rain. Retford, I am pleased to report, is a delightful and charming place even under the sort of oppressive grey clouds that make far more celebrated towns seem dreary and tired. Its centrepiece is an exceptionally large and handsome market square lined with a picturesque jumble of noble Georgian buildings. Beside the main church stood a weighty black cannon with a plaque saying 'Captured at Sevastopol 1865', which I thought a remarkable piece of initiative on the part of the locals – it's not every day, after all, that you find a Nottinghamshire market town storming a Crimean redoubt and bringing home booty – and the shops seemed prosperous and well ordered. I can't say that I felt like spending my holidays here, but I was pleased to have seen it at last and to have found it trim and likeable.

I had a cup of tea in a little shop, then caught a bus to Worksop, a place of similar size and tempo (and which, by the by, *does* get an entry in the *AA Book of British Towns*). Retford and Worksop apparently had had a contest to see which of them would house the headquarters of Bassetlaw District Council, and Worksop had clearly lost since the offices were there. They were predictably hideous and discordant, but the rest of the town seemed agreeable enough in a low-key sort of way.

I had come to Worksop not because I was aching to see it but because near by there was something I had wished to see for a long time: Welbeck Abbey, reputedly one of the finest homes in that curious compact region known as the Dukeries. The seats of five historic dukedoms – Newcastle, Portland, Kingston, Leeds and Norfolk – are all within twenty miles of each other in this obscure corner of the North Midlands, though Leeds and Portland are now extinct and the others, I gather, have mostly gone away. (The Duke of Newcastle, according to Simon Winchester in *Their Noble Lordships*, lives in a modest house in Hampshire, which I trust has taught *him* the folly of not investing in bouncing castles and miniature steam trains.)

Welbeck is the ancestral home of the Portland clan, though in fact they haven't lived there since 1954 on account of a similar unfortunate lack of prescience with regard to adventure playgrounds and petting zoos. The fifth Duke of Portland, one W.J.C. Scott-Bentinck (1800–1879), has long been something of a hero of mine. Old W.J.C., as I like to think of him, was one of history's great recluses and went to the most extraordinary lengths to avoid all forms of human contact. He lived in just one small corner of his stately home and communicated with his servants through notes passed to him through a special message box cut into the door to his rooms. Food was conveyed to him in the dining room by means of a miniature railway running from the kitchen. In the event of chance encounters, he would stand stock still and servants were instructed to pass him as they would a piece of furniture. Those who transgressed this instruction were compelled to skate on the duke's private skating-rink until exhausted. Sightseers were allowed to tour the house and grounds – 'so long,' as the duke put it, 'as you would be good enough not to *see* me.'

For reasons that can only be guessed at, the duke used his

considerable inheritance to build a second mansion underground. At its peak, he had 15,000 men employed on its construction, and when completed it included, among much else, a library nearly 250 feet long and the largest ballroom in England, with space for up to 2,000 guests – rather an odd thing to build if you never have guests. A network of tunnels and secret passageways connected the various rooms and ran for considerable distances out into the surrounding countryside. It was as if, in the words of one historian, 'he anticipated nuclear warfare'. When it was necessary for the duke to travel to London, he would have himself sealed in his horse-drawn carriage, which would be driven through a mile-and-a-half-long tunnel to a place near Worksop Station and loaded onto a special flatcar for the trip to the capital. There, still sealed, it would be driven to his London residence, Harcourt House.

When the duke died, his heirs found all of the above-ground rooms devoid of furnishings except for one chamber in the middle of which sat the duke's commode. The main hall was mysteriously floorless. Most of the rooms were painted pink. The one upstairs room in which the duke resided was packed to the ceiling with hundreds of green boxes, each of which contained a single dark brown wig. This was, in short, a man worth getting to know.

So in a state of some eagerness I strolled out of Worksop to the edge of Clumber Park, a neighbouring National Trust holding, and found what I hoped was a path to Welbeck Abbey, some three or four miles away. It was a long walk along a muddy woodland track. According to the footpath signs I was on something called the Robin Hood Way, but this didn't feel much like Sherwood Forest. It was mostly a boundless conifer plantation, a sort of farm for trees, and it seemed preternaturally still and lifeless. It was the kind of setting where you half expect to stumble on a body loosely covered with leaves, which is my great dread in life because the police would interview me and I would immediately become a suspect on account of an unfortunate inability to answer questions like 'Where were you on the afternoon of Wednesday the third of October at 4 p.m.?' I could imagine myself sitting in a windowless interview room, saying, 'Let's see, I think I might have been in Oxford, or maybe it was the Dorset coast path. Jeez, I don't know.' And the next thing you know I'd be banged up in Parkhurst or some place, and with my luck in the meantime they'd have replaced Michael Howard as Home Secretary so there wouldn't be any chance of just lifting the latch and letting myself out.

Things got stranger. An odd wind rose in the treetops, making them bend and dance, but didn't descend to earth so that at ground level everything was calm, which was a little spooky, and then I passed through a steep sandstone ravine with tree roots growing weirdly like vines along its face. Between the roots, the surface was covered with hundreds of carefully scratched inscriptions, with names and dates and occasional twined hearts. The dates covered an extraordinary span: 1861, 1962, 1947, 1990. This seemed a strange place indeed. Either this was a popular spot for lovers or some couple had been going steady for a very long time.

A bit further on I came to a lonely gatehouse with a machicolated roofline. Beyond it stood a sweep of open field full of stubbly winter wheat, and beyond that, just visible through a mantle of trees, was a large and many-angled green copper roof – Welbeck Abbey, or so at least I hoped. I followed the path around the periphery of the field, which was immense and muddy. It took me nearly three-quarters of an hour to make my way to a paved lane, but I was sure now that I had found the right place. The lane passed alongside a narrow, reedy lake, and this, according to my trusty OS map, was the only body of water for miles. I followed the lane for perhaps a mile until it ended at a rather grand entrance beside a sign saying PRIVATE – NO ENTRY, but with no other indication of what lay beyond.

I stood for a moment in a lather of indecision (the name I would like, incidentally, if I am ever ennobled: Lord Lather of Indecision) and decided to venture up the drive a little way – just enough to at least glimpse the house which I had come so far to see. I walked a little way. The grounds were meticulously and expensively groomed, but well screened with trees, so I walked a little further. After a few hundred yards the trees thinned a little and opened out into lawns containing a kind of assault course, with climbing nets and logs on stilts. What *was* this place? A bit further on, beside the lake, there was an odd paved area – like a car park in the middle of nowhere – which I realized, with a small cry of joy, was the duke's famous skating-rink. Now I was so far into the grounds that discretion hardly mattered. I strode on until I was square in front of the house. It was grand but curiously characterless and it had been clumsily graced with a number of new extensions. Beyond in the distance was a cricket pitch with an elaborate pavilion. There was no-one around, but there was a car park with several cars. This was clearly some kind of institution – perhaps a training centre for somebody like IBM. So why was it so anonymous? I was about to go up and have a look in the windows when a door opened and a man in a uniform emerged and strode towards me with a severe look on his face. As he neared me, I could see his jacket said 'MOD Security'. Oh-oh.

'Hello,' I said with a big foolish smile.

'Are you aware, sir, that you are trespassing on Ministry of Defence property?'

I wavered for a moment, torn between giving him my tourist-from-Iowa act ('You mean this isn't Hampton Court Palace? I just gave a cab driver £175') and fessing up. I fessed. In a small respect-ful voice I told him about my long fascination with the fifth Duke of Portland and how I had ached to see this place for years and couldn't resist just having a peep at it after coming all this way, which was exactly the right thing to do because he obviously had an affection for old W.J.C. himself. He escorted me smartishly to the edge of the property and kept up something of a bluff manner, but he seemed quietly pleased to have someone who shared his interests. He confirmed that the paved area was the skating-rink and pointed out where the tunnels ran, which was pretty much everywhere. They were still sound, he told me, though they weren't used any longer except for storage. The ballroom and other under-ground chambers, however, were still regularly employed for functions and as a gymnasium. The MOD had just spent a million pounds refurbishing the ballroom.

'What is this place anyway?' I asked.

'Training centre, sir,' was all he would say and in any case we had reached the end of the drive. He watched to make sure I went. I walked back across the big field, then paused at the far end to look at the Welbeck Abbey roof rising from the treetops. I was pleased to know that the Ministry of Defence had maintained the tunnels and underground rooms, but it seemed an awful shame that the place was so formidably shut to the public. It isn't every day after all that the British aristocracy produces someone of W.J.C. Scott-Bentinck's rare and extraordinary mental loopiness, though in fairness it must be said they give it their best shot.

And with this thought to chew on, I turned and began the long trudge back to Worksop.

CHAPTER SIXTEEN

I SPENT A PLEASANT NIGHT IN LINCOLN, WANDERING ITS STEEP AND ancient streets before and after dinner, admiring the squat, dark immensity of the cathedral and its two Gothic towers, and looking forward very much to seeing it in the morning. I like Lincoln, partly because it is pretty and well preserved but mostly because it seems so agreeably remote. H.V. Morton, in *In Search of England*, likened it to an inland St Michael's Mount standing above the great sea of the Lincolnshire plain, and that's exactly right. If you look on a map, it's only just down the road a bit from Nottingham and Sheffield, but it feels far away and quite forgotten. I like that very much.

Just about the time of my visit there was an interesting report in the *Independent* about a long-running dispute between the dean of Lincoln Cathedral and his treasurer. Six years earlier, it appears, the treasurer, along with his wife, daughter and a family friend, had taken the cathedral's treasured copy of the Magna Carta off to Australia for a six-month fund-raising tour. According to the *Independent*, the Australian visitors to the exhibition had contributed a grand total of just £938 over six months, which would suggest either that Australians are extraordinarily tight-fisted or that the dear old *Independent* was a trifle careless with its facts. In any case, what is beyond dispute is that the tour was a financial disaster. It lost over £500,000 – a pretty hefty bill, when you think about it, for four people and a piece of parchment. Most of this the Australian government had graciously covered, but the cathedral was still left nursing a £56,000 loss. The upshot is that the dean gave the story to the press, causing outrage among the cathedral chapter; the Bishop of Lincoln held an inquiry at which he commanded the chapter to resign; the chapter refused to resign; and now everybody was mad at pretty much everybody else. This had been going on for six years.

So when I stepped into the lovely, echoing immensity of Lincoln Cathedral the following morning I was rather hoping that there would be hymnals flying about and the unseemly but exciting sight of clerics wrestling in the transept, but in fact all was disappointingly calm. On the other hand, it was wonderful to be in a great ecclesiastical structure so little disturbed by shuffling troops of tourists. When you consider the hordes that flock to Salisbury, York, Canterbury, Bath and so many of the other great churches of England, Lincoln's relative obscurity is something of a small miracle. It would be hard to think of a place of equal architectural majesty less known to outsiders – Durham, perhaps.

The whole of the nave was filled with ranks of padded metal chairs. I've never understood this. Why can't they have wooden pews in these cathedrals? Every English cathedral I've ever seen has been like this, with semi-straggly rows of chairs that can be stacked or folded away. Why? Do they clear the chairs away for barn-dancing or something? Whatever the reason, they always look cheap and out of keeping with the surrounding splendour of soaring vaults, stained glass and Gothic tracery. What a heartbreak it is sometimes to live in an age of such consummate cost-consciousness. Still, it must be said that the modern intrusions do help you to notice how extravagantly deployed were the skills of medieval stonemasons, glaziers and woodcarvers, and how unstinting was the use of materials.

I would like to have lingered, but I had a vital date to keep. I needed to be in Bradford by mid-afternoon in order to see one of the most exciting visual offerings in the entire world, as far as I am concerned. On the first Saturday of every month, you see, Pictureville Cinema, part of the large and popular Museum of Photography, Film and Something Else, shows an original, uncut version of *This Is Cinerama*. It is the only place in the world now where you can see this wonderful piece of cinematic history, and this was the first Saturday of the month.

I can't tell you how much I was looking forward to this. I fretted all the way that I would miss my rail connection at Doncaster and then I fretted again that I would miss the one at Leeds, but I reached

Bradford in plenty of time – nearly three hours early, in fact, which made me tremble slightly, for what is one to do in Bradford with three hours to kill?

Bradford's role in life is to make every place else in the world look better in comparison, and it does this very well. Nowhere on this trip would I see a city more palpably forlorn. Nowhere would I pass more vacant shops, their windows soaped or covered with tattered posters for pop concerts in other, more vibrant communities like Huddersfield and Pudsey, or more office buildings festooned with TO LET signs. At least one shop in three in the town centre was empty and most of the rest seemed to be barely hanging on. Soon after this visit, Rackham's, the main department store, would announce it was closing. Such life as there was had mostly moved indoors to a characterless compound called the Arndale Centre. (And why is it, by the way, that Sixties shopping centres are always called the Arndale Centre?) But mostly Bradford seemed steeped in a perilous and irreversible decline.

Once this was one of the greatest congregations of Victorian architecture anywhere, but you would scarcely guess it now. Scores of wonderful buildings were swept away to make room for wide new roads and angular office buildings with painted plywood insets beneath each window. Nearly everything in the city suffers from well-intentioned but misguided meddling by planners. Many of the busier streets have the kind of pedestrian crossings that you have to negotiate in stages – one stage to get to an island in the middle, then another long wait with strangers before you are given four seconds to sprint to the other side – which makes even the simplest errands tiresome, particularly if you want to make a cater-corner crossing and have to wait at four sets of lights to travel a net distance of thirty yards. Worse still, along much of Hall Ings and Princes Way the hapless pedestrian is forced into a series of bleak and menacing subways that meet in large circles, open to the sky but always in shadow, and so badly drained, I'm told, that someone once drowned in one during a flash downpour.

You won't be surprised to hear that I used to wonder about these planning insanities a lot, and then one day I got a book from Skipton Library called *Bradford – Outline for Tomorrow* or something like that. It was from the late Fifties or early Sixties and it was full of black-and-white architect's drawings of gleaming pedestrian precincts peopled with prosperous, confidently striding, semi-stick figures, and office buildings of the type that loomed over me now, and I suddenly saw, with a kind of astonishing clarity, what they were trying to do. I mean to say, they genuinely thought they were building a new world – a Britain in which the brooding, soot-blackened buildings and narrow streets of the past would be swept away and replaced with sunny plazas, shiny offices, libraries, schools and hospitals, all linked with brightly tiled underground passageways where pedestrians would be safely segregated from the passing traffic. Everything about it looked bright and clean and fun. There were even pictures of women with pushchairs stopping to chat in the open-air subterranean circles. And what we got instead was a city of empty, peeling office blocks, discouraging roads, pedestrian drains and economic desolation. Perhaps it would have happened anyway, but at least we would have been left with a city of crumbling old buildings instead of crumbling new ones.

Nowadays, in a gesture that is as ironic as it is pathetic, the local authorities are desperately trying to promote their meagre stock of old buildings. In a modest cluster of narrow streets on a slope just enough out of the city centre to have escaped the bulldozer, there still stand some three dozen large and striking warehouses, mostly built between 1860 and 1874 in a confident neoclassical style that makes them look like merchant banks rather than wool sheds, which together make up the area known as Little Germany. Once there were many other districts like this – indeed, the whole of central Bradford as late as the 1950s consisted almost wholly of warehouses, mills, banks and offices single-mindedly dedicated to the woollen trade. And then – goodness knows how – the wool business just leaked away. It was, I suppose, the usual story of over-confidence and lack of investment followed by panic and retreat. In any case, the mills went, the offices grew dark, the once-bustling Wool Exchange dwindled to a dusty nothingness, and now you would never guess that Bradford had ever known greatness.

Of all the once thriving wool precincts in the city – Bermondsey, Cheapside, Manor Row, Sunbridge Road – only the few dark buildings of Little Germany survive in any number, and even this promising small neighbourhood seems bleak and futureless. At the time of my visit two-thirds of the buildings were covered in scaffolding, and the other third had TO LET signs on them. Those that had been renovated looked smart and well done, but they also looked permanently vacant, and they were about to be joined in their gleaming, well-preserved emptiness by the two dozen others now in the process of being renovated.

What a good idea it would be, I thought, if the Government ordered the evacuation of Milton Keynes and made all the insurance companies and other firms decamp to places like Bradford in order to bring some life back to real cities. Then Milton Keynes could become like Little Germany is now, an empty place that people could stroll through and wonder at. But it will never happen, of course. Obviously, the Government would never order such a thing, but it won't even happen through market forces because companies want big modern buildings with lots of car parking, and nobody wants to live in Bradford, and who can blame them? And anyway, even if by some miracle they find tenants for all these wonderful old relics, it will never be anything more than a small well-preserved enclave in the heart of a dying city.

Still, Bradford is not without its charms. The Alhambra Theatre, built in 1914 in an excitingly effusive style with minarets and towers, has been sumptuously and skilfully renovated and remains the most wonderful place (with the possible exception of the Hackney Empire) to see a pantomime. (Something I positively adore, by the way. Within weeks of this visit, I would be back to see Billy Pearce in *Aladdin*. Laugh? I soaked the seat.) The Museum of Film, Photography, Imax Cinema and Something Else (I can never remember the exact name) has brought a welcome flicker of life to a corner of the city that previously had to rely on the world's most appalling indoor ice rink for its diversion value, and there are some good pubs. I went in one now, the Mannville Arms, and had a pint of beer and a bowl of chilli. The Mannville is well known in Bradford as the place where the Yorkshire Ripper used to hang out, though it ought to be famous for its chilli, which is outstanding.

Afterwards, with an hour still to kill, I walked over to the Museum of Television, Photography and Whatever, which I admire, partly because it is free and partly because I think it is deeply commendable to put these institutions in the provinces. I had a look through the various galleries, and watched in some wonder as throngs of people parted with substantial sums of cash to see the two o'clock Imax show. I've been to these Imax screenings before and frankly I can't understand their appeal. I know the screen is massive and the visual reproduction stunning, but the films are always so incredibly *dull*, with their earnest, leaden commentaries about Man's conquest of this and fulfilling his destiny to do that – this latest offering which had the crowds flocking in was actually called *Destiny in Space* – when any fool can see that what

everybody really wants is to go on a roller-coaster ride and experience a little here-comes-my-lunch aerial dive-bombing.

The people at Cinerama Corporation understood this well some
forty years ago and made a death-defying roller-coaster ride the
focus of their advertising campaign. The first and last time I saw
This Is Cinerama was in 1956 on a family trip to Chicago. The
movie had been on general release since 1952 but such was its
popularity in the big cities, and its unavailability in places like
Iowa, that it ran for years and years, though it must be said that by
the time we saw it most of the audience consisted of people in bib
overalls chewing on stalks of grass. My memories of it were vague
– I was just four years old in the summer of 1956 – but fond, and
I couldn't wait to see it now.

Such was my eagerness that I hastened out of the Museum of
Various Things Involving Celluloid and across to the nearby
entrance of the Pictureville Cinema half an hour early and stood,
alone in a freezing drizzle, for fifteen minutes before the doors were
opened. I bought a ticket, stipulating a place in the centre of the
auditorium and with plenty of room for vomiting, and found my
way to my seat. It was a wonderful cinema, with plush seats and a
big curving screen behind velvet curtains. For a few minutes it
looked as if I was going to have the place to myself, but then others
started coming in and by two minutes to showtime it was pretty
well full.

At the stroke of two, the room darkened and the curtains opened
perhaps fifteen feet – a fraction of their total sweep – and the modest
portion of exposed screen filled with some introductory footage by
Lowell Thomas (a sort of 1950s American version of David
Attenborough but looking like George Orwell) sitting in a patently
fake study filled with globetrotting objects, preparing us for the
wonder we were about to behold. Now you must put this in its
historical context. Cinerama was created in a desperate response to
television which in the early 1950s was threatening to put
Hollywood clean out of business. So this prefatory footage, filmed
in black and white and presented in a modest rectangle the shape
of a television screen, was clearly intended to implant a subliminal
reminder that this was the sort of image we were used to looking at
these days. After a brief but not uninteresting rundown on the
history of the cinematic arts, Thomas told us to sit back and enjoy
the greatest visual spectacle the world had ever seen. Then he disappeared, rich orchestral music rose from every quarter, the

curtains drew back and back and back to reveal a majestic curved screen and suddenly we were in a world drenched in colour, on a roller-coaster on Long Island, and gosh was it good.

I was in heaven. The 3D effect was far better than you would expect with such a simple and ancient projection system. It really was like being on a roller-coaster, but with one incomparable difference: this was a 1951 roller-coaster, rising high above car parks full of vintage Studebakers and De Sotos and thundering terrifyingly past crowds of people in capacious trousers and colourful baggy shirts. This wasn't a movie. It was time travel.

I really mean that. Between the 3D wizardry, the stereophonic sound and the sparkling sharpness of the images, it was like being thrust magically back forty years in time. This had a particular resonance for me because in the summer of 1951, when this footage was being shot, I was curled up in my mother's abdomen, increasing body weight at a rate that I wouldn't match until I quit smoking thirty-five years later. This was the world I was about to be born into, and what a delightful, happy, promising place it seemed.

I don't think I have ever spent three such happy hours. We went all over the world, for *This Is Cinerama* wasn't a movie in a conventional sense but a travelogue designed to show this wonder of the age to best effect. We glided through Venice on gondolas, watched from the quaysides by people in capacious trousers and colourful baggy shirts; listened to the Vienna Boys Choir outside the Schönbrunn Palace; watched a regimental tattoo at Edinburgh Castle; saw a long segment of *Aida* at La Scala (bit boring, that); and concluded with a long aeroplane flight over the whole of America. We soared above Niagara Falls – a place I had been the summer before, but this was quite unlike the tourist-clogged nightmare I had visited, with its forests of viewing towers and international hotels. This Niagara Falls had a backdrop of trees and low buildings and thinly used car parks. We visited Cypress Gardens in Florida, flew low over the rippling farm fields of Middle America, and had an exciting landing at Kansas City Airport. We brushed over the Rockies, dropped into the staggering vastness of the Grand Canyon, and flew through the formidable, twisting gorges of Zion National Park while the plane banked sharply past alarming outcrops of rock and Lowell Thomas announced that such a cinematic feat had never before been attempted – and all of this to a swelling stereophonic rendition of 'God Bless America' by the Mormon Tabernacle Choir, which began with a melodic hum and rose to a full-throated let's-give-those-Krauts-a-licking crescendo. Tears of joy and pride welled in my sockets and it was all I could do to keep from climbing on to my seat and crying: 'Ladies and gentlemen, this is *my* country!'

And then it was over and we were shuffling out into the drizzly twilit bleakness of Bradford, which was something of a shock to the system, believe me. I stood by a bronze statue of J.B. Priestley (posed with coattails flying, which makes him look oddly as if he has a very bad case of wind) and stared at the bleak, hopeless city before me and thought: Yes, I am ready to go home.

But first, I additionally thought, I'll just have a curry.

CHAPTER SEVENTEEN

I FORGOT TO MENTION CURRY HOUSES EARLIER IN MY BRIEF LIST OF Bradford's glories, which was a terrible oversight. Bradford may have lost a wool trade but it has gained a thousand excellent Indian restaurants, which I personally find a reasonable swap as I have a strictly limited need for bales of fibre but can take about as much Indian food as you care to shovel at me.

The oldest of the Bradford curry houses, I'm told, and certainly one of the best and cheapest, is the Kashmir, just up the road from the Alhambra. There is a proper restaurant upstairs, with white tablecloths, gleaming cutlery and poised, helpful waiters, but *aficionados* descend to the basement where you sit with strangers at long Formica-topped tables. This place is so hard core that they don't bother with cutlery. You just scoop the food in with hunks of nan bread and messy fingers. For £3 I had a small feast that was rich, delicious and so hot that it made my fillings sizzle.

Afterwards, bloated and sated and with a stomach bubbling away like a heated beaker in a mad-scientist movie, I stepped out into the Bradford evening and wondered what to do with myself. It was just after six o'clock on a Saturday evening, but the place felt dead.

I was acutely and uncomfortably aware that my home and dear family were just over the next range of hills. For some reason I had it in my head that it would be cheating to go home now with the trip half finished, but then I thought: Sod it. I'm cold and lonesome and I'm not about to spend a night in a hotel twenty miles from my own home. So I walked to Forster Square Station, took a rattling, empty train to Skipton and a cab to the little Dales village where I live, and had the driver drop me down the road so that I could approach the house on foot.

What a joy it is to arrive after dark at a snug-looking house, its windows filled with welcoming light, and know that it is yours and that inside is your family. I walked up the drive and looked through the kitchen window, and there they all were gathered round the kitchen table playing Monopoly, bless their wholesome little hearts. I stared at them for ages, lost in a glow of affection and admiration and feeling like Jimmy Stewart in *It's a Wonderful Life* when he gets to spy on his own life. And then I went in.

Now I can't possibly write about this sort of thing without making it sound like an episode from *The Waltons*, so what I'm going to do is distract your attention for a moment from this animated and heartwarming reunion in a Yorkshire Dales kitchen and tell you a true but irrelevant story.

In the early 1980s, I was freelancing a lot in my spare time, principally for airline magazines. I got the idea to do an article on remarkable coincidences and sent off a query letter to one of these publications, which expressed serious interest and promised payment of $500 if published – a sum of money I could very handily have done with. But when I came to write the article, I realized that, although I had plenty of information about scientific studies into the probabilities of coincidence, I didn't have nearly enough examples of remarkable coincidences themselves to give the article sufficient zip or to fill 1,500 words of space. So I wrote a letter to the magazine saying I wouldn't be able to deliver and left it on the top of my typewriter to post the next day. Then I dressed myself in respectable clothing and drove to work at *The Times*.

Now in those days, Philip Howard, the kindly literary editor (I would, of course, say that, in view of his position, but in fact it is true: he's a proper gent), used to hold book sales for the staff a couple of times a year when his office became so filled with review copies that he'd lost his desk. These were always exciting occasions because you could acquire stacks of books for practically nothing. He charged something like 25p for hardbacks and 10p for paperbacks, and then passed the proceeds to the Cirrhosis Foundation or some other charity dear to the hearts of journalists. On this particular day, I arrived at work to find a notice by the lifts announcing a book sale at 4 p.m. It was 3.55, so I dumped my coat at my desk and eagerly hastened to his chamber. The place was already full of mingling people. I stepped into the mêlée and what should be the very first book my eyes fell on but a paperback called *Remarkable True Coincidences*. How's that for a remarkable true coincidence? But here's the uncanny thing. I opened it up and found that not only did it offer all the material I could possibly need, but the very first coincidence it discussed concerned a man named Bryson.

I've been telling this story for years in pubs and every time I've finished it, the people to whom I've told it have nodded thoughtfully for quite some time, then turned to each other and said: 'You know, it occurs to me there's another way to get to Barnsley without going anywhere near the M62. You know the Happy Eater roundabout at Guiseley? Well, if you take the second turning there . . .'

So anyway, I spent three days at home, immersed in the chaos of domestic life, happy as a puppy – romping with the little ones, bestowing affection indiscriminately, following my wife from room to room, doing widdles on a sheet of newspaper in the kitchen corner. I cleaned out my rucksack, attended to the mail, strode proprietorially around the garden, savoured the bliss of waking up each morning in my own bed.

I couldn't face the prospect of departing again so soon, so I decided to stay on a bit longer and make a couple of day trips. Thus it was that on the third morning I picked up my good friend and neighbour, the kindly and gifted artist David Cook – it is his painting that graces the jacket of this book – and went with him for a day's walk through Saltaire and Bingley, his native turf. It was awfully nice to have some company for a change and interesting to see this little corner of Yorkshire through the eyes of someone who had grown up in it.

I had never properly been to Saltaire before and what a splendid surprise it was to me. Saltaire, in case you don't know about it, is a model factory community built by Titus Salt between 1851 and 1876. It is a little difficult to know what to make of old Titus. On the one hand he was one of that unattractive breed of teetotalling, self-righteous, God-fearing industrialists in which the nineteenth century seemed to specialize – a man who didn't want merely to employ his workers but to own them. Workers at his mill were expected to live in his houses, worship in his church, follow his precepts to the letter. He would not allow a pub in the village and so saddled the local park with stern restrictions regarding noise, smoking, the playing of games and other indecorous activities that there was not much fun to be had in it. Workers were allowed to take boats out on the river – but only, for some reason, so long as there were never more than four out at any one time. Whether they liked it or not, in short, they were compelled to be sober, industrious and quiet.

On the other hand, Salt showed a rare degree of enlightenment in terms of social welfare, and there is no question that his employees enjoyed cleaner, healthier, more comfortable living conditions than almost any other industrial workers in the world at that time.

Though it has since been swallowed up by the great sprawl that is the Leeds–Bradford conurbation, when it was built Saltaire stood in clean, open countryside – a vast change from the unhealthy stew of central Bradford, where in the 1850s there were more brothels than churches and not a single yard of covered sewers. From bleak and grimy back-to-backs, Salt's workers came to airy, spacious cottages, each with a yard, private gas supply and at least two bedrooms. It must have seemed a very Eden.

On a sloping site overlooking the River Aire and Leeds to Liverpool Canal, Salt built a massive mill known as the Palace of Industry – in its day the largest factory in Europe – spreading over nine acres and graced with a striking Italianate campanile modelled on that of Santa Maria Gloriosa in Venice. He additionally built a park, a church, an institute for 'conversation, refreshment and education', a hospital, a school and 850 trim and tidy stone houses on a formal grid of cobbled streets, most of them named for Salt's wife and eleven children. The institute was perhaps the most remarkable of these undertakings. Built in the hope of distracting workers from the peril of drink, it contained a gymnasium, a laboratory, a billiards room, a library, a reading room, and a lecture and concert hall. Never before had manual workers been given a more lavish opportunity to better themselves, an opportunity that many scores enthusiastically seized. One James Waddington, an untutored woolsorter, became a world authority on linguistics and a leading light of the Phonetic Society of Great Britain and Ireland.

Today Saltaire remains miraculously intact, though the factory has long since ceased to manufacture cloth and the houses are now privately owned. One floor of the factory contains a wonderful –

and free – permanent exhibition of the works of David Hockney, and the rest is given over to retail space selling the most extraordinary range of designer clothes, posh and stylish housewares, books and arty postcards. It was a kind of miracle to find this place – this yuppie heaven – inhabiting a forgotten corner of metropolitan Bradford. And yet it seemed to be doing very well.

David Cook and I had an unhurried look around the gallery – I had never paid much attention to Hockney, but I'll tell you this: the boy can draw – then wandered through the streets of former workers' cottages, all of them snug and trim and lovingly preserved, before striking off through Roberts Park to Shipley Glen, a steep wooded dell leading to a sweep of open common land of the sort where you can usually find people exercising their dogs. It looks as if it has been wild and untended for ever, but in fact a century ago this was the site of a hugely successful amusement park – one of the world's first.

Among the many attractions were an aerial gondola ride, a big dipper and what was billed as 'The Largest, Wildest, Steepest Toboggan Slide Ever Erected on Earth'. I've seen pictures of these, filled with ladies with parasols and mustachioed men in stiff collars, and they do actually look pretty exciting, particularly the toboggan ride, which ran for perhaps a quarter of a mile down a formidably steep and perilous hill. One day in 1900, as a carful of smartly dressed tobogganers were being hauled up the hill to be despatched on another hair-raising descent, the winch cable snapped, sending the passengers hurtling out of control to a messy but exciting death at the bottom, and that was pretty much the end of the Shipley Glen Amusement Park. Today all that's left of these original thrills is the poky Glen Tramway, which goes up and down a nearby slope in a discreet and sedate fashion, as it has since 1895, but among the tall grass we did find a remnant of old track from the original toboggan ride, which thrilled us mildly.

The whole of this area is a kind of archaeological site of the not-too-distant past. A mile or so away, up an overgrown track, is the site of Milner Field, an ornate palace of stone built by Titus Salt Junior in 1870 at a time when the Salt family fortunes seemed boundless and perpetually secure. But weren't they in for a surprise? In 1893, the textile trade went into a sudden slump, leaving the Salts dangerously overextended, and the family abruptly lost control of the firm. In consternation and shame, they had to sell the house, mill and associated holdings. Then began a strange

and sinister series of events. Without apparent exception all the
subsequent owners of Milner Field suffered odd and devastating set-
backs. One whacked himself in the foot with a golf club and died
when the wound turned gangrenous. Another came home to find his
young bride engaged in an unseemly bout of naked bedtop wrestling
with a business associate. He shot the associate or possibly both of
them – accounts vary – but in any case he certainly made a mess of
the bedroom and was taken off to have his neck stretched.

Before long the house developed a reputation as a place where
you could reliably expect to come a cropper. People moved in and
abruptly moved out again, with ashen faces and terrible wounds.
By 1930, when the house went on the market one last time, no
buyer could be found for it. It stayed empty for twenty years, and
finally in 1950 it was pulled down. Now the site is overgrown
and weedy, and you could walk past it without ever guessing that
one of the finest houses in the North had once stood here. But if
you poke about in the tall grass, as we did now, you can find one
of the old conservatory floors, made of neatly patterned black and
white tiles. It was strangely reminiscent of the Roman mosaic I had
seen at Winchcombe, and scarcely less astonishing.

It seemed remarkable to think that a century ago Titus Salt
Junior could have stood on this spot, in a splendid house, looking
down the Aire Valley to the distant but formidable Salt's Mill,
clanging away and filling the air with steamy smoke, and beyond it
the sprawl of the richest centre of woollen trade in the world, and
that now it could all be gone. What would old Titus Senior think,
I wondered, if you brought him back and showed him that the
family fortune was spent and his busy factory was now full of
stylish chrome housewares and wooftah paintings of naked male
swimmers with glistening buttocks?

We stood for a long time on this lonely summit. You can see for
miles across Airedale from up there, with its crowded towns and
houses climbing up the steep hillsides to the bleak upland fells, and
I found myself wondering, as I often do when I stand on a northern
hillside, what all those people in all those houses do. There used to
be scores of mills all up and down Airedale – ten or more in Bingley
alone – and now they are virtually all gone, torn down to make
room for supermarkets or converted into heritage centres, blocks of
flats or shopping complexes. French's Mill, Bingley's last surviving
textile factory, had closed a year or two before and now sat forlorn
with broken windows.

One of the great surprises to me upon moving North was discovering the extent to which it felt like another country. Partly it
was from the look and feel of the North – the high, open moors and
big skies, the wandering drystone walls, the grimy mill towns, the
snug stone villages of the Dales and Lakes – and partly, of course,
it was to do with the accents, the different words, the refreshing if
sometimes startling frankness of speech. Partly it was also to do
with the way Southerners and Northerners were so extraordinarily,
sometimes defiantly, ignorant of the geography of the other end of
the country. It used to astonish me, working on newspapers in
London, how often you could call out a question like 'Which of the
Yorkshires is Halifax in?' and be met with a tableful of blank
frowns. And when I moved North and told people that I'd
previously lived in Surrey near Windsor, I often got the same look
– a kind of nervous uncertainty, as if they were afraid I was going
to say, 'Now you show me on the map just where that is.'

Mostly what differentiated the North from the South, however,
was the exceptional sense of economic loss, of greatness passed,
when you drove through places like Preston or Blackburn or stood
on a hillside like this. If you draw an angled line between Bristol
and the Wash, you divide the country into two halves with roughly
27 million people on each side. Between 1980 and 1985, in the
southern half they lost 103,600 jobs. In the northern half in
the same period they lost 1,032,000 jobs, almost exactly ten times
as many. And still the factories are shutting. Turn on the local television news any evening and at least half of it will be devoted to
factory closures (and the other half will be about a cat stuck up a
tree somewhere; there is truly nothing direr than local television
news). So I ask again: what do all those people in all those houses
do – and what, more to the point, will their children do?

We walked out of the grounds along another track towards
Eldwick, past a large and flamboyant gatehouse, and David made
a crestfallen noise. 'I used to have a friend who lived there,' he said.
Now it was crumbling, its windows and doorways bricked up, a
sad waste of a fine structure. Beside it, an old walled garden was
neglected and overgrown.

Across the road, David pointed out the house where Fred Hoyle
had grown up. In his autobiography (*It'll Start Getting Cold Any
Minute Now, Just You See*), Hoyle recalls how he used to see
servants in white gloves going in and out the gate of Milner Field,

but is mysteriously silent on all the scandal and tragedy that was happening beyond the high wall. I had spent £3 on his auto-biography in a second-hand bookshop in the certain expectation that the early chapters would be full of accounts of gunfire and midnight screams, so you can imagine my disappointment.

A bit further on, we passed three large blocks of council flats, which were not only ugly and remote but positioned in such an odd and careless way that, although they stood on an open hillside, the tenants didn't actually get a view. They had, David told me, won many architectural awards.

As we ambled into Bingley down a curving slope, David told me about his childhood there in the Forties and Fifties. He painted an attractive picture of happy times spent going to the pictures ('Wednesdays to the Hippodrome, Fridays to the Myrtle'), eating fish and chips out of newspapers, listening to *Dick Barton* and *Top of the Form* on the radio – a magic lost world of half-day closings, second posts, people on bicycles, endless summers. The Bingley he described was a confident, prosperous cog at the heart of a proud and mighty empire, with busy factories and a lively centre full of cinemas, tea-rooms and interesting shops, which was strikingly at odds with the dowdy, traffic-frazzled, knocked-about place we were passing into now. The Myrtle and Hippodrome had shut years before. The Hippodrome had been taken over by a Woolworth's, but that, too, was now long gone. Today there isn't a cinema in Bingley or much of anything else to make you want to go there. The centre of the town is towered over by the forbidding presence of the Bradford and Bingley Building Society – not a particularly awful building as these things go, but hopelessly out of scale with the town around it. Between it and a truly squalid 1960s brick shop-ping precinct, the centre of Bingley has had its character destroyed beyond repair. So it came as a pleasant surprise to find that beyond its central core Bingley remains a delightful spot.

We walked past a school and a golf course to a place called Beckfoot Farm, a pretty stone cottage in a dell beside a burbling beck. The main Bradford road was only a few hundred yards away, but it was another, pre-motorized century back here. We followed a shady riverside path, which was exceedingly fetching in the mild sunshine. There used to be a factory here where they rendered fat, David told me. It had the most awful smell, and the water always had a horrible rusty-creamy colour with a skin of frothy gunge on it. Now the river was sparkling green and healthy-looking and the

spot seemed totally untouched by either time or industry. The old
factory had been scrubbed up and gutted and turned into a block
of stylish flats. We walked up to a place called Five-Rise Locks,
where the Leeds-to-Liverpool Canal climbs a hundred feet or so in
five quick stages, and had a look at the broken windows beyond the
razor-wire perimeter of French's Mill. Then, feeling as if we had
exhausted pretty much all that Bingley had to offer, we went to a
convivial pub called the Old White Horse and drank a very large
amount of beer, which is what we had both had in mind all along.

The next day I went shopping with my wife in Harrogate – or
rather I had a look around Harrogate while she went shopping.
Shopping is not, in my view, something that men and women
should do together since all men want to do is buy something noisy
like a drill and get it home so they can play with it, whereas women
aren't happy until they've seen more or less everything in town and
felt at least 1,500 different textures. Am I alone in being mystified
by this strange compulsion on the part of women to finger things in
shops? I have many times seen my wife go twenty or thirty yards
out of her way to feel something – a mohair jumper or a velveteen
bed jacket or something.
    'Do you like that?' I'll say in surprise since it doesn't seem her
type of thing, and she'll look at me as if I'm mad.
    'That?' she'll say. 'No, it's hideous.'
    'Then why on earth,' I always want to say, 'did you walk all the
way over there to touch it?' But of course like all long-term
husbands I have learned to say nothing when shopping because no
matter what you say – 'I'm hungry', 'I'm bored', 'My feet are tired',
'Yes, that one looks nice on you, too', 'Well, have them both
then', 'Oh, for fuck sake', 'Can't we just go home?', 'Monsoon?
Again? Oh, for fuck sake', 'Where have I been? Where have you
been?', 'Then why on earth did you walk all the way over there to
touch it?' – it doesn't pay, so I say nothing.
    On this day, Mrs B. was in shoe-shopping mode, which means
hours and hours of making some poor guy in a cheap suit fetch endless boxes of more or less identical footwear and then deciding not
to have anything, so I wisely decided to clear off and have a look at
the town. To show her I love her, I took her for coffee and cake
at Betty's (and at Betty's prices you need to be pretty damn smitten),
where she issued me with her usual precise instructions for a
rendezvous. 'Three o'clock outside Woolworth's. But listen – stop

fiddling with that and listen – if Russell & Bromley don't have the shoes I want I'll have to go to Ravel, in which case meet me at 3.15 by the frozen foods in Marks. Otherwise I'll be in Hammick's in the cookery books section or possibly the children's books – unless I'm in Boots feeling toasters. But probably, in fact, I'll be at Russell & Bromley trying on all the same shoes all over again, in which case meet me outside Next no later than 3.27. Have you got that?'

'Yes.' No.

'Don't let me down.'

'Of course not.' In your dreams.

And then with a kiss she was gone. I finished my coffee and savoured the elegant, old-fashioned ambience of this fine institution where the waitresses still wear frilly caps and white aprons over black dresses. There really ought to be more places like this, if you ask me. It may cost an arm and a leg for a cafetière and a sticky bun, but it is worth every penny and they will let you sit there all day, which I seriously considered doing now as it was so agreeable. But then I thought I really ought to have a look around the town, so I paid the bill and hauled myself off through the shopping precinct to have a look at Harrogate's newest feature, the Victoria Gardens Shopping Centre. The name is a bit rich because they built it on *top* of Victoria Gardens, so it really ought to be called the Nice Little Gardens Destroyed By This Shopping Centre.

I wouldn't mind this so much, but they also demolished the last great public toilets in Britain – a little subterranean treasure house of polished tiles and gleaming brass in the aforementioned gardens. The Gents was simply wonderful and I've had good reports about the Ladies as well. I might not even mind this so much either but the new shopping centre is just heartbreakingly awful, the worst kind of pastiche architecture – a sort of Bath Crescent meets Crystal Palace with a roof by B&Q. For reasons I couldn't begin to guess at, a balustrade along the roofline had been adorned with life-sized statues of ordinary men, women and children. Goodness knows what this is meant to suggest – I suppose that this is some sort of Hall of the People – but the effect is that it looks as if two dozen citizens of various ages are about to commit mass suicide.

On the Station Parade side of the building, where the pleasant little Victoria Gardens and their pleasant little public toilets formerly existed, there is now a kind of open-air amphitheatre of steps, where I suppose it is intended for people to sit on those two or three days a year when Yorkshire is sunny, and high above the road there has been built a truly preposterous covered footbridge in the same Georgian/Italianate/Fuck-Knows style connecting the shopping centre to a multi-storey car park across the way.

Now, on the basis of my earlier remarks about Britain's treatment of its architectural heritage, you may foolishly have supposed that I would be something of an enthusiast for this sort of thing. Alas, no. If by pastiche you mean a building that takes some note of its neighbours and perhaps takes some care to match adjoining rooflines and echo the size and position of its neighbours' windows and door openings and that sort of thing, then yes, I am in favour of it. But if by pastiche you mean a kind of Disneyland version of Jolly Olde England like this laughable heap before me, then thank you but no.

You could argue, I suppose – and I dare say Victoria Gardens' architect would – that at least it shows some effort to inject traditional architectural values into the townscape and that it is less jarring to the sensibilities than the nearby glass-and-plastic box in which the Co-op is happy to reside (which is, let me say here, a building of consummate ugliness), but in fact it seems to me that it is just as bad as, and in its way even more uninspired and unimaginative than, the wretched Co-op building. (But let me also say that neither is even remotely as bad as the Maples building, a Sixties block that rises, like some kind of half-witted practical joke, a dozen or so storeys into the air in the middle of a long street of innocuous Victorian structures. Now how did *that* happen?)

So what are we to do with Britain's poor battered towns if I won't let you have Richard Seifert and I won't let you have Walt Disney? I wish I knew. More than this, I wish the architects knew. Surely there must be *some* way to create buildings that are stylish and forward-looking without destroying the overall ambience of their setting. Most other European nations manage it (with the notable and curious exception of the French). So why not here?

But enough of this tedious bleating. Harrogate is basically a very fine town, and far less scarred by careless developments than many other communities. It has in the Stray, a 215-acre sweep of parklike common land overlooked by solid, prosperous homes, one of the largest and most agreeable open spaces in the country. It has some nice old hotels, a pleasant shopping area and, withal, a genteel and well-ordered air. It is, in short, as nice a town as you will find anywhere. It reminds me, in a pleasantly English way, a little of Baden-Baden, which is, of course, not surprising since it was likewise a spa town in its day – and a very successful one, too. According to a leaflet I picked up at the Royal Pump Room Museum, as late as 1926 they were still dispensing as many as 26,000 glasses of sulphurous water in a single day. You can still drink the water if you want. According to a notice by the tap, it is reputedly very good for flatulence, which seemed an intriguing promise, and I very nearly drank some until I realized they meant it *prevented* it. What an odd notion.

I had a look around the museum and walked past the old Swan Hotel, where Agatha Christie went and hid after she found out that her husband was a philanderer, the beastly cad, then wandered up Montpellier Parade, a very pretty street filled with awesomely expensive antique shops. I examined the seventy-five-foot-high War Memorial, and went for a long, pleasantly directionless amble through the Stray, thinking how nice it must be to live in one of the big houses overlooking the park and be able to stroll to the shops.

You would never guess that a place as prosperous and decorous as Harrogate could inhabit the same zone of the country as Bradford or Bolton, but of course that is the other thing about the North – it has these pockets of immense prosperity, like Harrogate and Ilkley, that are even more decorous and flushed with wealth than their counterparts in the South. Makes it a much more interesting place, if you ask me.

Eventually, with the afternoon fading, I took myself back into the heart of the shopping area, where I scratched my head and, with a kind of panicky terror, realized I didn't have the faintest idea where or when I had agreed to meet my dear missis. I was standing there wearing an expression like Stan Laurel when he turns around to find that the piano he was looking after is rolling down a steep hill with Ollie aboard, legs wriggling, when by a kind of miracle my wife walked up.

'Hello, dear!' she said brightly. 'I must say, I never expected to find you here waiting for me.'

'Oh, for goodness' sake, give me a bit of credit, *please*. I've been here ages.'

And arm in arm we strode off into the wintry sunset.

CHAPTER EIGHTEEN

I TOOK A TRAIN TO LEEDS AND THEN ANOTHER TO MANCHESTER – A long, slow but not unpleasant ride through steep-sided dales that looked uncannily like the one I lived in except that these were thickly strewn with old mills and huddled, soot-blackened villages. The old mills seemed to come in three types: 1. Derelict with broken windows and TO LET signs. 2. Gone – just a grassless open space. 3. Something non-manufacturing, like a depot for a courier service or a B&Q Centre or similar. I must have passed a hundred of these old factories but not until we were well into the outskirts of Manchester did I see a single one that appeared to be engaged in the manufacture of anything.

I had left home late, so it was four o'clock and getting on for dark by the time I emerged from Piccadilly Station. The streets were shiny with rain, and busy with traffic and hurrying pedestrians, which gave Manchester an attractive big-city feel. For some totally insane reason, I had booked a room in an expensive hotel, the Piccadilly. My room was on the eleventh floor, but it seemed like about the eighty-fifth such were the views. If my wife had had a flare and an inclination to get up on the roof, I could just about have seen her. Manchester seemed enormous – a boundless sprawl of dim yellow lights and streets filled with slow-moving traffic.

I played with the TV, confiscated the stationery and spare tablet of soap, and put a pair of trousers in the trouser press – at these prices I was determined to extract full value from the experience – even though I knew that the trousers would come out with permanent pleats in the oddest places. (Is it me or are these things totally counter-productive?) That done, I went out for a walk and to find a place to eat.

There seems to be a kind of inverse ratio where dinner establishments and I are concerned – namely that the more of them there are, the harder it is for me to find one that looks even remotely adequate to my modest needs. What I really wanted was a little Italian place on a side-street – the kind with checked tablecloths and Chianti bottles with candles and a nice 1950s feel about them. British cities used to abound in these places, but they are deucedly hard to find now. I walked for some distance but the only places I could find were either the kind of national chains with big plastic menus and dismal food or hotel dining rooms where you had to pay £17.95 for three courses of pompous description and overcooked disappointment.

Eventually I ended up in Chinatown, which announces itself to the world with a big colourful arch and then almost immediately loses heart. There was a scattering of restaurants among big office buildings, but I can't say I felt as if I had wandered into a little corner of the Orient. The bigger, better-looking restaurants were packed, so I ended up going to some upstairs place, where the décor was tatty, the food barely OK and the service totally indifferent. When the bill came, I noticed an extra charge beside a notation marked 'S.C.'

'What's that?' I said to the waitress, who had, I should like to note, been uncommonly surly throughout.

'Suhvice chawge.'

I looked at her in surprise. 'Then why, pray, is there also a space here for a tip?'

She gave a bored, nothing-to-do-with-me shrug.

'That's terrible,' I said. 'You're just tricking people into tipping twice.'

She gave a heavy sigh, as if she had been here before. 'You got complaint? You want see manager?'

The offer was made in a tone that suggested that if I were to see the manager it would be with some of his boys in a back alley. I decided not to press the matter, and instead returned to the streets and had a long, purposeless walk through Manchester's dank and strangely ill-lit streets – I can't remember a darker city. I couldn't say where I went exactly because Manchester's streets always seem curiously indistinguishable to me. I never felt as if I were getting nearer to or farther from anything in particular but just wandering around in a kind of urban limbo.

Eventually I ended up beside the great dark bulk of the Arndale Centre (there's that name again). What a monumental mistake that was. I suppose it must be nice, in a place as rainy as Manchester, to be able to shop undercover and if you are going to have these things at all, much better to have them *in* the city than outside it. But at night it is just twenty-five acres of deadness, a massive impediment to anyone trying to walk through the heart of the city. I could see through the windows that they had tarted it up inside since the last time I had been there – and very nice it appeared now, too – but outside it was still covered in those awful tiles that make it look like the world's largest gents' lavatory, and indeed as I passed up Cannon Street three young men with close-cropped heads and abundantly tattooed arms were using an outside wall for that very purpose. They paid me scant heed, but it suddenly occurred to me that it was getting late and the streets were awfully empty of respectable-looking fellows like me, so I decided to get back to my hotel before some other late-night carousers put me to similar use.

I awoke early and hit the drizzly streets determined to form some fixed impression of the city. My problem with Manchester, you see, is that I have no image of it, none at all. Every other great British city has something about it, some central motif, that fixes it in my mind: Newcastle has its bridge, Liverpool has the Liver Buildings and docks, Edinburgh its castle, Glasgow the great sprawl of Kelvingrove Park and the buildings of Charles Rennie Mackintosh, even Birmingham has the Bull Ring (and very welcome it is to it, too). But Manchester to me is a perennial blank – an airport with a city attached. Mention Manchester to me and all that swims into my mind is a vague and unfocused impression of Ena Sharples, L.S. Lowry, Manchester United football club, some plan to introduce trams because they have them in Zurich or some place and they seem to work pretty well there, the Hallé Orchestra, the old *Manchester Guardian* and these rather touching attempts every four years or so to win the bid for the next summer Olympics, usually illustrated with ambitious plans to build a £400-million velodrome or a £250-million table tennis complex or some other edifice vital to the future of a declining industrial city.

Apart from Ena Sharples and L.S. Lowry, I couldn't name a single great Mancunian. It's clear from the abundance of statues outside the town hall that Manchester has produced its share of worthies in its time, though it is equally clear from all the frock coats and

mutton chops that it has either stopped producing worthies or
stopped producing statues. I had a look around them now and
didn't recognize a single name.

If I haven't got a very clear image of the city, it's not entirely my
fault. Manchester doesn't appear to have a very fixed image of
itself. 'Shaping Tomorrow's City Today' is the official local motto,
but in fact Manchester seems decidedly of two minds about its
place in the world. At Castlefield, they were busy creating *yesterday's* city today, cleaning up the old brick viaducts and warehouses,
recobbling the quaysides, putting fresh coats of glossy paint on the
old arched footbridges and scattering about a generous assortment
of old-fashioned benches, bollards and lampposts. By the time they
have finished, you will be able to see exactly what life was like in
nineteenth-century Manchester – or at least what it would have
been like if they had had wine-bars and cast-iron litter bins and
directional signs for heritage trails and the G-Mex Centre. At
Salford Quays, on the other hand, they have taken the opposite
tack and done everything they can to obliterate the past, creating a
kind of mini-Dallas on the site of the once-booming docks of the
Manchester Ship Canal. It's the most extraordinary place – a
huddle of glassy modern office buildings and executive flats in the
middle of a vast urban nowhere, all of them seemingly quite empty.

The one thing you have a job to find in Manchester is the one
thing you might reasonably expect to see – row after row of
huddled Coronation Streets. These used to exist in abundance, I'm
told, but now you could walk miles without seeing a single brick
terrace anywhere. But that doesn't matter because you can always
go and see the real *Coronation Street* on the Granada Studios Tour,
which is what I did now – along with, it seemed, nearly everyone
else in the North of England. For some distance along the road to
the studios there are massive waste-ground car and coach parks,
and even at 9.45 in the morning they were filling up. Coaches from
far and wide – from Workington, Darlington, Middlesbrough,
Doncaster, Wakefield, almost every northern town you could think
of – were decanting streams of sprightly white-haired people, while
from the car parks issued throngs of families, everyone looking
happy and good natured.

I joined a queue that was a good 150 yards long and three or four
people wide and wondered if this wasn't a mistake, but when the
turnstiles opened the line advanced pretty smartishly and within
minutes I was inside. To my deep and lasting surprise, it was

actually quite wonderful. I had expected it to consist of a stroll up the *Coronation Street* set and a perfunctory guided tour of the studios, but they have made it into a kind of amusement park and done it exceedingly well. It had one of those Motionmaster Cinemas, where the seats tilt and jerk, so that you actually feel as if you are being hurled through space or thrown off the edge of a mountain, and another cinema where you put on plastic glasses and watched a cherishably naff 3D comedy. There was an entertaining demonstration of sound effects, an adorably gruesome show about special effects make-up and a lively, hugely amusing debate in an ersatz House of Commons, presided over by a troupe of youthful actors. And the thing was, all of these were done not just with considerable polish but with great and genuine wit.

Even after twenty years here, I remain constantly amazed and impressed by the quality of humour you find in the most unlikely places – places where it would simply not exist in other countries. You find it in the patter of stallholders in places like Petticoat Lane and in the routines of street performers – the sort of people who juggle flaming clubs or do tricks on unicycles and keep up a steady stream of jokes about themselves and selected members of the audience – and in Christmas pantomimes and pub conversations and encounters with strangers in lonely places.

I remember once years ago arriving at Waterloo Station to find the place in chaos. A fire up the line at Clapham Junction had disrupted services. For an hour or so hundreds of people stood with incredible patience and implacable calm watching a blank departure board. Occasionally a rumour would rustle through the crowd that a train was about to leave from platform 7, and everyone would traipse off there only to be met at the gate by a new rumour that the train was, in fact, departing from platform 16 or possibly platform 2. Eventually, after visiting most of the station's platforms and sitting on a series of trains that went nowhere, I found myself in the guards' van of an express reputed to be departing for Richmond shortly. The van had one other occupant: a man in a suit sitting on a pile of mailbags. He had an enormous red beard – you could have stuffed a mattress with it – and the sort of world-weary look of someone who has long since abandoned hope of reaching home.

'Have you been here long?' I asked.

He exhaled thoughtfully and said: 'Put it this way. I was clean shaven when I got here.' I just love that.

Not too many months before this, I had been with my family to

Euro Disneyland. Technologically, it had been stunning. The amount of money invested by Disney in a single ride would make any part of the Granada Studios Tour look like amateur night in a village hall. But it occurred to me now, as I sat in the immense conviviality of Granada's mock House of Commons debate, that not once at Disneyland had there been a single laugh. Wit, and particularly the dry, ironic, taking-the-piss sort of wit, was completely beyond them. (Do you know that there isn't even an equivalent in American speech for 'taking the piss'?) Yet here in Britain it is such a fundamental part of daily life that you scarcely notice it. Just the day before at Skipton I had asked for a single to Manchester with a receipt. When the man in the window passed them to me he said: 'The ticket's free . . . but it's eighteen-fifty for the receipt.' If he had done that in America, the customer would have said: '*What?* What're ya saying? The ticket's *free*, but the receipt costs £18.50? What kind of cockamamy set-up is this?' If Disney had had a House of Commons debate, it would have been earnest, hokey, frighteningly competitive and over in three minutes. The people on the two sides of the chamber would have cared deeply, if briefly, about coming out on top. Here, things were so contrived that there wasn't the remotest possibility of anyone's winning. It was all about having a good time, and it was done so well, so cheerfully and cleverly, that I could hardly stand it. And I knew with a sinking feeling that I was going to miss this very much.

The one place you don't find any humour on the Granada Studios Tour is on Coronation Street, but that is because for millions of us it is a near-religious experience. I have a great fondness for *Coronation Street* because it was one of the first programmes I watched on British television. I had no idea what was going on, of course. I couldn't understand half of what the characters said or why they were all called Chuck. But I found myself strangely absorbed by it. Where I came from, soap operas were always about rich, ruthless, enormously successful people with $1,500 suits and offices high up in angular skyscrapers, and the main characters were always played by the sort of actors and actresses who, given a choice between being able to act and having really great hair, would always go for the hair. And here was this amazing programme about ordinary people living on an anonymous northern street, talking a language I could barely understand and never doing much of anything. By the time the first adverts came on, I was a helpless devotee.

Then I was cruelly forced into working nights on Fleet Street and fell out of the habit. Now I am not even permitted in the room when *Coronation Street* is on because I spend the whole time saying, 'Where's Ernie Bishop? So who's that then? I thought Deirdre was with Ray Langton? Where's Len? Stan Ogden is *dead*?' and after a minute I find myself shooed away. But, as I discovered now, you can go years without watching *Coronation Street* and still enjoy walking along the set because it's so obviously the same street. It's the real set, by the way – they close the park on most Mondays so that they can film on it – and it feels like a real street. The houses are solid and made of real bricks, though, like everyone else, I was disappointed to peer in the windows and find through gaps in the curtains that they were empty shells with nothing but electrical cables and carpenters' sawhorses inside. I was a bit confused to encounter a hairdresser's salon and a pair of modern houses, and the Kabin, to my clear distress, was much smarter and well ordered than it used to be, but I still felt uncannily on familiar and hallowed turf. Throngs of people walked up and down the street in a kind of reverential hush, identifying front doors and peering through lace curtains. I latched on to a friendly little lady with blue-rinsed hair under a transparent rain hat she seemed to have made from a bread wrapper, and she not only informed me who lived in which houses now, but who had lived in which houses way back when, so that I was pretty well brought up to speed. Pretty soon I found myself surrounded by a whole flock of little blue-haired ladies answering my shocked questions ('Deirdre with a toy boy? Never!') and assuring me with solemn nods that it was so. It is a profoundly thrilling experience to walk up and down this famous street – you may smirk, but you would feel just the same and you know it – and it comes as something of a shock to round the corner at either end and find yourself back in an amusement park.

I had only intended to stay an hour or so at the park, and hadn't got anywhere near the guided studio tour or the *Coronation Street* gift shop, when I glanced at my watch and discovered with a snort of alarm that it was nearly one o'clock. In a mild panic, I hastened from the park and back to my distant hotel, fearful that I would be charged for another day or, at the very least, that my trousers would be overcooked.

In consequence I found myself, three-quarters of an hour later, standing on the edge of Piccadilly Gardens with a heavy rucksack and a pretty near total uncertainty about where to go next. I had it vaguely in mind to head for the Midlands, since I had given this noble if challenging region of the country pretty short shrift on my previous foragings, but as I was standing there a faded red double-decker bus announcing WIGAN in its little destination window pulled up beside me and the matter was out of my hands. It happened that at this very moment I had *The Road to Wigan Pier* sticking out of my back pocket, so unhesitatingly – and wisely – I took this for a sign.

I bought a single and found my way to a seat midway along the back upstairs. Wigan can't be more than fifteen or sixteen miles from Manchester, but it took most of the afternoon to get there. We lurched and reeled through endless streets that never seemed to change character or gain any. They were all lined with tiny terrace houses, of which every fourth one seemed to be a hairdresser's, and dotted with garages and brick shopping precincts with an un-varying array of supermarkets, banks, video takeouts, pie and pea shops, and betting establishments. We went through Eccles and Worsley, then through a surprisingly posh bit, and on to Boothstown and Tyldesley and Atherton and Hindley and other such places of which I had never heard. The bus stopped frequently – every twenty feet in places, it seemed – and at nearly every stop there was a large exchange of people. They nearly all looked poor and worn out and twenty years older than I suspect they actually were. Apart from a sprinkling of old men in flat caps and dun-coloured, tightly zippered Marks & Spencer's jackets, the pas-sengers were nearly all middle-aged women with unlikely hairdos and the loose, phlegmy laughter of hardened smokers, but they were unfailingly friendly and cheerful and seemed happy enough with their lot. They all called each other 'darlin' and 'love'.

The most remarkable thing – or perhaps the least remarkable thing, depending on how you look at it – was how neat and well looked after were the endless terraces of little houses we passed. Everything about them bespoke an air of modesty and make-do, but every stoop shone, every window gleamed, every sill had a fresh, glossy coat of paint. I took out my copy of *The Road to Wigan Pier* and lost myself for a bit in another world, one that occupied the same space as these little communities we were pass-ing through, but was impossibly at odds with what my eyes were telling me when I glanced up from the pages.

Orwell – and let us never forget that he was an Eton boy from a fairly privileged background – regarded the labouring classes the way we might regard Yap Islanders, as a strange but interesting anthropological phenomenon. In *Wigan Pier* he records how one of the great panic moments of his boyhood years was when he found himself in the company of a group of working men and thought he would have to drink from a bottle they were passing round. Ever since I read this, I've had my doubts about old George frankly. Certainly he makes the working class of the 1930s seem disgustingly filthy, but in fact every piece of evidence I've ever seen shows that most of them were almost obsessively dedicated to cleanliness. My own father-in-law grew up in an environment of starkest poverty and used to tell the most appalling stories of deprivation – you know the kind of thing: father killed in a factory accident, thirty-seven brothers and sisters, nothing for tea but lichen broth and a piece of roofing slate except on Sundays when they might trade in a child for a penny's worth of rotten parsnips, and all that sort of thing – and *his* father-in-law, a Yorkshireman, used to tell even more appalling stories of hopping forty-seven miles to school because he only had one boot and subsisting on a diet of stale buns and snot butties. 'But,' they would both invariably add, 'we were always clean and the house was spotless.' And it must be said they *were* the most fastidiously scrubbed persons imaginable, as were all their countless brothers and sisters and friends and relatives.

It also happens that not long before this I had met Willis Hall, the author and playwright (and a very nice man into the bargain), and somehow we got to talking about this very matter. Hall grew up poor in Leeds, and he unhesitatingly confirmed that though the houses were barren and conditions hard, there was never the tiniest hint of dirtiness. 'When my mother was to be rehoused after the war,' he told me, 'she spent her last day there scrubbing it from top to bottom until it shone, even though she knew it was going to be torn down the next day. She just couldn't bear the thought of leaving it dirty – and I promise you that that wouldn't have been thought peculiar by anyone from that neighbourhood.'

For all his professed sympathy for the masses, you would never guess from reading Orwell that they were capable of any higher mental activities, and yet one Leeds neighbourhood alone produced Willis Hall, Keith Waterhouse and Peter O'Toole, while a similarly impoverished district of Salford that I know of produced Alistair Cooke and the artist Harold Riley, and I am sure the story was repeated countless times all up and down the country.

Such was the picture of appalling squalor Orwell painted that even now I was startled to find how neat and well maintained Wigan appeared to be as we entered it by means of a long hill. I got off at the bottom, pleased to return to the fresh air, and set off in search of the famous pier. Wigan Pier is an arresting landmark, yet – and here's another reason to be a bit cautious with regard to old George's reporting skills – after spending some days in the town, he concluded that the pier had been demolished. (So too, for that matter, did Paul Theroux in *Kingdom by the Sea*.) Now correct me if I'm wrong, but don't you think it a bit odd to write a book called *The Road to Wigan Pier* and to spend some days in the town and never once think to ask anybody whether the pier was still there or not?

In any case, you could hardly miss it now since there are cast-iron signposts pointing the way to it on almost every corner. The pier – it is really just an old coal shed on the side of the Leeds-to-Liverpool Canal – has (inevitably) been refurbished as a tourist attraction and incorporates a museum, gift shop, snack bar and a pub called, without evident irony, The Orwell. Alas for me, it was shut on Fridays, so I had to content myself with walking around it and peering in the windows at the museum displays, which looked reasonably diverting. Across the street was something nearly as arresting as the pier – a real working mill, a mountain of red bricks with the name Trencherfield Mill emblazoned across an upper storey. It's now part of Courtauld's, and is a sufficient rarity these days that it is something of a tourist attraction, too. There were signs out front telling you which way to go for the guided tours, the factory shop and the snack bar. It seemed a bit of an odd notion to me, the idea of joining a queue to watch people making duvets or whatever it is they do in there, but in any case it too appeared to be closed to the public on Fridays. The snack bar door was padlocked.

So I walked into the centre, a fair hike but a not unrewarding one. Such is Wigan's perennially poor reputation that I was truly astounded to find it has a handsome and well-maintained town centre. The shops seemed prosperous and busy and there were lots of public benches to sit on for the many people unable to take an active part in all the economic activity around them. Some talented architect had managed to incorporate a new shopping arcade into the existing fabric of the buildings in a simple but deceptively clever and effective way by making the glass canopy of the entrance match the line of the gables of the surrounding structures. The result was an entrance that was bright and modern but pleasantly harmonious – precisely the sort of thing I've been going on about for all these many pages – and I was delighted to think that if this sort of thing is going to happen just once in Britain that it should be in poor beleaguered Wigan.

To celebrate, I went off to have a cup of tea and a sticky bun at a place indoors called the Corinthia Coffee Lounge, which boasted, among its many other advertised features, a 'Georgian Potato Oven'. I asked the girl at the counter what that was and she looked at me as if I were very strange.

'It's for cooking potatoes and tha',' she said.

But of course. I took my tea and sticky bun to a table, where I spent a little time going 'Ooh, lovely,' and smiling inanely at some nice ladies at the next table, and afterwards, feeling strangely pleased with my day, went off to find the station.

CHAPTER NINETEEN

I TOOK A TRAIN TO LIVERPOOL. THEY WERE HAVING A FESTIVAL OF litter when I arrived. Citizens had taken time off from their busy activities to add crisp packets, empty cigarette boxes and carrier-bags to the otherwise bland and neglected landscape. They fluttered gaily in the bushes and brought colour and texture to pavements and gutters. And to think that elsewhere we stick these objects in rubbish bags.

In another bout of extravagant madness, I had booked a room in the Adelphi Hotel. I had seen it from the street on earlier visits and it appeared to have an old-fashioned grandeur about it that I was keen to investigate. On the other hand, it looked expensive and I wasn't sure my trousers could stand another session in the trouser press. So I was most agreeably surprised when I checked in to discover that I was entitled to a special weekend rate and that there would be money spare for a nice meal and a parade of beer in any of the many wonderful pubs in which Liverpool specializes.

And so, soon afterwards, I found myself, like all fresh arrivals in Liverpool, in the grand and splendorous surroundings of the Philharmonic, clutching a pint glass and rubbing shoulders with a happy Friday-evening throng. The Phil (you can call it this if you have been there twice) was in fact a bit too crowded for my liking. There was nowhere to sit and scarcely any room to stand, so I drank two pints, just enough at my time of life to need a pee – for there is no place in the world finer for a pee than the ornate gents' room of the Philharmonic – then went off to find some place a little quieter.

I ended up back in a place called The Vines, which was nearly as ornate as the Philharmonic but infinitely quieter. Apart from me, there were only three other customers, which was a mystery to me because it was a very fine pub with wood panelling by some Grinling Gibbons wannabe and a plaster ceiling even more ornate than the panelling. As I was sitting there drinking my beer and savouring my plush surroundings, some guy came in with a collecting tin from which the original label had been clumsily scratched, and asked me for a donation for handicapped children.

'Which handicapped children?' I asked.

'Ones in wheelchairs like.'

'I mean which organization do you represent?'

'It's, er, the, er, Handicapped Children's Organization like.'

'Well, as long as it's totally legitimate,' I said and gave him 20p. And that is what I like so much about Liverpool. The factories may be gone, there may be no work, the city may be pathetically dependent on football for its sense of destiny, but the Liverpudlians still have character and initiative, and they don't bother you with preposterous ambitions to win the bid for the next Olympics.

So nice was The Vines that I drank two more pints and then realized that I really ought to get something in my stomach lest I grow giddy and end up staggering into street furniture and singing 'Mother Machree'. Outside, the hill on which the pub stood seemed suddenly and unaccountably steep and taxing, until it dawned on me, in my mildly addled state, that I had come down it before whereas now I was going up it, which seemed to put everything in a new light. I found myself, after no great distance, standing outside a Greek restaurant and surveying the menu with a hint of a sway. I'm not much of one for Greek food – no disrespect to a fine cuisine, you understand, but I always feel as if I could boil my own leaves if I had a taste for that sort of thing – but the restaurant was so forlornly empty and the proprietress beckoned at me with such imploring eyes that I found myself wandering in. Well, the meal was wonderful. I have no idea what I ate, but it was abundant and delicious and they treated me like a prince. Foolishly I washed it all down with many additional draughts of beer. By the time I finished and settled the bill, leaving a tip of such lavishness as to bring the whole family to the kitchen door, and began the long process of stabbing an arm at a mysteriously disappearing jacket sleeve, I was, I fear, pretty nearly intoxicated. I staggered out into the fresh air, feeling suddenly queasy and largely incapable.

Now the second rule of excessive drinking (the first, of course, is don't take a sudden shine to a woman larger than Hoss Cartwright) is never to drink in a place on a steep slope. I walked down the hill on unfamiliar legs that seemed to snap out in front of me like whipped lengths of rope. The Adelphi, glowing beckoningly at the foot of the hill, managed the interesting trick of being both near by and astonishingly distant. It was like looking at it through the wrong end of a telescope – a sensation somewhat enhanced by the fact that my head was a good seven or eight yards behind my manically flopping appendages. I followed them helplessly, and by a kind of miracle they hurtled me down the hill, safely across the road and up the steps to the entrance to the Adelphi, where I celebrated my arrival by making a complete circuit in the revolving door so that I emerged into open air once again, before plunging back in and being flung with a startling suddenness into the Adelphi's grand and lofty lobby. I had one of those where-am-I moments, then grew aware that the night staff were silently watching me. Summoning as much dignity as I could and knowing that the lifts would be quite beyond me, I went to the grand staircase and managed – I know not how – to fall up them in a manner uncannily reminiscent of a motion picture run in reverse. All I know is that at the very end I leapt backwards to my feet and announced to the craning faces that I was quite all right, and then embarked on a long search for my room among the Adelphi's endless and mysteriously numbered corridors.

Here's a piece of advice for you. Don't go on the Mersey ferry unless you are prepared to have the famous song by Gerry and the Pacemakers running through your head for about eleven days afterwards. They play it when you board the ferry and they play it when you get off and for quite a lot of time in between. I went on it the following morning thinking a bit of a sitdown and a cruise on the water would be just the way to ease myself out of a killer hangover, but in fact the inescapable sound of 'Ferry 'cross the Mersey' only worsened my cranial plight. Apart from that, it must be said that the Mersey ferry is an agreeable, if decidedly breezy, way of passing a morning. It's a bit like the Sydney Harbour cruise, but without Sydney.

When they weren't playing 'Ferry 'cross the Mersey', they played a soundtrack outlining the famous sights from the deck, but the acoustics were terrible and 80 per cent of whatever was said was instantly blown away on the wind. All I could hear were snatches of things like 'three million' and 'world's biggest' but whether they were talking about oil refinery capacity or Derek Hatton's suits I couldn't say. But the gist of it was that *this* was once a great city and now it's Liverpool.

Now don't get me wrong. I'm exceedingly fond of Liverpool. It's probably my favourite English city. But it does rather feel like a place with more past than future. Leaning on a deck rail gazing out on miles of motionless waterfront, it was impossible to believe that until quite recently – and for 200 proud and prosperous years before that – Liverpool's ten miles of docks and shipyards provided employment for 100,000 people, directly or indirectly. Tobacco from Africa and Virginia, palm oil from the South Pacific, copper from Chile, jute from India, and almost any other commodity you could care to name passed through here on its way to being made into something useful. So too, no less significantly, did some 10 million people bound for a new life in the new world, drawn by stories of streets paved with gold and the possibility of accumulating immense personal wealth, or in the case of my own forebears by the giddy prospect of spending the next century and a half dodging tornadoes and shovelling snow in Iowa.

Liverpool became the third richest city in the empire. Only London and Glasgow had more millionaires. By 1880 it was generating more tax revenue than Birmingham, Bristol, Leeds and Sheffield together even though collectively they had twice the population. Cunard and White Star Lines had their headquarters in Liverpool, and there were countless other lines, now mostly forgotten – Blue Funnel, Bank Line, Coast Line, Pacific Steam Line, McAndrews Lines, Elder Dempster, Booth. There were more lines operating out of Liverpool then than there are ships today, or so at least it can seem when there is nothing much along the waterfront but the ghostly warble of Gerry Marsden's voice.

The decline happened in a single generation. In 1966, Liverpool was still the second busiest port in Britain, after London. By 1985, it had fallen so low that it was smaller and quieter than even Tees and Hartlepool, Grimsby and Immingham. But in its heyday it was something special. Maritime commerce brought Liverpool not just wealth and employment, but an air of cosmopolitanism that few cities in the world could rival, and it still has that sense about it. In Liverpool, you still feel like you are some place.

I walked from the ferry to the Albert Dock. There were plans at one time to drain it and turn it into a car park – it seems a miracle sometimes that there is anything at all left in this poor, stumbling country – but now, of course, they have been scrubbed up and gentrified, the old warehouses turned into offices, flats and restaurants for the sort of people who carry telephones in their briefcases. It also incorporates an outpost of the Tate Gallery and the Merseyside Maritime Museum.

I love the Merseyside Maritime Museum, not merely because it is well done but because it gives such a potent sense of what Liverpool was like when it was a great port – indeed, when the world was full of a productive busyness and majesty of enterprise that it seems utterly to have lost now. How I'd love to have lived in an age when you could walk to a waterfront and see mighty ships loading and unloading great squares of cotton fibre and heavy brown bags of coffee and spices, and when every sailing involved hundreds of people – sailors and dockers and throngs of excited passengers. Today, you go to a waterfront and all you find is an endless expanse of battered containers and one guy in an elevated cabin shunting them about.

Once there was infinite romance in the sea, and the Merseyside Maritime Museum captures every bit of it. I was particularly taken with an upstairs room full of outsized ships' models – the sort that must once have decorated executive boardrooms. Gosh, they were wonderful. Even as models they were wonderful. All the great Liverpool ships were here – the *Titanic*, the *Imperator*, the RMS *Majestic* (which began life as the *Bismarck* and was seized as war reparations) and the unutterably lovely TSS *Vauban*, with its broad decks of polished maple and its jaunty funnels. According to its label, it was owned by the Liverpool, Brazil and River Plate Steam Navigation Company Limited. Just reading those words, I was seized with a dull ache at the thought that never again will we see such a beautiful thing. J.B. Priestley called them the greatest constructions of the modern world, our equivalent of cathedrals, and he was absolutely right. I was appalled to think that never in my life would I have an opportunity to stride down a gangplank in a panama hat and a white suit and go looking for a bar with a revolving ceiling fan. How crushingly unfair life can sometimes be.

I spent two hours wandering through the museum, looking with care at all the displays. I would happily have stayed longer, but I had to check out of the hotel, so I regretfully departed and walked back through central Liverpool's fine Victorian streets to the Adelphi, where I grabbed my things and checked out.

I had a slight hankering to go to Port Sunlight, the model community built in 1888 by William Lever to house his soap workers, as I was interested to see how it compared with Saltaire. So I went to Liverpool Central and caught a train. At Rock Ferry we were informed that because of engineering works we would have to complete the journey by bus. This was OK by me because I was in no hurry and you can always see more from a bus. We rode along the Wirral peninsula for some time before the driver announced the stop for Port Sunlight. I was the only person to get off, and the most striking thing about it was that this was patently not Port Sunlight. I tapped on the front doors and waited for them to gasp open.

'Excuse me,' I said, 'but this doesn't look like Port Sunlight.'

'That's because it's Bebington,' he said. 'It's as close as I can get to Port Sunlight because of a low bridge.'

Oh.

'So where exactly is Port Sunlight then?' I asked but it was to a cloud of blue smoke. I hooked my rucksack over a shoulder and set off along a road that I hoped might be the right one – and no doubt would have been had I taken another. I walked for some distance, but the road seemed to go nowhere, or at least nowhere that looked Port Sunlightish. After a time an old man in a flat cap came doddering along and I asked him if he could point me the way to Port Sunlight.

'*Port Sunlight!*' he replied in the bellow of someone who thinks the world is going deaf with him, and with a hint that that was a bloody daft place to want to go. 'You want a *boose*!'

'A bus?' I said in surprise. 'How far am I then?'

'I say you want a *boose*!' he repeated, but more vehemently.

'I understand that. But which way is it exactly?'

He jabbed me with a bony finger in a tender spot just below the shoulder. It hurt. '*It's a boose you're wanting!*'

'I understand that.' You tedious deaf old fart. I raised my voice to match his and bellowed near his ear: 'I need to know which way to go!'

He looked at me as if I were unsustainably stupid. 'A bloody boose! You want a bloody boose!' And then he shuffled off, working his jaw wordlessly.

'Thank you. Die soon,' I called after him, rubbing my shoulder.

I returned to Bebington where I sought directions in a shop, which I should have done in the first place, of course. Port Sunlight, it turned out, was just down the road, under a railway bridge and over a junction – or perhaps it was the other way round. I don't know because it was now pissing down with rain and I tucked my head so low into my shoulders that I didn't see much of anything.

I walked for perhaps half a mile, but it was worth every sodden step. Port Sunlight was lovely, a proper little garden community, and much cheerier in aspect than the huddled stone cottages of Saltaire. This had open green spaces and a pub and pretty little houses half hidden behind drifts of foliage. There wasn't a soul about and nothing seemed to be open – neither the shops nor the pub nor the heritage centre nor the Lady Lever Art Gallery, all of which was a bit of a pisser – but I made the best of things by having a long slog around the rainy streets. I was a bit surprised to see a factory still there, still churning out soap as far as I could tell, and then I realized that I had exhausted all that Port Sunlight had to offer on a rainy Saturday out of season. So I trudged back to the bus-stop where I had so recently alighted and waited an hour and a quarter in a driving rain for a bus onward to Hooton, which was even less fun than it sounds.

Hooton offered the world not only a mildly ridiculous name, but the dumpiest British Rail station I ever hope to sneeze in. The shack-like platform waiting-rooms were dripping wet, which didn't matter a great deal as I was soaked already. With six others, I waited a small eternity for a train to Chester, where I changed to another for Llandudno.

The Llandudno train was gratifyingly empty, so I took a seat at a table for four, and contented myself with the thought that I would soon be in a nice hotel or guesthouse where I could have a hot bath followed by a generously apportioned dinner. I spent a little time watching the scenery, then pulled out my copy of *Kingdom by the Sea* to see if Paul Theroux had said anything about the vicinity that I might steal or modify to my own purposes. As always, I was amazed to find that as he rattled along these very tracks he was immersed in a lively conversation with his fellow passengers. How *does* he do it? Quite apart from the consideration that my carriage was nearly empty, I don't know how you strike up conversations with strangers in Britain. In America, of course, it's easy. You just offer a hand and say, 'My name's Bryson. How much money did you make last year?' and the conversation never looks back from there.

But in England – or in this instance Wales – it's so hard, or at least it is for me. I've never had a train conversation that wasn't disastrous or at least regretted. I either blurt the wrong thing ('Excuse me, I can't help notice the exceptional size of your nose') or it turns out that the person whose companionship I've encouraged has a serious mental disorder that manifests itself in murmurings and prolonged helpless weeping, or is a sales rep for the Hoze-Blo Stucco Company who mistakes your polite interest for keenness and promises to drop by for an estimate the next time he's in the Dales, or who wants to tell you all about his surgery for rectal cancer and then makes you guess where he keeps his colostomy bag ('Give up? Look, it's here under my arm. Go on, have a squeeze') or is a recruiter for the Mormons or any of ten thousand other things I would sooner be spared. Over a long period of time it gradually dawned on me that the sort of person who will talk to you on a train is almost by definition the sort of person you don't want to talk to on a train, so these days I mostly keep to myself and rely for conversational entertainment on books by more loquacious types like Jan Morris and Paul Theroux.

So there is a certain neat irony that as I was sitting there minding my own business some guy in a rustling anorak came by, spied the book, and cried, 'Aha, that Thoreau chap!' I looked up to find him taking a perch on a seat opposite me. He looked to be in his early sixties, with a shock of white hair and festive, lushly overgrown eyebrows that rose in pinnacles, like the tips of whipped meringue. They looked as if somebody had been lifting him up by grabbing hold of them. 'Doesn't know his trains, you know,' he said.

'Sorry?' I answered warily.

'Thoreau.' He nodded at my book. 'Doesn't know his trains at all. Or if he does he keeps it to himself.' He laughed heartily at this and enjoyed it so much that he said it again and then sat with his hands on his knees and smiling as if trying to remember the last time he and I had had this much fun together.

I gave an economical nod of acknowledgement for his quip and returned my attention to my book in a gesture that I hoped he would correctly interpret as an invitation to fuck off. Instead, he reached across and pulled the book down with a crooked finger – an action I find deeply annoying at the best of times. 'Do you know that book of his – *Great Railway what's-it*? All across Asia. You know the one?'

I nodded.

'Do you know that in that book he goes from Lahore to Islamabad on the *Delhi Express* and never once mentions the make of engine.'

I could see that I was expected to comment, so I said, 'Oh?'

'Never mentioned it. Can you imagine that? What use is a railway book if you don't talk about the engines.'

'You like trains then?' I said and immediately wished I hadn't.

The next thing I knew the book was on my lap and I was listening to the world's most boring man. I didn't actually much listen to what he said. I found myself riveted by his soaring eyebrows and by the discovery that he had an equally rich crop of nose hairs. He seemed to have bathed them in Miracle-Gro. He wasn't just a trainspotter, but a train-talker, a far more dangerous condition.

'Now *this* train,' he was saying, 'is a Metro-Cammel self-sealed unit built at the Swindon works, at a guess I'd say between July 1986 and August, or at the very latest September, of '88. At first I thought it couldn't be a Swindon 86–88 because of the cross-stitching on the seatbacks, but then I noticed the dimpled rivets on the side panels, and I thought to myself, I thought, What we have here, Cyril my old son, is a hybrid. There aren't many certainties in this world but Metro-Cammel dimpled rivets never lie. So where's your home?'

It took me a moment to realize that I had been asked a question. 'Uh, Skipton,' I said, only half lying.

'You'll have Crosse & Blackwell cross-cambers up there,' he said or something similarly meaningless to me. 'Now me, I live in Upton-on-Severn—'

'The Severn bore,' I said reflexively, but he missed my meaning.

'That's right. Runs right past the house.' He looked at me with a hint of annoyance, as if I were trying to distract him from his principal thesis. 'Now down there we have Z-46 Zanussi spin cycles with Abbott & Costello horizontal thrusters. You can always tell a Z-46 because they go *patoosh-patoosh* over seamed points rather than *katoink-katoink*. It's a dead giveaway every time. I bet you didn't know that.'

I ended up feeling sorry for him. His wife had died two years before – suicide, I would guess – and he had devoted himself since then to travelling the rail lines of Britain, counting rivets, noting breastplate numbers, and doing whatever else it is these poor people do to pass the time until God takes them away to a merciful death. I had recently read a newspaper article in which it was reported that a speaker at the British Psychological Society had described train-spotting as a form of autism called Asperger's syndrome.

He got off at Prestatyn – something to do with a Faggots & Gravy twelve-ton blender tender that was rumoured to be coming through in the morning – and I waved to him from the window as the train pulled out, then luxuriated in the sudden peace. I listened to the train rushing over the tracks – it sounded to me like it was saying *Asperger's syndrome Asperger's syndrome* – and passed the last forty minutes to Llandudno idly counting rivets.

CHAPTER TWENTY

FROM THE TRAIN, NORTH WALES LOOKED LIKE HOLIDAY HELL – ENDLESS ranks of prison-camp caravan parks standing in fields in the middle of a lonely, windbeaten nowhere, on the wrong side of the railway line and a merciless dual carriageway, with views over a boundless estuary of moist sand dotted with treacherous-looking sinkholes and, far off, a distant smear of sea. It seemed an odd type of holiday option to me, the idea of sleeping in a tin box in a lonesome field miles from anywhere in a climate like Britain's and emerging each morning with hundreds of other people from identical tin boxes, crossing the rail line and dual carriageway and hiking over a desert of sinkholes in order to dip your toes in a distant sea full of Liverpool turds. I can't put my finger on what exactly, but something about it didn't appeal to me.

Then suddenly the caravan parks thinned, the landscape around Colwyn Bay took on a blush of beauty and grandeur, the train made a sharp jag north and minutes later we were in Llandudno.

It is truly a fine and handsome place, built on a generously proportioned bay and lined along its broad front with a huddle of prim but gracious nineteenth-century hotels that reminded me in the fading light of a line-up of Victorian nannies. Llandudno was purpose-built as a resort in the mid-1800s, and it cultivates a nice old-fashioned air. I don't suppose that Lewis Carroll, who famously strolled this front with little Alice Liddell in the 1860s, telling her captivating stories of white rabbits and hookah-smoking caterpillars and asking between times if he could borrow her knickers to wipe his fevered brow and possibly take a few innocuous snaps of her in the altogether, would notice a great deal of change today, except of course that the hotels were now lit with electricity and Alice would be – what? – 127 years old and perhaps less of a distraction to a poor, perverted mathematician.

To my consternation, the town was packed with weekending pensioners. Coaches from all over were parked along the side-streets, every hotel I called at was full and in every dining room I could see crowds – veritable oceans – of nodding white heads spooning soup and conversing happily. Goodness knows what had brought them to the Welsh seaside at this bleak time of year.

Further on along the front there stood a clutch of guesthouses, large and virtually indistinguishable, and a few of them had vacancy signs perched in their windows. I had eight or ten to choose from, which always puts me in a mild fret because I have an unerring instinct for choosing badly. My wife can survey a row of guesthouses and instantly identify the one run by a white-haired widow with a kindly disposition and a fondness for children, snowy sheets and sparkling bathroom porcelain, whereas I can generally count on choosing the one run by a guy with a grasping manner, a drooping fag and the sort of cough that makes you wonder where he puts the phlegm. Such, I felt gloomily certain, would be the case tonight.

All the guesthouses had boards out front listing their many amenities – 'Colour TV', '*En Suite* All Rooms', 'Hospitality Trays', 'Full CH' – which only heightened my sense of unease and doom. How could I possibly choose intelligently among such a welter of options? One offered satellite TV and a trouser press and another boasted, in special jaunty italics, '*Current Fire Certificate*' – something I had never thought to ask for in a B & B. It was so much easier in the days when the very most you could hope for was H & C in all rooms.

I selected a place that looked reasonable enough from the outside – its board promised a colour TV and coffee-making facilities, about all I require these days for a lively Saturday night – but from the moment I set foot in the door and drew in the mildewy pong of damp plaster and peeling wallpaper, I knew it was a bad choice. I was about to turn and flee when the proprietor emerged from a back room and stayed my retreat with an unenthusiastic 'Yes?' A short conversation revealed that a single room with breakfast could be had for £19.50 – little short of a swindle. It was entirely out of the question that I would stay the night in such a dismal place at such a larcenous price, so I said, 'That sounds fine,' and signed in. Well, it's so hard to say no.

My room was everything I expected it to be – cold and cheerless, with melamine furniture, grubbily matted carpet and those mysterious ceiling stains that bring to mind a neglected corpse in the room above. Fingers of icy wind slipped through the single ill-fitting sash window. I drew the curtains and was not surprised that they had to be yanked violently before they would budge and came nowhere near meeting in the middle. There was a tray of coffee things but the cups were – let me be charitable – disgusting and the spoon was stuck to the tray. The bathroom, faintly illuminated by a distant light activated by a length of string, had curling floor tiles and years of accumulated muck packed into every corner and crevice. I peered at the yellowy grouting round the bath and sink and realized what the landlord did with his phlegm. A bath was out of the question, so I threw some cold water on my face, dried it with a towel that had the texture of a Weetabix and gladly took my leave.

I had a long stroll along the prom to boost my appetite and pass an hour. It felt wonderful. The air was still and sharp and there wasn't a soul about, though there were still lots of white heads in the hotel lounges and dining rooms, all bobbing merrily about. Perhaps they were having a Parkinson's convention. I walked nearly the length of The Parade, enjoying the chill autumn air and the trim handsomeness of the setting: a soft glow of hotels to the left, an inky void of restless sea to my right and a scattered twinkling of lights on the near and far headlands of Great and Little Ormes.

I couldn't help notice – it seemed so obvious now – that nearly all the hotels and guesthouses looked markedly superior to mine. Almost without exception they had names that bore homage to other places – 'Windermere', 'Stratford', 'Clovelly', 'Derby', 'St Kilda', even 'Toronto' – as if their owners feared that it would be too much of a shock to the system to remind visitors that they were in Wales. Only one place, with a sign that said 'Gwely a Brecwast/Bed and Breakfast', gave any hint that I was, at least in a technical sense, abroad.

I dined simply at a small nondescript restaurant off Mostyn Street and afterwards, feeling disinclined to return to my dingy room in a state of stark sobriety, went hunting for a pub. Llandudno had surprisingly few of these vital institutions. I walked for some time before I found one that looked even vaguely approachable. It was a typical town pub inside – maroon-plush, stale-odoured, smoky – and it was busy, mostly with young people. I took a seat at the bar, thinking I might be able to eavesdrop on my neighbours and receive more immediate attention when my glass was empty, but neither of these was to be. There was too much music and background noise to discern what my neighbours were saying and too much clamour for service at a spot near the till for the single harried server to notice an empty glass and a beggarly face up at my end.

So I sat and drank beer when I could get some and instead watched, as I often do in these circumstances, the interesting process by which customers, upon finishing a pint, would present the barman with a glass of clinging suds and golden dribble, and that this would be carefully filled to slightly overflowing, so that the excess froth, charged with an invisible load of bacteria, spittle and micro-fragments of loosened food, would run down the side of the glass and into a slop tray, where it would be carefully – I might almost say scientifically – conveyed by means of a clear plastic tube back to a barrel in the cellar. There these tiny impurities would drift and float and mingle, like flaky pooh in a goldfish bowl, awaiting summons back to someone else's glass. If I am to drink dilute dribble and mouth rinsings, then I do rather wish I could do it in a situation of comfort and cheer, seated in a Windsor chair by a blazing fire, but this appears to be an increasingly elusive dream. As sometimes also happens in these circumstances, I had a sudden urge not to drink any more beer, so instead I hauled myself from my barside perch and returned to my seafront lodgings for an early night.

In the morning, I emerged from the guesthouse into a world drained of colour. The sky was low and heavy and the sea along the front vast, lifeless and grey. As I walked along, rain began to fall, dimpling the water. By the time I reached the station it was coming down steadily. Llandudno Station is closed on Sundays – that the largest resort in Wales has no Sunday rail services is too preposterous and depressing to elaborate on – but there was a bus to Blaenau Ffestiniog from the station forecourt at eleven. There was no bench or shelter by the bus-stop, nowhere to get out of the rain. If you travel much by public transport in Britain these days you soon come to feel like a member of some unwanted sub-class, like the handicapped or unemployed, and that everyone essentially wishes you would just go away. I felt a bit like that now – and I am rich and healthy and immensely good-looking. What must it be like to be permanently poor or disabled or otherwise unable to take a full and active part in the nation's headlong rush for the sunny slopes of Mt Greedy?

It is remarkable to me how these matters have become so thoroughly inverted in the past twenty years. There used to be a kind of unspoken nobility about living in Britain. Just by existing, by going to work and paying your taxes, catching the occasional bus and being a generally decent if unexceptional soul, you felt as if you were contributing in some small way to the maintenance of a noble enterprise – a generally compassionate and well-meaning society with health care for all, decent public transport, intelligent television, universal social welfare and all the rest of it. I don't know about you, but I always felt rather proud to be part of that, particularly as you didn't actually have to *do* anything – you didn't have to give blood or buy the *Big Issue* or otherwise go out of your way – to feel as if you were a small contributory part. But now, no matter what you do, you end up stung with guilt. Go for a ramble in the country and you are reminded that you are inexorably adding to congestion in the national parks and footpath erosion on fragile hills. Try to take a sleeper to Fort William or a train on the Settle-to-Carlisle line or a bus from Llandudno to Blaenau on a Sunday and you begin to feel shifty and aberrant because you know that these services require vast and costly subsidization. Go for a drive in your car, look for work, seek a place to live, and all you are doing is taking up valuable space and time. And as for needing health care – well, how thoughtless and selfish can you possibly be? ('We *can* treat your ingrown toenails, Mr Smith, but it will of course mean taking a child off a life-support machine.')

I dread to think how much it cost Gwynedd Transport to convey me to Blaenau Ffestiniog on this wet Sunday morning since I was the only customer, apart from a young lady who joined us at Betws-y-Coed and left us soon after at the interestingly named Pont-y-Pant. I had been looking forward to the journey for the chance to see a little of Snowdonia, but the rain was soon falling so hard, and the bus windows so beaded with dirty droplets, that I could see almost nothing – just blurry expanses of dead, rust-coloured ferns dotted here and there with motionless, seriously discontented-looking sheep. Rain pattered against the windows like thrown pebbles and the bus swayed alarmingly under gusts of wind. It was like being on a ship in rough seas. The bus lumbered with grinding reluctance up twisting mountain roads, its windscreen wipers flapping wildly, to a plateau in the clouds and then embarked on a precipitate, seemingly out-of-control descent into Blaenau Ffestiniog through steep defiles covered with numberless slagheaps of broken, rain-shiny slate. This was once the heart of the Welsh slate-mining industry, and the scattered rejects and remnants, which covered virtually every inch of ground, gave the landscape an unearthly and eerie aspect like nothing else I had seen before in Britain. At the epicentre of this unearthliness squatted the village of Blaenau, itself a kind of slate slagheap, or so it seemed in the teeming rain.

The bus dropped me in the centre of town near the terminus of the famous Blaenau Ffestiniog Railway, now a private line run by enthusiasts and which I hoped to take through the cloudy mountains to Porthmadog. The station platform was open, but all the doors to waiting-rooms, toilets and ticket halls were padlocked, and there was no-one around. I had a look at the winter timetable hanging on the wall and discovered to my dismay that I had just missed – literally just missed – a train. Puzzled, I dragged my crumpled bus timetable from my pocket and discovered with further dismay that the bus was actually scheduled to arrive just in time to miss the one midday train out of Blaenau. Running a finger down the rail timetable, I learned that the next train would not be for another four hours. The next bus would follow that by minutes. How could that be possible and, more to the point, what on earth was I supposed to do with myself in this God-forsaken, rain-sodden place for four hours? There was no possibility of staying on the platform. It was cold and the rain was falling at such a treacherous slant that there was no place to escape it even in the furthest corners.

Muttering uncharitable thoughts about Gwynedd Transport, the Blaenau Ffestiniog Railway Company, the British climate and my own mad folly, I set off through the little town. This being Wales and this being Sunday, there was nothing open and no life on the narrow streets. Nor, as far as I could see, were there any hotels or guesthouses. It occurred to me that perhaps the train wasn't running at all in this weather, in which case I would be truly stuck. I was soaked through, cold and deeply, deeply gloomy. At the far end of town, there was a little restaurant called Myfannwy's and by a miracle it was open. I hastened into its beckoning warmth, where I peeled off my sodden jacket and sweater and went with a headful of suddenly enlivened hair to a table by a radiator. I was the only customer. I ordered a coffee and a little something to eat and savoured the warmth and dryness. Somewhere in the background Nat King Cole sang a perky tune. I watched the rain beat down on the road outside and told myself that one day this would be twenty years ago.

If I learned just one thing in Blaenau that day it was that no matter how hard you try you cannot make a cup of coffee and a cheese omelette last four hours. I ate as slowly as I could and ordered a second cup of coffee, but after nearly an hour of delicate eating and sipping, it became obvious that I was either going to have to leave or pay rent, so I reluctantly gathered up my things. At the till, I explained my plight to the kindly couple who ran the place and they both made those sympathetic oh-dear noises that kindly people make when confronted with someone else's crisis.

'He might go to the slate mine,' suggested the woman to the man.

'Yes, he might go to the slate mine,' agreed the man and turned to me. 'You might go to the slate mine,' he said as if thinking I might somehow have missed the foregoing exchange.

'Oh, and what's that exactly?' I said, trying not to sound too doubtful.

'The old mine. They do guided tours.'

'It's very interesting,' said his wife.

'Yes, it's very interesting,' said the man. 'Mind, it's a fair hike,' he added.

'And it may not be open on a Sunday,' said his wife. 'Out of season,' she explained.

'Of course, you could always take a cab up there if you don't fancy the walk in this weather,' said the man.

I looked at him. A cab? Did he say 'a *cab*'? This seemed too miraculous to be taken in. 'You have a cab service in Blaenau?'

'Oh, yes,' said the man as if this were one of Blaenau's more celebrated features. 'Would you like me to order one to take you to the mine?'

'Well,' I sought for words; I didn't want to sound ungrateful when these people had been so kind, but on the other hand I found the prospect of an afternoon touring a slate mine in damp clothes about as appealing as a visit to the proctologist. 'Do you think the cab would take me to Porthmadog?' I wasn't sure how far it was, and I dared not hope.

'Of course,' said the man. So he called a cab for me and the next thing I knew I was departing to a volley of good wishes from the proprietors and stepping into a cab, feeling like a shipwreck victim being winched to unexpected safety. I cannot tell you with what joy I beheld the sight of Blaenau disappearing into the distance behind me.

The cab driver was a friendly young man and on the twenty-minute ride to Porthmadog he filled me in on much important economic and sociological data with regard to the Dwyfor peninsula. The most striking news was that the peninsula was dry on Sundays. You couldn't get an alcoholic drink to save your life between Porthmadog and Aberdaron. I didn't know such pockets of rectitude still existed in Britain, but I was so glad to be getting out of Blaenau that I didn't care.

Porthmadog, squatting beside the sea under a merciless downpour, looked a grey and forgettable place, full of wet pebbledash and dark stone. Despite the rain, I examined the meagre stock of local hotels with some care – I felt entitled to a spell of comfort and luxury after my night in a cheerless Llandudno guesthouse – and I chose an inn called the Royal Sportsman. My room was adequate and clean, if not exactly outstanding, and suited my purposes. I made a cup of coffee and, while the kettle boiled, changed into dry clothes, then sat on the edge of the bed with a coffee and a Rich Tea biscuit, and watched a soap opera on television called *Pobol Y Cwm*, which I enjoyed very much. I had no idea what was going on, of course, but I can say with some confidence that it had better acting, and certainly better production values, than any programme ever made in, say, Sweden or Norway – or Australia come to that. At least the walls didn't wobble when someone shut a door. It was an odd experience watching people who existed in a recognizably British milieu – they drank tea and wore Marks & Spencer's cardigans – but talked in Martian. Occasionally, I was interested to note, they dropped in English words – 'hi ya', 'right then', 'OK' – presumably because a Welsh equivalent didn't exist, and in one memorable encounter a character said something like 'Wlch ylch aargh ybsy cwm dirty weekend, look you,' which I just loved. How sweetly endearing of the Welsh not to have their own term for an illicit bonk between Friday and Monday.

By the time I finished my coffee and returned to the streets, the rain had temporarily abated, but the streets were full of vast puddles where the drains were unable to cope with the volume of water. Correct me if I'm wrong, but you would think that if one nation ought by now to have mastered the science of drainage,

Britain would be it. In any case, cars aquaplaned daringly through these temporary lakes and threw sheets of water over nearby houses and shops. Mindful of my experience with puddles in Weston, and aware that this was a place where there truly was nothing to do on a Sunday, I proceeded up the High Street in a state of some caution.

I nosed around the tourist information centre, where I picked up a leaflet that informed me that Porthmadog was built in the early nineteenth century as a port for Blaenau slate by one Alexander Maddocks and that by late in the century a thousand ships a year were entering the port to carry off 116,000 tones of Welsh stone. Today the quayside is, inevitably, a renovated zone for yuppies, with cobbles and smart flats. I had a polite look at it, then followed a back lane through a harbourside neighbourhood of small boat-yards and other marine businesses, and up one side of a residential hill and down the other until I found myself in the tranquil hamlet of Borth-y-Gest, a pretty village of brick villas on a horseshoe bay with gorgeous views across Traeth Bach to Harlech Point and Tremadoc Bay beyond. Borth-y-Gest had an engaging old-fashioned feel about it. In the middle of the village, overlooking the bay, was a sub-post office with a blue awning announcing on the dangling part 'SWEETS' and 'ICES' and near by was an establishment called the Sea View Café. This place might have been lifted whole from *Adventures on the Island*. I was charmed at once.

I followed a grassy path out above the sea towards a headland. Even under low cloud, the views across the Glaslyn estuary and Snowdon range beyond were quite majestic. The wind was gusting and down below the sea battered the rocks in an impressively tempestuous way, but the rain at least held off and the air was sweet and fresh in that way you only get when you are beside the sea. The light was failing and I was afraid of ending up joining the waves on the rocks far below, so I headed back into town. When I got there, I discovered that the few businesses that had been open were now shut. Only one small beacon of half-light loomed from the enclosing darkness. I went up to see what it was and was inter-ested to find that it was the southern terminus and operational HQ for the famous Blaenau Ffestiniog Railway.

Interested to see the nerve centre of this organization which had caused me so much distress and discomfort earlier, I went in. Though it was well after five, the station bookshop was still open and liberally sprinkled with silent browsers, so I went in and had a nose around. It was an extraordinary place, with shelf after shelf of books, all with titles like *Railways of the Winion Valley and Mawddach Estuary* and *The Complete Encyclopaedia of Signal Boxes*. There was a multi-volume series of books called *Trains in Trouble*, each consisting of page after page of photographs of derailments, crashes and other catastrophes – a sort of train-spotter's equivalent of a snuff movie, I suppose. For those seeking more animated thrills, there were scores of videos. I took down one at random, called *The Hunslet and Hundreds Steam Rally 1993*, which bore a bold label promising '50 Minutes of Steam Action!' Under that there was a sticker that said: 'Warning: Contains explicit footage of a Sturrock 0-6-0 Heavy Class coupling with a GWR Hopper.' Actually, I just made that last part up, but I did notice, with a kind of profound shock, that all the people around me were browsing with precisely the same sort of self-absorbed, quiet breathing concentration that you would find in a porno shop and I suddenly wondered if there was an extra dimension to this train-spotting lark that had never occurred to me.

According to a plaque on the wall in the ticket hall, the Blaenau Ffestiniog Railway was formed in 1832 and is the oldest still running in the world. I also learned from the plaque that the railway society has 6,000 members, a figure that staggers me from every possible direction. Though the last train of the day had finished its run some time ago, there was still a man in the ticket booth, so I went over and interrogated him quietly about the lack of co-ordination between the train and bus services in Blaenau. I don't know why, because I was charm itself, but he got distinctly huffy, as if I were being critical of his wife, and said in a petulant tone: 'If Gwynned Transport want people to catch the midday train from Blaenau, then they should have the buses set off earlier.'

'But equally,' I persisted, 'you could have the train leave a few minutes later.'

He looked at me as if I were being outrageously presumptuous, and said: 'But why should we?'

And there, you see, you have everything that is wrong with these train enthusiast types. They are irrational, argumentative, danger-ously fussy and often, as here, have an irritating little Michael Fish moustache that makes you want to stick out two forked fingers and pop them in the eyes. Moreover, thanks to my journalistic sleuthing in the bookshop, I think we can safely say that there is a prima facie case to presume that they perform unnatural acts with steam videos. For their own good, and for the good of society, they should be taken away and interned behind barbed wire.

I thought about making a citizen's arrest there and then – 'I detain you in the name of Her Majesty the Queen for the offence of being irritatingly intractable about timetables, and also for having an annoying and inadequate little moustache' – but I was feeling generous and let him go with a hard look and an implied warning that it would be a cold day in hell before I ventured anywhere near *his* railway again. I think he got the message.

CHAPTER TWENTY-ONE

IN THE MORNING, I WALKED TO PORTHMADOG STATION — NOT THE Blaenau Ffestiniog let's-play-at-trains one, but the real British Rail one. The station was closed, but there were several people on the platform, all studiously avoiding each other's gaze and standing, I do believe, on the same spot on which they stood every morning. I am pretty certain of this because as I was standing there minding my own business, a man in a suit arrived and looked at first surprised and then cross to find me occupying what was evidently his square metre of platform. He took a position a few feet away and regarded me with an expression not a million miles from hate. How easy it is sometimes, I thought, to make enemies in Britain. All you have to do is stand in the wrong spot or turn your car round in their driveway – this guy had NO TURNING written all over him – or inadvertently take their seat on a train, and they will quietly hate you to the grave.

Eventually a two-carriage Sprinter train came in and we all shuffled aboard. They really are the most comfortless, utilitarian, deeply unlovely trains, with their hard-edged seats, their mystifyingly simultaneous hot and cold draughts, their harsh lighting and, above all, their noxious colour scheme with all those orange stripes and hopelessly jaunty chevrons. Why would anyone think that train passengers would like to be surrounded by a lot of orange, particularly first thing in the morning? I longed for one of those old-style trains that you found when I first came to Britain, the ones that had no corridors but consisted of just a series of self-contained compartments, each a little world unto itself. There was always a frisson of excitement as you opened the carriage door because you never knew what you would find on the other side. There was something pleasingly intimate and random about sitting in such close proximity with total strangers. I remember once I was on one of these trains when one of the other passengers, a shy-looking young man in a trench coat, was abruptly and lavishly sick on the floor – it was during a flu epidemic – and then had the gall to stumble from the train at the next station, leaving three of us to ride on into the evening in silence, with pinched faces and tucked-in toes and behaving, in that most extraordinary British way, as if nothing had happened. On second thoughts perhaps it is just as well that we don't have those trains any more. But I'm still not happy with the orange chevrons.

We followed a coastal route past broad estuaries and craggy hills beside the grey, flat expanse of Cardigan Bay. The towns along the way all had names that sounded like a cat bringing up a hairball: Llwyngwril, Morfa Mawddach, Llandecwyn, Dyffryn Ardudwy. At Penrhyndeudraeth the train filled with children of all ages, all in school uniforms. I expected shouting and smoking and things to be flying about, but they were impeccably behaved, every last one of them. They all departed at Harlech and the interior suddenly felt empty and quiet – quiet enough that I could hear the couple behind me conversing in Welsh, which pleased me. At Barmouth we crossed another broad estuary, on a rickety-looking wooden causeway. I had read somewhere that this causeway had been closed for some years and that Barmouth had until recently been the end of the line. It seemed a kind of miracle that BR had invested the money to repair the causeway and keep the line open, but I bet that if I were to come back in ten years, this trundling, half-forgotten line to Porthmadog will be in the hands of enthusiasts like those of the Blaenau Ffestiniog Railway and that some twit with a fussy little moustache will be telling me that I can't make a connection at Shrewsbury because it doesn't suit the society's timetable.

So I was pleased, three hours and 105 miles after setting off, to make a connection at Shrewsbury while the chance was still there. My intention was to turn north and resume my stately progress towards John O'Groats, but as I was making my way through the station, I heard a platform announcement for a train to Ludlow, and impulsively I boarded it. For years I had heard that Ludlow was a delightful spot, and it suddenly occurred to me that this might be my last chance to see it. Thus it was that I found myself, some twenty minutes later, alighting on to a lonely platform at Ludlow and making my way up a long hill into the town.

Ludlow was indeed a charming and agreeable place on a hilltop high above the River Teme. It appeared to have everything you could want in a community – bookshops, a cinema, some appealing-looking tearooms and bakeries, a couple of 'family butchers' (I always want to go in and say, 'How much to do mine?'), an old-fashioned Woolworth's and the usual assortment of chemists, pubs, haberdashers and the like, all neatly arrayed and respectful of their surroundings. The Ludlow Civic Society had thoughtfully put plaques up on many of the buildings announcing who had once lived there. One such hung on the wall of the Angel, an old coaching inn on Broad Street now sadly – and I hoped only temporarily – boarded up. According to the plaque, the famous Aurora coach once covered the hundred or so miles to London in just over twenty-seven hours, which just shows you how much we've progressed. Now British Rail could probably do it in half the time.

Near by I chanced upon the headquarters of an organization called the Ludlow and District Cats Protection League, which intrigued me. Whatever, I wondered, did the people of Ludlow do to their cats that required the setting up of a special protective agency? Perhaps I'm coming at this from the wrong angle, but short of setting cats alight and actually throwing them at me, I can't think of what you would have to do to drive me to set up a charity to defend their interests. There is almost nothing, apart perhaps from a touching faith in the reliability of weather forecasts and the universal fondness for jokes involving the word 'bottom', that makes me feel more like an outsider in Britain than the nation's attitude to animals. Did you know that the National Society for the Prevention of Cruelty to Children was formed sixty years after the founding of the Royal Society for the Prevention of Cruelty to Animals, and as an offshoot of it? Did you know that in 1994 Britain voted *for* a European Union directive requiring statutory rest periods for transported animals, but *against* statutory rest periods for factory workers?

But even against this curious background, it seemed extraordinary to me that there could be a whole, clearly well-funded office dedicated just to the safety and well-being of Ludlow and District cats. I was no less intrigued by the curiously specific limits of the society's self-imposed remit – the idea that they were interested only in the safety and well-being of Ludlow and District cats.

What would happen, I wondered, if the members of the league found you teasing a cat just outside the district boundaries? Would they shrug resignedly and say, 'Out of our jurisdiction'? Who can say? Certainly not I, because when I approached the office with a view to making enquiries, I found that it was shut, its members evidently – and I wish you to read nothing into this – out to lunch.

Which is where I decided to be. I went across the road to a pleasant little salad bar restaurant called the Olive Branch, where I quickly made myself into a pariah by taking a table for four. The place was practically empty when I arrived and as I was struggling with a rucksack and a tippy tray, I took the first empty table. But immediately I sat down people poured in from all quarters and for the rest of my brief lunch period I could feel eyes burrowing into me from people who turned from the till to find me occupying a space obviously not designed for a solitary diner and that they would have to take their trays to the unpopular More Seating Upstairs section, evidently a disagreeable option. As I sat there, trying to eat quickly and be obscure, a man from two tables away came and asked me in a pointed tone if I was using one of the chairs, and took it without awaiting my reply. I finished my food and slunk from the place in shame.

I returned to the station and bought a ticket for the next train to Shrewsbury and Manchester Piccadilly. Because of a points failure somewhere along the line, the train was forty minutes late arriving. It was packed and the passengers were testy. I found a seat by disturbing a tableful of people who gave up their space grudgingly and glared at me with disdain – more enemies! What a day I was having! – and sat crammed into a tiny space in my overcoat in an overheated carriage with my rucksack on my lap. I had vague hopes of getting to Blackpool, but I couldn't move a muscle and couldn't get at my rail timetable to see where I needed to change trains, so I just sat and trusted that I could catch an onward train at Manchester.

British Rail was having a bad day. We crept a mile or so out of the station, and then sat for a long time for no evident reason. Eventually, a voice announced that because of faults further up the line this train would terminate at Stockport, which elicited a general groan. Finally, after about twenty minutes, the train falteringly started forward and limped across the green countryside. At each station the voice apologized for the delay and announced anew that the train would terminate at Stockport. When at last we reached Stockport, ninety minutes late, I expected everyone to get off, but no-one moved, so neither did I. Only one passenger, a Japanese fellow, dutifully disembarked, then watched in dismay as the train proceeded on, without explanation and without him, to Manchester.

At Manchester I discovered that I needed a train to Preston, so I had a look at a television screen, but these only gave the final destination and not the stations in between. So I went off and joined a queue of travellers asking a BR guard for directions to various places. It was unfortunate for him that there were no stations in Britain called Fuck Off because that was clearly what he wanted to tell people. He told me to go to platform 13, so I set off for it, but the platforms ended at 11. So I went back to the guy and informed him that I couldn't find a platform 13. It turned out that platform 13 was up some secret stairs and over a footbridge. It appeared to be the platform for missing trains. There was a whole crowd of travellers standing there looking lost and doleful, like the people in that *Monty Python* milkman sketch. Eventually we were sent back to platform 3. The train, when it arrived, was of course a two-carriage Sprinter. The usual 700 people squeezed onto it.

Thus it was, fourteen hours after setting off from Porthmadog that morning, that I arrived tired, dishevelled, hungry and full of woe, in Blackpool, a place that I didn't particularly want to be in anyway.

CHAPTER TWENTY-TWO

BLACKPOOL – AND I DON'T CARE HOW MANY TIMES YOU HEAR THIS, IT never stops being amazing – attracts more visitors every year than Greece and has more holiday beds than the whole of Portugal. It consumes more chips per capita than anywhere else on the planet. (It gets through forty acres of potatoes a day.) It has the largest concentration of roller-coasters in Europe. It has the continent's second most popular tourist attraction, the forty-two-acre Pleasure Beach, whose 6.5 million annual visitors are exceeded in number only by those going to the Vatican. It has the most famous illuminations. And on Friday and Saturday nights it has more public toilets than anywhere else in Britain; elsewhere they call them doorways.

Whatever you may think of the place, it does what it does very well – or if not very well at least very successfully. In the past twenty years, during a period in which the number of Britons taking traditional seaside holidays has declined by a fifth, Blackpool has increased its visitor numbers by 7 per cent and built tourism into a £250-million-a-year industry – no small achievement when you consider the British climate, the fact that Blackpool is ugly, dirty and a long way from anywhere, that its sea is an open toilet, and its attractions nearly all cheap, provincial and dire.

It was the illuminations that had brought me there. I had been hearing and reading about them for so long that I was genuinely keen to see them. So, after securing a room in a modest guesthouse on a back street, I hastened to the front in a sense of some expectation. Well, all I can say is that Blackpool's illuminations are nothing if not splendid, and they are not splendid. There is, of course, always a danger of disappointment when you finally encounter something you have wanted to see for a long time, but in terms of letdown it would be hard to exceed Blackpool's light show. I thought there would be lasers sweeping the sky, strobe lights tattooing the clouds and other gasp-making dazzlements. Instead there was just a rumbling procession of old trams decorated as rocket ships or Christmas crackers, and several miles of paltry decorations on lampposts. I suppose if you had never seen electricity in action, it would be pretty breathtaking, but I'm not even sure of that. It all just seemed tacky and inadequate on rather a grand scale, like Blackpool itself.

What was no less amazing than the meagreness of the illuminations were the crowds of people who had come to witness the spectacle. Traffic along the front was bumper to bumper, with childish faces pressed to the windows of every creeping car, and there were masses of people ambling happily along the spacious promenade. At frequent intervals hawkers sold luminous necklaces and bracelets or other short-lived diversions, and were doing a roaring trade. I read somewhere once that half of all visitors to Blackpool have been there at least ten times. Goodness knows what they find in the place. I walked for a mile or so along the prom, and couldn't understand the appeal of it – and I, as you may have realized by now, am an enthusiast for tat. Perhaps I was just weary after my long journey from Porthmadog, but I couldn't wake up any enthusiasm for it at all. I wandered through brightly lit arcades and peered in bingo halls, but the festive atmosphere that seemed to seize everyone failed to rub off on me. Eventually, feeling very tired and very foreign, I retired to a fish restaurant on a side-street, where I had a plate of haddock, chips and peas, and was looked at like I was some kind of southern pansy when I asked for tartare sauce, and afterwards took yet another early night.

In the morning, I got up early to give Blackpool another chance. I liked it considerably better by daylight. The promenade had some nice bits of cast iron and elaborate huts with onion domes selling rock, nougat and other sticky things, which had escaped me in the darkness the night before, and the beach was vast and empty and very agreeable. Blackpool's beach is seven miles long and the curious thing about it is that it doesn't officially exist. I am not making this up. In the late 1980s, when the European Community issued a directive about minimum standards of ocean-borne sewage, it turned out that nearly every British seaside town failed to come anywhere near even the minimum levels. Most of the bigger places like Blackpool went right off the edge of the turdometer, or whatever it is they measure these things with. This presented an obvious problem to the Government, which was loath to spend money on British beaches when there were perfectly good beaches for rich people in Mustique and Barbados, so it drew up a policy under which it officially decreed – this is so bizarre I can hardly stand it, but I swear it is true – that Brighton, Blackpool, Scarborough and many other leading resorts did not have, strictly speaking, bathing beaches. Christ knows what they then termed these expanses of sand – intermediate sewage buffers, I suppose – but in any case it disposed of the problem without either solving it or costing the Exchequer a penny, which is, of course, the main thing, or in the case of the present Government, the only thing.

But enough of political satire! Let us away in haste to Morecambe. I went there next, on a series of rattling Sprinters, partly to make poignant comparisons with Blackpool, but mostly because I like Morecambe. I'm not at all sure why, but I do.

Looking at it now, it is hard to believe that not so very long ago Morecambe rivalled Blackpool. In fact, starting in about 1880 and for many decades afterwards, Morecambe was *the* northern English seaside resort. It had Britain's first seaside illuminations. It was the birthplace of bingo, lettered rock and the helter-skelter. During the celebrated Wakes Weeks, when whole northern factory towns went on holiday together (they called Morecambe Bradford-by-Sea), up to 100,000 visitors at a time flocked to its boarding-houses and hotels. At its peak it had two mainline railway stations, eight music halls, eight cinemas, an aquarium, a funfair, a menagerie, a revolving tower, a boating garden, a Summer Pavilion, a Winter Gardens, the largest swimming-pool in Britain, and two piers. One of these, the Central Pier, was one of the most beautiful and elaborate in Britain, with fabulous towers and domed roofs – an Arabian palace afloat on Morecambe Bay.

It had over a thousand boarding-houses catering for the masses, but also classier diversions for those with more extravagant ambitions. The Old Vic and Sadler's Wells spent whole seasons there. Elgar conducted orchestras in the Winter Gardens and Nellie Melba sang. And it was the home of many hotels that were the equal of any in Europe, like the Grand and the Broadway, where in the early 1900s well-heeled patrons could choose between a dozen types of hydro bath, including 'Needle, Brine, Foam, Plombière and Scotch Douche'.

I know all this because I had been reading a book called *Lost Resort: The Flow and Ebb of Morecambe*, by a local vicar named Roger K. Bingham, which was not only exceptionally well written (and it is quite extraordinary, let me say here, how much good local history there is in this country) but full of photos of Morecambe from its heyday that were just staggeringly at variance with the scene I found before me now as I stepped from the train, one of only three passengers to alight, and ambled out into the sunny but breathtakingly faded charms of Marine Road.

It is hard to say when or why Morecambe's decline started. It remained popular well into the 1950s – as late as 1956 it had 1,300 hotels and guesthouses, ten times the number it has today – but its descent from greatness had begun long before. The famous Central Pier was extensively damaged by a fire in the 1930s, then gradually sank into an embarrassing wreck. By 1990 the town officials had removed it from the local map – simply pretended that the derelict heap projecting into the sea, dominating the front, wasn't there. The West End Pier, meanwhile, was swept away by a winter storm in 1974. The magnificent Alhambra music hall burned down in 1970 and the Royalty Theatre was razed to make way for a shopping centre two years later.

By the early 1970s Morecambe's decline was precipitate. One by one the local landmarks vanished – the venerable swimming-pool in 1978, the Winter Gardens in 1982, the truly sumptuous Grand Hotel in 1989 – as people abandoned Morecambe for Blackpool and the Spanish Costas. By the late 1980s, according to Bingham, you could buy a large, once-proud seafront hotel like the five-storey Grosvenor for the same price as a semi-detached house in London.

Today Morecambe's tattered front consists largely of little-used bingo halls and amusement arcades, everything-for-£1 shops, and the kind of cut-price boutiques where the clothes are so cheap and undesirable that they can be safely put outside on racks and left unattended. Many of the shops are empty, and most of the rest look temporary. It has become once again – irony of ironies – Bradford-by-Sea. So low had Morecambe's fortunes sunk that the previous summer the town couldn't even find someone to take on the deckchair concession. When a seaside resort can't find anyone willing to set up deckchairs, you know that business is bad.

And yet Morecambe has its charms. Its seafront promenade is handsome and well maintained and its vast bay (174 square miles, if you're taking notes) is easily one of the most beautiful in the world, with unforgettable views across to the green and blue Lakeland hills: Scafell, Coniston Old Man, the Langdale Pikes.

Today almost all that remains of Morecambe's golden age is the Midland Hotel, a jaunty, cheery, radiant white art deco edifice with a sweeping, streamlined frontage erected on the seafront in 1933. Concrete structures were all the rage in 1933, but concrete apparently was beyond the capabilities of local builders, so it was built of Accrington brick and rendered in plaster so that it *looked* like concrete, which I find very endearing. Today the hotel is gently crumbling around the edges and streaked here and there with rust stains. Most of the original interior fittings were lost during periodic and careless refurbishments over the years, and several large Eric Gill statues that once graced the entranceway and public rooms simply disappeared, but it still has an imperishable 1930s charm.

I couldn't begin to guess where the Midland gets its custom these days. There didn't seem to be any custom of any sort when I went in now and had a cup of coffee in an empty sun lounge overlooking the bay. One of the small endearments of modern Morecambe is that wherever you go they are grateful for your patronage. I enjoyed superb service and a nice view, two things wholly unobtainable in Blackpool as far as I can tell. As I was departing, my eye was caught by a large white plaster statue by Gill of a mermaid in the empty dining room. I went and had a look at it and found that the tail of the statue, which I presume is worth a small fortune, was held on with a mass of sticky tape. It seemed a not inappropriate symbol for the town.

I took a room in a seafront guesthouse, where I was received with a kind of startled gratitude, as if the owners had forgotten that all those empty rooms upstairs were to let, and spent the afternoon strolling around with Roger Bingham's book looking at the sights, trying to imagine the town in its heyday, and occasionally bestowing my patronage on pathetically grateful tea-rooms.

It was a mild day and there were a number of people, mostly elderly, walking along the promenade, but little sign of anyone spending money. With nothing better to do, I took a long walk along the front nearly to Carnforth and then walked back along the sands since the tide was out. The surprising thing about

Morecambe, it occurred to me, isn't that it declined, but that it ever prospered. It would be hard to imagine a less likely place for a resort. Its beaches consist of horrible gooey mud and its vast bay spends large periods devoid of water thanks to the vagaries of the tides. You can walk six miles across the bay to Cumbria when the tide is out, but they say it is dangerous to do so without a guide, or sand pilot as they are known hereabouts. I once spent some time with one of these pilots, who told alarming stories about coaches and horses that tried to cross the bay at low tide and disappeared into the treacherous quicksands, never to be seen again. Even now people sometimes stroll out too far and then get cut off when the tide comes in, about as disagreeable a way to finish an afternoon as I could imagine.

Feeling daring, I walked a few hundred yards out on to the sands now, studying worm casts and the interesting corrugated imprints left by the receding waters, and keeping an eye out for quicksand – which isn't really sand at all, but silty mud and it really does hoover you up if you blunder into it. The tides at Morecambe don't rush in and out like the Severn bore, but creep in from various angles, which is all the more menacing since you can easily find, if you are the sort to get lost in thought, that you are suddenly stranded on a large but insidiously shrinking sandbar in the middle of a great wet bay, so I kept my eyes out and didn't venture too far.

It was quite wonderful – certainly better than anything Blackpool could offer. It is an odd sensation to be walking about on a seabed and to think that any time now this could be under thirty feet of water. I especially liked the solitude. One of the hardest things to adjust to, if you come from a large country, is that you are seldom really alone out of doors in England – that there is scarcely an open space where you could, say, safely stand and have a pee without fear of appearing in some birdwatcher's binoculars or having some matronly rambler bound round the bend – so the sense of aloneness on the open sands was rather luxurious.

From a few hundred yards out, Morecambe looked quite fetching in the late afternoon sun, and even up close, as I left the sands and clambered up some mossy concrete steps to the prom, it didn't look half bad away from the desolate bingo parlours and novelty shops. The line of guesthouses along the eastern length of Marine Road looked neat and trim and sweetly hopeful. I felt sorry for the owners who had invested their hopes and found themselves now in a dying resort. The decline that began in the Fifties and accelerated out of control in the Seventies must have seemed bewildering and inexplicable to these poor people as they watched Blackpool, just twenty miles to the south, going from strength to strength.

Foolishly, but not unnaturally, Morecambe responded by trying to compete with Blackpool. It built an expensive dolphinarium and a new outdoor swimming-pool, and recently there had been some half-assed plan to open a Mr Blobby amusement park. But really its charm, and certainly its hope, lies in being *not* Blackpool. That is what I liked about it – that it is quiet and friendly and well behaved, that there is plenty of room in the pubs and cafés, that you aren't bowled off the kerb by swaggering youths and don't go sidewalk surfing on abandoned styrofoam chip platters and vomit slicks.

One day, I would like to think, people will rediscover the charms of a quiet break at the seaside, the simple pleasures of strolling along a well-kept front, leaning on railings, drinking in views, sitting in a café with a book, just pottering about. Then perhaps Morecambe can thrive again. How nice it would be if the Government actually erected a policy to this end, took steps to restore fading places like Morecambe – rebuilt the pier to its original plans, gave a grant for a new Winter Gardens, insisted on the restoration of seafront buildings, perhaps moved a division of the Inland Revenue or some other bureaucracy to the town to give it a bit of year-round life.

With a little priming and a thoughtful long-term plan, I am sure you could attract the sort of people who would want to open bookshops, little restaurants, antique shops, galleries, maybe even tapas bars and the odd boutique hotel. Well, why not?

Morecambe could become a little northern English equivalent of Sausalito or St Ives. You may smirk at the thought of it, but what other possible future is there for a place like Morecambe? People could come for weekends to eat quality meals in new seafront restaurants overlooking the bay and perhaps take in a play or concert at the Winter Gardens. Yuppie fell walkers could spend the night there and thus ease pressure on the Lake District. It would all make eminent sense. But of course it will never happen, and partly, if I may say so, because you smirk.

CHAPTER TWENTY-THREE

I HAVE A SMALL, TATTERED CLIPPING THAT I SOMETIMES CARRY WITH ME and pull out for purposes of private amusement. It's a weather forecast from the *Western Daily Mail* and it says, *in toto*: 'Outlook: Dry and warm, but cooler with some rain.'

There you have in a single pithy sentence the English weather captured to perfection: dry but rainy with some warm/cool spells. The *Western Daily Mail* could run that forecast every day – for all I know, it may – and scarcely ever be wrong.

To an outsider the most striking thing about the English weather is that there isn't very much of it. All those phenomena that elsewhere give nature an edge of excitement, unpredictability and danger – tornadoes, monsoons, raging blizzards, run-for-your-life hailstorms – are almost wholly unknown in the British Isles, and this is just fine by me. I like wearing the same type of clothing every day of the year. I appreciate not needing air conditioning or mesh screens on the windows to keep out the kind of insects and flying animals that drain your blood or eat away your face while you are sleeping. I like knowing that so long as I do not go walking up Ben Nevis in carpet slippers in February I will almost certainly never perish from the elements in this soft and gentle country.

I mention this because as I sat eating my breakfast in the dining room of the Old England Hotel in Bowness-on-Windermere, two days after leaving Morecambe, I was reading an article in *The Times* about an unseasonable snowstorm – a 'blizzard', *The Times* called it – that had 'gripped' parts of East Anglia. According to *The Times* report, the storm had covered parts of the region with 'more than two inches of snow' and created 'drifts up to six inches high'. In response to this, I did something I had never done before: I pulled out my notebook and drafted a letter to the editor in which I pointed out, in a kindly, helpful way, that two inches of snow cannot possibly constitute a blizzard and that six inches of snow is not a drift. A blizzard, I explained, is when you can't get your front door open. Drifts are things that make you lose your car till spring. Cold weather is when you leave part of your flesh on doorknobs, mailbox handles and other metal objects. And then I crumpled the letter up because I realized I was in serious danger of turning into one of the Colonel Blimp types who sat around me in considerable numbers, eating cornflakes or porridge with their blimpish wives, and without whom hotels like the Old England would not be able to survive.

I was in Bowness because I had two days to kill until I was to be joined by two friends from London with whom I was going to spend the weekend walking. I was looking forward to that very much, but rather less to the prospect of another long, purposeless day in Bowness, pottering about trying to fill the empty hours till tea. There are, I find, only so many windowsful of tea-towels, Peter Rabbit dinnerware and patterned jumpers I can look at before my interest in shopping palls, and I wasn't at all sure that I could face another day of poking about in this most challenging of resorts.

I had come to Bowness more or less by default since it is the only place inside the Lake District National Park with a railway station. Besides, the idea of spending a couple of quiet days beside the tranquil beauty of Windermere, and wallowing in the plump comforts of a gracious (if costly) old hotel, had seemed distinctly appealing from the vantage of Morecambe Bay. But now, with one day down and another to go, I was beginning to feel stranded and fidgety, like someone at the end of a long period of convalescence. At least, I reflected optimistically, the unseasonable two inches of snow that had brutally lashed East Anglia, causing chaos on the roads and forcing people to battle their way through perilous snowdrifts, some of them as high as their ankletops, had mercifully passed this corner of England by. Here the elements were benign and the world outside the dining-room window sparkled weakly under a pale wintry sun.

I decided to take the lake steamer to Ambleside. This would not only kill an hour and let me see the lake, but deliver me to a place rather more like a real town and less like a misplaced seaside resort than Bowness. In Bowness, I had noted the day before, there are no fewer than eighteen shops where you can buy jumpers and at least twelve selling Peter Rabbit stuff, but just one butcher's. Ambleside on the other hand, though hardly unfamiliar with the manifold possibilities for enrichment presented by hordes of passing tourists, did at least have an excellent bookshop and any number of outdoor shops, which I find hugely if inexplicably diverting – I can spend hours looking at rucksacks, kneesocks, compasses and survival rations, then go to another shop and look at precisely the same things all over again. So it was with a certain animated keenness that I made my way to the steamer pier shortly after breakfast. Alas, there I discovered that the steamers run only in the summer months, which seemed shortsighted on this mild morning because even now Bowness gently teemed with trippers. So I was forced, as a fallback, to pick my way through the scattered, shuffling throngs to the little ferry that shunts back and forth between Bowness and the old ferry house on the opposite shore. It travels only a few hundred yards, but it does at least run all year.

A modest line-up of cars was patiently idling on the ferry approach, and there were eight or ten walkers as well, all with Mustos, rucksacks and sturdy boots. One fellow was even wearing shorts – always a sign of advanced dementia in a British walker. Walking – walking, that is, in the British sense – was something that I had come into only relatively recently. I was not yet at the point where I would wear shorts with many pockets, but I had taken to tucking my trousers into my socks (though I have yet to find anyone who can explain to me what benefits this actually confers, other than making one look serious and committed).

I remember when I first came to Britain wandering into a bookstore and being surprised to find a whole section dedicated to 'Walking Guides'. This struck me as faintly bizarre and comical – where I came from people did not as a rule require written instructions to achieve locomotion – but then gradually I learned that there are, in fact, two kinds of walking in Britain, namely the everyday kind that gets you to the pub and, all being well, back home again, and the more earnest type that involves stout boots, Ordnance Survey maps in plastic pouches, rucksacks with sandwiches and flasks of tea, and, in its terminal phase, the wearing of khaki shorts in inappropriate weather.

For years, I watched these walker types toiling off up cloud-hidden hills in wet and savage weather and presumed they were genuinely insane. And then my old friend John Price, who had grown up in Liverpool and spent his youth doing foolish things on sheer-faced crags in the Lakes, encouraged me to join him and a couple of his friends for an amble – that was the word he used – up Haystacks one weekend. I think it was the combination of those two untaxing-sounding words, 'amble' and 'Haystacks', and the promise of lots of drink afterwards, that lulled me from my natural caution.

'Are you sure it's not too hard?' I asked.

'Nah, just an amble,' John insisted.

Well, of course it was anything but an amble. We clambered for hours up vast, perpendicular slopes, over clattering scree and lumpy tussocks, round towering citadels of rock, and emerged at length into a cold, bleak, lofty nether world so remote and forbidding that even the sheep were startled to see us. Beyond it lay even greater and remoter summits that had been quite invisible from the ribbon of black highway thousands of feet below. John and his chums toyed with my will to live in the cruellest possible way; seeing me falling behind, they would lounge around on boulders, smoking and chatting and resting, but the instant I caught up with them with a view to falling at their feet, they would bound up refreshed and, with a few encouraging words, set off anew with large, manly strides, so that I had to stumble after and never got a rest. I gasped and ached and sputtered, and realized that I had never done anything remotely this unnatural before and vowed never to attempt such folly again.

And then, just as I was about to lie down and call for a stretcher, we crested a final rise and found ourselves abruptly, magically, on top of the earth, on a platform in the sky, amid an ocean of swelling summits. I had never seen anything half so beautiful before. 'Fuck me,' I said in a moment of special eloquence and realized I was hooked. Ever since then I had come back whenever they would have me, and never complained and even started tucking my trousers in my socks. I couldn't wait for the morrow.

The ferry docked and I shuffled on board with the others. Windermere looked serene and exceedingly fetching in the gentle sunshine. Unusually there wasn't a single pleasure boat disturbing its glassy calmness. To say that Windermere is popular with boaters is to flirt recklessly with understatement. Some 14,000 powerboats – let me repeat that number: *14,000* – are registered to use the lake. On a busy summer's day, as many as 1,600 powerboats may be out on the water at any one time, a good many of them zipping along at up to 40 mph with water-skiers in tow. This is in addition to all the thousands of other types of floating objects that may be out on the water and don't need to register – dinghies, sailboats, sailboards, canoes, inflatables, li-los, various excursion steamers and the old chugging ferry I was on now – all of them searching for a boat-sized piece of water. It is all but impossible to stand on a lakeside bank on an August Sunday watching water-skiers slicing through packed shoals of dinghies and other floating detritus and not end up with your mouth open and your hands on your head.

I had spent some weeks in the Lakes a year or so before working on an article for *National Geographic* and one of the passing thrills of the experience was being taken out for a morning on the lake on a national park launch. To show me just how dangerous it could be to let high-powered craft race around in this kind of crowded environment, the park warden pootled the launch out into the middle of the lake, told me to hang on – I smiled at this: listen, I do 90 on the motorways – then opened the throttle. Well, let me say this: 40 mph in a boat is nothing like 40 mph on a road. We took off with a velocity that snapped me back in the seat and had me clutching on for dear life with both hands, and bounced across the water like a flat stone fired from a gun. I have seldom been so petrified. Even on a quiet morning out of season, Windermere was clogged with impediments. We shot between little islands and skittered sideways past headlands that loomed up with alarming suddenness, like frights on a funfair ride. Imagine sharing this space with 1,600 other similarly dashing craft, most of them in the control of some pot-bellied urban halfwit with next to no experience of powered craft, plus all the floating jetsam of rowboats, kayaks, pedalos and the like and it is a wonder that there aren't bodies all over the water.

The experience taught me two things – first, that vomit vaporizes at 40 mph in an open boat and second that Windermere is an exceedingly compact body of water. And here we come to the point of all this. Britain is, for all its topographical diversity and timeless majesty, an exceedingly small-scale place. There isn't a single natural feature in the country that ranks anywhere in world terms – no Alp-like mountains, no stunning gorges, not even a single great river. You may think of the Thames as a substantial artery, but in world terms it is little more than an ambitious stream.

Put it down in North America and it wouldn't even make the top one hundred. It would come in at number 108, to be precise, out-classed by such relative obscurities as the Skunk, the Kuskokwim and even the little Milk. Windermere may have pride of place among English lakes, but for each twelve square inches of Windermere's surface, Lake Superior offers 268 square *feet* of water. There is in Iowa a body of water called Dan Green Slough, which even most Iowans have never heard of, and it is bigger than Windermere. The Lake District itself takes up less space than the Twin Cities.

I think that's just wonderful – not that these features are modest in their dimensions but that they are modest, in the middle of a densely crowded island and still wonderful. What an achievement that is. Do you have any idea, other than in a vague theoretical sense, just how desperately crowded Britain is? Did you know, for instance, that to achieve the same density of population in America you would have to uproot the entire populations of Illinois, Pennsylvania, Massachusetts, Minnesota, Michigan, Colorado and Texas and pack them all into Iowa? Twenty million people live within a day-trip of the Lake District and 12 million, roughly a quarter of England's population, come to the Lakes each year. No wonder on some summer weekends it can take two hours to get through Ambleside and that you could almost walk across Windermere by stepping from boat to boat.

And yet even at its worst, the Lake District remains more charm-ing and less rapaciously commercialized than many famed beauty spots in more spacious countries. And away from the crowds – away from Bowness, Hawkshead and Keswick, with their tea towels, tea-rooms, teapots and endless Beatrix Potter shit – it retains pockets of sheer perfection, as I found now when the ferry nosed into its landing and we tumbled off. For a minute the land-ing area was a hive of activity as one group of cars got off, another got on and the eight or ten foot passengers departed in various directions. And then all was blissful silence. I followed a pretty, wooded road around the lake's edge before turning inland and heading for Near Sawrey.

Near Sawrey is the home of Hilltop, the cottage where the inescapable Potter drew her sweet little watercolours and contrived her soppy stories. For most of the year, it is overrun with tourists from far and wide. Much of the village is given over to large (but discreetly sited) car parks and the tea-room even has a sign out front advertising its fare in Japanese, egads. But the approaches to the village – actually, it's just a hamlet (and do you know the difference, by the way, between 'village' and 'hamlet'? Surprisingly few people do, but it's quite simple really: one is a place where people live and the other is a play by Shakespeare) – from every direction are exquisite and unspoiled: a meadowy green Eden laced with wandering slate walls, woodland clumps and low white farms against a backdrop of blue, beckoning hills. Even Near Sawrey itself has a beguiling, well-concocted charm that belies the over-whelming hordes who come to shuffle through its most famous residence. Such indeed is Hilltop's alarming popularity that the National Trust doesn't even actively advertise it any more. Yet still the visitors come. Two coaches were disgorging chattering white-haired occupants when I arrived and the main car park was already nearly full.

I had been to Hilltop the year before, so I wandered past it and up a little-known track to a tarn on some high ground behind it. Old Mrs Potter used to come up to this tarn regularly to thrash about on it in a rowing-boat – whether for healthful exercise or as a kind of flagellation I don't know – but it was very lovely and seemingly quite forgotten. I had the distinct feeling that I was the first visitor to venture up there for years. Across the way, a farmer was mending a stretch of fallen wall and I stood and watched him for a while from a discreet distance, because if there is one thing nearly as soothing to the spirit as mending a drystone wall it is watching someone else doing it. I remember once, not long after we moved to the Yorkshire Dales, going for a stroll and happening across a farmer I knew slightly rebuilding a wall on a remote hill. It was a rotten January day full of drifting fog and rain and the thing is there wasn't any discernible point in his rebuilding the wall. He owned the fields on either side and in any case there was a gate that stood permanently open between the two so it wasn't as if the wall had any real function. I stood and watched him awhile and finally asked him why he was standing out in a cold rain rebuilding the wall. He looked at me with that special pained look Yorkshire farmers save for onlookers and other morons and said: 'Because it's fallen *down*, of course.' From this I learned, first of all, never to ask a Yorkshire farmer any question that can't be answered with 'pint of Tetley's' and that one of the primary reasons so much of the British landscape is so unutterably lovely and timeless is that most farmers, for whatever reason, take the trouble to keep it that way.

It certainly has very little to do with money. Did you know that the Government spends less per person each year on national parks than you spend on a single daily newspaper, that it gives more to the Royal Opera House at Covent Garden than it does to all ten national parks together? The annual budget for the Lake District National Park, an area widely perceived as the most beautiful and environmentally sensitive in England, is £2.4 million, about the same as for a single large comprehensive school. From that sum the park authorities must manage the park, run ten information centres, pay 127 full-time staff and forty part-time staff in summer, replace and maintain equipment and vehicles, fund improvements to the landscape, implement educational programmes *and* act as the local planning authority. That the Lakes are so generally wonderful, so scrupulously maintained, so seldom troubling to mind and spirit is a ringing testament to the people who work in them, the people who live in them and the people who use them. I recently read that more than half of Britons surveyed couldn't think of a single thing about their country to be proud of. Well, be proud of that.

I spent a happy few hours tramping about through the sumptuous and easygoing landscape between Windermere and Coniston Water, and would gladly have stayed longer except that it began to rain – a steady, dispiriting rain that I foolishly had not allowed for in regard to my walking apparel – and anyway I was growing hungry, so I made my way back to the ferry and Bowness.

Thus it was that I found myself an hour or so and an overpriced tuna sandwich later, back in the Old England, staring out at the wet lake through a large window and feeling bored and listless in that special way peculiar to wet afternoons spent in plush surroundings. To pass a half-hour, I went to the residents' lounge to see if I couldn't scare up a pot of coffee. The room was casually strewn with ageing colonels and their wives, sitting amid carelessly folded *Daily Telegraphs*. The colonels were all shortish, round men with tweedy jackets, well-slicked silvery hair, an outwardly gruff manner that concealed within a heart of flint, and, when they walked, a rakish limp. Their wives, lavishly rouged and powdered, looked as if they had just come from a coffin fitting. I felt seriously out of my element, and was surprised to find one of them – a grey-haired lady who appeared to have put on her lipstick during an earth tremor – addressing me in a friendly, conversational manner. It always takes me a moment to remember in these circumstances that I am now a reasonably respectable-looking middle-aged man and not a gangly young rube straight off the banana boat.

We began, in the customary fashion, with a few words about the beastliness of the weather, but when the woman discovered I was an American she went off on some elaborate tangent about a trip she and Arthur – Arthur, I gathered, being the shyly smiling clot beside her – had recently taken to visit friends in California, and this gradually turned into what appeared to be a well-worn rant about the shortcomings of Americans. I never understand what people are thinking when they do this. Do they think I'll appreciate their candour? Are they winding me up? Or have they simply for-gotten that I am one of the species myself? The same thing often happens when people talk about immigration in front of me.

'They're so forward, don't you think?' the lady sniffed and took a sip of tea. 'You've only to chat to a stranger for five minutes and they think you've become *friends*. I had some man in Encino – a retired postal worker or some such thing – asking my address and promising to call *round* next time he's in England. Can you imagine it? I'd never met the man in my life.' She took a sip of tea and grew momentarily thoughtful. 'He had the most extraordinary belt buckle. All silver and little gemstones.'

'It's the food that gets me,' said her husband, raising himself a little to embark on a soliloquy, but it quickly became evident that he was one of those men who never get to say anything beyond the first sentence of a story.

'Oh yes, the food!' cried his wife, seizing the point. 'They have the most *extraordinary* attitude to food.'

'What, because they like it tasty?' I enquired with a thin smile.

'No, my dear, the *portions*. The portions in America are positively *obscene*.'

'I had a steak one time,' the man began with a little chortle.

'And the things they do to the language! They simply cannot speak the Queen's English.'

Now wait a minute. Say what you will about American portions and friendly guys with colourful belt buckles, but mind what you say about American English. 'Why should they speak the Queen's English?' I asked a trifle frostily. 'She's not their queen, after all.'

'But the words they use. And their accents. What's that word you so dislike, Arthur?'

'Normalcy,' said Arthur. 'I met this one fellow.'

'But normalcy isn't an Americanism,' I said. 'It was coined in Britain.'

'Oh, I don't think so, dear,' said the woman with the certainty of stupidity and bestowed a condescending smile. 'No, I'm sure not.'

'In 1687,' I said, lying through my teeth. Well, I was right in the fundamentals – normalcy *is* an anglicism. I just couldn't recall the details. 'Daniel Defoe in *Moll Flanders*,' I added in a flash of inspiration. One of the things you get used to hearing when you are an American living in Britain is that America will be the death of English. It is a sentiment expressed to me surprisingly often, usually at dinner parties, usually by someone who has had a little too much to drink, but sometimes by a semi-demented, overpowdered old crone like this one. There comes a time when you lose patience with this sort of thing. So I told her – I told them both, for her husband looked as if he was about to utter another fraction of thought – that whether they appreciated it or not British speech has been enlivened beyond measure by words created in America, words that they could not do without, and that one of these words was moron. I showed them my teeth, drained my coffee, and with a touch of hauteur excused myself. Then I went off to write another letter to the editor of *The Times*.

By eleven the next morning, when John Price and a very nice fellow named David Partridge rolled up at the hotel in Price's car, I was waiting for them by the door. I forbade them a coffee stop in Bowness on the grounds that I could stand it no longer, and made them drive to the hotel near Bassenthwaite where Price had booked us rooms. There we dumped our bags, had a coffee, acquired three packed lunches from the kitchen, accoutred ourselves in stylish fellware and set off for Great Langdale. Now this was more like it.

Despite threatening weather and the lateness of the year, the car parks and verges along the valley were crowded with cars. Everywhere people delved for equipment in boots or sat with car doors open pulling on warm socks and stout boots. We dressed our feet, then fell in with a straggly army of walkers, all with rucksacks and knee-high woolly socks, and set off for a long, grassy humpback hill called the Band. We were headed for the fabled summit of Bow Fell, at 2,960 feet the sixth highest of the Lakeland hills. Walkers ahead of us formed well-spaced dots of slow-moving colour leading to an impossibly remote summit, lost in cloud. As ever, I was quietly astounded to find that so many people had been

seized with the notion that struggling up a mountainside on a damp
Saturday on the winter end of October was fun.

We climbed through the grassy lower slopes into ever-bleaker
terrain, picking our way over rocks and scree, until we were up
among the ragged shreds of cloud that hung above the valley floor
perhaps a thousand feet below. The views were sensational – the
jagged peaks of the Langdale Pikes rising opposite and crowding
against the narrow and gratifyingly remote valley, laced with tiny,
stonewalled fields, and off to the west a swelling sea of hefty brown
hills disappearing in mist and low cloud.

As we pressed on the weather severely worsened. The air filled
with swirling particles of ice that hit the skin like razor nicks. By
the time we neared Three Tarns the weather was truly menacing,
with thick fog joining the jagged sleet. Ferocious gusts of wind
buffeted the hillside and reduced our progress to a creeping plod.
The fog cut visibility to a few yards. Once or twice we briefly lost
the path, which alarmed me as I didn't particularly want to die up
here – apart from anything else, I still had 4,700 unspent Profiles
points on my Barclaycard. Out of the murk ahead of us emerged
what looked disconcertingly like an orange snowman. It proved on
closer inspection to be a hi-tech hiker's outfit. Somewhere inside it
was a man.

'Bit fresh,' the bundle offered understatedly.

John and David asked him if he'd come far.

'Just from Blea Tarn.' Blea Tarn was ten miles away over taxing
terrain.

'Bad over there?' John asked in what I had come to recognize was
the abbreviated speech of fell walkers.

'Hands-and-knees job,' said the man.

They nodded knowingly.

'Be like that here soon.'

They nodded again.

'Well, best be off,' announced the man as if he couldn't spend the
whole day jabbering, and trundled off into the white soup. I
watched him go, then turned to suggest that perhaps we should
think about retreating to the valley, to a warm hostelry with hot
food and cold beer, only to find Price and Partridge dematerializing
into the mists thirty feet ahead of me.

'Hey, wait for me!' I croaked and scrambled after.

We made it to the top without incident. I counted thirty-three
people there ahead of us, huddled among the fog-whitened

boulders with sandwiches, flasks and madly fluttering maps, and tried to imagine how I would explain this to a foreign onlooker – the idea of three dozen English people having a picnic on a mountain top in an ice storm – and realized there was no way you could explain it. We trudged over to a rock, where a couple kindly moved their rucksacks and shrank their picnic space to make room for us. We sat and delved among our brown bags in the piercing wind, cracking open hard-boiled eggs with numbed fingers, sipping warm pop, eating floppy cheese-and-pickle sandwiches, and staring into an impenetrable murk that we had spent three hours climbing through to get here, and I thought, I seriously thought: God, I love this country.

CHAPTER TWENTY-FOUR

I WAS HEADING FOR NEWCASTLE, BY WAY OF YORK, WHEN I DID another impetuous thing. I got off at Durham, intending to poke around the cathedral for an hour or so and fell in love with it instantly in a serious way. Why, it's wonderful – a perfect little city – and I kept thinking: 'Why did no-one tell me about this?' I knew, of course, that it had a fine Norman cathedral but I had no idea that it was so *splendid*. I couldn't believe that not once in twenty years had anyone said to me, 'You've never been to Durham? Good God, man, you must go at once! Please – take my car.' I had read countless travel pieces in Sunday papers about weekends away in York, Canterbury, Norwich, even Lincoln, but I couldn't remember reading a single one about Durham, and when I asked friends about it, I found hardly any who had ever been there. So let me say it now: if you have never been to Durham, go at once. Take my car. It's wonderful.

The cathedral, a mountain of reddish-brown stone standing high above a lazy green loop of the River Wear, is, of course, its glory. Everything about it was perfect – not just its setting and execution but also, no less notably, the way it is run today. For a start there was no nagging for money, no 'voluntary' admission fee. Outside, there was simply a discreet sign announcing that it cost £700,000 a year to maintain the cathedral and that it was now engaged on a £400,000 renovation project on the east wing and that they would very much appreciate any spare money that visitors might give them. Inside, there were two modest collecting boxes and nothing else – no clutter, no nagging notices, no irksome bulletin boards or

stupid Eisenhower flags, nothing at all to detract from the unutterable soaring majesty of the interior. It was a perfect day to see
it. Sun slanted lavishly through the stained-glass windows, high-
lighting the stout pillars with their sumptuously grooved patterns
and spattering the floors with motes of colour. There were even
wooden pews.

I'm no judge of these things, but the window at the choir end
looked to me at least the equal of the more famous one at York, and
this one at least you could see in all its splendour since it wasn't
tucked away in a transept. And the stained-glass window at the
other end was even finer. Well, I can't talk about this without
babbling because it was just so wonderful. As I stood there, one of
only a dozen or so visitors, a verger passed and issued a cheery
hello. I was charmed by this show of friendliness and captivated to
find myself amid such perfection, and I unhesitatingly gave Durham
my vote for best cathedral on planet Earth.

When I had drunk my fill, I showered the collection pot with
coins and wandered off for the most fleeting of looks at the old
quarter of town, which was no less ancient and beguiling, and
returned to the station feeling simultaneously impressed
and desolate at just how much there was to see in this little
country and what folly it had been to suppose that I might see anything more than a fraction of it in seven flying weeks.

I took an intercity train to Newcastle and then a local to
Pegswood, eighteen miles to the north, where I emerged into more
splendid, unseasonal sunshine and hiked a mile or two along an
arrow-straight road to Ashington.

Ashington has long called itself the biggest mining village in the
world, but there is no mining any more and, with a population of
23,000, it is scarcely a village. It is famous as the birthplace of a
slew of footballers – Jackie and Bobby Charlton, Jackie Milburn
and some forty others skilled enough to play in the first division, a
remarkable outpouring for a modest community – but I was drawn
by something else: the once famous and now largely forgotten
pitmen painters.

In 1934, under the direction of an academic and artist from
Durham University named Robert Lyon, the town formed a painting club called the Ashington Group, consisting almost exclusively
of miners who had never painted – in many cases had never seen a
real painting – before they started gathering in a hut on Monday
evenings. They showed an unexpected amount of talent and

'carried the name of Ashington over the grey mountains', as a critic for the *Guardian* (who clearly knew fuck-all about football) later put it. In the 1930s and '40s particularly, they attracted huge attention, and were the frequent focus of articles in national papers and art magazines, as well as exhibitions in London and other leading cities. My friend David Cook had an illustrated book by William Feaver called *Pitmen Painters*, which he had once shown me. The illustrations of the paintings were quite charming, but it was the photographs of burly miners, dressed up in suits and ties and crowded into a little hut, earnestly hunched over easels and drawing-boards, that stuck in my mind. I had to see it.

Ashington was nothing like I expected it to be. In the photographs from David's book it appeared to be a straggly, overgrown village, surrounded by filthy waste heaps and layered with smoke from the three local pits, a place of muddy lanes hunched under a perpetual wash of sooty drizzle, but what I found instead was a modern, busy community swimming in clean, clear air. There was even a new business park with fluttering pennants, spindly new trees and an impressive brick gateway on what was clearly reclaimed ground. The main street, Station Road, had been smartly pedestrianized and its many shops appeared to be doing a good trade. It was obvious that there was not a great deal of money in Ashington – most of the shops were of the Price Busters/ Superdrug/Wotta Loada Crap variety, their windows papered with strident promises of special offers within – but at least they appeared to be thriving in a way that those of Bradford, for instance, were not.

I went to the town hall to ask the way to the site of the once-famous hut, and set off down Woodhorn Road in search of the old Co-op building behind which it had stood. The fame of the Ashington Group, it must be said, rested on a large measure of well-meaning but faintly objectionable paternalism. Reading the old accounts of their exhibitions in places like London and Bath, it is hard to escape the conclusion that the Ashington artists were regarded by critics and other aesthetes rather like Dr Johnson's performing dog: the wonder was not that they did it well but that they did it at all.

Yet the Ashington painters represented only a small fragment of a greater hunger for betterment in places like Ashington, where most people were lucky to come away with more than a few years of primary education. It is quite astonishing, seeing it now, to

realize just how rich life was, and how enthusiastically opportunities were seized, in Ashington in the years before the war. At
one time the town boasted a philosophical society, with a busy year-
round programme of lectures, concerts and evening classes; an
operatic society; a dramatic society; a workers' educational association; a miners' welfare institute with workshops and yet more
lecture rooms; and gardening clubs, cycling clubs, athletics clubs,
and others in similar vein almost beyond counting. Even the work-
ingmen's clubs, of which Ashington boasted twenty-two at its peak,
offered libraries and reading-rooms for those who craved more
than a pint or two of Federation Ale. The town had a thriving
theatre, a ballroom, five cinemas, and a concert chamber called
the Harmonic Hall. When, in the 1920s, the Bach Choir from
Newcastle performed on a Sunday afternoon at the Harmonic Hall,
it drew an audience of 2,000. Can you imagine anything remotely
like that now?

And then, one by one, they faded away – the Thespians, the
Operatic Society, the reading-rooms and lecture halls. Even the five
cinemas all quietly closed their doors. Today the liveliest diversion
in Ashington is a Noble's amusement arcade, which I passed now
on my way to the Co-op building, which wasn't hard to find. At the
back of the Co-op stood a large, unpaved car park surrounded by
a scattering of low buildings – a builder's merchants, a boy scout
hut, a DHS compound, a Veterans' Institute building made of wood
and painted a bright veridian green. I knew from William Feaver's
book that the Ashington Group hut had stood beside the Veterans'
Institute, but on which side I didn't know and now there was no
telling.

The Ashington Group was one of the last local institutions to go,
though its decline was slow and painful. Throughout the 1950s, its
numbers inexorably fell as the older members died off and younger
people decided that it was naff to put on a suit and tie and ponce
about with paintboxes. For the last several years, only two surviving members, Oliver Kilbourn and Jack Harrison, regularly showed
up on Monday nights. In the summer of 1982, they received a
notice that the ground rent on the hut was to be raised from 50p a
year to £14. 'That,' as Feaver notes, 'plus the £7 standing quarterly
charge for electricity seemed too much.' In October 1983, just short
of its fiftieth anniversary and for want of £42 a year in running
costs, the Ashington Group was disbanded and the hut pulled
down.

Now there is nothing to look at but a car park, but the paintings are faithfully preserved in the Woodhorn Colliery Museum another mile or so up Woodhorn Road. I walked there now, past endless ranks of former miners' cottages. The old colliery still looks like a colliery, its brick buildings intact, its old winding wheel hanging in the air like some kind of curious and forlorn fairground ride. Rusting iron tracks still curve across the grounds. But all is quiet now and the marshalling yards have been turned to tidy green lawns. I was almost the only visitor.

The Woodhorn Colliery closed down in 1981, seven years short of its hundredth anniversary. Once it was one of 200 pits in Northumberland, and of some 3,000 in the country as a whole. In the 1920s, at the industry's peak, 1.2 million men worked in British coal mines. Now, at the time of my visit, there were just sixteen working pits in the country and the number employed had fallen by 98 per cent.

All of which seems a little sad until you step into the museum and are reminded through photographs and accident statistics just how harsh and draining the work was, and how carefully it systematized generations of poverty. It's no wonder the town produced so many footballers; for decades there was no other way out.

The museum was free and full of cleverly engaging displays showing life down the pits and in the busy village above it. I had no idea, other than in a loose notional sense, just how hard life was in the mines. Well into this century, more than a thousand men a year died in mines and every pit had at least one fabled disaster. (Woodhorn's was in 1916 when thirty men died in an explosion caused by criminally lax supervision; the mine's owners were sternly told not to let it happen again or next time they would *really* get told off.) Until 1847, children as young as four – can you believe this? – worked in the mines for up to ten hours a day, and until relatively recent times boys of ten were put to work as trapper lads, confined in total darkness in a small space with nothing to do but open and shut ventilation traps when a coal cart passed by. One boy's shift ran from 3 a.m. to 4 p.m. six days a week. And those were the soft jobs.

Goodness knows how people found the time or strength to haul themselves off to lectures and concerts and painting clubs, but they most assuredly did. In a brightly lit room hang thirty or forty paintings executed by members of the Ashington Group. So modest were the group's resources that many are painted with walpamur, a kind of primitive emulsion, on paper, card or fibreboard. Hardly any are on canvas. It would be cruelly misleading to suggest that the Ashington Group harboured a budding Tintoretto, or even a Hockney, but the paintings provide a compelling record of life in a mining community over a period of fifty years. Nearly all depict local scenes – 'Saturday Night at the Club', 'Whippets' – or life down the pits, and seeing them in the context of a mining museum, rather than in some gallery in a metropolis, adds appreciably to their lustre. For the second time in a day I was impressed and captivated.

And here's a small, incidental point. As I was leaving, I noticed on a label recording the mine's owners that one of the principal beneficiaries of all this sweat and toil at the coalface was none other than our old friend W.J.C. Scott-Bentinck, the fifth Duke of Portland, and it occurred to me, not for the first time, what a remarkably, cherishably small world Britain is.

That is its glory, you see – that it manages at once to be intimate and small-scale and at the same time packed to bursting with incident and interest. I am constantly filled with admiration at this – at the way you can wander through a town like Oxford and in the space of a few moments pass the home of Christopher Wren, the buildings where Halley found his comet and Boyle his first law, the track where Roger Bannister ran the first sub-four-minute mile, the meadow where Lewis Carroll strolled; or how you can stand on Snow's Hill at Windsor and see, in a single sweep, Windsor Castle and the playing-fields of Eton, the churchyard where Gray wrote his elegy, the site where *The Merry Wives of Windsor* was first performed. Can there anywhere on earth be, in such a modest span, a landscape more packed with centuries of busy, productive attainment?

I returned to Pegswood lost in a small glow of admiration and caught a train to Newcastle, where I found a hotel and passed an evening in a state of some serenity, walking till late through the echoing streets, surveying the statues and buildings with fondness and respect, and I finished the day with a small thought, which I shall leave you with now. It was this:

How is it possible, in this wondrous land where the relics of genius and enterprise confront you at every step, where every realm of human possibility has been probed and challenged and generally extended, where many of the very greatest accomplishments of industry, commerce and the arts find their seat, how is it possible in such a place that when at length I returned to my hotel and switched on the television it was *Cagney and Lacey* again?

CHAPTER TWENTY-FIVE

AND SO I WENT TO EDINBURGH. CAN THERE ANYWHERE BE A MORE beautiful and beguiling city to arrive at by train early on a crisp, dark Novembery evening? To emerge from the bustling, subterranean bowels of Waverley Station and find yourself in the very heart of such a glorious city is a happy experience indeed. I hadn't been to Edinburgh for years and had forgotten just how captivating it can be. Every monument was lit with golden floodlights – the castle and Bank of Scotland headquarters on the hill, the Balmoral Hotel and the Scott Monument down below – which gave them a certain eerie grandeur. The city was abustle with end-of-day activity. Buses swept through Princes Street and shop and office workers scurried along the pavements, hastening home to have their haggis and cock-a-leekie soup and indulge in a few skirls or whatever it is Scots do when the sun goes doon.

I'd booked a room in the Caledonian Hotel, which was a rash and extravagant thing to do, but it's a terrific building and an Edinburgh institution and I just had to be part of it for one night, so I set off for it down Princes Street, past the Gothic rocket ship of the Scott Monument, unexpectedly exhilarated to find myself among the hurrying throngs and the sight of the castle on its craggy mount outlined against a pale evening sky.

To a surprising extent, and far more than in Wales, Edinburgh felt like a different country. The buildings were thin and tall in an un-English fashion, the money was different, even the air and light felt different in some ineffable northern way. Every bookshop window was full of books about Scotland or by Scottish authors.

And of course the voices were different. I walked along, feeling as if I had left England far behind, and then I would pass something familiar and think in surprise, Oh, look, they have Marks & Spencer here, as if I were in Reykjavik or Stavanger and oughtn't to expect to find British things. It was most refreshing.

I checked into the Caledonian, dumped my things in the room, and immediately returned to the streets, eager to be out in the open air and to take in whatever Edinburgh had to offer. I trudged up a long, curving back hill to the castle, but the grounds were shut for the night, so I contented myself with a shuffling amble down the Royal Mile, which was nearly empty of life and very handsome in a dour, Scottish sort of way. I passed the time browsing in the windows of the many tourist shops that stand along it, reflecting on what a lot of things the Scots have given the world – kilts, bagpipes, tam-o'-shanters, tins of oatcakes, bright yellow jumpers with big diamond patterns of the sort favoured by Ronnie Corbett, plaster casts of Greyfriars Bobby looking soulful, sacks of haggis – and how little anyone but a Scot would want them.

Let me say right here, flat out, that I have the greatest fondness and admiration for Scotland and her clever, cherry-cheeked people. Did you know that Scotland produces more university students per capita than any other nation in Europe? And it has churned out a rollcall of worthies far out of proportion to its modest size – Stevenson, Watt, Lyell, Lister, Burns, Scott, Conan Doyle, J.M. Barrie, Adam Smith, Alexander Graham Bell, Thomas Telford, Lord Kelvin, John Logie Baird, Charles Rennie Mackintosh and Ian McCaskill, to name but a few. Among much else we owe the Scots are whisky, raincoats, rubber wellies, the bicycle pedal, the telephone, tarmac, penicillin and an understanding of the active principles of cannabis, and think how insupportable life would be without those. So thank you, Scotland, and never mind that you seem quite unable to qualify for the World Cup these days.

At the bottom of the Royal Mile, I came up against the entrance to the Palace of Holyroodhouse, and picked my way to the centre of things along a series of darkened back lanes. Eventually I ended up in an unusual pub on St Andrew Square called Tiles – an apt name since every inch of it from floor to ceiling was covered in elaborate, chunky, Victorian tiles. It felt a bit like drinking in Prince Albert's loo – a not disagreeable experience, as it happens. In any case, something about it must have appealed to me because I drank a foolish amount of beer and emerged to find that nearly all the restaurants round about were closed, so I toddled back to my hotel, where I winked at the night staff and put myself to bed.

In the morning, I awoke feeling famished, perky and unusually clear-headed. I presented myself in the entrance to the dining room of the Caledonian. Would I like breakfast? asked a man in a black suit.

'Does the Firth have a Forth?' I replied drolly and nudged him in the ribs. I was shown to a table and was so hungry that I dispensed with the menu and told the man to bring me the full whack, whatever it might consist of, then sat back happily and idly glanced at the menu, where I discovered that the full cooked breakfast was listed at £14.50. I snared a passing waiter.

'Excuse me,' I said, 'but it says here that the breakfast is fourteen-fifty.'

'That's right, sir.'

I could feel a sudden hangover banging on the cranial gates. 'Are you telling me,' I said, 'that on top of the lavish sum I paid for a room I must additionally pay fourteen-fifty for a fried egg and an oatcake?'

He allowed that this was, in essence, so. I withdrew my order and asked instead for a cup of coffee. Well, honestly.

Perhaps it was this sudden early blot on my happiness that put me in a grumpy mood or perhaps it was the drippy rain I emerged into, but Edinburgh didn't look half so fine in daylight as it had appeared the night before. Now people plodded through the streets with umbrellas and cars swished through puddles with a noise that sounded testy and impatient. George Street, the core of the New Town, presented an unquestionably fine, if damp, prospect with its statues and stately squares, but far too many of the Georgian buildings had been clumsily abused by the addition of modern frontages. Just around the corner from my hotel was an office supply shop with plate-glass windows that had been grafted onto an eighteenth-century frontage in a way that was nothing short of criminal, and there were others in like vein here and there along the surrounding streets.

I wandered around looking for some place to eat, and ended up on Princes Street. It, too, seemed to have changed overnight. Then, with homeward-bound workers scurrying past, it had seemed beguiling and vibrant, exciting even, but now in the dull light of day it merely seemed listless and grey. I shuffled along it looking for a café or bistro, but with the exception of a couple of truly dumpy discount woollens places where the goods seemed to have been drop-kicked onto display counters or were spontaneously climbing out of bins, Princes Street appeared to offer nothing but the usual array of chain establishments – Boots, Littlewoods, Virgin Records, BHS, Marks & Spencer, Burger King, McDonald's. What central Edinburgh lacked, it seemed to me, was a venerable and much-loved institution – a Viennese-style coffeehouse or treasured tea-room, some place with newspapers on gripper rods, potted palms and perhaps a fat little lady playing a grand piano.

In the end, fractious and impatient, I went into a crowded McDonald's, waited a century in a long, ragged line, which made me even more fractious and impatient, and finally ordered a cup of coffee and an Egg McMuffin.

'Do you want an apple turnover with that?' asked the spotty young man who served me.

'I'm sorry,' I said, 'do I appear to be brain-damaged?'

'Pardon?'

'Correct me if I'm wrong, but I didn't ask for an apple turnover, did I?'

'Uh . . . no.'

'So do I look as if I have some mental condition that would render me unable to request an apple turnover if I wanted one?'

'No, it's just that we're told to ask everyone like.'

'What, you think everyone in Edinburgh is brain-damaged?'

'We're just told to ask everyone like.'

'Well, I don't want an apple turnover, which is why I didn't ask for one. Is there anything else you'd like to know if I don't want?'

'We're just told to ask everyone.'

'Do you remember what I *do* want?'

He looked in confusion at his till. 'Uh, an Egg McMuffin and a cup of coffee.'

'Do you think I might have it this morning or shall we talk some more?'

'Oh, uh, right, I'll just get it.'

'Thank you.'

Well, honestly.

Afterwards, feeling only fractionally less fractious, I stepped out to find the rain beating down. I sprinted across the road and, on an impulse, ducked into the Royal Scottish Academy, a grand pseudo-hellenic edifice with banners suspended between the columns, which make it look a little like a lost outpost of the Reichstag. I paid £1.50 for a ticket and, shaking myself dry like a dog, shuffled in. They were having their autumn show or perhaps it was their winter show or perhaps it was their annual show. I couldn't say because I didn't notice any signs and the pictures were labelled with numbers. You had to pay an extra £2 for a catalogue to find out what was what, which frankly annoys me when I have just parted with £1.50. (The National Trust does this, too – puts numbers on the plants and trees in its gardens and so on, so that you have to buy a catalogue – which is one reason why I won't be leaving my fortune to the National Trust.) The works in the RSA exhibition extended over many rooms and appeared to fall chiefly into four categories: (1) boats on beaches, (2) lonely crofts, (3) half-clad girl-friends engaged in their toilette, and, for some reason, (4) French street scenes, always with at least one shop front saying BOULANGERIE or EPICERIE so that there was no possibility of mistaking the setting for Fraserburgh or Arbroath.

Many of the pictures – indeed most – were outstanding, and when I saw red gummed circles attached to some of them I not only realized that they were for sale but developed a sudden, strange hankering to buy one myself. So I started making trips to the lady at the front desk and saying, 'Excuse me, how much is number 125?' She would look it up and state a figure several hundred pounds beyond what I was prepared to pay, so I would wander off again and after a bit come back and say, 'Excuse me, how much is number 47?' At one point, I saw a picture I particularly liked – a painting of Solway Firth by a fellow named Colin Park – and she looked it up and told me that it was £125. This was a good price and I was prepared to buy it then and there even if I had to carry it all the way to John O'Groats under my arm, but then she discovered that she had read the wrong line, that the £125 picture was a little thing about three inches square and that the Colin Park was very considerably more than that, so I went off again. Eventually, when my legs began to tire, I tried a new tack and asked her what she had for £50 or less, and when it turned out there was nothing, I left, discouraged in my quest but £2 richer in regard to the catalogue.

Then I went to the Scottish National Gallery, which I liked even better and not just because it was free. The Scottish National Gallery is tucked away behind the RSA and doesn't look much from outside, but inside it was very grand in an imperial, nineteenth-century sort of way, with red baize walls, outsized pictures in extravagant frames, scattered statues of naked nymphs and furniture trimmed in gilt, so that it rather brought to mind a stroll through Queen Victoria's boudoir. The pictures were not only outstanding, but they had labels telling you their historical background and what the people in them were doing, which I think is to be highly commended and in fact should be made mandatory everywhere.

I read these instructive notes gratefully, pleased to know, for instance, that the reason Rembrandt looked so glum in his self-portrait was that he had just been declared insolvent, but in one of the salons I noticed that there was a man, accompanied by a boy of about thirteen, who didn't need the labels at all.

They were from what I suspect the Queen Mother would call the lower orders. Everything about them murmured poorness and material want – poor diet, poor income, poor dentistry, poor prospects, even poor laundering – but the man was describing the pictures with a fondness and familiarity that were truly heart-warming and the boy was raptly attentive to his every word. 'Now this is a later Goya, you see,' he was saying in a quiet voice. 'Just look at how controlled those brush strokes are – a complete change in style from his earlier work. D'ye remember how I told you that Goya didn't paint a single great picture till he was nearly fifty? Well, this is a great picture.' He wasn't showing off, you understand; he was sharing.

I have often been struck in Britain by this sort of thing – by how mysteriously well educated people from unprivileged backgrounds so often are, how the most unlikely people will tell you plant names in Latin or turn out to be experts on the politics of ancient Thrace or irrigation techniques at Glanum. This is a country, after all, where the grand final of a programme like *Mastermind* is frequently won by cab drivers and footplatemen. I have never been able to decide whether that is deeply impressive or just appalling – whether this is a country where engine drivers know about Tintoretto and Leibniz or a country where people who know about Tintoretto and Leibniz end up driving engines. All I know is that it exists more here than anywhere else.

Afterwards, I climbed up the steep slope to the castle grounds, which seemed oddly, almost spookily, familiar. I hadn't been here before, so I couldn't think why this should be, and then I realized that a regimental tattoo from Edinburgh Castle had been one of the features of *This Is Cinerama* back in Bradford. The castle precinct was just as it had been in the film, apart from a change of weather and a merciful absence of strutting Gordon Highlanders, but one other thing had changed mightily since 1951 – the view of Princes Street from the terrace.

In 1951, Princes Street remained one of the world's great streets, a gracious thoroughfare lined along its northern side with solid, weighty Victorian and Edwardian edifices that bespoke confidence, greatness and empire – the North British Mercantile Insurance Company, the sumptuous, classical New Club building, the old Waverley Hotel. And then, one by one, they were unaccountably torn down, and replaced for the most part with grey concrete bunkers. At the eastern end of the street the whole of St James' Square, an open green space surrounded by a crowd of eighteenth-century tenements, was bulldozed to make way for one of the squattest, ugliest shopping centre/hotel complexes ever to spill from an architect's pen. Now about all that is left of Princes Street's age of confident grandeur are odd fragments like the Balmoral Hotel and the Scott Monument and part of the front of Jenners Department Store.

Later, when I was back home, I found in my *AA Book of British Towns* an artist's illustration of central Edinburgh as it might be seen from the air. It showed Princes Street lined from end to end with nothing but fine old buildings. The same was true of all the other artists' impressions of British cities – Norwich and Oxford and Canterbury and Stratford. You can't do that, you know. You can't tear down fine old structures and pretend they are still there. But that is exactly what has happened in Britain in the past thirty years, and not just with buildings.

And on that sour note, I went off to try to find some real food.

CHAPTER TWENTY-SIX

SO LET'S TALK ABOUT SOMETHING HEARTENING. LET'S TALK ABOUT John Fallows. One day in 1987 Fallows was standing at a window in a London bank waiting to be served when a would-be robber named Douglas Bath stepped in front of him, brandished a handgun and demanded money from the cashier. Outraged, Fallows told Bath to 'bugger off' to the back of the line and wait his turn, to the presumed approving nods of others in the queue. Unprepared for this turn of events, Bath meekly departed from the bank empty-handed and was arrested a short distance away.

I bring this up here to make the point that if there is one golden quality that characterizes the British it is an innate sense of good manners and you defy it at your peril. Deference and a quiet consideration for others are such a fundamental part of British life, in fact, that few conversations could even start without them. Almost any encounter with a stranger begins with the words 'I'm terribly sorry but' followed by a request of some sort – 'could you tell me the way to Brighton,' 'help me find a shirt my size,' 'get your steamer trunk off my foot.' And when you've fulfilled their request, they invariably offer a hesitant, apologetic smile and say sorry again, begging forgiveness for taking up your time or carelessly leaving their foot where your steamer trunk clearly needed to go. I just love that.

As if to illustrate my point, when I checked out of the Caledonian late the next morning, I arrived to find a woman ahead of me wearing a helpless look and saying to the receptionist: 'I'm terribly sorry but I can't seem to get the television in my room to work.' She had come all the way downstairs, you understand, to apologize to *them* for their TV not working. My heart swelled with feelings of warmth and fondness for this strange and unfathomable country.

And it is all done so instinctively, that's the other thing. I remember when I was still new to the country arriving at a railway station one day to find that just two of the dozen or so ticket windows were open. (For the benefit of foreign readers, I should explain that as a rule in Britain no matter how many windows there are in a bank, post office or rail station, only two of them will be open, except at very busy times, when just one will be open.) Both ticket windows were occupied. Now, in other countries one of two things would have happened. Either there would be a crush of customers at each window, all demanding simultaneous attention, or else there would be two slow-moving lines, each full of gloomy people convinced that the other line was moving faster.

Here in Britain, however, the waiting customers had spontaneously come up with a much more sensible and ingenious arrangement. They had formed a single line a few feet back from both windows. When either position became vacant, the customer at the head of the line would step up to it and the rest of the line would shuffle forward a space. It was a wonderfully fair and democratic approach and the remarkable thing was that no-one had commanded it or even suggested it. It just happened.

Much the same sort of thing occurred now, for when the lady with the recalcitrant TV set had finished with her apology (which the receptionist, I must say, accepted with uncommonly good grace, going so far as to hint that if anything else in the woman's room was found to be out of order, she wasn't to blame herself for a minute), the receptionist turned to me and another gentleman who was also waiting and said, 'Who's next?' and he and I went through an elaborate after-you, no-after-you, but-I-insist, well-that's-most-gracious-of-you routine, which made my heart swell further.

And so, on my second morning in Edinburgh, I stepped from the hotel in happy spirits, at one with the world, buoyed by this cheerful and civilized encounter, to find the sun shining and the city transformed yet again. On this day, George Street and Queen Street looked positively ravishing, their stone fronts burnished with sunlight, the damp, brooding darkness that had suffused them the day before banished utterly. The Firth of Forth gleamed in the distance and the little parks and squares seemed alive with green. I trudged up The Mound to the Old Town terraces to take in the view and was astonished to see how different the city looked. Princes Street was still a scar of architectural regrettabilities, but beyond it the hills were thronged with jaunty roofs and thrusting steeples that gave the city a character and graciousness that had entirely escaped me the day before.

I spent the morning doing touristy things – I went to St Giles' Cathedral and had a look at Holyroodhouse, climbed to the top of Calton Hill – and finally fetched my pack and returned to the station, happy to have made my peace with Edinburgh and pleased to be on the move again.

And what a fine thing a train journey is. I was instantly lulled by the motion of the train as we lumbered out through Edinburgh and its quiet suburbs and over the Forth Bridge. (And, gosh, what a mighty structure it is; suddenly I understood why the Scots are always on about it.) The train was mostly empty and rather splendidly posh. It was done up in restful blues and greys, which provided a sharp contrast to all the Sprinters I had been on in recent days and proved so deeply soothing that soon my eyelids were growing unsustainably heavy and my neck seemed to be turning to a rubbery material. In no time at all, my head was slumped on my chest and I was engaged in the quiet, steady manufacture of several gallons of saliva – all of them, alas, spare.

Some people simply should not be allowed to fall asleep on a train, or, having fallen asleep, should be discreetly covered with a tarpaulin, and I'm afraid I am one of them. I awoke, some indeterminate time later, with a rutting snort and a brief, wild flail and lifted my head from my chest to find myself mired in a cobweb of drool from beard to belt buckle, and with three people gazing at me in a curiously dispassionate manner. At least I was spared the usual experience of waking to find myself stared at open-mouthed by a group of small children who would flee with shrieks at the discovery that the dribbling hulk was alive.

Shrinking from my audience and daubing myself discreetly with the sleeve of my jacket, I attended to the view. We were rattling through an open landscape that was pleasant rather than dramatic – arable farmland running off to big round hills – under a sky that seemed ready to collapse under its own weight of grey. From time to time we stopped in some inert little town with a dead little station – Ladybank, Cupar, Leuchars – before eventually entering a larger, fractionally more active world at Dundee, Arbroath and Montrose. And then, some three hours after leaving

Edinburgh, we were sliding into Aberdeen in a thin and fast-fading light.

I pressed my face to the glass keenly. I had never been to Aberdeen before and didn't know anyone who had. I knew almost nothing about it, other than that it was dominated by the North Sea oil industry and proudly called itself the 'Granite City'. It had always seemed to me exotically remote, a place I was unlikely ever to get to, so I was eager to see it.

I had booked into a hotel which was warmly described in my guidebook (a tome that later went for kindling), but turned out to be a dreary, overpriced back-street block. My room was small and ill-lit, with battered furniture, a narrow, prison-cell bed with a thin blanket and a single grudging pillow, and wallpaper doing its best to flee a damp wall. Once, in a moment of ambition, the management had installed a bedside console that operated lights, radio and TV, and incorporated an alarm clock, but none of these appeared to work. The alarm clock knob came off in my hand. With a sigh, I dumped my stuff on the bed and returned to the dark streets of Aberdeen looking for food, drink and granite splendour.

One thing I have learned over the years is that your impressions of a city are necessarily coloured by the route you take into it. Enter London by way of the leafy suburbs of Richmond, Barnes and Putney and alight at, say, Kensington Gardens or Green Park and you would think that you were in the midst of some vast, well-tended Arcadia. Enter it by way of Southend, Romford and Liverpool Street and you would perceive it in another way altogether. So perhaps it was simply the route I took from my hotel. All I know is that I walked for nearly three hours up streets and down and I couldn't find anything remotely adorable about Aberdeen. There were some briefly diverting vignettes – an open pedestrianized space around the Mercat Cross, an interesting-looking little museum called John Dun's House, some imposing university buildings – but no matter how many times I crisscrossed through its heart, all I seemed to encounter was a vast, glossy new shopping centre that was a damnable nuisance to circumnavigate (I kept ending up, muttering and lost, in dead-end delivery bays and collecting compounds for cardboard boxes) and a single broad end-less street lined with precisely the same stores I had seen in every other city for the last six weeks. It was like anywhere and nowhere – like a small Manchester or a random fragment of Leeds. In vain I sought a single place where I could stand with hands on hips and

say, 'Aha, so *this* is Aberdeen.' Perhaps, too, it was the dreary time
of year. I had read somewhere that Aberdeen had won the Britain
in Bloom competition nine times, but I saw hardly any gardens or
green spaces. Above all, I had scant sense of being in the midst of a
rich, proud city built of granite.

On top of that, I couldn't settle on a place to eat. I hankered for
something different, something I hadn't encountered a hundred
times already on this trip – Thai or Mexican, perhaps, or maybe
Indonesian or even Scottish – but there seemed nothing but the
usual scattering of Chinese and Indian establishments, usually on a
side-street, usually up a flight of stairs that looked as if they had
been recently used for a motorcycle rally, and I couldn't bring
myself to make that terrible climb into the unknown. In any case, I
knew exactly what would be up there – low lighting, a reception
area with a padded bar, twangy Asian music, tables covered with
glasses of lager and stainless-steel plate warmers. I couldn't face it.
In the end, I engaged in a desperate session of eenie meenie minie
mo on a street corner and opted for an Indian. It was, in every
degree, exactly like every Indian meal I had had in the previous
weeks. Even the post-dinner burp tasted exactly the same. I
returned to my hotel in a dim and restless frame of mind.

In the morning, I went for a walk around the town sincerely hoping that I would like it better, but alas, alas. It wasn't that there was
anything *wrong* with Aberdeen exactly, more that it suffered from
a surfeit of innocuousness. I had a shuffle round the new shopping
centre and ranged some distance out into the surrounding streets,
but they all seemed equally colourless and forgettable. And then I
realized that the problem really wasn't with Aberdeen so much as
with the nature of modern Britain. British towns are like a deck of
cards that have been shuffled and endlessly redealt – same cards,
different order. If I had come to Aberdeen fresh from another
country, it would probably have seemed pleasant and agreeable. It
was prosperous and clean. It had bookshops and cinemas and a
university and pretty much everything else you could want in a
community. It is, I've no doubt, a nice place to live. It's just that it
was so much like everywhere else. It was a British city. How could
it be otherwise?

Once I had packed this small thought into my head I liked
Aberdeen much better. I can't say I ached to up sticks and move
there – but then why should I when I could get exactly the same
things, the same shops and libraries and leisure centres, the

same pubs and television programmes, the same phone boxes, post offices, traffic lights, park benches, zebra crossings, marine air and post-Indian-dinner burps anywhere else? In an odd way the very things that had made Aberdeen seem so dull and predictable the night before now made it seem comfortable and rather homey. But I still never had the slightest sense that I was in the midst of a lot of granite, and it was without regret that I fetched my things from the hotel and returned to the station to resume my stately progress north.

The train was again very clean and nearly empty, with more soothing blues and greys. It was just two carriages, but it had a trolley service, which impressed me. The difficulty was that the young chap in charge was obviously keen – I had the impression that he had just started the job and was still at the point where it was fun to dispense teas and make change – but as there were only two other passengers and just sixty yards of carriage to patrol, he came by about once every three minutes. Still, the constant ruckus of the passing trolley kept me from nodding off and falling into a state of embarrassing hyper-salivation.

We rode through a pleasant but unexciting landscape. All my previous experience of the Highlands was up the more dramatic west coast, and this was decidedly muted in comparison – rounded hills, flat farms, occasional glimpses of an empty, steel-grey sea – but by no means disagreeable. Nothing of incident happened except that at Nairn a big plane took off and did all kinds of astonishing things in the sky, climbing vertically for hundreds of feet, then slowly tipping over and plunging towards earth before pulling out in a steep bank at nearly the last moment. I supposed it was some sort of a test base for RAF planes, but it was more exciting to imagine that it had been hijacked by a suicidal madman. And then an arresting thing happened. The plane began coming towards the train, really bearing down on it, as if the pilot had spotted us and thought that it would be interesting to take us with him. It got larger and larger and nearer and nearer – I looked around uneasily but there was no-one to share the experience with – until it nearly filled the window and then the train went into a cutting and the plane disappeared from view. I bought a cup of coffee and a packet of biscuits from the trolley to steady my nerves and waited for Inverness to appear.

I liked Inverness immediately. It is never going to win any beauty contests, but it has some likeable features – an old-fashioned little cinema called La Scala, a well-preserved market arcade, a large and adorably over-the-top nineteenth-century sandstone castle on a hill, some splendid river walks. I was particularly taken with the dim-lit market arcade, an undercover thoroughfare apparently locked in a perpetual 1953. It had a barbershop with a revolving pole out front and pictures inside of people who looked like they had modelled their hairstyles on *Thunderbirds* characters. There was even a joke shop selling useful and interesting items that I hadn't seen for years: sneezing powder and plastic vomit (very handy for saving seats on trains) and chewing-gum that turns the teeth black. It was shut, but I made a mental note to return in the morning to stock up.

Above all, Inverness has an especially fine river, green and sedate and charmingly overhung with trees, lined on one side by big houses, trim little parks and the old sandstone castle (now the home of the regional sheriff's courts) and on the other by old hotels with steep-pitched roofs, more big houses and the stolid, Notre Dame-like grandeur of the cathedral, standing on a broad lawn beside the river. I checked into a hotel at random and immediately set off for a walk through the gathering twilight. The river was lined on both sides by gracious promenades thoughtfully punctu-ated with benches, which made it very agreeable for an evening stroll. I walked for some distance, perhaps two miles, on the Haugh Road side of the river, past little islands reached by Victorian suspension footbridges.

Nearly all the houses on both sides of the river were rambling places built for an age of servants. What, I wondered, had brought all this late Victorian wealth to Inverness, and who supported these handsome heaps today? Not far from the castle, on spacious grounds in what I suppose a developer would call a prime location, stood a particularly grand and elaborate mansion, with turrets and towers. It was a wonderful, spacious house, the kind you could imagine riding a bicycle around in, and it was boarded, derelict and up for sale. I couldn't think how such a likeable place could have ended up in such a neglected state. As I walked along, I lost myself in a reverie of buying it for a song, doing it up, and living happily ever after on these large grounds beside this deeply fetching river, until I realized what my family would say if I told them we weren't after all going to the land of shopping malls, 100-channel television and hamburgers the size of a baby's head, but instead to the damp north of Scotland.

And anyway, I regret to say that I could never live in Inverness because of two sensationally ugly modern office buildings that stand by the central bridge and blot the town centre beyond any hope of redemption. I came upon them now as I returned to the town centre and was positively riveted with astonishment to realize that an entire town could be ruined by two inanimate structures. Everything about them – scale, materials, design – was madly inappropriate to the surrounding scene. They weren't just ugly and large but so ill-designed that you could actually walk around them at least twice without ever finding the front entrance. In the larger of the two, on the river side where there might have been a restaurant or terrace or at least shops or offices with a view, much of the road frontage had been given over to a huge delivery bay with overhead metal doors. This in a building that overlooked one of the handsomest rivers in Britain. It was awful, awful beyond words.

I had recently been to Hobart in Tasmania, where the Sheraton chain had built a hotel of stunning plainness on its lovely waterfront. I had been told that the architect hadn't actually visited the site and had put the hotel restaurant at the back, where diners couldn't see the harbour. Since then, I had thought that was the most brainless thing I had ever heard of architecturally. I don't suppose this pair could possibly have been designed by the same architect – it was terrifying to think that there could be two architects in the world this bad – but he could certainly have worked for the firm.

Of all the buildings that I would deeply love to blow up in Britain – the Maples building in Harrogate, the Hilton Hotel in London, the Post Office building in Leeds, a lucky dip among almost any structure owned by British Telecom – I have no hesitation in saying that my first choice would be either of these two.

And here is the cruncher. Guess who inhabits these two piles of heartbreak? Well, I'll tell you. The larger is the regional headquarters of the Highland Enterprise Board and the other is the home of Inverness and Nairn Enterprise Board, the two bodies entrusted with the attractiveness and well-being of this lovely and vital corner of the country. God.

CHAPTER TWENTY-SEVEN

I HAD BIG PLANS FOR THE MORNING: I WAS GOING TO GO TO THE BANK, buy some plastic vomit, have a look at the local art gallery, perhaps take another stroll along the lovely River Ness, but I woke late and had no time to do anything but fumble my way into clothes, check out of the hotel and waddle in a sweat to the station. Beyond Inverness trains run infrequently – just three times a day to Thurso and Wick – so I couldn't afford to be late.

As it happened, the train was waiting, humming quietly, and left right on time. We slid out of Inverness against a backdrop of round mountains and the cold flatness of the Beauly Firth. The train was soon rattling along at a fair old clip. There were more passengers this time, and there was a trolley service again – all credit to BR – but no-one wanted anything from it because the other passengers were almost all pensioners and they had brought their own provisions.

I bought a tandoori chicken sandwich and a coffee. How far things have come. I can remember when you couldn't buy a British Rail sandwich without wondering if this was your last act before a long period on a life-support machine. And anyway you couldn't buy one because the buffet car was nearly always closed. And now here I was sitting eating a tandoori chicken sandwich and drinking a creditable cup of coffee brought to me in my seat by a friendly and presentable young man on a two-carriage train across the Highlands.

Here's an interesting statistic for you, which is kind of boring but must be taken in. Rail infrastructure spending per person per year in Europe is £20 in Belgium and Germany, £31 in France, more than £50 in Switzerland, and in Britain a slightly less than munificent £5. Britain spends less per capita on rail improvements than any other country in the European Union except Greece and Ireland. Even Portugal spends more. And the thing is, despite this paucity of support you actually have an excellent train service in this country, all things considered. Trains are now much cleaner than they used to be and staff generally more patient and helpful. Ticket people always say please and thank you, bless them, and you can eat the food.

So I ate my tandoori chicken sandwich and drank my cup of coffee with pleasure and gratification, and passed the time between nibbles watching a white-haired couple at a table across the way delving among their travelling fare, setting out little plastic boxes of pork pies and hard-boiled eggs, lifting out flasks, unscrewing lids, finding little salt and pepper shakers. It's amazing, isn't it, how you can give a couple of old people a canvas holdall, an assortment of Tupperware containers and a Thermos flask and they can amuse themselves for hours. They worked away with well-ordered precision and total silence, as if they had been preparing for this event for years. When the food was laid out, they ate for four minutes with great delicacy, then spent most of the rest of the morning quietly packing everything away. They looked very happy.

They reminded me in an odd but heartwarming way of my mother, as she is something of a Tupperware devotee herself. She doesn't picnic on trains, since there are no passenger trains in her part of the country any more, but she does like to put stray items of food in plastic containers of various sizes and file them away in the fridge. It's an odd thing about mothers generally, I believe. As soon as you leave home they merrily throw away everything that you cherished through childhood and adolescence – your valuable collection of baseball cards, a complete set of *Playboys* from 1966–75, your high-school yearbooks – but give them half a peach or a spoonful of leftover peas and they will put it in a Tupperware container at the back of the fridge and treasure it more or less for ever.

And so the long ride to Thurso passed. We rattled on through an increasingly remote and barren landscape, treeless and cold, with heather clinging to the hillsides like lichen on rock and thinly scattered with sheep that took fright and scampered off when the train passed. Now and then we passed through winding valleys

speckled with farms that looked romantic and pretty from a
distance, but bleak and comfortless up close. Mostly they were
smallholdings with lots of rusted tin everywhere – tin sheds, tin hen
huts, tin fences – looking rickety and weatherbattered. We were
entering one of those weird zones, always a sign of remoteness from
the known world, where nothing is ever thrown away. Every farm-
yard was cluttered with piles of cast-offs, as if the owner thought
that one day he might need 132 half-rotted fenceposts, a ton of
broken bricks and the shell of a 1964 Ford Zodiac.

Two hours after leaving Inverness, we came to a place called
Golspie. It was a good-sized town with big council estates and
winding streets of those grey pebbledash bungalows that seem to
have been modelled on public toilets and for which they have a
strange fondness in Scotland, but no sign of factories or workplaces. What, I wondered, do all the people in all those houses do
for a living in a place like Golspie? Then came Brora, another good-
sized community, with a seafront but no harbour, as far as I could
see, and no factories. What *do* they *do* in these little places in the
middle of nowhere?

After that, the landscape became quite empty, with neither farmhouses nor field animals. We rode for a seeming eternity through a
great Scottish void, full of miles of nothingness, until, in the middle
of this great emptiness, we came to a place called Forsinard, with
two houses, a railway station and an inexplicably large hotel. What
a strange lost world this was. And then at long last we arrived in
Thurso, the northernmost town on the British mainland, the end of
the line in every sense of the word. I stepped from the little station
on slightly unsteady legs and set off down the long main street
towards the centre.

I had no idea what to expect, but my initial impressions were
favourable. It seemed a tidy, well-ordered place, comfortable rather
than showy, considerably larger than I had expected, and with
several small hotels. I took a room in the Pentland Hotel, which
seemed a nice enough place in a deathly quiet, end-of-the-world
sort of way. I accepted a key from the pleasant receptionist, conveyed my things to a distant room reached through spooky,
winding corridors, then went out to have a look around.

The big event in Thurso, according to civic records, was in 1834
when Sir John Sinclair, a local worthy, coined the term 'statistics' in
the town, though things have calmed down pretty considerably
since. When he wasn't contriving neologisms, Sinclair also

extensively rebuilt the town, endowing it with a splendid library in a cautiously baroque style and a small square with a little park in the middle. Around the square today stands a modest district of small, useful, friendly looking shops – chemists and butchers, a wine merchant, a ladies' boutique or two, a scattering of banks, lots of hair salons (why is there always an abundance of hair salons in little out-of-the-way communities?) – pretty well everything, in short, you would hope to find in a model community. There was a small old-fashioned Woolworth's, but apart from that and the banks, nearly everything else appeared to be locally owned, which gave Thurso a nice, homey feel. It had the air of a real, self-contained community. I liked it very much.

I pottered about for a bit among the shopping streets, then followed some back lanes down to the waterfront, where there was a lonely fish warehouse marooned in an acre of empty car park and a vast empty beach with thunderous crashing waves. The air was fresh and vigorously abundant in the blowy way of the seaside, and the world was bathed in an ethereal northern light that gave the sea a curious luminescence – indeed, gave everything an odd, faint bluish cast – that intensified my sense of being a long way from home.

At the far end of the beach there stood a spectral tower, a fragment of old castle, and I set off to investigate. A rocky stream stood between me and it, so I had to backtrack to a footbridge some distance from the beach, then pick my way along a muddy path liberally strewn with litter. The castle tower was derelict, its lower windows and door openings bricked over. A notice beside it announced that the coastal path was closed because of soil erosion. I stood for a long time by this little headland gazing out to sea, then turned to face the town and wondered what to do next.

Thurso was to be my home for the next three days and I wasn't at all sure how I was going to fill such an expanse of empty time. Between the smell of sea air and the sense of utter remoteness, I had a moment of quiet panic at finding myself alone here at the top of the earth, where there was no-one to talk to and the most exciting diversion was an old bricked-up tower. I wandered back into town the way I had come and, for want of anything better to do, had another pottering look in the shop windows. And then, outside a greengrocer's, it happened – something that sooner or later always happens to me on a long trip away from home. It is a moment I dread.

I started asking myself unanswerable questions.

Prolonged solitary travel, you see, affects people in different ways. It is an unnatural business to find yourself in a strange place with an underutilized brain and no particular reason for being there, and eventually it makes you go a little crazy. I've seen it in others often. Some solitary travellers start talking to themselves: little silently murmured conversations that they think no-one else notices. Some desperately seek the company of strangers, striking up small talk at shop counters and hotel reception desks and then lingering for an uncomfortably long period before finally departing. Some become ravenous, obsessive sightseers, tramping from sight to sight with a guidebook in a lonely quest to see everything. Me, I get a sort of interrogative diarrhoea. I ask private, internal questions – scores and scores of them – for which I cannot supply answers. And so as I stood by a greengrocer's in Thurso, looking at its darkened interior with pursed lips and a more or less empty head, from out of nowhere I thought, Why do they call it a grape-fruit? and I knew that the process had started.

It's not a bad question, as these things go. I mean to say, why *do* they call it a grapefruit? I don't know about you, but if someone presented me with an unfamiliar fruit that was yellow, the size of a cannonball and tasted sour I don't believe I would think: Well, you know, it rather puts me in mind of a grape.

The trouble is that once these things start there is no stopping them. A couple of doors away was a shop that sold jumpers and I thought: Why do the British call them jumpers? I've actually been wondering this for years, off and on, usually in lonely places like Thurso, and I would sincerely like to know. Do they make you want to jump? Do you think to yourself when you put one on in the morning: Now not only shall I be warm all day, no small con-sideration in a nation where central heating still cannot be assumed, but if I should be required to do some jumping I shall be suitably attired.

And so it went on. I proceeded through the streets under a meteor shower of interrogations. Why do they call them milk floats? They don't float at all. Why do we foot a bill rather than, say, head it? Why do we say that our nose is *running*? (Mine slides.) Who ate the first oyster and how on earth did anyone ever figure out that ambergris would make an excellent fixative for perfumes?

When this happens, I know from years of experience, it takes a special distraction to shock the mind from this solitary torment, and fortunately Thurso had one. On a side-street, as I was just beginning to wonder why we say we are head over heels when we are happy when in fact our head normally *is* over our heels, I happened on an extraordinary little establishment called the Fountain Restaurant, which offered three complete but different menus – a Chinese menu, an Indian menu and a 'European' menu. Thurso evidently couldn't maintain three separate restaurants, so it had one restaurant offering three kinds of cuisines.

Immediately taken with this concept, I went in and was shown to a table by a pretty young lady who left me with a menu that ran to many pages. It was apparent from the title page that all three kinds of meals were cooked by a single Scottish chef, so I pored through the entries hoping to find 'sweet-and-sour oatcakes' or 'haggis vindaloo', but the dishes were strictly conventional. I opted for Chinese, then sat back and enjoyed a state of blissful mindlessness.

When it came, the food tasted, I have to say, like a Chinese meal cooked by a Scottish chef – which is not to say that it wasn't good. It was just curiously unlike any Chinese meal I had ever had. The more I ate it the more I liked it. At least it was different, and that, by this stage of the trip, was all I craved.

When I emerged, I felt much better. Lacking anything better to do, I strolled back down to the vicinity of the fish warehouse to take the evening air. As I stood there in the darkness, listening to the pounding surf and gazing contentedly at the great starry dome of sky above me, I thought, Who decided that Hereford and Worcester would make a zippy name for a county? and I knew then that it was time for bed.

In the morning, I was roused early by my alarm clock and rose reluctantly, for I was having my favourite dream – the one where I own a large, remote island, not unlike those off this section of Scottish coast, to which I invite carefully selected people, like the guy who invented the Christmas tree lights that go out when one bulb blows, the person in charge of escalator maintenance at Heathrow Airport, nearly anyone who has ever written a user's manual for a personal computer, and of course John Selwyn Gummer, let them loose with a *very* small amount of survival rations, and then go out with braying dogs and mercilessly hunt them down – but then I remembered that I had a big, exciting day in front of me. I was going to John O'Groats.

I had been hearing about John O'Groats for years, but I had not the faintest idea of what it would be like. It seemed exotic beyond words and I ached to see it. So I breakfasted in a spirit of keenness at the Pentland Hotel, the only person in the dining room, and then repaired at the stroke of nine to William Dunnet's, the local Ford dealer, where I had arranged by phone some days earlier to hire a car for the day, since there was no other way to get to John O'Groats at this time of year.

It took the man in the showroom a moment to recall the arrangement. 'Ah, you're the chap from down south,' he said, remembering, which threw me a little. It isn't often you hear Yorkshire referred to as down south.

'Isn't every place down south from here?' I asked.

'Yes. Why, yes, I suppose it is,' he said as if I had stumbled on a rare profundity.

He was a friendly fellow – everyone in Thurso is friendly – and while he scratched away at the voluminous paperwork that would put me in charge of two tons of dangerous metal, we chatted amiably about life in this remote outpost of civilization. He told me it took sixteen hours to drive to London, not that anyone much ever did. For most people, Inverness, four hours to the south by car, was the southern limit of the known world.

It seemed like months since I had had a conversation, and I babbled away at him with questions. What did people in Thurso do for a living? How did the castle come to be derelict? Where did they go if they wanted to buy a sofa, see a movie, have a Chinese meal not cooked by a Scotsman or otherwise experience something beyond the modest range of pleasures available locally?

Thus I learned that the local economy was underpinned by the Dounreay nuclear reactor down the road, that the castle had once been a thing of well-maintained beauty but had been allowed to fall into decrepitude by an eccentric owner, that Inverness was the seat of all forms of excitement. I must have betrayed a flutter of astonishment at this because he smiled and said drily, 'Well, it has a Marks & Spencer.'

Then he took me outside, sat me in the driver's seat of a Ford Thesaurus (or something; I'm not very good at car names), gave me a quick rundown on all the many moveable stalks and dashboard buttons, and then stood by with a kind of nervous frozen smile while I activated controls that made the seatback jettison away from my back, the boot pop open and the windscreen wipers go into monsoon mode. And then, with a worrisome grinding of gears and several jerky movements, I blazed a trail from the car park by a novel and lavishly bumpy route and took to the road.

Moments later, for such is Thurso's diminutive size, I was out on the open highway and cruising with a light heart towards John O'Groats. It was an arrestingly empty landscape, with nothing much but fields of billowy winter-bleached grass running down to a choppy sea and the hazy Orkneys beyond, but the feeling of spaciousness was exhilarating and for the first time in years I felt comparatively safe behind a wheel. There was absolutely nothing to crash into.

You really are on the edge of a great deal of emptiness when you reach the far north of Scotland. Only 27,000 people live in the whole of Caithness – roughly the population of Haywards Heath or Eastleigh in an area considerably larger than most English counties. More than half of that population is accounted for by just two towns, Thurso and Wick, and none of it by John O'Groats since John O'Groats isn't a community at all but just a place to stop and buy postcards and ice-creams.

It is named for Jan de Groot, a Dutchman who ran a ferry service from there to somewhere else (Amsterdam if he had any sense) in the fifteenth century. He charged 4d a trip apparently, and they will tell you in these parts that that sum became known ever after as a groat, but alas it is a pathetic fiction. It is more probable that Groot was named Groat after the money rather than it for he. But anyway who gives a shit?

Today John O'Groats consists of a capacious car park, a little harbour, a lonely white hotel, a couple of ice-cream kiosks and three or four shops selling postcards, sweaters and videos by a singer named Tommy Scott. I thought there was supposed to be a famous finger-sign telling you how far it was to Sydney and Los Angeles, but I couldn't find it; perhaps they take it in out of season so that people like me don't carry it off as a souvenir. Only one of the shops was open. I went in and was surprised to find that there were three middle-aged ladies working there, which seemed a bit excessive as I was obviously the only tourist for 400 miles. The ladies were exceedingly cheerful and chipper and greeted me warmly with those wonderful Highland accents – so clinically precise and yet so dulcet. I unfolded some jumpers so that they would have something to do after I left, watched open-mouthed a demo video for Tommy Scott singing perky Scottish tunes on various blowy headlands (I'm saying nothing), bought some postcards, had a lingering cup of coffee, chatted with the ladies about the weather, then stepped out into the

gusty car park and realized that I had about exhausted the
possibilities presented by John O'Groats.

I wandered around above the harbour, peered with hooded hands
into the windows of the little museum, which was closed till spring,
looked appreciatively at the view across the Pentland Firth to
Stroma and the Old Man of Hoy, and then wandered back to the
car. You probably know this already, but John O'Groats is not the
northernmost point of the Scottish mainland. That distinction
belongs to a spot called Dunnet Head, five or six miles away down
a nearby single-lane road, so I went there now. Dunnet Head offers
even less to the world in the way of diversions than John O'Groats,
but it has a handsome unmanned lighthouse and sensational sea
views, and a nice sense of being a long way from anywhere.

I stood on the gusty eminence gazing at the view for a long time,
waiting for some profundity to steal over me, since this was the end
of the line, as far as I was going. Part of me longed to catch a ferry
to the outward islands, to follow the scattered outcrops of stone all
the way up to distant Shetland, but I was out of time and anyway
there didn't seem a great deal of need. Whatever its bleak and airy
charms, Shetland would still be just another piece of Britain, with
the same shops, the same television programmes, the same people
in the same Marks & Spencer cardigans. I didn't find this depressing at all – rather the contrary – but I didn't feel any pressing need
to see it just now. It would still be there next time.

I had one more port of call in my hired Ford. Six or seven miles
south of Thurso lies the village of Halkirk, now forgotten but
famous during the Second World War as a deeply, *deeply* unpopular
posting for British soldiers on account of its remoteness and the
reputed unfriendliness of the locals. The soldiers sang a charming
little refrain that went

> *This fucking town's a fucking cuss*
> *No fucking trams, no fucking bus,*
> *Nobody cares for fucking us*
> *In fucking Halkirk*
>
> *No fucking sport, no fucking games,*
> *No fucking fun. The fucking dames*
> *Won't even give their fucking names*
> *In fucking Halkirk*

and carries on in a similarly affectionate spirit for another ten stanzas. (In answer to the obvious question, I'd looked earlier and, no, it wasn't one of Tommy Scott's standards.) So I went to Halkirk now, along the lonely B874. Well, there was nothing much to Halkirk – just a couple of streets on a road to nowhere, with a butcher's, a builder's merchants, two pubs, a little grocery, and a village hall with a war memorial. There was no sign that Halkirk had ever been more than a dreary little interruption to the general emptiness around it, but the memorial contained the names of sixty-three dead from the First World War (nine of them named Sinclair and five named Sutherland) and eighteen from the Second World War.

You could see for miles across grassy plains from the edges of the village, but there was no sign anywhere of tumbledown army barracks. In fact, there was no sign that there had ever been anything in this district but endless grassy plains. I went into the grocery in investigative mood. It was the strangest grocery – a large shed-like room, barely lit and nearly empty except for a couple of racks of metal shelves near the door. These, too, were nearly empty but for a few scattered packets of odds and ends. There was a man on the till and an old guy ahead of me making some small purchase, so I asked them about the army camp.

'Oh, aye,' said the proprietor. 'Big POW camp. We had fourteen thousand Germans here at the end of the war. There's a book here all about it.' To my small astonishment, given the meagreness of the other stocks, he had a stack of picture books by the till called *Caithness in the War* or something like that and he handed me one to examine. It was full of the usual pictures of bombed-out houses and pubs with people standing around scratching their heads in consternation or looking at the camera with those idiot grins that people in disaster pictures always wear, as if they're thinking, Well, at least we'll be in *Picture Post*. I didn't find any pictures of soldiers looking bored in Halkirk, and there wasn't any mention of the village in the index. The book was ambitiously priced at £15.95.

'Lovely book,' said the proprietor encouragingly. 'Good value.'

'We had fourteen thousand Germans here during the war,' said the old boy in a deaf bellow.

I couldn't think of a tactful way of asking about Halkirk's dire reputation. 'It must have been pretty lonely for the British soldiers, I bet,' I suggested speculatively.

'Oh, no, I don't think so,' disagreed the man. 'There's Thurso just down the road, you see, and Wick if you fancy a change. There was dancing back then,' he added a trifle ambiguously, then nodded at the book in my hands. 'Good value, that.'

'Is there anything left of the old base?'

'Well, the buildings are gone, of course, but if you go out the back way' – he gestured in the appropriate direction – 'you can still see the foundations.' He was silent for a moment and then he said, 'So will you be having the book?'

'Oh – well, I might come back for it,' I lied and handed it back.

'It's good value,' said the man.

'Fourteen thousand Germans there was,' called the older man as I left.

I had another look around the surrounding countryside on foot, and then drove around for a bit in the car, but I couldn't find any sign of a prison camp, and gradually it dawned on me that it hardly mattered, so in the end I drove back to Thurso and returned the car to the Ford dealer, to the frank surprise of the friendly fellow since it was only a little after two in the afternoon.

'Are you sure there isn't anywhere else you want to go?' he said. 'It seems a shame when you've hired the car for the day.'

'Where else could I go?' I asked.

He thought for a minute. 'Well, nowhere really.' He looked a little downcast.

'It's all right,' I said, 'I've seen plenty,' and I meant it in the broadest sense.

CHAPTER TWENTY-EIGHT

NOW HERE IS WHY I WILL ALWAYS STAY AT THE PENTLAND HOTEL WHEN I am in Thurso. The night before I left I asked the kindly lady at the checkout desk for a wake-up call at 5 a.m. as I had to catch an early train south. And she said to me – perhaps you should sit down if you are not sitting already – she said, 'Would you like a cooked breakfast?'

I thought she must be a bit dim, frankly, so I said: 'I'm sorry, I meant five *a*.m. I'll be leaving at half-past five, you see. Half-past five a.m. In the morning.'

'Yes, dear. Would you like a cooked breakfast?'

'At five a.m.?'

'It's included in the room rate.'

And damn me if this wonderful little establishment didn't fix me up with a handsome plate of fried food and a pot of hot coffee at 5.15 the following pre-dawn.

And so I left the hotel a happy and fractionally fatter man, and waddled up the road in darkness to the station and there met my second surprise of the morning. The place was packed with women, all standing around on the platform in festive spirits, filling the chill, dark air with clouds of breath and happy Highland chatter, and waiting patiently for the guard to finish his fag and open the train doors.

I asked a lady what was up and she told me they were all off to Inverness to do their shopping. It was like this every Saturday. They would ride for the best part of four hours, stock up on Marks & Spencer's knickers and plastic vomit and whatever else Inverness had that Thurso hadn't, which was quite a lot, then catch the 6 p.m. train home, arriving back in time for bed.

And so we rode through the misty early morning, a great crowd of us, crammed snugly together on a two-carriage train, in happy, expectant mood. At Inverness the train terminated and we all piled off, the ladies to do their shopping, I to catch the 10.35 to Glasgow. As I watched them go, I found to my small surprise that I rather envied them. It seemed an extraordinary business, the idea of rising before dawn to do a little shopping in a place like Inverness and then not getting home till after ten, but on the other hand I don't think I had ever seen such a happy band of shoppers.

The little train to Glasgow was nearly empty and the countryside lushly scenic. We went through Aviemore, Pitlochry, Perth and on to Gleneagles, with a pretty station, now sadly boarded. And then at last, some eight hours after rising from my bed that morning, we were in Glasgow. It seemed odd after so many long hours of travelling to step from Queen Street Station and find myself still in Scotland.

At least it wasn't a shock to the system. I remember when I first came to Glasgow in 1973 stepping from this very station and being profoundly stunned at how suffocatingly dark and soot-blackened the city was. I had never seen a place so choked and grubby. Everything in it seemed black and cheerless. Even the local accent seemed born of clinkers and grit. St Mungo's Cathedral was so dark that even from across the road it looked like a two-dimensional cut-out. And there were no tourists – none at all. Glasgow may be the largest city in Scotland, but my *Let's Go* guide to Europe didn't even mention it.

In the subsequent years Glasgow has, of course, gone through a glittering and celebrated transformation. Scores of old buildings in the city centre have been sandblasted and lovingly buffed, so that their granite surfaces gleam anew, and dozens more were vigorously erected in the heady boom years of the 1980s – more than £1 billion of new offices in the previous decade alone. The city acquired one of the finest museums in the world in the Burrell Collection and one of the most intelligent pieces of urban renewal in the Princes Square shopping centre. Suddenly the world began cautiously to come to Glasgow and thereupon discovered to its delight that this was a city densely endowed with splendid museums, lively pubs, world-class orchestras, and no fewer than seventy parks, more than any other city of its size in Europe. In

1990, Glasgow was named European City of Culture, and no-one laughed. Never before had a city's reputation undergone a more dramatic and sudden transformation – and none, as far as I am concerned, deserves it more.

Among the city's many treasures, none shines brighter, in my view, than the Burrell Collection. After checking into my hotel, I hastened there now by taxi, for it is a long way out.

'D'ye nae a lang roon?' said the driver as we sped along a motorway towards Pollok Park by way of Clydebank and Oban.

'I'm sorry,' I said for I don't speak Glaswegian.

'D'ye dack ma fanny?'

I hate it when this happens – when a person from Glasgow speaks to me. 'I'm so sorry,' I said and floundered for an excuse. 'My ears are very bad.'

'Aye, ye nae hae doon a lang roon,' he said, which I gathered meant 'I'm going to take you a very long way around and look at you a lot with these menacing eyes of mine so that you'll begin to wonder if perhaps I'm taking you to a disused warehouse where friends of mine are waiting to beat you up and take your money,' but he said nothing further and delivered me at the Burrell without incident.

How I like the Burrell Collection. It is named for Sir William Burrell, a Scottish shipowner, who in 1944 left the city his art collection on the understanding that it be placed in a country setting within the city boundaries. He was worried – not unreasonably – about air pollution damaging his artworks. Unable to decide what to do with this sumptuous windfall, the city council did, astonishingly, nothing. For the next thirty-nine years, some truly exceptional works of art lay crated away in warehouses, all but forgotten. Finally in the late 1970s, after nearly four decades of dithering, the city engaged a gifted architect named Barry Gasson, who designed a trim and restrained building noted for its airy rooms set against a woodland backdrop and for the ingenious way architectural features from Burrell's Collection – medieval doorways and lintels and the like – were incorporated into the fabric of the building. It opened in 1983 to widespread acclaim.

Burrell was not an especially rich man, but goodness me he could select. The gallery contains only 8,000 items but they come from all over – from Mesopotamia, Egypt, Greece and Rome – and nearly every one of them (with the exception of some glazed porcelain figurines of flower girls, which he must have picked up during a fever) is stunning. I spent a long, happy afternoon wandering through the many rooms, pretending, as I sometimes do in these circumstances, that I had been invited to take any one object home with me as a gift from the Scottish people in recognition of my fineness as a person. In the end, after much agonizing, I settled on a Head of Persephone from fifth-century-BC Sicily, which was not only as stunningly flawless as if it had been made yesterday, but would have looked just perfect on top of the TV. And thus late in the afternoon, I emerged from the Burrell and into the leafy agreeability of Pollok Park in a happy frame of mind.

It was a mild day, so I decided to walk back to town even though I had no map and only the vaguest idea of where the distant centre of Glasgow lay. I don't know if Glasgow is truly a wonderful city for walking or whether I have just been lucky there, but I have never wandered through it without encountering some memorable surprise – the green allure of Kelvingrove Park, the Botanic Gardens, the fabulous Necropolis cemetery with its ranks of ornate tombs – and so it was now. I set off hopefully down a broad avenue called St Andrews Drive and found myself adrift in a handsome district of houses of substance and privilege with a comely park with a little lake. At length I passed the Scotland Street Public School, a wonderful building with airy stairwells that I presumed was one of Mackintosh's, and soon after found myself in a seamier but no less interesting district, which I eventually concluded must be the Gorbals. And then I got lost.

I could see the Clyde from time to time, but I couldn't figure out how to get to it or, more crucially, over it. I wandered along a series of back lanes and soon found myself in one of those dead districts that consist of windowless warehouses and garage doors that say NO PARKING – GARAGE IN CONSTANT USE. I took a series of turns that seemed to lead ever further away from society before finally bumbling into a short street that had a pub on the corner. Fancying a drink and a sitdown, I wandered inside. It was a dark place, and battered, and there were only two other customers, a pair of larcenous-looking men sitting side by side at the bar drinking in silence. There was no-one behind the bar. I took a stance at the far end of the counter and waited for a bit, but no-one came. I drummed my fingers on the counter and puffed my cheeks and made assorted puckery shapes with my lips the way you do when you are waiting. (And just why do we do that, do you suppose? It isn't even privately entertaining in the extremely low-level way that, say, peeling a blister or cleaning your fingernails with a thumbnail is.) I cleaned my nails with a thumbnail and puffed my cheeks some more, but still no-one came. Eventually I noticed one of the men at the bar eyeing me.

'Hae ya nae hook ma dooky?' he said.

'I'm sorry?' I replied.

'He'll nay be doon a mooning.' He hoiked his head in the direction of a back room.

'Oh, ah,' I said and nodded sagely, as if that explained it.

I noticed that they were both still looking at me.

'D'ye hae a hoo and a poo?' said the first man to me.

'I'm sorry?' I said.

'D'ye hae a hoo and a *poo*?' he repeated. It appeared that he was a trifle intoxicated.

I gave a small, apologetic smile and explained that I came from the English-speaking world.

'D'ye nae hae in May?' the man went on. 'If ye dinna dock ma donny.'

'Doon in Troon they croon in June,' said his mate, then added: 'Wi' a spoon.'

'Oh, ah.' I nodded thoughtfully again, pushing my lower lip out slightly, as if it was all very nearly clear to me now. Just then, to my small relief, the barman appeared, looking unhappy and wiping his hands on a tea towel.

'Fuckin muckle fucket in the fuckin muckle,' he said to the two men, and then to me in a weary voice: 'Ah hae the noo.' I couldn't tell if it was a question or a statement.

'A pint of Tennent's, please,' I said hopefully.

He made an impatient noise, as if I were avoiding his question. 'Hae ya nae hook ma dooky?'

'I'm sorry?'

'Ah hae the noo,' said the first customer, who apparently saw himself as my interpreter.

I stood for some moments with my mouth open, trying to imagine what they were saying to me, wondering what mad impulse had bidden me to enter a pub in a district like this, and said in a quiet voice: 'Just a pint of Tennent's, I think.'

The barman sighed heavily and got me a pint. A minute later, I realized that what they were saying to me was that this was the worst pub in the world in which to order lager since all I would get was a glass of warm soap suds, dispensed from a gasping, reluctant tap, and that really I should flee with my life while I could. I drank two sips of this interesting concoction, and, making as if I were going to the Gents', slipped out a side door.

And so I returned to the twilit streets along the south bank of the Clyde and tried to find my way back to the known world. It's nearly impossible to imagine what the Gorbals must have been like before they started tarting it up and inviting daring yuppies to move into smart new blocks of flats around its fringes. After the war, Glasgow did the most extraordinary thing. It built vast estates of shiny tower blocks out in the countryside and decanted tens of thousands of people from inner-city slums like the Gorbals into them, but it forgot to provide any infrastructure. Forty thousand people were moved to the Easterhouse estate alone and when they got there they found smart new flats with indoor plumbing, but no cinemas, no shops, no banks, no pubs, no schools, no jobs, no health centres, no doctors. So every time they wanted anything, like a drink or work or medical attention, they had to climb aboard a bus and ride for miles back into the city. In consequence of this and other considerations like lifts that were forever breaking down (and why, incidentally, does Britain alone among nations have so much difficulty with moving conveyances like escalators and lifts? I think some heads should roll, frankly) they grew peevish and turned them into new slums. The result is that Glasgow has some of the worst housing problems in the developed world. Glasgow Council is the largest landlord in Europe. Its 160,000 houses and flats represent half the city's total housing stock. By its own estimates the council needs to spend something like £3 billion to bring the housing up to standard. That doesn't include provisions for new housing, but simply making existing housing habitable. At the moment its entire housing budget is about £100 million a year.

At length, I found my way over the river and back into the gleaming centre. I had a look at George Square, which is to my mind the handsomest in Britain, and then trudged uphill to Sauchiehall Street, where I remembered my favourite Glasgow joke. (Also my only Glasgow joke.) It's not a very good one, but I like it. A policeman collars a thief at the corner of Sauchiehall and Dalhousie, then drags him by the hair for a hundred yards to Rose Street to book him.

'Oi, why'd ye do *tha*'?' asks the aggrieved culprit, rubbing his head.

'Because I can spell Rose Street, ye thieving cunt,' says the policeman.

That's the thing about Glasgow. It has all this newfound prosperity and polish, but right at the very edge of things there is always this sense of grit and menace, which I find oddly exhilarating. You can wander through the streets on a Friday night, as I did now, and never know when you turn a corner whether you are going to bump into a group of tony revellers in dinner jackets or a passle of idle young yobboes who might decide to fall upon you and carve their initials in your forehead for purposes of passing amusement. Gives the place a certain tang.

CHAPTER TWENTY-NINE

I SPENT ANOTHER DAY IN GLASGOW POKING ABOUT, NOT SO MUCH because I wanted to be there, but because it was a Sunday and I couldn't get a train home beyond Carlisle. (The Settle-to-Carlisle service doesn't run on Sundays in winter because there is no demand for its services. That there may be no demand for its services because it doesn't run appears not to have occurred to British Rail.) So I wandered far and wide through the wintry streets, and had a respectful look round the museums, Botanic Gardens and Necropolis, but really all I wanted to do was go home, which was understandable, I think, because I missed my family and my own bed and, besides, when I walk around my home I don't have to watch out for dog shit and vomit slicks with every step I take.

And so the following morning, in a state of giddy excitement, I boarded the 8.10 from Glasgow Central to Carlisle and there, after a refreshing cup of coffee in the station buffet, caught the 11.40 train to Settle.

The Settle-to-Carlisle line is the most celebrated obscure line in the world. British Rail has been wanting to close it down for years on the grounds that it doesn't pay its way, which is the most mad and preposterous line of argument imaginable.

We've been hearing this warped reasoning for so long about so many things that it has become received wisdom, but when you think about it for even a nanosecond it is perfectly obvious that most worthwhile things don't begin to pay for themselves. If you followed this absurd logic any distance at all, you would have to get rid of traffic lights, lay-bys, schools, drains, national parks, museums, universities, old people and much else besides. So why on earth should something as useful as a railway line, which is generally much more agreeable than old people, and certainly less inclined to bitch and twitter, have to demonstrate even the tiniest measure of economic viability to ensure its continued existence? This is a line of thinking that must be abandoned at once.

Having said that, it can't be denied that the Settle-to-Carlisle line has always had something of the air of folly about it. In 1870, when James Allport, general manager of the Midland Railway, took it into his head to build a main line north, there was already an east coast line and a west coast line, so he decided to drive one up the middle, even though it went from nowhere much to nowhere much by way of nothing at all. The whole thing cost £3.5 million, which doesn't sound much now, but translates to some fantastic sum like £487 trillion billion or something. Anyway, it was enough to convince everyone who knew anything about railways that Allport was totally off his head – as in fact he was.

Because the line went through an insanely bleak and forbidding stretch of the Pennines, Allport's engineers had to come up with all kinds of contrivances to make it work, including twenty viaducts and twelve tunnels. This wasn't some eccentric, pootling narrow-gauge line, you understand; this was the nineteenth century's bullet train, something that would allow passengers to fly across the Yorkshire Dales – if, that is, anyone had wanted to, and hardly anyone did.

So from the very beginning it lost money. But who cares? It is a wonderful line, gorgeous in every respect, and I intended to enjoy every minute of my one-hour-and-forty-minute, 71¾-mile journey. Even when you live near Settle, it isn't often you find a reason to use the line, so I sat with my face close to the glass and waited eagerly for the line's famous landmarks – Blea Moor Tunnel, almost 2,300 yards long; Dent Station, the highest in the country; the glorious Ribblehead Viaduct, a quarter of a mile long, 104 feet high and with twenty-four graceful arches – and in between I enjoyed the scenery, which is not just spectacular and unrivalled but speaks to me with a particular siren voice.

I suppose everybody has a piece of landscape somewhere that he finds captivating beyond words and mine is the Yorkshire Dales. I can't altogether account for it because you can easily find more dramatic landscapes elsewhere, even in Britain. All I can say is that the Dales seized me like a helpless infatuation when I first saw them and will not let me go. Partly, I suppose, it is the exhilarating contrast between the high fells, with their endless views, and the relative lushness of the valley floors, with their clustered villages and green farms. To drive almost anywhere in the Dales is to make a constant transition between these two hypnotic zones. It is wonderful beyond words. And partly it is the snug air of self-containment that the enclosing hills give, a sense that the rest of the world is far away and unnecessary, which is something you come to appreciate very much when you live there.

Every dale is a little world of its own to an extraordinary degree. I remember one sunny afternoon when we were new to our dale a car overturned in the road outside our gate with a frightful bang and a noise of scraping metal. The driver, it turned out, had clipped a grass bank and run up against a field wall, which had flipped the car onto its roof. I rushed out to find a local woman hanging upside down by her seatbelt, bleeding gently from a scalp wound and muttering dazed sentiments along the lines of having to get to the dentist and that this wouldn't do at all. While I was hopping around and making hyperventilating noises, two farmers arrived in a Land-Rover and climbed out. They gently hauled the lady from the car and sat her down on a rock. Then they righted the car and manoeuvred it out of the way. While one of them led the lady off to have a cup of tea and get her head seen to by his wife, the other scattered sawdust on an oil slick, directed traffic for a minute till the road was clear, then winked at me and climbed into his Land-Rover and drove off. The whole thing was over in less than five minutes and never involved the police or ambulance services or even a doctor. An hour or so later someone came along with a tractor and hauled the car away and it was as if it had never happened.

They do things differently in the Dales, you see. For one thing, people who know you come right in your house. Sometimes they knock once and shout 'Hullo!' before sticking their head in, but often they don't even do that. It's an unusual experience to be standing at the kitchen sink talking to yourself animatedly and doing lavish, raised-leg farts and then turning around to find a fresh pile of mail lying on the kitchen table. And I can't tell you the number of times I've had to dart into the pantry in my underpants at the sound of someone's approach and cowered breathless while they've shouted, 'Hullo! Hullo! Anyone t'home?' For a couple of minutes you can hear them clumping around in the kitchen, examining the messages on the fridge and holding the mail to the light. Then they come over to the pantry door and in a quiet voice they say, 'Just taking six eggs, Bill – all right?'

When we announced to friends and colleagues in London that we were moving to a village in Yorkshire, a surprising number made a sour face and said: 'Yorkshire? What, with Yorkshire people? How very . . . interesting.' Or words to that effect.

I've never understood why Yorkshire people have this terrible reputation for being mean-spirited and uncharitable. I've always found them to be decent and open, and if you want to know your shortcomings, you won't find more helpful people anywhere. It's true that they don't exactly smother you with affection, which takes a little getting used to if you hail from a more gregarious part of the world, like anywhere else. Where I come from in the American Midwest if you move into a village or little town everybody comes to your house to welcome you like this is the happiest day in the history of the community – and everyone brings you a pie. You get apple pies and cherry pies and chocolate-cream pies. There are people in the Midwest who move house every six months just to get the pies.

In Yorkshire, that would never happen. But gradually, little by little, they find a corner for you in their hearts, and begin to acknowledge you when they drive past with what I call the Malhamdale wave. This is an exciting day in the life of any new arrival. To make the Malhamdale wave, pretend for a moment that you are grasping a steering wheel. Now very slowly extend the index finger of your right hand as if you were having a small in-voluntary spasm. That's it. It doesn't look like much, but it speaks volumes, believe me, and I shall miss it very much.

I lost myself in a little reverie along these lines and then, with a start, I realized I was in Settle and my wife was waving to me from the platform. Suddenly my trip was over. I hastened from the train in a state of confusion, like someone wakened in the middle of the night by an emergency, and felt as if this was somehow not the right termination at all. This was all too abrupt.

We drove home over the tops, a winding, six-mile drive of unutterable loveliness, up on to the *Wuthering Heights*-like expanses around Kirkby Fell, with boundless views of Northern glory, and then began the descent into the serene, cupped majesty of Malhamdale, the little lost world that had been my home for seven years. Halfway down, I had my wife stop the car by a field gate. My favourite view in the world is there, and I got out to have a look. You can see almost the whole of Malhamdale; sheltered and snug beneath steep, imposing hills, with its arrow-straight drystone walls climbing up impossibly ambitious slopes, its clustered hamlets, its wonderful little two-room schoolhouse, the old church with its sycamores and tumbling tombstones, the roof of my local pub, and in the centre of it all, obscured by trees, our old stone house, which itself is far older than my native land.

It looked so peaceful and wonderful that I could almost have cried, and yet it was only a tiny part of this small, enchanted island. Suddenly, in the space of a moment, I realized what it was that I loved about Britain – which is to say, all of it. Every last bit of it, good and bad – Marmite, village fêtes, country lanes, people saying 'mustn't grumble' and 'I'm terribly sorry but', people apologizing to *me* when I conk them with a careless elbow, milk in bottles, beans on toast, haymaking in June, stinging nettles, seaside piers, Ordnance Survey maps, crumpets, hot-water bottles as a necessity, drizzly Sundays – every bit of it.

What a wondrous place this was – crazy as fuck, of course, but adorable to the tiniest degree. What other country, after all, could possibly have come up with place names like Tooting Bec and Farleigh Wallop, or a game like cricket that goes on for three days and never seems to start? Who else would think it not the least odd to make their judges wear little mops on their heads, compel the Lord Chancellor to sit on something called the Woolsack, or take pride in a naval hero whose dying wish was to be kissed by a fellow named Hardy? ('Please, Hardy, full on the lips, with just a bit of tongue.') What other nation in the world could possibly have given us William Shakespeare, pork pies, Christopher Wren, Windsor Great Park, the Open University, *Gardeners' Question Time* and the chocolate digestive biscuit? None, of course.

How easily we lose sight of all this. What an enigma Britain will seem to historians when they look back on the second half of the twentieth century. Here is a country that fought and won a noble war, dismantled a mighty empire in a generally benign and enlightened way, created a far-seeing welfare state – in short, did nearly everything right – and then spent the rest of the century looking on itself as a chronic failure. The fact is that this is still the best place in the world for most things – to post a letter, go for a walk, watch television, buy a book, venture out for a drink, go to a museum, use the bank, get lost, seek help, or stand on a hillside and take in a view.

All of this came to me in the space of a lingering moment. I've said it before and I'll say it again. I like it here. I like it more than I can tell you. And then I turned from the gate and got in the car and knew without doubt that I would be back.

NOTES from a BIG COUNTRY

CONTENTS

ACKNOWLEDGEMENTS

I am deeply indebted to the following people for various expressions of kindness, patience, generosity and drink: Simon Kelner and all his dear, wonderful colleagues on *Night & Day*, including Tristan Davies, Kate Carr, Ian Johns, Rebecca Carswell and Nick Donaldson; Alan Baker for his ever-droll and inventive illustrations to the column; Patrick Janson-Smith, Marianne Velmans, Alison Tulett, Larry Finlay, Katrina Whone and Emma Dowson, among many, many others, at Transworld Publishers; my agent Carol Heaton; my old pal David Cook for yet another brilliant jacket; Allan Sherwin and Brian King for letting me write columns when I should have been doing work for them; and above all – way above all – my wife, Cynthia, and children, David, Felicity, Catherine and Sam, for so graciously letting me drag them into all this.

And a special thanks to little Jimmy, whoever he may be.

INTRODUCTION

In the late summer of 1996 Simon Kelner, who is both an old friend and an exceptionally nice fellow, rang me up in New Hampshire and asked me if I would write a weekly column about America for the *Mail on Sunday*'s *Night & Day* magazine, to which he had recently been appointed editor.

At various times over the years Simon had persuaded me to do all kinds of work that I didn't have time to do, but this was way out of the question.

'No,' I said. 'I can't. I'm sorry. It's just not possible.'

'So can you start next week?'

'Simon, you don't seem to understand. I can't do it.'

'We thought we'd call it "Notes from a Big Country".'

'Simon, you'll have to call it "Blank Space at the Start of the Magazine" because I cannot do it.'

'Great,' he said, but a trifle absently. I had the impression that he was doing something else at the time – reviewing models for a swimsuit issue would be my guess. In any case, he kept covering up the phone and issuing important editor-type instructions to other people in the vicinity.

'So we'll send you a contract,' he went on when he came back to me.

'No, Simon, don't do that. I can't write a weekly column for you. It's as simple as that. Are you taking this in? Simon, tell me you are taking this in.'

'Wonderful. I'm so pleased. Well, must run.'

'Simon, please listen to me. I can't do a weekly column. Just not possible. Simon, are you listening? Simon? Hello? Simon, are you there? Hello? Bugger.'

So here are seventy-eight columns from the first eighteen months of 'Notes from a Big Country'. And the thing is, I really *didn't* have time for this.

COMING HOME

I ONCE JOKED IN A BOOK THAT THERE ARE THREE THINGS YOU CAN'T do in life. You can't beat the phone company, you can't make a waiter see you until he's ready to see you, and you can't go home again. For the last seventeen months I have been quietly, even gamely, reassessing point number three.

A year ago last May, after nearly two decades in England, I moved back to the States with my wife and children. Returning home after such an absence is a surprisingly unsettling business, a little like waking from a long coma. You quickly discover that time has wrought changes that leave you feeling mildly foolish and out of touch. You proffer hopelessly inadequate sums when making small purchases. You puzzle over vending machines and pay-phones, and are quite astounded to discover, by means of a stern grip on your elbow, that gas station road maps are no longer free.

In my case, the problem was intensified by the fact that I had left as a youth and was returning in middle age. All those things one does as an adult – take out mortgages, have children, accumulate pension plans, develop an interest in household wiring – I had only ever done in England. Things like furnaces and screened windows were, in an American context, the preserve of my father.

So finding myself suddenly in charge of an old New England home, with its mysterious pipes and thermostats, its temperamental garbage disposal and life-threatening automatic garage door, was both unnerving and rather exhilarating.

Moving home after many years away is like that in most respects – an odd blend of the comfortably familiar and oddly unknown. It is disconcerting to find yourself so simultaneously in your element and out of it. I can enumerate all manner of minutiae that mark me out as an American – which of the fifty states has a unicameral legislature, what a squeeze play is in baseball, who played Captain Kangaroo on TV. I even know about two-thirds of the words to 'The Star-Spangled Banner', which is more than some people who have sung it publicly.

But send me to the hardware store and even now I am totally lost. For months I had conversations with the sales clerk at our local True-Value that went something like this:

'Hi. I need some of that stuff you fill holes in walls with. My wife's people call it Polyfilla.'

'Oh, you mean spackle.'

'Very possibly. And I need some of those little plastic things that you use to hold screws in the wall when you put shelves up. I know them as Rawlplugs.'

'Well, we call them *anchors*.'

'I shall make a mental note of it.'

Really, I could hardly have felt more foreign if I had stood there dressed in lederhosen. All this was a shock to me. Although I was always very happy in Britain, I never stopped thinking of America as home, in the fundamental sense of the term. It was where I came from, what I really understood, the base against which all else was measured.

In a funny way nothing makes you feel *more* like a native of your own country than to live where nearly everyone is not. For twenty years being an American was my defining quality. It was how I was identified, differentiated. I even got a job on the strength of it once when, in a moment of youthful audacity, I asserted to a senior editor of *The Times* that I would be the only person on the staff who could reliably spell Cincinnati. (And it was so.)

Happily, there is a flipside to this. The many good things about America also took on a bewitching air of novelty. I was as dazzled as any foreigner by the famous ease and convenience of daily life, the giddying abundance of absolutely everything, the wondrous un-fillable vastness of an American basement, the delight of encountering waitresses who seemed to be enjoying themselves, the curiously astounding notion that ice is not a luxury item.

As well, there has been the constant, unexpected joy of re-encountering those things I grew up with but had largely for-gotten: baseball on the radio, the deeply satisfying *whoing-bang* a number of such breathtaking complexity? If every neutrino in the universe, every particle of matter between here and the furthest wisp of receding Big Bang gas, somehow acquired a computer from this company there would still be plenty of spare numbers under such a system.

Intrigued, I began to look at all the numbers in my life, and nearly every one of them was absurdly excessive. My Barclaycard number, for instance, has thirteen digits. That's enough for almost 2 *trillion* potential customers. Who are they trying to kid? My Budget Rent-a-Car card has no fewer than seventeen digits. Even my local video shop appears to have 1.999 billion customers on its rolls (which may explain why *L.A. Confidential* is always out).

The most impressive by far is my Blue Cross/Blue Shield medical card – that is the card every American must carry if he doesn't want to be left at an accident site – which not only identifies me as No. YGH475907018 00, but also as a member of Group 02368. Presumably, then, each group has a person in it with the same number as mine. You can almost imagine us having reunions.

Now all this is a long way of getting round to the main point of this discussion, which is that one of the great improvements in American life in the last twenty years is the advent of phone numbers that any fool can remember. Let me explain.

For complicated historical reasons, on American telephones all the punch buttons except 1 and 0 also come with three of the letters of the alphabet on them. Button 2 has ABC on it, button 3 has DEF, and so on.

A long time ago people realized that you could remember numbers more easily if you relied on the letters rather than the numbers. In my hometown of Des Moines, for instance, if you wanted to call time – or the talking clock as you people so charm-ingly term it – the official number was 244-5646, which of course no-one could recall. But if you dialled BIG JOHN you got the same number, and everybody could remember that (except, curiously, my mother, who was a bit hazy on the Christian name part, and so generally ended up asking the time of strangers whom she had just woken, but that's another story).

Then at some point in the last twenty years big businesses discovered that they could make everyone's life easier, and generate lots of lucrative calls for themselves, if they based their numbers on catchy letter combinations. So now any time you make almost any call to a commercial enterprise you dial 1-800-FLY TWA, or

244-GET PIZZA, or whatever. Not many changes in the last twenty years have made life immeasurably better for simple folk like me, but this unquestionably has.

So while you, poor thing, are listening to a schoolmarmish voice telling you that the code for Chippenham is now 01724750, except with a four-figure number, when it is 9, I am eating pizza, booking airline tickets and feeling considerably less churlish about modern telecommunications.

Now here is my big idea. I think we should all have one number for everything. Mine, of course, would be 1-800-BILL. This number would do for everything – it would make my phone ring, it would appear on my cheques, it would adorn my passport, it would get me a video.

Of course, it would mean rewriting a lot of computer programs, but I'm sure it could be done. I intend to take it up with my own computer company, just as soon as I can get at that serial number again.

WELL, DOCTOR, I WAS JUST
TRYING TO LIE DOWN . . .

HERE'S A FACT FOR YOU. ACCORDING TO THE LATEST *STATISTICAL Abstract of the United States*, every year more than 400,000 Americans suffer injuries involving beds, mattresses or pillows. Think about that for a minute. That is more people than live in greater Coventry. That is almost 2,000 bed, mattress or pillow injuries a day. In the time it takes you to read this article, four Americans will somehow manage to be wounded by their bedding.

My point in raising this is not to suggest that Americans are somehow more inept than the rest of the world when it comes to lying down for the night (though clearly there are thousands who could do with additional training), but rather to observe that there is scarcely a statistic to do with this vast and scattered nation that doesn't in some way give one pause.

I had this brought home to me the other day when I was in our local library looking up something else altogether in the aforesaid *Abstract* and happened across 'Table No. 206: Injuries Associated with Consumer Products'. I have seldom passed a more diverting half-hour.

Consider this intriguing fact: almost 50,000 Americans are injured each year by pencils, pens and other desk accessories. How do they do it? I have spent many long hours sat at desks when I would have greeted almost any kind of injury as a welcome diversion, but never once have I come close to achieving actual bodily harm.

So I ask again: how do they do it? These are, bear in mind,

injuries severe enough to warrant a trip to an emergency room. Putting a staple in the tip of your index finger (which I *have* done quite a lot, sometimes only semi-accidentally) doesn't count. I am looking around my desk now and unless I put my head in the laser printer or stab myself with the scissors I cannot see a single source of potential harm within ten feet.

But then that's the thing about household injuries, if Table No. 206 is any guide – they can come at you from almost anywhere. Consider this one. In 1992 (the latest year for which figures are available) more than 400,000 people in the United States were injured by chairs, sofas and sofabeds. What are we to make of this? Does it tell us something trenchant about the design of modern furniture or merely that Americans are exceptionally careless sitters? What is certain is that the problem is worsening. The number of chair, sofa and sofabed injuries showed an increase of 30,000 over the previous year, which is quite a worrying trend even for those of us who are frankly fearless with regard to soft furnishings. (That may, of course, be the nub of the problem – overconfidence.)

Predictably, 'stairs, ramps and landings' was the most lively category, with almost 2 million startled victims, but in other respects dangerous objects were far more benign than their reputations might lead you to predict. More people were injured by sound-recording equipment (46,022) than by skateboards (44,068), trampolines (43,655), or even razors and razorblades (43,365). A mere 16,670 over-exuberant choppers ended up injured by hatchets and axes, and even saws and chainsaws claimed a relatively modest 38,692 victims.

Paper money and coins (30,274) claimed nearly as many victims as scissors (34,062). I can just about conceive how you might swallow a dime and then wish you hadn't ('You guys want to see a neat trick?'), but I cannot for the life of me construct hypothetical circumstances involving folding money and a subsequent trip to the ER. It would be interesting to meet some of these people.

I would also welcome a chat with almost any of the 263,000 people injured by ceilings, walls and inside panels. I can't imagine being hurt by a ceiling and not having a story worth hearing. Likewise, I could find time for any of the 31,000 people injured by their 'grooming devices'.

But the people I would really like to meet are the 142,000 hapless souls who received emergency-room treatment for injuries inflicted by their clothing. What *can* they be suffering from? Compound pyjama fracture? Sweatpants haematoma? I am powerless to speculate.

I have a friend who is an orthopaedic surgeon and he told me the other day that one of the occupational hazards of his job is that you get nervous about doing almost anything since you are constantly mending people who have come a cropper in unlikely and unpredictable ways. (Only that day he had treated a man who had a moose come through the windscreen of his car, to the consternation of both.) Suddenly, thanks to Table 206, I began to see what he meant.

Interestingly, what had brought me to the *Statistical Abstract* in the first place was the wish to look up crime figures for the state of New Hampshire, where I now live. I had heard that it is one of the safest places in America – and indeed the *Abstract* bore this out. There were just four murders in the state in the latest reporting year – compared with over 23,000 for the country as a whole – and very little serious crime.

All that this means, of course, is that statistically in New Hampshire I am far more likely to be hurt by my ceiling or underpants – to cite just two potentially lethal examples – than by a stranger, and frankly I don't find that comforting at all.

TAKE ME OUT TO THE BALL PARK

PEOPLE SOMETIMES ASK ME, 'WHAT IS THE DIFFERENCE BETWEEN baseball and cricket?'

The answer is simple. Both are games of great skill involving balls and bats, but with this crucial difference: baseball is exciting and when you go home at the end of the day you know who won.

I'm joking, of course. Cricket is a wonderful game, full of deliciously scattered micro-moments of real action. If a doctor ever instructs me to take a complete rest and not get over-excited, I shall become a fan at once. In the meantime, however, I hope you will understand when I tell you that my heart belongs to baseball.

It's what I grew up with, what I played as a boy, and that of course is vital to any meaningful appreciation of a sport. I had this brought home to me many years ago in England when I went out onto a football pitch with a couple of guys to knock a ball around.

I had watched football on TV and thought I had a fair idea of what was required, so when one of them lofted a ball in my direction, I decided to flick it casually into the net with my head, the way I had seen Kevin Keegan do it. I thought that it would be like heading a beachball – that there would be a gentle 'ponk' sound and that the ball would lightly leave my brow and drift in a pleasing arc into the net. But of course it was like heading a bowling ball. I have never felt anything so startlingly not like I expected it to feel. I walked around for four hours on wobbly legs with a big red circle and the word MITRE imprinted on my forehead, and vowed never again to do anything so foolish and painful.

I bring this up here because the World Series has just started and

I want you to know why I am very excited about it. The World Series, I should perhaps explain, is the annual baseball contest between the champion of the American League and the champion of the National League.

Actually, that's not quite true because they changed the system some years ago. The trouble with the old way of doing things was that it only involved two teams. Now you don't have to be a brain surgeon to work out that if you could somehow contrive to include more teams there would be a lot more money in the thing.

So each league divided itself into three divisions of four or five teams. Now, the World Series is not a contest between the two best teams in baseball – at least not necessarily – but rather between the winners of a series of playoff games involving the Western, Eastern and Central divisional champions of each league, plus (and this was particularly inspired, I think) a pair of 'wild card' teams that didn't win anything at all.

It is all immensely complicated, but essentially it means that practically every team in baseball except the Chicago Cubs gets a chance to go to the World Series.

The Chicago Cubs don't get to go because they never manage to qualify even under a system as magnificently accommodating as this. Often they *almost* qualify, and sometimes they are in such a commanding position that you cannot believe they won't qualify, but always in the end they doggedly manage to come up short. Whatever it takes – losing seventeen games in a row, letting easy balls go through their legs, crashing comically into each other in the outfield – you can be certain the Cubs will manage it.

They have been doing this, reliably and efficiently, for over half a century. They haven't been in a World Series since, I believe, 1938. Mussolini had good years more recently than that. This heartwarming annual failure by the Cubs is almost the only thing in baseball that hasn't changed in my lifetime, and I appreciate that very much.

It's not easy being a baseball fan because baseball fans are a hopelessly sentimental bunch, and there is no room for sentiment in something as wildly lucrative as an American sport. I haven't space here to elucidate all the misguided things they have done to my beloved game in the past forty years, so I'll just tell you the worst: they've torn down nearly all the great old stadiums and replaced them with big characterless, multi-purpose arenas.

It used to be that every big American city had a venerable ball park. Generally these were dank and creaky, but they had character. You would get splinters from the seats, the soles of your shoes would congeal to the floor from all the years of sticky stuff that had been spilled during exciting moments, and your view would inevitably be obscured by a cast-iron column supporting the roof, but that was all part of the glory.

There are only four of these old parks left. One is Fenway Park in Boston, home of the Red Sox. I won't say that Fenway's proximity was the absolute decisive consideration in our settling in New England, but it was a factor. Now the owners want to tear it down and build a new stadium. I keep saying that when they raze Fenway I won't go to the new stadium, but I know I'm lying because I am hopelessly addicted to the game.

All of which increases my respect and admiration for the hapless Chicago Cubs. To their eternal credit, the Cubs have never threatened to leave Chicago and continue to play at Wrigley Field. They even still play mostly day games – the way God intended baseball to be played. A day game at Wrigley Field is, believe me, one of the great American experiences.

And here's the problem. Nobody deserves to go to the World Series more than the Chicago Cubs. But they can't go because that would spoil their tradition of never going. It is an irreconcilable conflict. You see what I mean when I say that it is not easy being a baseball fan.

DUMB AND DUMBER

A FEW YEARS AGO AN ORGANIZATION CALLED THE NATIONAL ENDOWMENT for the Humanities tested 8,000 American high-school seniors and found that a very large number of them didn't know, well, anything.

Two-thirds had no idea when the US Civil War took place or which president penned the Gettysburg Address. Roughly the same proportion could not identify Joseph Stalin, Winston Churchill or Charles de Gaulle. A third thought that Franklin Roosevelt was president during the Vietnam War and that Columbus sailed to America after 1750. Forty-two per cent – this is my favourite – couldn't name a single country in Asia.

I am always a little dubious about these surveys because I know how easy it would be to catch me out. ('The study found that Bryson couldn't understand simple instructions for assembling a household barbecue and nearly always inadvertently washed both the front and back windscreens when driving round corners.') Still, there is a kind of emptiness of thought at large these days that is hard to overlook. The phenomenon is now widely known as the Dumbing Down of America.

I first noticed it myself a few months ago when I was watching something called the Weather Channel on TV and the meteorologist said, 'And in Albany today they had twelve inches of snow,' then brightly added, 'That's about a foot.'

No, actually that *is* a foot, you poor sad imbecile.

On the same night I was watching a documentary on the Discovery Channel (little realizing that I would be able to watch this same documentary on the Discovery Channel up to six times a month for the rest of eternity) when the narrator intoned: 'Owing to wind and rain, the Sphinx eroded by three feet in just three hundred years,' then paused and solemnly added: 'That's a rate of one foot a century.'

See what I mean? It sometimes feels as if nearly the whole nation has taken Nytol and that the effects haven't quite worn off. This isn't just some curious, occasional aberration. It happens all the time.

I was recently on a cross-country flight with Continental Airlines (suggested slogan: 'Not Quite the Worst') and, goodness knows why, I was reading that 'Letter from the President' that you get at the front of every airline magazine – the one that explains how they are constantly striving to improve services, evidently by making everyone change planes at Newark. Well, this one was about how they had just conducted a survey of their customers to find out their needs.

What the customers wanted, according to the incisive prose of Mr Gordon Bethune, President and CEO, was 'a clean, safe and reliable airline that took them where they wanted to go, on time and with their luggage'.

Gosh! Let me get a pen and a notebook! Did you say '*with* their luggage'? Wow!

Now don't get me wrong. I don't for a moment think that Americans are inherently more stupid or brain-dead than anyone else. It's just that they are routinely provided with conditions that spare them the need to think, and so they have got out of the habit.

Partly you can attribute it to what I call the 'London, England' syndrome, after the American newspaper practice of specifying the country as well as the city in datelines. If, say, the *New York Times* were to report on a British general election, it would dateline the story 'London, England', so that no reader anywhere would have to think: 'London? Now let's see, is that in Nebraska?'

American life is full of these little crutches, sometimes to a quite astonishing degree. A few months ago a columnist in the *Boston Globe* wrote a piece about unwittingly ridiculous advertisements and announcements – things like a notice in an optometrist's shop saying 'Eyes Examined While You Wait' – then carefully explained what was wrong with each one. ('Of course, it would be difficult to have your eyes examined *without* being there.')

It was excruciating, but hardly unusual. Just a couple of weeks ago a writer in the *New York Times* magazine did almost precisely the same thing, writing an essay on amusing linguistic misunderstandings and then explaining each in turn. For example, he noted that a friend of his had always thought the Beatles' lyric was 'the girl with colitis goes by', then chucklingly explained that in fact the lyric was— But *you* don't need me to tell you that, do you?

The idea is to spare the audience having to think. At all. Ever. I was recently asked by an American publication to remove a reference to David Niven 'because he's dead and we don't think he'll be familiar to some of our younger readers'.

Oh, but of course.

On another occasion when I made reference to someone in Britain attending a state school, an American researcher said to me: 'But I didn't think they had states in Britain.'

'I meant state in the rather broader sense of nation-state.'

'So you mean public schools?'

'Well, no, because public schools in Britain are private schools.'

Long pause. 'You're kidding.'

'It's a well-known fact.'

'So let me get this straight. They call private schools public schools in Britain?'

'Correct.'

'Then what do they call public schools?'

'State schools.'

Another long pause. 'But I didn't think they had states in Britain.'

But let us finish with my favourite inanity of the moment. It is the reply given by Bob Dole when he was asked to define the essence of his campaign.

'It's about the future,' he replied gravely, 'because that's where we're going.'

The scary thing is, he's right.

DRUG CULTURE

DO YOU KNOW WHAT I REALLY MISS NOW THAT I LIVE IN AMERICA? I miss coming in from the pub about midnight in a blurry frame of mind and watching Open University on TV. Honestly.

If I were to come in about midnight now all I would find on the TV is a series of nubile actresses disporting in the altogether, plus the Weather Channel, which is diverting in its way, I grant you, but it doesn't begin to compare with the hypnotic fascination of the Open University after six pints of beer. I'm quite serious about this.

I'm not at all sure why, but I always found it strangely compelling to turn on the TV late at night and find a guy who looked as if he had bought all the clothes he would ever need during one shopping trip to C&A in 1977 (so that he would be free to spend the rest of his waking hours around oscilloscopes) saying in an oddly characterless voice, 'And so we can see, adding two fixed-end solutions gives us another fixed-end solution.'

Most of the time I had no idea what he was talking about – that was a big part of what made it so compelling somehow – but very occasionally (well, once) the topic was something I could actually follow and enjoy. I'm thinking of an unexpectedly diverting documentary I chanced upon three or four years ago comparing the marketing of proprietary healthcare products in Britain and the United States.

The gist of the programme was that the same product had to be sold in entirely different ways in the two markets. An advertisement in Britain for a cold-relief capsule, for instance, would promise no more than that it might make you feel a bit better. You would still have a red nose and be in your dressing gown, but you would be smiling again, if wanly.

A commercial for the same product in America would guarantee total, instantaneous relief. An American who took this miracle compound would not only throw off his dressing gown and get back to work at once, he would feel better than he had for years and finish the day having the time of his life at a bowling alley.

The drift of all this was that the British don't expect over-the-counter drugs to change their lives, whereas Americans will settle for nothing less. The passing of the years has not, I can assure you, dulled the nation's touching faith in the notion.

You have only to watch any television channel for ten minutes, flip through a magazine or stroll along the groaning shelves of any drugstore to realize that Americans expect to feel more or less perfect all the time. Even our household shampoo, I notice, promises to 'change the way you feel'.

It is an odd thing about Americans. They expend huge efforts exhorting themselves to 'Say No to Drugs', then go to the drugstore and buy them by the armloads. Americans spend almost $75 billion a year on medicines of all types, and pharmaceutical products are marketed with a vehemence and forthrightness that can take a little getting used to.

In one commercial running on television at the moment, a pleasant-looking middle-aged lady turns to the camera and says in a candid tone: 'You know, when I get diarrhoea I like a little comfort.' (To which I always say: 'Why wait for diarrhoea?')

In another a man at a bowling alley (men are pretty generally at bowling alleys in these things) grimaces after a poor shot and mutters to his partner, 'It's these haemorrhoids again.' And here's the thing. The buddy has some haemorrhoid cream in his pocket! Not in his gym bag, you understand, not in the glovebox of his car, but in his shirt pocket, where he can whip it out at a moment's notice and call the gang round. Extraordinary.

But the really amazing change in the last twenty years is that now even prescription drugs are advertised. I have before me a popular magazine called *Health* that is just chock-full of ads with bold head-lines saying things like 'Why take two tablets when you can take one? Prempro is the only prescription tablet that combines Premarin and a progestin in one tablet,' or, 'Introducing Allegra, the new prescription seasonal allergy medicine that lets you get out there.'

Another more rakishly asks, 'Have you ever treated a vaginal yeast infection in the middle of nowhere?' (Not knowingly!) A fourth goes to the economic heart of the matter and declares, 'The doctor told me I'd probably be taking blood pressure pills for the rest of my life. The good news is how much I might save since he switched me to Adalat CC (nifedipine) from Procardia XL (nifedipine).'

The idea is that you read the advert, then badger your doctor (or 'healthcare professional') to prescribe it for you. It seems a curious concept to me, the idea of magazine readers deciding what medications are best for them, but then Americans appear to know a great deal about drugs. Nearly all the adverts assume an impressively high level of biochemical familiarity. The vaginal yeast ad confidently assures the reader that Diflucan is 'comparable to seven days of Monistat 7, Gyne-Lotrimin, or Mycelex-7', while the ad for Prempro promises that it is 'as effective as taking Premarin and a progestin separately'.

When you realize that these are meaningful statements for thousands and thousands of Americans, the idea of your bowling buddy carrying a tube of haemorrhoid unguent in his shirt pocket perhaps doesn't seem quite so ridiculous.

I don't know whether this national obsession with health is actually worth it. What I do know is that there is a much more agreeable way to achieve perfect inner harmony. Drink six pints of beer and watch Open University for ninety minutes before retiring. It has never failed for me.

MAIL CALL

ONE OF THE PLEASURES OF LIVING IN A SMALL, OLD-FASHIONED NEW England town is that you usually get a small, old-fashioned post office. Ours is particularly agreeable. It's in an attractive federal-style brick building, grand but not flashy, that looks like a post office ought to. It even smells nice – a combination of gum adhesive and old central heating turned up a little too high.

The counter staff are always briskly efficient and pleased to give you an extra piece of sticky tape if it looks as if your envelope flap might peel open. Moreover, American post offices deal only with postal matters – they don't concern themselves with pensions, car tax, family allowances, TV licences, passports, lottery tickets or any of the hundred other things that make a visit to any British post office such a popular, all-day event and provide a fulfilling and reliable diversion for chatty people who enjoy nothing so much as a good long hunt in their purses and handbags for exact change. Here there are never any queues and you are in and out in minutes.

Best of all, once a year every American post office has a Customer Appreciation Day. Ours was yesterday. I had never heard of this wonderful custom, but I was taken with it immediately. The employees had hung up banners, put out a long table with a nice checkered cloth and laid on a generous spread of doughnuts, pastries and hot coffee – all of it free.

It seemed a wonderfully improbable notion, the idea of a faceless government bureaucracy thanking me and my fellow townspeople for our patronage, but I was impressed and grateful – and, I must say, it was good to be reminded that postal employees are not just

mindless automatons who spend their days mangling letters and
whimsically sending my royalty cheques to a guy in Vermont
named Bill Bubba, but rather are dedicated, highly trained individuals who spend their days mangling letters and sending my
royalty cheques to a guy in Vermont named Bill Bubba.

Anyway, I was won over utterly. Now I would hate for you to
think that my loyalty with respect to postal delivery systems can be
cheaply bought with a chocolate twirl doughnut and a styrofoam cup
of coffee, but in fact it can. Much as I admire the Royal Mail, it has
never once offered me a morning snack, so I have to tell you that as
I strolled home from my errand, wiping crumbs from my face, my
thoughts towards American life in general and the US Postal Service
in particular were pretty incomparably favourable.

But, as nearly always with government services, it couldn't last.
When I got home, the day's mail was on the mat. There among the
usual copious invitations to acquire new credit cards, save a rain-
forest, become a life member of the National Incontinence
Foundation, add my name (for a small fee) to the *Who's Who of
People Named Bill in New England*, examine without obligation
Volume One of *Great Explosions*, help the National Rifle
Association with its Arm-a-Toddler campaign and the scores of
other unsought inducements, special offers and solicitations involving naff little adhesive rectangles with my name and address
already printed on them which arrive each day at every American
home – and you really cannot believe the volume of junk mail that
you receive in this country nowadays – well, among all this clutter
and detritus was a forlorn and mangled letter that I had sent forty-
one days earlier to a friend in California, care of his place of
employment, and that was now being returned to me marked
'Insufficient Address – Get Real and Try Again' or words to that
effect.

At the sight of this I issued a small despairing sigh, and not
merely because I had just sold the US Postal Service my soul for a
doughnut. It happens that I had recently read an article on
wordplay in the *Smithsonian* magazine in which the author asserted
that some puckish soul had once sent a letter addressed, with playful ambiguity, to

HILL
JOHN
MASS

and it had got there after the American postal authorities worked out that it was to be read as 'John Underhill, Andover, Mass.' (Get it?)

It's a nice story, and I would truly like to believe it, but the fate of my letter to California, freshly returned after a forty-one-day adventure trip to the west, seemed to suggest a need for caution with regard to the postal service and its sleuthing abilities.

The problem with my letter was that I had addressed it to my friend merely 'c/o Black Oak Books, Berkeley, California', without a street name or number because I didn't know either. I appreciate that that is not a complete address, but it is a lot more explicit than 'Hill John Mass' and anyway Black Oak Books is a Berkeley institution. Anyone who knows the city – and I had assumed in my quaintly naïve way that that would include the local postal authorities – would know Black Oak Books. But oh no. (Goodness knows, incidentally, what my letter had been *doing* in California for nearly six weeks, though it came back with a nice tan and an urge to get in touch with its inner feelings.)

Now just to give this plaintive tale a little heartwarming perspective, let me tell you that not long before I departed from England, the Royal Mail had brought me, within forty-eight hours of its posting in London, a letter addressed to 'Bill Bryson, Writer, Yorkshire Dales', which is a pretty impressive bit of sleuthing. (And never mind that the correspondent was a trifle off his head.)

So here I am, my affections torn between a postal service that never feeds me but can tackle a challenge, and one that gives me free sticky tape and prompt service but won't help me out when I can't remember a street name. The lesson to draw from this, of course, is that when you move from one country to another you have to accept that there are some things that are better and some things that are worse, and there's nothing you can do about it. That may not be the profoundest of insights, but I did get a free doughnut as well, so on balance I guess I'm happy.

Now if you will excuse me I have to drive to Vermont and collect some mail from a Mr Bubba.

HOW TO HAVE FUN AT HOME

MY WIFE THINKS NEARLY EVERYTHING ABOUT AMERICAN LIFE IS wonderful. She loves having her groceries bagged for her. She adores free iced water and bookmatches. She thinks home-delivered pizza is a central hallmark of civilization. I haven't the heart to tell her that waitresses in the States urge everyone to have a nice day.

Personally, while I am fond of America and grateful for its many conveniences, I am not quite so slavishly uncritical. Take the matter of having your groceries bagged for you. I appreciate the gesture, but when you come down to it what does it actually achieve except give you an opportunity to stand there and watch your groceries being bagged? It's not as if it buys you some quality time. I don't want to get heavy here, but given the choice between free iced water at restaurants and, let us say, a national health service, I have to say my instinct is to go with the latter.

However, there are certain things that are so wonderful in American life that I can hardly stand it myself. Chief among these, without any doubt, is the garbage disposal. A garbage disposal is everything a labour-saving device should be and so seldom is – noisy, fun, extremely hazardous, and so dazzlingly good at what it does that you cannot imagine how you ever managed without one. If you had asked me eighteen months ago what the prospects were that shortly my chief hobby would be placing assorted objects down a hole in the kitchen sink, I believe I would have laughed in your face, but in fact it is so.

I have never had a garbage disposal before, so I have been learning its tolerances through a process of trial and error.

Chopsticks give perhaps the liveliest response (this is not recommended, of course, but there comes a time with every piece of machinery when you just have to see what it can do), but cantaloupe rinds make the richest, throatiest sound and result in less 'down time'. Coffee grounds in quantity are the most likely to provide a satisfying 'Vesuvius effect', though for obvious reasons it is best not to attempt this difficult feat until your wife has gone out for the day, and to have a mop and stepladder standing by.

The most exciting event with a garbage disposal, of course, is when it jams and you have to reach in and unclog it, knowing that at any moment it might spring to life and abruptly convert your arm from a useful grasping tool into a dibber. Don't try to tell me about living life on the edge.

Equally satisfying in its way, and certainly no less ingenious, is the little-known fireplace ashpit. This is simply a metal plate – a kind of trapdoor – built into the floor of the living-room fireplace above a deep, brick-lined pit. When you clean the fireplace, instead of sweeping the ash into a bucket and then trailing the dribblings through the house, you manoeuvre it into this hole and it disappears for ever. Brilliant.

In theory the ashpit must eventually fill up, but ours seems to be bottomless. Down in the basement there's a small metal door in the wall that allows you to see how the pit is doing, and occasionally I go down to have a look. It isn't really necessary, but it gives me an excuse to go down in the basement, and I always welcome that because basements are the third great feature of American life. They are wonderful chiefly because they are so amazingly, so spaciously, useless.

Now basements I know because I grew up with one. Every American basement is the same. They all have a clothesline that is rarely used, a trickle of water from an indeterminable source running diagonally across the floor, and a funny smell – a combination of old magazines, camping gear that should have been aired and wasn't, and something to do with a guinea pig named Mr Fluffy that escaped down a central heating grate six months ago and has not been seen since (and presumably would now be better called Mr Bones).

Basements are so monumentally useless, in fact, that you seldom go down there, so it always comes as a surprise to remember that you have one. Every dad who ever goes down in a basement pauses at some point and thinks: Gee, we really ought to do something with all this space. We could have a cocktail cabinet and a pool table and maybe a jukebox and a jacuzzi and a couple of pinball machines . . . But of course it's just one of those things that you intend to do one day, like learn Spanish or take up home barbering, and never do.

Oh, occasionally, especially in starter homes, you will find that some young gung-ho dad has converted the basement into a play-room for the children, but this is always a mistake as no child will play in a basement. This is because no matter how loving your parents, no matter how much you would like to trust them, there is always the thought that they will quietly lock the door at the top of the stairs and move to Florida. No, basements are deeply and inescapably scary – that's why they always feature in spooky movies, usually with a shadow of Joan Crawford carrying an axe thrown on the far wall. That may be why even dads don't go down there very often.

I could go on and on cataloguing other small, unsung glories of American household life – refrigerators that dispense iced water and make their own icecubes, walk-in closets, electrical sockets in bathrooms – but I won't. I'm out of space and anyway Mrs B has just gone out to do some shopping and it has occurred to me that I have not yet seen what the disposal can do with a juice carton. I'll get back to you on this one.

DESIGN FLAWS

I HAVE A TEENAGED SON WHO IS A RUNNER. HE HAS, AT A CONSERVATIVE estimate, 6,100 pairs of running shoes, and every one of them represents a greater investment of cumulative design effort than, say, Milton Keynes.

These shoes are amazing. I was just reading a review in one of his running magazines of the latest in 'sport utility sneakers', as they are called here, and it was full of passages like this: 'A dual-density EVA midsole with air units fore and aft provides stability while a gel heel-insert absorbs shock, but the shoe makes a narrow foot-print, a characteristic that typically suits only the biomechanically efficient runner.' Alan Shepard went into space with less science at his disposal than that.

So here is my question. If my son can have his choice of a seemingly limitless range of scrupulously engineered, biomechanically efficient footwear, why does my computer keyboard suck? This is a serious enquiry.

My computer keyboard has 102 keys – almost double what my old manual typewriter had – which on the face of it seems awfully generous. Among other typographical luxuries, I can choose between three styles of bracket and two kinds of colon. I can dress my text with carets (^) and cedillas (¸). I can have slashes that fall to the left or to the right, and goodness knows what else.

I have so many keys, in fact, that over on the right-hand side of the keyboard there are whole communities of buttons of whose function I haven't the tiniest inkling. Occasionally I hit one by accident and subsequently discover that several paragraphs of my

w9rk n+w look l*ke th?s, or that I have written the last page and a
half in an interesting but unfortunately non-alphabetic font called
Wingdings, but otherwise I haven't the faintest idea what those
buttons are there for.

Never mind that many of these keys duplicate the functions of
other keys, while others apparently do nothing at all (my favourite
in this respect is one marked 'Pause', which when pressed does
absolutely nothing, raising the interesting metaphysical question of
whether it is therefore doing its job), or that several keys are
arrayed in slightly imbecilic places. The delete key, for instance, is
right beside the overprint key, so that often I discover, with a trill
of gay laughter, that my most recent thoughts have been devouring,
Pacman-like, everything I had previously written. Quite often, I
somehow hit a combination of keys that summons a box which
says, in effect, 'This Is a Pointless Box. Do You Want It?' which is
followed by another that says, 'Are You *Sure* You Don't Want the
Pointless Box?' Never mind all that. I have known for a long time
that the computer is not my friend.

But here is what gets me. Out of all the 102 keys at my disposal,
there is no key for the fraction ½. Typewriter keyboards always used
to have a key for ½. Now, however, if I wish to write ½, I have to
bring down the font menu and call up a directory called 'WP
Characters', then hunt through a number of sub-directories until I
remember or more often blunder on the particular one, 'Typographic
Symbols', in which hides the furtive ½ sign. This is irksome and
pointless and it doesn't seem right to me.

But then most things in the world don't seem right to me. On the
dashboard of our family car is a shallow indentation about the size
of a paperback book. If you are looking for somewhere to put your
sunglasses or spare change, it is the obvious place, and it works
extremely well, I must say, so long as the car is not actually moving.
As soon as you put the car in motion, however, and particularly
when you touch the brakes, turn a corner, or go up a gentle slope,
everything slides off. There is, you see, no lip round this dashboard
tray. It is just a flat space, with a dimpled bottom. It can hold
nothing that has not been nailed to it.

So I ask you: what, then, is it *for*? Somebody had to design it. It didn't
just appear spontaneously. Some person – perhaps, for all I know,
a whole committee of people in the Dashboard Stowage Division –
had to invest time and thought in incorporating into the design of
this vehicle (it's a Dodge Excreta, if you're wondering) a storage

tray that will actually hold nothing. That is really quite an achievement.

But it is nothing, of course, compared with the manifold design achievements of those responsible for the modern video recorder. Now I am not going to go on about how impossible it is to programme the typical video recorder because you know that already. Nor will I observe how irritating it is that you must cross the room and get down on your belly to confirm that it is actually recording. But I will just make one small passing observation. I recently bought a video recorder and one of the selling points – one of the things the manufacturer boasted about – was that it was capable of recording programmes up to twelve months in advance. Now think about this for a moment and tell me any circumstance – and I mean any circumstance at all – in which you can envision wanting to set a video machine to record a programme one year from now.

I don't want to sound like some old guy who is always moaning. I freely acknowledge that there are many excellent, well-engineered products that didn't exist when I was a boy – the pocket calculator and kettles that switch off automatically are two that fill me yet with gratitude and wonder – but it does seem to me that an awful lot of things out there have been designed by people who cannot possibly have stopped to think how they will be used.

Just think for a moment of all the everyday items you have to puzzle over – fax machines, photocopiers, central heating thermostats, airline tickets, television remote control units, hotel showers and alarm clocks, microwave ovens, almost any electrical product owned by someone other than you – because they are ill thought out.

And why are they so ill thought out? Because all the best designers are making running shoes. Either that, or they are just idiots. In either case, it really isn't fair.

WIDE-OPEN SPACES

HERE ARE A COUPLE OF THINGS TO BEAR IN MIND AS YOU GO THROUGH life: Daniel Boone was an idiot, and it's not worth trying to go to Maine for the day from Hanover, New Hampshire. Allow me to explain.

I was fooling around with a globe the other night (one of the benefits of the awfulness of American television is that you find yourself fooling around with a lot of new things) and I was mildly astounded to realize that here in Hanover I am much closer to our old house in Yorkshire than to many other parts of the United States. Indeed, from where I sit to Attu, the westernmost of Alaska's Aleutian Islands, is almost 4,000 miles. Put another way, you are closer to Johannesburg than I am to the outermost tip of my own country.

Of course, you could argue that Alaska is not a fair comparison because there is so much non-American territory between here and there, but even if you confine yourself to the mainland US, the distances are impressive. From my house to Los Angeles is about the same as from your house to Lagos. We are, in a word, talking big scale here.

Here is another arresting fact to do with scale. In the past twenty years (a period in which, let the record show, I was doing my breeding elsewhere), the population of the United States increased by almost exactly the equivalent of a Great Britain. I find that quite amazing, too, not least because I don't know where all these new people are.

A remarkable thing about America, if you have been living for a long time in a snug little place like the UK, is how very big and very empty so much of it is. Consider this: Montana, Wyoming and North and South Dakota have an area twice the size of France but a population less than that of south London. Alaska is bigger still and has even fewer people. Even my own adopted state of New Hampshire, in the relatively crowded Northeast, is 85 per cent forest, and most of the rest is lakes. You can drive for very long periods in New Hampshire and never see anything but trees and mountains – not a house or a hamlet or even, quite often, another car.

I am constantly caught out by this. Not long ago, I had a couple of friends over from England and we decided to take a drive over to the lakes of western Maine. It had the makings of a nice day out. All we had to do was cross New Hampshire – which is after all the fourth tiniest state in America – and go a little way over the state line into our lovely, moose-strewn neighbour to the east. I figured it would take about two to two and a half hours.

Well, of course you have anticipated the punchline. Seven hours later we pulled up exhausted at the shore of Rangeley Lake, took two pictures, looked at each other, and wordlessly got back in the car and drove home. This sort of thing happens all the time.

The curious thing is that nearly all Americans, as far as I can tell, don't see it this way. They think the country is way too crowded. Moves are constantly afoot to restrict access to national parks and wilderness areas on the grounds that they are dangerously overrun. Parts of them *are* unquestionably crowded, but that is only because 98 per cent of visitors arrive by car, and 98 per cent of those venture no more than 400 yards from their metallic wombs. Elsewhere, however, you can have whole mountains to yourself even in the most crowded parks on the busiest days. Yet I may soon find myself barred from hiking in many wilderness areas, unless I had the foresight to book a visit weeks beforehand, because of perceived overcrowding.

Even more ominously, there is a growing belief that the best way of dealing with this supposed crisis is by expelling most of those not born here. There is an organization whose name escapes me (it may be Dangerously Small-Minded Reactionaries for a Better America) that periodically runs earnest, carefully reasoned ads in the *New York Times* and other important publications calling for an end to immigration because, as one of its ads explains, it 'is devastating our environment and the quality of our lives'. Give me a break.

Elsewhere it adds, 'Primarily because of immigration we are rushing at breakneck speed towards an environmental and economic disaster.'

You could, I suppose, make a case for cutting back on immigration, but not on the grounds that the country is running out of room. Anti-immigration arguments conveniently overlook the fact that America already expels a million immigrants a year, and that those who are here mostly do jobs that are too dirty, dangerous or low-paying for Americans to do. Getting rid of immigrants is not suddenly going to open employment opportunities for the locals; all it's going to do is leave a lot of dishes unwashed and a lot of fruit unpicked. Still less is it going to miraculously create a lot more breathing space for the rest of us.

America already has one of the lowest proportions of immigrants in the developed world. Just 6 per cent of people in the United States are foreign born compared with, for instance, 8 per cent in Britain and 11 per cent in France. America may or may not be heading for an environmental and economic disaster, but if so it certainly isn't because six people in every hundred were born somewhere else. But try telling that to most Americans.

The fact is America is already one of the least crowded countries on earth with an average of just sixty-eight people per square mile, compared with 256 in France and over 600 in Britain. Altogether, only 2 per cent of the United States is classified as 'built up'.

Of course, Americans have always tended to see these things in a different way. Daniel Boone famously is supposed to have looked out of his cabin window one day, seen a wisp of smoke rising from a homesteader's dwelling on a distant mountain, and announced his intention to move on, complaining bitterly that the neighbourhood was getting too crowded.

Which is why I say Daniel Boone was an idiot. I just hate to see the rest of my country going the same way.

RULE NUMBER 1: FOLLOW ALL RULES

I DID A FOOLISH THING THE OTHER EVENING. I WENT INTO ONE OF OUR local bars and seated myself without permission. You just don't do this in America, but I had an important recurring thought that I wanted to scribble down before it left my head (namely, 'There is *always* a little more toothpaste in the tube. Think about it'), and anyway the place was practically empty, so I just took a table near the door.

After a couple of minutes the hostess – the Customer Seating Manager – came up to me and said in a level tone, 'I see you've seated yourself.'

'Yup,' I replied proudly. 'Dressed myself too.'

'Didn't you see the sign?' She tilted her head at a big sign that said 'Please Wait to Be Seated'.

I have been in this bar about 150 times. I have seen the sign from every angle but supine.

'Is there a sign?' I said innocently. 'Gosh, I didn't notice it.'

She sighed. 'Well, the server in this section is *very* busy, so you may have to wait some time for her to get to you.'

There was no other customer within fifty feet, but that wasn't the point. The point was that I had disregarded a posted notice and would have to serve a small sentence in purgatory in consequence.

It would be entirely wrong to say that Americans love rules, but they have a certain regard for them. They behave towards rules in much the way the British behave towards queues – as something that is fundamental to the maintenance of a civilized and orderly society. I had, in effect, queue-jumped the 'Wait to Be Seated' sign.

I expect it may be something to do with our Germanic stock. On the whole I have no quibble with that. There are times, I have to say, when a little Teutonic order wouldn't go amiss in England – like when people take two spaces in a car park (the one offence for which, if I may speak freely here, I would welcome back capital punishment).

Sometimes, however, the American devotion to order goes too far. Our local public swimming-pool, for example, has twenty-seven posted rules – twenty-seven! – of which my favourite is 'Only One Bounce Per Dive on Diving Board'. And they're enforced.

What is frustrating – no, maddening – is that it almost never matters whether these rules make any sense or not. A year or so ago, as a way of dealing with the increased threat of terrorism, America's airlines began requiring passengers to present photographic identification when checking in for a flight. The first I heard of this was when I showed up to catch a plane at an airport 120 miles from my home.

'I need to see some picture ID,' said the clerk, who had the charm and boundless motivation you would expect to find in someone whose primary employment perk is a nylon tie.

'Really? I don't think I have any,' I said and began patting my pockets, as if that would make a difference, and then pulling cards from my wallet. I had all kinds of identification – library card, credit cards, Social Security card, health insurance card, airline ticket – all with my name on them, but nothing with a picture. Eventually, at the back of the wallet I found an old Iowa driver's licence that I had forgotten I even had.

'This is expired,' he sniffed.

'Then I won't ask to drive the plane,' I replied.

'Anyway, it's fifteen years old. I need something more up to date.'

I sighed and rooted through my belongings. Finally it occurred to me that I had a copy of one of my own books with my picture on the jacket. I handed it to him proudly and with some relief.

He looked at the book and then hard at me and then at a printed list. 'That's not on our list of Permissible Visual Cognitive Imagings,' he said, or something similarly vacuous.

'I'm sure it isn't, but it's still me. It couldn't *be* more me.' I lowered my voice and leaned closer to him. 'Are you seriously suggesting that I had this book specially printed so I could sneak onto a flight to Buffalo?'

He stared hard at me for another minute, then called in another clerk for consultation. They conferred and summoned a third party. Eventually we ended up with a crowd scene involving three check-in clerks, their supervisor, the supervisor's supervisor, two baggage handlers, several nosy bystanders straining to get a better view and a guy selling jewellery out of an aluminium case.

My flight was due to take off in minutes and froth was starting to form at the corners of my mouth. 'What is the point of all this anyway?' I said to the head supervisor. 'Why do you need a picture ID?'

'FAA rule,' he said, staring unhappily at my book, my invalid driver's licence and the list of permissible photo options.

'But *why* is it the rule? Do you honestly believe that you are going to thwart a terrorist by requiring him to show you a laminated photograph of himself? Do you think a person who could plan and execute a sophisticated hijacking would be thrown off his quest by a demand to see his driver's licence? Has it occurred to you that it might be more productive, vis-à-vis terrorism, if you employed someone who was actually awake, and perhaps with an IQ above that of a small mollusc, to monitor the TV screens on your X-ray machines?' I may not have said all this in exactly those words, but that was the drift of my sentiment.

But you see the requirement is not simply to identify yourself, but to identify yourself in a way that *precisely matches a written instruction*.

Anyway, I changed tack and begged. I promised never again to turn up at an airport without adequate ID. I took on an attitude of complete contrition. I don't suppose anyone has ever shown such earnest, remorseful desire to be allowed to proceed to Buffalo.

Eventually, with misgivings, the supervisor nodded at the clerk and told him to check me in, but warned me not to try anything as slippery as this again, and then departed with his colleagues.

The check-in clerk issued me a boarding pass and I started towards the gate, then turned back, and in a low, confidential tone shared with him a helpful afterthought.

'There is always a little more toothpaste in the tube,' I said. 'Think about it.'

THE MYSTERIES OF CHRISTMAS

ONE OF THE MANY SMALL MYSTERIES I HOPED TO RESOLVE WHEN I FIRST moved to England was this: when British people sang 'A-Wassailing We'll Go', where was it they went and what exactly did they do when they got there?

Throughout an American upbringing I heard this song every Christmas without ever finding anyone who had the faintest idea of how to go about the obscure and enigmatic business of wassailing. Given the perky lilt of the carol and the party spirit in which it was always sung, it suggested to my youthful imagination rosy-cheeked wenches bearing flagons of ale in a scene of general merriment and abandon before a blazing yule log in a hall decked with holly, and with this in mind I looked forward to my first English Christmas with a certain frank anticipation. In my house, the most exciting thing you could hope for in the way of seasonal recklessness was being offered a cookie shaped like a Christmas tree.

So you may conceive my disappointment when my first Christmas in England came and went and not only was there no wassailing to be seen but no-one I quizzed was any the wiser as to its arcane and venerable secrets. In fact, in nearly twenty years in England I never did find anyone who had ever gone a-wassailing, at least not knowingly. Nor, while we are at it, did I encounter any mumming, still less any hodening (a kind of organized group begging for coins with a view to buying drinks at the nearest public house, which I think is an outstanding idea), or many of the other traditions of an English Christmas that were expressly promised in the lyrics of carols and the novels of authors like Jane Austen and Charles Dickens.

It wasn't until I happened on a copy of T.G. Crippen's scholarly and ageless *Christmas and Christmas Lore*, published in London in 1923, that I finally found that *wassail* was originally a salutation. From the Old Norse *ves heil*, it means 'in good health'. In Anglo-Saxon times, according to Crippen, it was customary for someone offering a drink to say 'Wassail!' and for the recipient to respond 'Drinkhail!' and for the participants to repeat the exercise until comfortably horizontal.

It is clear from Crippen's tome that in 1923 this and many other ancient and agreeable Christmas customs were still commonly encountered in Britain. Now, alas, they appear to be gone for good.

Even so, Christmas in Britain is wonderful, far better than Christmas in America, and for all kinds of reasons. To begin with, in Britain – or at least in England – you still pretty much pack all your festive excesses (eating, drinking, gift-giving, more eating and drinking) into Christmas, whereas we in America spread ours out over three separate holidays.

In America, the big eating holiday is Thanksgiving, at the end of November. Thanksgiving is a great holiday – probably the very best holiday in America, if you ask me. (In case you've always wondered, it commemorates the first harvest feast at which the pilgrims sat down with the Indians to thank them for all their help and tell them, 'Oh, and by the way, we've decided we want the *whole* country.') It is a great holiday because you don't have to give gifts or send cards or do anything but eat until you begin to look like a balloon that has been left on a helium machine too long.

The trouble is that it comes less than a month before Christmas. So when on 25 December Mom brings out another turkey, you don't go, 'Turkey! YIPPEEE!' but rather, 'Ah, turkey again is it, Mother?' Under such an arrangement Christmas dinner is bound to come as an anticlimax.

Also, Americans don't drink much at Christmas, as a rule. Indeed, I suspect most people in America would think it faintly unseemly to imbibe anything more than, say, a small sherry before lunch on Christmas Day. Americans save their large-scale drinking for New Year's Eve.

Nor, come to that, do we have many of the standard features of Christmas that you take for granted. There are no Christmas pantomimes in America. No mince pies and hardly any Christmas puddings. There's no bellringing on Christmas Eve. No crackers. No big double issue of the *Radio Times*. No brandy butter. No little dishes full of nuts. No hearing 'Merry Xmas Everybody' by Slade at least once every twenty minutes. Above all, there is no Boxing Day.

On 26 December, everybody in the United States goes back to work. In fact, Christmas as a noticeable phenomenon pretty well ends about midday on 25 December. There's nothing special on TV, and most large stores and shopping malls now open for the afternoon (so that people can exchange all the things they got but didn't want). You can go to the movies on Christmas Day in America. You can go *bowling*. It doesn't seem right somehow.

As for Boxing Day, most people in America have never heard of it, or at best have only the vaguest idea of what it is. It may surprise you to hear, incidentally, that Boxing Day is actually quite a modern invention. The *Oxford English Dictionary* can trace the term back no further than 1849. Its roots go back at least to medieval times, when it was the custom to break open church alms boxes at Christmas and distribute the contents to the poor, but as a holiday Boxing Day only dates from the last century, which explains why you have it and we don't.

Personally, I much prefer Boxing Day to Christmas, largely because it has all the advantages of Christmas (lots of food and drink, general goodwill towards all, a chance to doze in an armchair during daylight hours) without any of the disadvantages like spending hours on the floor trying to assemble doll's houses and bicycles from instructions written in Taiwan or the uttering of false professions of gratitude to Aunt Gladys for a hand-knitted jumper that even Gyles Brandreth wouldn't wear. ('No honestly, Glad, I've been looking everywhere for a jumper with a unicorn motif.')

No, if there is one thing I miss from England it's Boxing Day. That and of course hearing 'Merry Xmas Everybody' by Slade over and over. Apart from anything else, it makes you appreciate the rest of the year so much more.

THE NUMBERS GAME

THE UNITED STATES CONGRESS, WHICH NEVER CEASES TO BE AMAZING, recently voted to give the Pentagon $11 billion more than it had asked for.

Do you have any idea how much $11 billion is? Of course you don't. Nobody does. It is not possible to conceive of a sum that large.

No matter where you turn with regard to America and its economy you are going to bump into figures that are so large as to be essentially incomprehensible. Consider just a few figures that I pulled from this past Sunday's papers. The annual gross domestic product of the United States is $6.8 trillion. The federal budget is $1.6 trillion. The federal deficit is nearly $200 billion. California alone has an economy worth $850 billion.

It's easy to lose sight of just how enormous these figures really are. America's cumulative debt at last count, according to *Time* magazine, was 'a hair' under $4.7 trillion. The actual figure was $4.692 trillion, so that statement is hard to argue with, yet it represents a difference of $8 billion – a pretty large hair in anybody's book.

I worked long enough on the business news desk of a national newspaper to know that even the most experienced financial journalists often get confused when dealing with terms like *billion* and *trillion*, and for two good reasons. First, they've usually had quite a lot to drink at lunch, and, second, such numbers really are confusing.

And that is the whole problem. Big numbers are simply beyond what we are capable of grasping. On Sixth Avenue in New York there is an electronic hoarding, erected and paid for by some anonymous source, that announces itself as 'The National Debt Clock'. When I was last there, in November, it listed the national debt at $4,533,603,804,000 – that's $4.5 trillion – and the figure was growing by $10,000 every second, or so fast that the last three digits on the electronic meter were just a blur. But what does $4.5 trillion actually *mean*?

Well, let's just try for a trillion. Imagine that you were in a vault with the whole of America's national debt and you were told you could keep each dollar bill you initialled. Say, too, for the sake of argument that you could initial one dollar bill each second and that you worked straight through without stopping. How long do you think it would take to count a trillion dollars? Go on, humour me and take a guess. Twelve weeks? Five years?

If you initialled one dollar per second, you would make $1,000 every seventeen minutes. After twelve days of non-stop effort you would acquire your first $1 million. Thus it would take you 120 days to accumulate $10 million and 1,200 days – something over three years – to reach $100 million. After 31.7 years, you would become a billionaire, and after almost a thousand years you would be as wealthy as Bill Gates, the founder of Microsoft. But not until after 31,709.8 years would you count your trillionth dollar (and then you would be less than one-fourth of the way through the pile of money representing America's national debt).

That is what $1 trillion is.

What is interesting is that it is becoming increasingly evident that most of these inconceivably vast sums that get bandied about by economists and policy makers are almost certainly miles out anyway. Take gross domestic product, the bedrock of modern economic policy. GDP was a concept originated in the 1930s by the economist Simon Kuznets. It is very good at measuring physical things – tonnes of steel, board feet of lumber, potatoes, tyres, and so on. That was all very well in a traditional industrial economy. But now the greater part of output for nearly all developed nations is in services and ideas – things like computer software, tele-communications, financial services – which produce wealth but don't necessarily, or even generally, result in a product that you can load on a pallet and ship out to the marketplace.

Because such activities are so difficult to measure and quantify, no-one really knows what they amount to. Many economists now believe that America may have been underestimating its rate of GDP growth by as much as two to three percentage points a year for several years. That may not seem a great deal, but if that is correct then the American economy – which obviously is already staggeringly enormous – may be one-third larger than anyone had thought. In other words, there may be several hundred *billions* of dollars floating around in the American economy that no-one ever suspected was there. Incredible.

Here's another arresting thought. None of this really matters because GDP is in any case a perfectly useless measurement. All that it is, literally, is a crude measure of national income – 'the dollar value of finished goods and services', as the textbooks put it – over a given period.

Any kind of economic activity adds to the gross domestic product. It doesn't matter whether it's a good activity or a bad one. It has been estimated, for instance, that the O.J. Simpson trial added $200 million to America's GDP through lawyers' fees, court costs, hotel bills for the press, and so on, but I don't think many people would argue that the whole costly spectacle made America a noticeably greater, nobler place.

In fact, bad activities often generate more GDP than good activities. I was recently in Pennsylvania at the site of a zinc factory whose airborne wastes were formerly so laden with pollutants that they denuded an entire mountainside. From the factory fence to the top of the mountain there was not a single scrap of growing vegetation to be seen. From a GDP perspective, however, this was wonderful. First there was the gain to the economy from all the zinc the factory had refined and sold over the years. Then there was the gain from the tens of millions of dollars the Government must spend to clean up the site and restore the mountain. Finally, there will be a continuing gain from medical treatments for workers and townspeople made chronically ill by living amid all those contaminants.

In terms of conventional economic measurement, all of this is gain, not loss. So too is overfishing of lakes and seas. So too is deforestation. In short, the more recklessly we use up natural resources, the more the GDP glows.

As the economist Herman Daly once put it: 'The current national accounting system treats the earth as a business in liquidation.' Or as three other leading economists drily observed in an article in the *Atlantic Monthly* last year: 'By the curious standard of the GDP, the nation's economic hero is a terminal cancer patient who is going through a costly divorce.'

So why do we persist with this preposterous gauge of economic performance? Because it's the best thing that economists have come up with yet. Now you know why they call it the dismal science.

ROOM SERVICE

SOMETHING I HAVE LONG WANTED TO DO – AND IF THIS COLUMN CAME with expenses I'd be doing it right now – is visit the Motel Inn in San Luis Obispo, California.

On the face of it, this might seem an odd quest since the Motel Inn is not, by all accounts, a particularly prepossessing establishment. Built in 1925 in the Spanish colonial style much beloved by Californians, Zorro and almost no-one else, it sits in the shadow of a busy elevated freeway amid a cluster of gas stations, fast-food outlets and other more modern motor inns.

Once, however, it was a famous stopping place on the coastal highway between Los Angeles and San Francisco. A Pasadena architect named Arthur Heineman gave it its exuberant style, but his most inspired legacy lies in the name he chose for it. Playing around with the words *motor* and *hotel*, he dubbed it a *mo-tel*, hyphenating the word to emphasize its novelty.

America already had lots of motels by then, but they were all called something else – *auto court, cottage court, hotel court, tour-o-tel, auto hotel, bungalow court, cabin court, tourist camp, tourist court, trav-o-tel*. For a long time it looked like *tourist court* would become the standard designation. It wasn't until about 1950 that *motel* achieved generic status.

I know all this because I have just been reading a book on the history of the motel in America called, with dazzling originality, *The Motel in America*. Written by three academics, it is an awfully dull piece of work, full of sentences like 'The needs of both consumers and purveyors of lodging strongly influenced the development of organized systems of distribution,' but I bought it and devoured it anyway because I love everything about motels.

I can't help myself. I still get excited every time I slip a key into a motel room door and fling it open. It is just one of those things – airline food is another – that I get excited about and should know better.

The golden age of motels was also, as it happens, the golden age of me – the 1950s – and I suppose that's what accounts for my fascination. For anyone who didn't travel around America by car in the 1950s, it is almost impossible now to imagine how thrilling they were. For one thing, the national chains like Holiday Inn and Ramada barely existed. As late as 1962, 98 per cent of motels were individually owned, so each one had its own character.

Essentially they were of two types. The first type were the good ones. These nearly always had a homely, cottagey air. Typically, they were built around a generous lawn with shady trees and a flowerbed decorated with a wagon wheel painted white. (The owners, for some reason, generally liked to paint all their rocks white, too, and array them along the edge of the drive.) Often they had a swimming-pool and a gift shop or coffee shop.

Indoors they offered measures of comfort and elegance that would have the whole family cooing – thick carpet, purring air-conditioner, a nightstand with a private phone and a built-in radio, a TV at the foot of the bed, a private bath, sometimes a dressing area, Vibro-matic beds, which gave you a massage for a quarter.

The second kind of motels were the appalling ones. We always stayed at these. My father, who was one of history's great cheapskates, was of the view that there was no point in spending money on . . . well, on anything really, and certainly not on anything that you were mostly going to be asleep in.

In consequence, we normally camped in motel rooms where the beds sagged and the furnishings were battered, and where you could generally count on being awakened in the night by a piercing shriek, the sounds of splintering furniture and a female voice pleading, 'Put the gun down, Vinnie. I'll do anything you say.' I don't wish to suggest that these experiences left me scarred and embittered, but I can remember watching Janet Leigh being hacked up in the Bates Motel in *Psycho* and thinking, At least she got a shower curtain.

All of this, even at its worst, gave highway travel a kind of exhilarating unpredictability. You never knew what quality of comfort you would find at the end of the day, what sort of small pleasures might be on offer. It gave road trips a piquancy that the homogenized refinements of the modern age cannot match.

That changed very quickly with the rise of motel chains. Holiday Inn, for instance, went from seventy-nine outlets in 1958 to almost 1,500 in less than twenty years. Today just five chains account for one-third of all the motel rooms in America. Travellers these days don't want uncertainty in their lives. They want to stay in the same place, eat the same food, watch the same TV wherever they go.

Recently, while driving from Washington, DC, to New England with my own family, I tried explaining this to my children, and got the idea that we should stop for the night at an old-fashioned family-run place. Everyone thought this was an immensely stupid idea, but I insisted that it would be a great experience.

Well, we looked everywhere. We passed scores of motels, but they were all part of national chains. Eventually, after perhaps ninety minutes of futile hunting, I pulled off the interstate for the seventh or eighth time and – lo! – there shining out of the darkness was the Sleepy Hollow Motel, a perfect 1950s sort of place.

'There's a Comfort Inn across the street,' one of my children pointed out.

'We don't want a Comfort Inn, Jimmy,' I explained, temporarily forgetting in my excitement that I don't have a child named Jimmy. 'We want a real motel.'

My wife, being English, insisted on having a look at the room. It was awful, of course. The furnishings were battered and threadbare. The room was so cold you could see your breath. There was a shower curtain, but it hung by just three rings.

'It's got character,' I insisted.

'It's got nits,' said my wife. 'We'll be across the road at the Comfort Inn.'

In disbelief, I watched them troop out. 'You'll stay, won't you, Jimmy?' I said, but even he left without a backward glance.

I stood there for about fifteen seconds, then switched off the light, returned the key and went across to the Comfort Inn. It was very bland and just like every Comfort Inn I had ever stayed in. But it was clean, the TV worked and, it must be said, the shower curtain was very nice.

OUR FRIEND THE MOOSE

MY WIFE HAS JUST CALLED UP THAT DINNER IS ON THE TABLE (I'D RATHER it was on plates, but there you are), so this week's column may be shorter than usual.

In our house, you see, if you don't get to the table within five minutes there's nothing left but gristle and that greyish piece of string they use to hold the joint together. But at least – and here's a nice thing about living in America these days, or indeed anywhere other than Britain – we can eat beef here without having to wonder if when we rise from the table we will walk sideways into the wall.

I was recently back in the UK and I noticed that a lot of you are eating beef again, which makes me conclude that you didn't watch the recent excellent *Horizon* two-parter on BSE or read John Lanchester's equally excellent account in the *New Yorker* on same. If you had, believe me, you'd never wish to eat beef again. (But not as much as you'd wish you hadn't eaten it at all between 1986 and 1988. I ate it then too and boy are *we* in for it!)

However, my purpose today is not to make you feel bad about your future prospects (though having said that, my advice is to get your affairs in order while you can still hold a pen), but rather to suggest an alternative use for all those poor cows that are being sent to slaughter.

My idea is that we should ship all those cows over here and set them loose in the Great North Woods which extend across northern New England from Vermont to Maine, and let America's hunters at them. My thinking is that this might distract the hunters from shooting moose.

Goodness knows why anyone would want to shoot an animal as harmless and retiring as the moose, but thousands do – so many, in fact, that states now hold lotteries to decide who gets a licence. Maine last year received 82,000 applications for 1,500 permits. Over 12,000 out-of-staters happily parted with a non-refundable $20 just to be allowed to take part in the draw.

Hunters will tell you that a moose is a wily and ferocious forest creature. In fact, a moose is a cow drawn by a three-year-old. That's all there is to it. Without doubt, the moose is the most improbable, endearingly hopeless creature ever to live in the wilds. It is huge – as big as a horse – but magnificently ungainly. A moose runs as if its legs have never been introduced to each other. Even its antlers are hopeless. Other creatures grow antlers with sharp points that look wonderful in profile and command the respect of adversaries. Moose grow antlers that look like oven gloves.

Above all what distinguishes the moose is its almost boundless lack of intelligence. If you are driving down a highway and a moose steps from the woods ahead of you, he will squint at you for a long minute, then abruptly hie off down the road away from you, legs flailing in eight directions at once. Never mind that there are perhaps 10,000 square miles of safe, dense forest on either side of the highway. Clueless as to where he is and what exactly is going on, the moose doggedly follows the highway halfway to New Brunswick before his peculiar gait inadvertently steers him back into the woods, where he immediately stops and takes on a perplexed expression that says, 'Hey – woods. Now how the heck did I get here?'

Moose are so monumentally muddle-headed, in fact, that when they hear a car or truck approaching they will often bolt *out* of the woods and on to the highway in the curious hope that this will bring them to safety. Every year in New England about 1,000 moose are fatally struck by cars or trucks. (Since a moose weighs 2,000 pounds and is exactly built so that a car bonnet will take its spindly legs out from under it while leaving the bulk of it to fall through the windscreen, collisions are often equally fatal to the motorist.) When you see how quiet and empty are the roads that run through the northern woods and realize how manifestly unlikely it is that any creature could emerge onto the highway just as a vehicle is passing, you will appreciate just how amazing those numbers are.

More amazing still, given the moose's lack of cunning and

curiously blunted survival instincts, is that it is one of the longest-surviving creatures in North America. When mastodons walked the earth, moose were there with them. Woolly mammoths, sabre-toothed tigers, mountain lions, wolves, caribou, wild horses and even camels all once thrived in the eastern United States but gradually stumbled into extinction, while the moose just plodded on, untroubled by ice ages, meteor impacts, volcanic eruptions and shifting continents.

It hasn't always been so. At the turn of the century it was estimated that there were no more than a dozen moose in the whole of New Hampshire and probably none at all in Vermont. Today New Hampshire has an estimated 5,000 moose, Vermont 1,000 more and Maine anything up to 30,000.

It is because of these robust and growing numbers that hunting has been gradually re-introduced as a way of keeping the numbers from getting out of hand. However, there are two problems with this. First, the population numbers are really just guesses. Moose clearly don't line up for censuses. At least one leading naturalist thinks the population numbers may have been overstated by as much as 20 per cent, which would mean that moose aren't so much being selectively culled as carelessly slaughtered.

Even more pertinent, to my mind, is the thought that there is just something wrong about hunting and killing an animal as dopily unassuming as a moose. Shooting a moose is not an achievement. I have encountered moose in the wild and can tell you that you could just about go up and kill one with a folded newspaper. The fact that over 90 per cent of hunters manage to bag a moose in a season that lasts only a week is testament to the ease with which they can be hunted down.

Which is why I suggest that you send all your poor addled bovines to us. It would provide our hunters with the sort of manly challenge they evidently long for, and, as I say, might help save the odd moose.

So send those mad cows over. Address them to Bob Smith. He's one of our New Hampshire senators, and if his voting record is any guide he's already at ease with disorders of the mind.

Now if you will excuse me I have to go see if there is any meat left on that greyish piece of string.

CONSUMING PLEASURES

I BELIEVE I HAVE JUST SECURED DEFINITIVE PROOF THAT AMERICA IS THE ultimate shopping paradise. It came in a video catalogue that arrived unsolicited with the morning mail. There, among the usual diverse offerings – *Fiddler on the Roof*, *T'ai Chi for Health and Fitness*, every movie ever made by John Wayne – was a self-help video called *Do the Macarena Totally Nude*, which promises to guide the naked home viewer through 'the hot moves of this Latin-influenced dance that is sweeping the nation'.

Among the catalogue's other intriguing offerings were a documentary called *Antique Farm Tractors*, a boxed set representing the complete oeuvre of Don Knotts, and an interesting compilation entitled *Nude Housewives of America* (Vols 1&2), depicting ordinary housewives 'doing their daily chores in the buff!'

And to think I asked for a socket wrench for Christmas.

My point is that there is almost nothing you cannot buy in this remarkable country. Of course, shopping has been the national sport in America for decades, but three significant retailing developments in recent years have elevated the shopping experience to a higher, giddier plane. They are:

• **Telemarketing**. This is an all-new business in which platoons of salespeople phone up complete strangers, more or less at random, and doggedly read to them a prepared script promising a free set of steak knives or AM–FM radio if they buy a certain product or service. These people have become positively relentless.

The possibility that I would buy a time-share in Florida from a stranger over the telephone is about as likely as the possibility that I would change religion on the basis of a doorstep visit from a brace of Mormons, but evidently this feeling is not universal. According to the *New York Times*, telemarketing in America is now worth $35 *billion* a year. That figure is so amazing that I cannot think about it without getting a headache, so let us move on to retail development number two:

• **Outlet malls.** These are malls in which companies like Ralph Lauren and Calvin Klein sell their own lines at discounts. They are, in short, clusters of shops where everything is permanently on sale, and they have become huge.

In many cases, outlet malls are not malls at all, but rather whole communities that have been taken over by outlet stores. Easily the most remarkable of these is Freeport, Maine, home of L.L. Bean, a popular supplier of outdoor apparel and sporting equipment for yuppies.

We stopped there last summer on the way through Maine and I am still trembling from the experience. The procedure for a visit to Freeport is unvarying. You creep into town in a long line of traffic, spend forty minutes hunting for a parking space, then join a crowd of thousands shuffling along Main Street past a succession of shops selling every known brand name that ever was or will be.

At the centre of it all is the L.L. Bean store, which is enormous. It is open twenty-four hours a day, 365 days a year. You can buy a kayak there at 3 a.m. if you want. People apparently do. My brain is beginning to hurt again.

• **Finally, catalogues.** Shopping by post has been around for a long time, but it has proliferated to a degree that is just beyond astounding. Almost from the moment we arrived in America catalogues began plopping unbidden onto our mat with the daily mail. Now we get perhaps a dozen a week, sometimes more – catalogues for videos, gardening implements, lingerie, books, camping and fishing gear, things to make your bathroom a more stylish and convivial place, you name it.

For a long time I tossed these out with the rest of the unsolicited mail. What a fool I was. I now realize they not only provide hours of reading pleasure, but open up a world of possibilities I scarcely knew existed.

Just today, along with the aforementioned nude macarena

brochure, we received a catalogue called *Tools for Serious Readers*. It was full of the usual assortment of blotters and desk tidies, but what particularly caught my eye was something called the Briefcase Valet – a small wheeled trolley that sits about four inches off the floor.

Available in dark or natural cherry and attractively priced at $139, it is designed to alleviate one of the most intractable office storage problems of our age. As the catalogue copy explains: 'Most of us are faced with the same nagging problem of what to do with our briefcase when we put it down at home or in the office. That's why we designed our Briefcase Valet. It holds your briefcase up off the floor, making it easier to insert and retrieve things as the day progresses.'

I especially like those last four words, 'as the day progresses'. How many times have I got to the end of a working day myself and thought: Oh, what I'd give for a small wheeled device in a choice of wood tones to save me reaching those last four inches.

The scary thing is that often these descriptions are written so artfully that you are almost taken in by them. I was just reading in another catalogue about a fancy kitchen accessory from Italy called a *portarotolo di carta*, which boasts 'a spring tension arm', 'stainless-steel guide', 'crafted brass finial' and 'rubber gasket for exceptional stability' – all for just $49.95 – when I realized that it was a paper towel holder.

Obviously the catalogue couldn't say, 'No matter how you look at it, this is just a paper towel dispenser and you'd be a sap to buy it,' so they must try to dazzle you with its exotic pedigree and technical complexity.

In consequence, even the most mundane catalogue items boast more design features than a 1954 Buick. I have before me a glossy book from another company announcing with undisguised pride that their flannel shirts feature, among much else, gauntlet buttons, extra-long sleeve plackets, two-ply 40S yarn construction ('for a superior nap'), boxed back pleat, double stitching at stress points, handy locker loop and non-fused collar, whatever all that may be. Even socks come with lengthy, scientific-sounding descriptions extolling their seamless closures, one-to-one fibre loops and hand-linked yarns.

I confess I have sometimes been briefly tempted by these seductive blandishments to make a purchase, but in the end I realize that given a choice between paying $37.50 for a shirt with a superior nap and just having a nap, I will always go for the latter.

However, let me say right here that if anyone comes up with a Totally Nude Macarena Socket-Wrench Home Workout Video with handy locker loop in a choice of colours, I am ready to buy.

JUNK FOOD HEAVEN

I DECIDED TO CLEAN OUT THE FRIDGE THE OTHER DAY. WE DON'T USUALLY clean out our fridge – we just box it up every four or five years and send it off to the Center for Disease Control in Atlanta with a note to help themselves to anything that looks scientifically promising – but we hadn't seen one of the cats for a few days and I had a vague recollection of having glimpsed something furry on the bottom shelf towards the back. (Turned out to be a large piece of Gorgonzola.)

So there I was, down on my knees unwrapping pieces of foil and peering cautiously into Tupperware containers, when I came across an interesting product called a breakfast pizza and I examined it with a kind of rueful fondness, as you might regard an old photograph of yourself dressed in clothes that you cannot believe you ever thought were stylish. The breakfast pizza, you see, represented the last surviving relic of a bout of very serious retail foolishness on my part.

Some weeks ago I announced to my wife that I was going to the supermarket with her next time she went because the stuff she kept bringing home was – how can I put this? – not fully in the spirit of American eating. Here we were living in a paradise of junk food – the country that gave the world cheese in a spray can – and she kept bringing home healthy stuff like fresh broccoli and packets of Ryvita.

It was because she was English, of course. She didn't really understand the rich, unrivalled possibilities for greasiness and goo that the American diet offers. I longed for artificial bacon bits, melted cheese in a shade of yellow unknown to nature, and creamy chocolate fillings, sometimes all in the same product. I wanted food that squirts when you bite into it or plops onto your shirt front in such gross quantities that you have to rise carefully from the table and limbo over to the sink to clean yourself up. So I accompanied her to the supermarket and while she was off squeezing melons and pricing shiitake mushrooms I made for the junk food section – which was essentially all the rest of the store. Well, it was heaven.

The breakfast cereals alone could have occupied me for most of the afternoon. There must have been 200 types, and I am not exaggerating. Every possible substance that could be dried, puffed and coated with sugar was there. The most immediately arresting was a cereal called Cookie Crisp, which tried to pretend it was a nutritious breakfast but was really just chocolate chip cookies that you put in a bowl and ate with milk. Brilliant.

Also of note were cereals called Peanut Butter Crunch, Cinnamon Mini Buns, Count Chocula ('with Monster Marsh-mallows'), and a particularly hardcore offering called Cookie Blast Oat Meal, which contained *four* kinds of cookies. I grabbed one of each of the cereals and two of the oatmeal – how often I've said that you shouldn't start a day without a big steaming bowl of cookies – and sprinted with them back to the trolley.

'What's that?' my wife asked in the special tone of voice with which she often addresses me in retail establishments.

I didn't have time to explain. 'Breakfast for the next six months,' I panted as I dashed past, 'and don't even *think* about putting any of it back and getting muesli.'

I had no idea how the market for junk food had proliferated. Everywhere I turned I was confronted with foods guaranteed to make you waddle, most of which were entirely new to me – jelly creme pies, moon pies, pecan spinwheels, peach mellos, root beer buttons, chocolate fudge devil dogs and a whipped marshmallow sandwich spread called Fluff, which came in a tub large enough to bath a baby in.

You really cannot believe the bounteous variety of non-nutritious foods available to the American supermarket shopper these days or the quantities in which they are consumed. I recently read that the average American eats 17.8 *pounds* of pretzels every year.

Aisle seven ('Food for the Seriously Obese') was especially productive. It had a whole section devoted exclusively to a product called Toaster Pastries, which included, among much else, eight different types of toaster strudel. And what exactly is toaster strudel? Who cares? It was coated in sugar and looked drippy. I grabbed an armload.

I admit I got a little carried away – but there was so much and I had been away so long.

It was the breakfast pizza that finally made my wife snap. She looked at the box and said, 'No.'

'I beg your pardon, my sweet?'

'You are not bringing home something called breakfast pizza. I will let you have' – she reached into the trolley for some specimen samples – 'root beer buttons and toaster strudel and . . .' She lifted out a packet she hadn't noticed before. 'What's this?'

I looked over her shoulder. 'Microwave pancakes,' I said.

'Microwave pancakes,' she repeated, but with less enthusiasm.

'Isn't science wonderful?'

'You're going to eat it all,' she said. 'Every bit of everything that you don't put back on the shelves now. You do understand that?'

'Of course,' I said in my sincerest voice.

And do you know she actually made me eat it. I spent weeks working my way through a symphony of American junk food, and it was all awful. Every bit of it. I don't know whether American junk food has got worse or whether my taste buds have matured, but even the treats I'd grown up with now seemed discouragingly pallid or disgustingly sickly.

The most awful of all was the breakfast pizza. I tried it three or four times, baked it in the oven, zapped it with microwaves, and once in desperation served it with a side of marshmallow Fluff, but it never rose beyond a kind of limp, chewy listlessness. Eventually I gave up altogether and hid the box in the Tupperware graveyard on the bottom shelf of the fridge.

Which is why, when I came across it again the other day, I regarded it with mixed feelings. I started to chuck it out, then hesitated and opened the lid. It didn't smell bad – I expect it was pumped so full of chemicals that there wasn't any room for bacteria – and I thought about keeping it a while longer as a reminder of my folly, but in the end I discarded it. And then, feeling peckish, I went off to the larder to see if I couldn't find a nice plain piece of Ryvita and maybe a stick of celery.

TALES OF THE NORTH WOODS

ABOUT A YEAR AGO, IN THE DEPTHS OF WINTER, A YOUNG COLLEGE student left a party in a village near the small town in New Hampshire in which I live to walk to his parents' house a couple of miles away. Foolishly – for it was dark and he had been drinking – he decided to take a shortcut through the woods. He never made it.

The next day when his disappearance became known hundreds of volunteers took to the woods to search for him. They searched for days, but without success. It wasn't until spring that someone walking in the woods stumbled on his body.

Five weeks ago, something broadly similar happened. A small private jet with two people aboard had to abort its approach as it came in to land at our local airport in poor weather. As the pilot swung round to the northeast to make a new approach, he radioed his intentions to the control tower.

A moment later the little green blip that was his plane disappeared from the airport radar screen. Somewhere out there, abruptly and for reasons unknown, the plane came down in the woods.

Again a large-scale search was mounted, this time with a dozen planes and eleven helicopters augmenting more than 200 volunteer searchers on the ground. Again they searched for days, and again without luck. The missing jet was an eighteen-seater, so it must have made quite an impact, yet there were no signs of strewn wreckage, no crash paths through the trees. The plane had simply vanished without trace.

I don't mean to imply that we live on the edge of some kind of

Bermuda triangle of the deciduous world, merely that the woods of New Hampshire are a rather strange and sinister place.

To begin with they are full of trees – and I don't mean that as a joke. I spent some weeks last summer hiking in these woods and I can tell you that the one thing you see in numbers beyond imagining is trees. At times it's actually unsettling because it is essentially just one endlessly repeated scene. Every bend in the path presents a prospect indistinguishable from every other, and it remains like that no matter how far you go. If you somehow lost the path, you could easily find yourself – very probably would find yourself – helplessly bereft of bearings. You could walk to the point of exhaustion before realizing that your route described a large and sadly pointless circle.

Knowing this, it's much less surprising to learn that the woods sometimes swallow aircraft whole or keep for ever people unfortunate enough to get lost in their featureless embrace. New Hampshire is as big as Wales and is 85 per cent forest. There's a lot of forest out there to get lost in. Every year at least one or two people on foot go missing, sometimes never to be seen again.

Yet here's a remarkable thing. Until only about a century ago, and less than that in some areas, most of these woods didn't exist. Nearly the whole of rural New England – including all the area around our part of New Hampshire – was open, meadowy farmland.

I had this brought home to me with a certain potency the other week when our local council sent us, as a kind of New Year's present, a calendar containing old photographs of the town from the local archives. One of the pictures, a hilltop panorama taken in 1874, showed a scene that looked vaguely familiar, though I couldn't tell why. It showed a corner of the Dartmouth College campus and a dirt road, leading off into some distant hills. The rest was spacious farm fields.

It took me some minutes to work out that I was looking at the future site of my own neighbourhood. It was odd because our street looks like a traditional New England street, with clapboard houses shaded by tall and shapely trees, but in fact nearly all of it dates from the early 1920s, half a century after the photograph. The hill from which the picture was taken is now a twenty-acre wood and nearly all the landscape from the back of our houses to the distant hills is swathed in dense, mature forest, but hardly a twig of it existed in 1874.

The farms disappeared because the farmers moved west, to richer lands in places like Illinois and Ohio, or moved to the burgeoning industrial cities, where earnings were more reliable and generous. The farms they left behind – and sometimes the villages that supported them – sank into the ground and gradually returned to wilderness. All over New England if you go for a walk in the woods you will come across the remains of old stone walls and the foundations of abandoned barns and farmhouses hidden in the ferns and bracken of the forest floor.

Near our house is a woodland path that follows the route of an eighteenth-century post road. For eighteen miles the path winds through dark, tangled, seemingly ancient woodland, yet there are people alive who remember when all that land was farmland. Just off the old post road, four miles or so from here, there once stood a village called Quinntown, which had a mill and a school and several houses. You can find it on old Geological Survey maps.

I've looked out for Quinntown a couple of times as I've passed, but even with a good map the site is deucedly hard to find because the woods are so lacking in distinguishing landmarks. I know a man who has looked for Quinntown off and on for years and still not found it.

Last weekend I decided to try again. There was a fresh fall of snow, which always makes the woods agreeable. Naturally the thought flitted through my mind that I might stumble on some sign of the missing jet. I didn't *really* expect to find anything – I was seven or eight miles from the presumed crash site – but on the other hand the plane has to be out there somewhere and it was altogether possible that no-one had looked in this area.

So I went out in the woods and had a good tramp around. I got a lot of healthy fresh air and exercise, and the woods were stunning in their snowy softness. It was strange to think that in all that vast stillness there were the remains of a once-thriving village, and stranger still that somewhere out there with me was a crumpled, unfound plane with two bodies aboard.

I would love to be able to tell you that I found Quinntown or the missing plane or both, but alas I did not. Sometimes life has inconclusive endings.

Columns, too.

HAIL TO THE CHIEF

IT'S PRESIDENTS DAY TOMORROW IN AMERICA. I KNOW. I CAN HARDLY stand the excitement either.

Presidents Day is a new holiday to me. When I was growing up, we had two presidential holidays in February – Lincoln's Birthday on 12 February and Washington's Birthday on 22 February. I may not be exactly right on those dates, or indeed even very close, because frankly it's been a long time since I was growing up and anyway they weren't very interesting holidays. You didn't receive presents or get to go on a picnic or anything.

The problem with birthdays, as I am sure you have noticed yourself, is that they can fall on any day of the week, whereas most people like to have their public holidays on Mondays so that they get a nice long weekend.

So for a while America celebrated Washington's Birthday and Lincoln's Birthday on the Mondays nearest the appropriate dates. However, this bothered some people of a particular nature, so it was decided to have a single holiday on the third Monday of February and call it Presidents Day.

The idea now is to honour all the presidents, whether they were good or bad, which I think is swell because it gives us an opportunity to commemorate the more obscure or peculiar presidents – people like Grover Cleveland, who, according to legend, had the interesting habit of relieving himself out of his office window, or Zachary Taylor, who never voted in an election and didn't even vote for himself.

All things considered, America has produced quite a few great presidents – Washington, Lincoln, Jefferson, Franklin and Teddy Roosevelt, Woodrow Wilson, John F. Kennedy. It has also produced several great men who incidentally became president, among them James Madison, Ulysses S. Grant and – you may be surprised to hear me say this – Herbert Hoover.

I have a certain regard for Hoover – fondness would be much too strong a word – because he was from Iowa, and so am I. Besides, you have to feel a little sorry for the poor man. He was the only person in American history for whom attaining the White House was a bad career move. Nowadays when people think of Hoover at all, it is as the man who gave the world the Great Depression. Hardly anyone remembers the half-century of remarkable, even heroic, achievements that preceded it.

Consider his CV: orphaned at eight, he put himself through college (he was in the first graduating class from Stanford University) and became a successful mining engineer in the western United States. He then went off to Australia, where he more or less started the mining industry in Western Australia – still one of the most productive regions in the world – and eventually ended up in London, where he became a vastly wealthy and influential pillar of the business community.

Such was his stature that at the outbreak of the First World War he was invited to join the British Cabinet, but declined and instead took on the job of directing famine relief throughout Europe, which he managed with such distinction that he is estimated to have saved 10 million lives. By the end of the war he was one of the most admired and respected men in the world, known everywhere as the Great Humanitarian.

Returning to America, he became a trusted adviser to Woodrow Wilson, then served as Secretary of Commerce under Harding and Coolidge, where he oversaw a 58 per cent rise in American exports in eight years. When he ran for president in 1928, he was elected in a record landslide.

In March 1929 he was inaugurated. Seven months later Wall Street crashed and the economy went into freefall. Contrary to common belief, Hoover responded at once. He spent more money on public works and unemployment relief than all his predecessors combined, provided $500 million in assistance to troubled banks, even donated his own salary to charity. But he lacked the common touch and alienated the electorate by insisting repeatedly that recovery was just around the corner. In 1932 he was defeated as resoundingly as he had been elected four years before, and has been remembered ever since as an abject failure.

Still, at least he is remembered for something, which is more than can be said for many of our chief executives. Of the forty-one men who have risen to the office of president, at least half served with such lack of eminence as to be almost totally forgotten now, which I think is deserving of the warmest approbation. To be President of the United States and not accomplish anything is, after all, a kind of accomplishment in itself.

By almost universal agreement, the most vague and ineffectual of all our leaders was Millard Fillmore, who succeeded to the office in 1850 upon the death of Zachary Taylor, and spent the next three years demonstrating how the country would have been run if they had just propped Taylor up in a chair with cushions. However, Fillmore has become so celebrated for his obscurity that he is no longer actually obscure, which rather disqualifies him from serious consideration.

Far more noteworthy to my mind is the great Chester A. Arthur, who was sworn in as president in 1881, posed for an official photograph and then, as far as I can make out, was never heard from again. If Arthur's goal in life was to grow rather splendid facial hair and leave plenty of room in the history books for the achievements of other men, then his presidency can be ranked a sterling success.

Also admirable in their way were Rutherford B. Hayes, who was president from 1877 to 1881 and whose principal devotions in life were the advocacy of 'hard money' and the repeal of the Bland–Allison Act, both of which were so pointless and abstruse that no-one can remember now what they were, and Franklin Pierce, whose term of office from 1853 to 1857 was an interlude of indistinction between two longer periods of anonymity. He spent virtually the whole of his incumbency hopelessly intoxicated, prompting the affectionate slogan 'Franklin Pierce, the Hero of Many a Well-Fought Bottle'.

My favourites, however, are the two Presidents Harrison. The first was William Henry Harrison, who heroically refused to don an overcoat for his inaugural ceremony in 1841, contracted pneumonia and with engaging swiftness expired. He was president for just thirty days, nearly all of it spent unconscious. Forty years later his grandson, Benjamin Harrison, was elected president, and succeeded in the challenging ambition of achieving as little in four years as his grandfather had in a month.

As far as I am concerned, all these men deserve public holidays of their own. So you may imagine my dismay at news that moves are afoot in Congress to abolish Presidents Day and return to observing Lincoln's and Washington's birthdays separately, on the grounds that Lincoln and Washington were truly great men and, moreover, didn't pee out of the window. Can you believe that? Some people have no sense of history.

LIFE IN A COLD CLIMATE

SOMETHING DARING THAT I LIKE TO DO AT THIS TIME OF YEAR IS TO GO out without putting on my coat or gloves or any other protection against the elements and walk the thirty or so yards to the bottom of our drive to bring in the morning paper from a little box on a post.

Now you might say that that doesn't sound very daring at all, and in a sense you would be right because it only takes about twenty seconds there and back, but here is the thing that makes it special: sometimes I hang around out there just to see how long I can stand the cold.

I don't want to sound boastful, but I have devoted much of my life to testing the tolerance to extremes of the human body, often with very little thought to the potential long-term peril to myself – for instance, allowing a leg to go fast asleep in a cinema and then seeing what happens if I try to go for popcorn, or wrapping an elastic band around my index finger to see if I can make it explode. It is through this work that I have made some important break-throughs, notably the discovery that very hot surfaces don't necessarily look hot, and that temporary amnesia can be reliably induced by placing the head immediately beneath an open drawer.

I expect your instinct is to regard such behaviour as foolhardy, but let me remind you of all those occasions when you yourself have stuck a finger into a small flame just to see what would happen (and what exactly *did* happen, eh?) or stood first on one leg and then on the other in a scalding bath waiting for an inflow of cold water to moderate the temperature, or sat at a kitchen table quietly absorbed with letting melted candle wax drip onto your fingers, or a great deal else I could mention.

At least when I engage in these matters it is in a spirit of serious scientific enquiry. Which is why, as I say, I like to go for the morning paper in the least encumbering apparel that decency and Mrs Bryson will allow.

This morning when I set off it was minus 19°F (minus 28°C) out there – cold enough to reconfigure the anatomy of a brass monkey, as I believe the saying has it. Unless you have a particularly vivid imagination, or are reading this in a chest freezer, you may find such extreme chilliness difficult to conceive. So let me tell you just how cold it is: *very*.

When you step outside in such weather, for the first instant it is startlingly invigorating – not unlike the experience of diving into cold water, a sort of wake-up call to every corpuscle. But that phase passes quickly. Before you have trudged a few yards your face feels as it would after a sharp slap, your extremities are aching, and every breath you take hurts. By the time you return to the house your fingers and toes are throbbing with a gentle but insistent pain and you notice with interest that your cheeks yield no sensation at all. The little residual heat you brought from the house is long gone, and your clothes have ceased to have any insulating value. It is decidedly uncomfortable.

Nineteen degrees below zero is unusually cold even for northern New England, so I was interested to see how long I could bear such an exposure, and the answer was thirty-nine seconds. I don't mean that that's how long it took for me to get bored with the idea, or to think, Gracious, it is rather chilly; I guess I'll go in now. I mean that's how long it took me to be so cold that I would have climbed over my mother to get inside first.

New Hampshire is famous for its harsh winters, but in fact there are plenty of places much worse. The coldest temperature ever recorded here was minus 46°F, back in 1925, but twenty other states – nearly half – have had lower lows than that. The bleakest thermometer reading yet seen in the US was at Prospect Creek, Alaska, in 1971, when the temperature fell to minus 79.8°F.

Of course, almost any place can have a cold snap. The real test of a winter is in its duration. In International Falls, Minnesota, the winters are so long and ferocious that the mean annual temperature is just 36.5°F (2.5°C), which is very mean indeed. Near by there is a town called (honestly) Frigid, where I suspect the situation is even worse but they are just too depressed to report.

However, the record for the most wretched inhabited place ever must surely go to Langdon, North Dakota, which in the winter of 1935–6 recorded 176 consecutive days of below-freezing temperatures, including sixty-seven consecutive days in which the temperature fell below 0°F (i.e., into the shrieking brass monkey zone) for at least part of the day, and forty-one consecutive days when the temperature did not rise above 0°F.

Just to put that in perspective, 176 days is the span of time that lies between February and August. Personally, I would find it very hard to spend 176 consecutive days in North Dakota at any time, but I guess that is another matter.

In any case, I have all I can handle right here in New Hampshire. I was dreading the long, cruel winters in New England, but to my surprise they delight me. Partly it is because they are so shocking. There really is something exhilarating about the sharpness of the cold, the cleanness of the air. And winters here are stunningly pretty. Every rooftop and mailbox wears a jaunty cap of snow for months on end. Nearly every day the sun shines, so there is none of the oppressive grey gloom that characterizes winter in so many other places. And when the snow begins to get trampled or dirty, there is generally a big new fall that fluffs it up again.

People here actually get excited about winter. There is skiing and ice skating and sledging on the local golf course. One of our neighbours floods his back garden and turns it into a skating pond for the kids on our street. The local college has a winter carnival, with ice sculptures on the college green. It is all very cheery.

Best of all, you know that winter is just one in an endless cycle of reliable, well-defined seasons. When the cold starts to get to you, there is the reassurance of knowing that a good hot summer is just around the corner. Apart from anything else, it means a whole new set of interesting experimental challenges involving sunburn, poison ivy, infectious deer tics, electric hedge clippers and – this goes without saying – barbecue lighter fluid. I can't wait.

DROWNING IN RED TAPE

I'M NOT EVEN GOING TO BEGIN TO TELL YOU ABOUT THE FRUSTRATION OF trying to get a foreign-born spouse or other loved one registered as a legal resident in the United States because I haven't space and anyway it is much too boring. Also, I can't talk about it without weeping copiously. Also, you would think I was making most of it up.

You would scoff, I am quite sure, if I told you that an acquaintance of ours – an academic of high standing – sat open-mouthed while his daughter was asked such questions as 'Have you ever engaged in any unlawful commercial vice, including, but not limited to, illegal gambling?' and 'Have you ever been a member of, or in any way affiliated with, the Communist Party or any other totalitarian party?' and – my particular favourite – 'Do you plan to practise polygamy in the US?' His daughter, I should point out, was five years old.

You see, I am weeping already.

There is something seriously wrong with a country that asks such questions of any person, not simply because the questions are intrusive and irrelevant, and not because enquiries into one's political affinities fly in the face of the American Constitution, but because they are such a monumental waste of everyone's time. Who, after all, when asked if he intends to engage in genocide, espionage, hijacking, multiple marriages or any other of an extremely long and interestingly paranoid list of undesirable activities is going to say: 'I certainly do! Say, will this harm my chances of getting in?'

If all that was involved was answering a list of pointless

questions under oath, then I would just sigh and let it be. But it is infinitely more than that. Acquiring legal status in America involves fingerprints, medical examinations, blood tests, letters of affidavit, birth and marriage certificates, employment records, proof of financial standing, and much else – and all of it must be assembled, validated, presented and paid for in very specific ways. My wife recently had to make a 250-mile round trip to give a blood sample at a clinic recognized by the US Immigration and Naturalization Service even though one of the finest teaching hospitals in America is here in the town in which we live.

There are endless forms to fill in, each with pages of instructions, which often contradict other instructions and almost always lead to the need for more forms. Here is a typical fragment of instructions regarding the presentation of fingerprints:

'Submit a complete set of fingerprints on Form FD-258 . . . Complete the information on the top of the chart and write your A# (if any) in the space marked "Your no. OCA" or "Miscellaneous no. MNU".'

If you don't have form FD-258 (and you don't) or aren't sure which is your MNU number (and you aren't), you can spend days repeatedly dialling a phone number that is forever engaged, only to be told when you finally do get through that you must call another number, which the person tells you once in a mumble and you don't quite catch before you are cut off. It is like this with every encounter you have with every branch of the American government. After a while you begin to understand why flinty-eyed cowpokes in places like Montana turn their ranches into fortresses and threaten to shoot any government officer fool enough to walk into the cross-hairs.

And it's no good just filling in the forms to the best of your ability, because if anything is even a tiny bit out of order, it is all sent back. My wife had her file returned once because the distance between her chin and hairline on a passport-sized photograph was out by one-eighth of an inch.

This has been going on for two years for us. Understand, my wife does not want to practise brain surgery, engage in espionage, assist or collude in the trafficking of drugs, participate in the overthrow of the American government (though frankly I would not stand in her way), or take part in any other proscribed activity. She just wants to do a little shopping and be legally resident with her family. Doesn't seem too much to ask.

Goodness knows what the hold-up is. Occasionally we get a request for some additional document. Every few months I write to ask what is happening, but I never get a response. Three weeks ago we received a letter from the INS office in London, which we thought must be the official approval at last. Good joke! It was a computer-generated letter saying that because her application had been inactive for twelve months it was being cancelled.

All this is a very roundabout way of getting to a story concerning some British friends of ours here in Hanover. The husband is a professor at the local university, and has been for some years. Eighteen months ago, he and his family went back to England for a year's sabbatical. When they arrived at Heathrow, excited to be home, the immigration officer asked them how long they were staying.

'A year,' my friend answered brightly.

'And what about the American child?' the officer asked with a cocked eyebrow.

Their youngest, you see, had been born in America, and they had never bothered to register him as British. He was only four, so it wasn't as if he would be looking for work or anything.

They explained the situation. The immigration man listened gravely, then went off to consult a supervisor.

It had been eight years since my friends had left Britain, and they weren't sure just how much more like America it might have grown in that period. So they waited uneasily. After a minute the immigration man returned, followed by his supervisor, and said to them in a low voice, 'My supervisor is going to ask you how long you intend to stay in Britain. Say, "Two weeks."'

So the supervisor asked them how long they intended to stay, and they said, 'Two weeks.'

'Good,' said the supervisor, then added as if by way of afterthought, 'It might be an idea to register your child as British within the next day or two, in case you should decide to extend your stay.'

'Of course,' said my friend.

And they were in. And that is why I love Britain. That and the pubs and Branston pickle and country churchyards and a great deal else, but mostly because you still have a public service that is capable of genuine humanity and doesn't act as if it loathes you.

And on that note, I am going to go off and stock up on ammo.

THE WASTELAND

I HAVE BEEN WATCHING A MOVIE CALLED *MAGNIFICENT OBSESSION* lately. Made in 1954 and starring Rock Hudson and Jane Wyman, it is one of those stupefyingly mediocre movies they made in abundance in the early 1950s when people would still watch almost anything (as opposed to now when you have to put in lots of fiery explosions and at least one scene involving the hero abseiling down a liftshaft).

Anyway, if I've got it right, *Magnificent Obsession* involves a handsome young racing-car driver played by Rock who carelessly causes Ms Wyman to go blind in a car crash. Rock is so consumed with guilt at this that he goes off and studies eye medicine at the 'University of Oxford, England', or some place, then comes back to Perfectville under an assumed name and dedicates his life to restoring Jane's sight. Only of course she doesn't know it's him on account of she is blind, as well as apparently a little slow with regard to recognizing the voices of people who have left her maimed.

Needless to say, they fall in love and she gets her sight back. The best scene is when Rock removes her bandages and she says, 'Why, it's . . . *you*!' and slumps into a comely faint, but unfortunately does not strike her head a sharp blow and lose her vision again, which would have improved the story considerably, if you ask me. Also, Jane has a ten-year-old daughter played by one of those syrupy, pigtailed, revoltingly precocious child actors of the Fifties that you just ache to push out of a high window. I expect also Lloyd Nolan is in there somewhere because Lloyd Nolan is always in 1950s movies with parts for doctors.

I may not have all the details right because I have not been watching this movie in order, or even on purpose. I have been watching it because one of our cable channels has shown it at least fifty-four times in the last two months, and I keep coming across it while trawling around looking for something I actually want to watch.

You cannot believe – you really cannot believe – the awfulness, the jaw-slackening direness, of American television. Oh, I know that British TV can be pretty appalling itself. I lived in England for twenty years, so I am well acquainted with the dismay that comes when you look at the television listings and discover that the featured highlights for the evening are *Carry On Ogling*, a nature special on ice maggots of Lake Baikal, and a new Jeremy Beadle series called *Ooh, I Think I May Be Sick*. But even at its grimmest – even when you find yourself choosing between *Prisoner: Cell Block H* and Peter Snow being genuinely interested in European farm subsidies – British TV cannot begin to touch American television for the capacity to make you want to go out and lie down on a motorway.

We get about fifty channels in our house – it is possible on some systems now to get up to 200, I believe – so you think at first that you are going to be spoiled for choice, but you gradually realize that the idea of TV here is simply to fill up the air with any old sludge.

Programmes that even Sky One would be embarrassed to put on (I know, it hardly seems possible, but it is so) here get lavish air-time. It is as if the programmers just pull down a cassette from the shelves and slap it into the machine. I have watched 'current affairs' investigations that were ten years old. I have seen Barbara Walters interviewing people who died a dozen years ago, and weren't that interesting to begin with. Seven nights a week you can watch Johnny Carson shows that were witless in 1976 and now are witless and dated.

There is almost no concept that TV might, just sometimes, be innovative and good. On this very evening, under the category of 'Drama', my cable channel magazine lists as its most sublime and compelling offerings *Matlock* and *Little House on the Prairie*. Tomorrow it recommends *The Waltons* and *Dallas*. The next day it is *Dallas* again and *Murder, She Wrote*.

You begin to wonder who watches it all. One of our channels is a twenty-four-hour cartoon network. That there are people out there who wish to watch cartoons through the night is remarkable enough, but what is truly astounding to me is that the channel carries commercials. What could you possibly sell to people who voluntarily watch *Deputy Dawg* at 2.30 a.m.? Bibs?

But perhaps the most mind-numbing feature of American television is that the same programmes are shown over and over at the same times each night. Tonight at 9.30 p.m. on Channel 20 we can watch the *Munsters*. Last night at 9.30 p.m. on Channel 20 it was the *Munsters*. Tomorrow night at 9.30 p.m. on Channel 20 it will be – did you guess correctly? – the *Munsters*. Each *Munsters* showing is preceded by an episode of *Happy Days* and followed by an episode of the *Mary Tyler Moore Show*. It has been like this for years, as far as I can tell, and will stay like this for ever.

And it is like this on virtually every channel for every time slot. If you turn on the Discovery Channel and find a programme on Hollywood stunts (and you will), you can be certain that the next time you turn to the Discovery Channel at the same hour, it will be a programme on Hollywood stunts. Probably it will be the same episode.

With so many channels to choose from, and nearly all of it so hopelessly undiverting, you don't actually watch anything. And that is the scary part of all this. Although American television is totally imbecilic, although it makes you weep and rend your hair and throw soft foods at the screen, it is also strangely irresistible. As a friend once explained to me, you don't watch television here to see what is on, you watch it to see what else is on. And the one thing to be said for American TV is that there is always something else on. You can trawl infinitely. By the time you have reached the fiftieth channel you have forgotten what was on the first, so you start the cycle again in the pathetically optimistic hope that you might find something absorbing this time through.

I haven't begun to cover this topic. TV is my life, so we'll be coming back to this a lot in future months. But I must leave you now. I notice that *Magnificent Obsession* is about to start and I really would like to see Jane Wyman lose her sight. It's the best part. Besides, I keep thinking that if I watch long enough Lloyd Nolan will shove that little girl out of an upstairs window.

COMMERCIALS, COMMERCIALS, COMMERCIALS

THERE IS AN ADVERT RUNNING ON TELEVISION AT THE MOMENT THAT says something like 'The new Dodge Backfire. Rated number one against the Chrysler Inert for handling. Rated number one against the Plymouth Repellent for mileage. Rated number one against the Ford Eczema for repair costs.'

As you will notice, because luckily for you your brain has not been dented and dimmed by years of over-exposure to rapid-fire American advertising, in each category the Dodge is rated against only one other competitor, which makes comparisons a trifle hollow, if not actually suspect. I mean to say, if the Dodge were rated top against ten or twelve or fifteen competitors in any of these categories, then presumably the ad would have said so. Because it doesn't say so, one must naturally conclude that the Dodge performed worse than all its competitors except the one cited. Ergo, it is effectively inviting you to think twice before buying a Dodge.

The flimsiness of commercial assertions here is something that often leaves me quietly boggled. Last year some other manufacturer proudly boasted that its vehicles had been rated 'tops for reliability among cars manufactured or assembled in the United States', which seemed to me positively to invite the audience to go out and buy a foreign car. But clearly audiences don't see it that way.

Being carefully selective with the truth is a venerable tradition in American advertising. I retain a special fondness for a series of ads run by an insurance company in which 'real people in real situations' discussed their personal finances. When a journalist asked the company who these 'real people' were, a spokesman replied that actually they were actors and 'in that sense they are not real people'. That tells you about as much as you need to know about the American approach to advertising.

To be fair, not all American commercials are vacuous or misleading. Quite a lot of them – well, two of them – are droll and original. I am particularly taken at the moment with a commercial for pizza by the foot in which a deliveryman with an overlong pizza destroys everything he comes in contact with. (My least favourite, for the record, is one in which a gorgeous-and-don't-I-know-it young woman turns to the camera and says, 'Don't hate me because I'm beautiful.' To which I always reply, 'Oh, I don't. I hate you because you make me gip.')

No, the problem with American commercials is that they are simply so constant. Most channels have a commercial break about every five or six minutes. CNN, as far as I can tell, has nothing but commercial breaks.

It occurred to me that this is rather a sweeping statement, so I have just taken a half-hour, at no extra cost to you, to monitor a typical CNN programme, and here are my findings. In a single thirty-minute period, CNN interrupted its programme five times to show twenty commercials. Altogether it showed ten minutes of commercials in a thirty-minute slot. Apart from a seven-minute span at the start of the programme, the longest period without commercials was four minutes and fifty-nine seconds. The shortest interval between commercials was two minutes. For the benefit of people who suffered a serious brain injury during the programme, three of the commercials were repeated.

This, I hasten to add, is completely typical. Last night, one of the networks showed the movie *The Fugitive*, and I did a similar exercise. In order to watch about a hundred minutes of movie, it was necessary to sit through almost fifty minutes of commercials, spread over about twenty interruptions. (One every seven minutes, on average.)

According to Neil Postman in his book *Amusing Ourselves to Death*, the average American is exposed to 1,000 television commercials a week. By the time he is eighteen, the typical American child has sat goggle-eyed through no fewer than 350,000 television adverts.

Increasingly nowadays even when you are not watching commercials you are watching commercials, so to speak. For example, the ABC network recently aired a special on the making of the Disney movie *The Hunchback of Notre Dame*. According to the *New York Times*, several ABC stations also devoted a portion of their evening news broadcasts to 'a gala celebration that Disney threw for the movie in New Orleans'. It just happens that ABC owns the Disney Company.

Meanwhile, the History Channel unveiled plans to run a series called *The Spirit of Enterprise* celebrating the history and achievements of corporations like Boeing, DuPont and General Motors. The programmes were to be made by – yup – the corporations themselves. The History Channel later cancelled the series when it was brought to its attention that the whole undertaking was just too, too tacky.

Less troubled by considerations of credibility and impartiality was CNBC, another cable network, which announced the launch of a weekly news magazine called *Scan*. This programme was to report on all the latest developments in technology – or, to be slightly more precise, on all the latest developments that met with the approval of its sponsor, IBM, to which it had handed editorial control. 'This is not hard news,' a CNBC spokesman explained. 'It is a feature programme.' Oh, well, that makes it all right, then.

In short, commercials are inescapable here – and not just at home. I am appalled to report that many thousands of schools across America now rely, at least in part, on educational materials provided by corporations, so that pupils are learning about nutrition from McDonald's and conservation and the environment from Exxon, among others. Since 1989, a company called Channel One has been beaming educational programmes to schools via a closed-circuit system. The programmes are free but they are interspersed with commercials aimed specifically at young audiences. Now I would call that obviously, palpably unacceptable and exploitative, but this is evidently a minority view. Channel One has been a big hit; its sets are in 350,000 classrooms.

Even Sesame Street programmes – this is truly heartbreaking – have become, in the words of the *Boston Globe*, 'uninterrupted thirty-minute commercials'. As the *Globe* points out, Sesame Street products generate over $800 million in retail sales every year, and its executives enjoy salaries of up to $200,000 a year. Yet because the programme is aired on public television here, it receives an annual government subsidy of $7 million.

I was about to say think what would happen if that $7 million were spent instead on inner-city schools, but then it occurred to me that what would happen is that they would go out and buy more TVs to hook more classrooms into Channel One.

Inevitably, this has made my brain throb, so I'm off to take a Tylenol. I understand that in a survey it was preferred over other brands by two to one. Or maybe I'm thinking of Pepsi.

FRIENDLY PEOPLE

I WAS INTENDING THIS WEEK TO WRITE ABOUT SOME EXASPERATION OR other of modern American life when Mrs Bryson (who is, may I say, a dear woman) brought me a cup of coffee, read the first few lines off the computer screen, and muttered, 'Bitch, bitch, bitch,' and shuffled off.

'Pardon, my dewy English rose?' I called.

'You're always complaining in that column.'

'But the world needs righting, my luscious, cherry-cheeked daughter of Boadicea,' I rejoined tranquilly. 'Besides, complaining is what I do.'

'Complaining is all you do.'

Well, excuse me, but not quite. I believe on these very pages I once said a few words of praise for American garbage disposal units and I clearly recall commending our local post office for providing me with a free doughnut on Customer Appreciation Day. But perhaps she had a point.

There are many wonderful things about the United States of America that deserve praise – the Bill of Rights, the Freedom of Information Act and free bookmatches are three that leap to mind – but none is more outstanding than the friendliness of the people.

When we moved to this little town in New Hampshire, people received us as if the one thing that had kept them from total happiness to this point was the absence of us in their lives. They brought us cakes and pies and bottles of wine. Not one of them said, 'So you're the people who paid a fortune for the Smith place,' which I believe is the traditional greeting in England. Our next-door neighbours, upon learning that we were intending to go out to eat, protested that it was too dreary to dine in a strange restaurant on one's first night in a new town and insisted we come to them for dinner there and then, as if feeding six extra mouths was the most trifling of burdens.

When word got round that our furniture was on a container ship making its way from Liverpool to Boston, evidently by way of Port Said, Mombasa and the Galápagos Islands, and that we were temporarily without anything to sleep on, sit on, or eat from, a stream of friendly strangers (many of whom I have not seen since) began traipsing up the walk with chairs, lamps, tables, even a microwave oven.

It was dazzling, and it has remained so. At Christmas this year we went to England for ten days and returned home late at night and hungry to find that a neighbour had stocked the fridge with both essentials and goodies, and filled vases with fresh flowers. This sort of thing happens all the time.

Recently I went with one of my children to a local college basketball game. We arrived just before game time and joined a queue at one of the ticket windows. After a minute a man came up to me and said, 'Are you waiting to buy tickets?'

No, I wanted to reply, I'm standing here to make the line more impressive, but of course all I said was, 'Yes, I am.'

'Because you can have these,' he said and thrust two tickets at me.

My immediate thought, born of years of stupidly misreading situations, was that he was a tout and that there must be some catch. 'How much?' I said warily.

'No, no, you can have them. For free. We can't go to the game, you see.' He indicated a car outside with the motor running and a woman in the passenger seat.

'Really?' I said. 'Well, thank you very much.' And then I was struck by a thought. 'Did you make a special trip here to give away two tickets?'

'They were going to go to waste otherwise,' he said apologetically. 'Enjoy the game.'

I could go on and on about this sort of thing – about the young man who returned my son's lost wallet with nearly all his summer's wages in it and wouldn't take a reward, about the employees of the cinema who go out if it starts to rain and roll up all the windows of cars parked along nearby streets on the assumption that at least some of them will belong to cinema customers who don't know it is raining, how after the wife of the local police chief lost her hair during chemotherapy treatment every member of the force had his head shaved to raise money for a cancer charity and to make the chief's wife feel less conspicuous.

That people leave their cars unlocked and the windows open tells you something more about the town, of course. The fact is, there is no crime here. None. People will casually leave a $500 bicycle propped against a tree and go off to do their shopping. If someone did steal it, I am almost certain the victim would run after the thief shouting, 'Could you please return it to 32 Wilson Avenue when you've finished? And watch out for the third gear – it sticks.'

No-one locks anything. I remember being astounded by this on my first visit when an estate agent took me out to look at houses (and there's another thing – estate agents in America know how to stand up and move around) and she kept leaving her car unlocked, even when we went into a restaurant for lunch and even though there was a portable phone on the seat and some shopping in the back.

At one of the houses she discovered she had brought the wrong key. 'Back door'll be unlocked,' she announced confidently, and it was. I subsequently realized that there was nothing unusual in this. We know people who go away on holiday without locking their doors, don't know where their house key is, aren't even sure if they still have one.

Now you might reasonably wonder why, then, this is not a thief's paradise. There are two reasons, I believe. First, there is no market for stolen goods here. If you sidled up to anyone in New Hampshire and said, 'Wanna buy a car stereo?' the person would look at you as if you were off your head and say, 'No, I already have a car stereo.' Then they would report you to the police and – here is the second thing – the police would come and shoot you.

But of course the police don't shoot people here because they don't need to because there is no crime. It is a rare and heart-warming example of a virtuous circle. We have grown used to this now, but when we were still new in town and I expressed wonder about it all to a woman who grew up in New York City but has lived here for twenty years, she laid a hand on my arm and said, as if imparting a great secret, 'Honey, you're not in the real world any longer. You're in New Hampshire.'

ON THE HOTLINE

I CAME ACROSS SOMETHING IN OUR BATHROOM THE OTHER DAY WHICH has occupied my thoughts off and on since. It was a little dispenser of dental floss.

It isn't the floss itself that is of interest to me, but that the container has a freephone number printed on it. You can call the company's Floss Hotline twenty-four hours a day. But here is the question: Why would you need to? I keep imagining some guy calling up and saying in an anxious voice, 'OK, I've got the floss. Now what?'

As a rule of thumb, I would submit that if you need to call your floss provider, for any reason, you are probably not ready for this level of oral hygiene.

My curiosity aroused, I had a look through all our cupboards and discovered with interest that nearly all household products in America carry a hotline number. You can, it appears, ring up for guidance on how to use soap and shampoo, gain helpful tips on where to store ice cream so that it doesn't turn to soup and run out of the bottom of the container, and receive professional advice on which parts of your body you can most successfully and stylishly apply nail polish. ('So let me get this straight. You're saying *not* on my forehead?')

For those who do not have access to a telephone, or who perhaps have a telephone but have not yet mastered its use, most products also carry helpful printed tips such as 'Remove Shells Before Eating' (on peanuts) and 'Caution: Do Not Re-Use as Beverage Container' (on a bleach bottle). We recently bought an electric iron which admonished us, among other things, not to use it in conjunction with explosive materials. In a broadly similar vein, I read a couple of weeks ago that computer software companies are considering re-writing the instruction 'Strike Any Key When Ready' because so many people have been calling in to say they cannot find the 'Any' key.

Until a few days ago my instinct would have been to chortle richly at people who need this sort of elemental guidance, but then three things happened that made me modify my views.

First, I read in the paper how John Smoltz, a pitcher for the Atlanta Braves baseball team, showed up at a training session one day with a painful-looking red welt across his chest and, when pressed for an explanation, sheepishly admitted that he had tried to iron a shirt while he was wearing it.

Second, it occurred to me that although I have never done any-thing quite so foolish as that, it was only because I had not thought of it.

Third, and perhaps most conclusively, two nights ago I went out to run two small errands – specifically, to buy some pipe tobacco and post some letters. I bought the tobacco, carried it straight across the street to a post office letter box, opened the lid, and deposited it. I won't tell you how far I walked before it dawned on me that this was not a 100 per cent correct execution of my original plans.

You see my problem. People who need labels on pillar boxes say-ing 'Not for Deposit of Tobacco or Other Personal Items' can't very well smirk at others, even those who iron their chests or have to seek lathering guidance from a shampoo hotline.

I mentioned all this at dinner the other night and was appalled to see the enthusiasm and alacrity with which all the members of the family began suggesting labels that would be particularly apt for me, like 'Caution: When Door Says "Pull" It's Absolutely No Use Pushing' and 'Warning: Do Not Attempt to Remove Sweater Over Head While Walking Among Chairs and Tables'. A particular favourite was 'Caution: Ensure That Shirt Buttons Are in Correct Holes Before Leaving House'. This went on for some hours.

I concede that I am somewhat inept with regard to memory, personal grooming, walking through low doorways, and much else, but the thing is it's my genes. Allow me to explain.

I recently tore out of the newspaper an article concerning a study at the University of Michigan, or perhaps it was the University of Minnesota (at any rate it was somewhere cold with 'University' in the title), which found that absent-mindedness is a genetically inherited trait. I put it in a file marked 'Absent-Mindedness' and, of course, immediately mislaid the file.

However, in searching for it this morning I found another file intriguingly marked 'Genes and So On', which is just as interesting and – here was the lucky part – not altogether irrelevant. In it I found a copy of a report from the 29 November 1996 issue of the journal *Science* entitled 'Association of Anxiety-Related Traits with a Polymorphism in the Serotonin Transporter Gene Regulatory Region'.

Now to be perfectly frank, I don't follow polymorphism in serotonin transporters as closely as I ought, at least not during basketball season, but when I saw the sentence 'By regulating the magnitude and duration of serotonergic responses, the 5-HT transporter (5-HTT) is central to the fine-tuning of brain serotonergic neurotransmission,' I thought, Hey, these fellows could be on to something.

The upshot of the study is that scientists have located a gene (specifically gene number SLC6A4 on chromosome 17q12, in case you want to experiment at home) which determines whether you are a born worrier or not. To be absolutely precise, if you have a long version of the SLC6A4 gene, you are very probably easy-going and serene, whereas if you have the short version you can't leave home without saying at some point, 'Stop the car. I think I left the bathwater running.'

What this means in practice is that if you are not a born worrier then you have nothing to worry about (though of course you wouldn't be worrying anyway), whereas if you *are* a worrier by nature there is absolutely nothing you can do about it, so you may as well stop worrying, except of course you can't. Now put this together with the aforementioned findings about absent-mindedness at the University of Somewhere Cold, and I think you can see that our genes have a great deal to answer for.

Here's another interesting fact from my 'Genes and So On' file. According to Richard Dawkins in *The Blind Watchmaker*, each one of the 10 trillion cells in the human body contains more genetic information than the entire *Encyclopedia Britannica* (and without sending a salesman to your door), yet it appears that 90 per cent of all our genetic material doesn't do anything at all. It just sits there, like Uncle Fred and Aunt Muriel when they drop by on a Sunday.

From this I believe we can draw four important conclusions,

namely: (1) Even though your genes don't do much they can let you down in a lot of embarrassing ways, (2) always post your letters first, then buy the tobacco, (3) never promise a list of four things if you can't remember the fourth one, and (4).

THOSE BORING FOREIGNERS

JULIAN BARNES, IN A LINE I INTEND TO MAKE MY OWN WHEN THE moment is right, once observed that any foreigner visiting the United States can perform an easy magic trick: 'Buy a newspaper and see your own country disappear.'

Actually, you don't need to read a newspaper. You can read a magazine or watch TV or just talk to people. My son recently reported to me that in a current affairs quiz in one of his high-school classes only one person was able to name the British Prime Minister, and he was that person. I am quite certain that not one American in 500 has any idea that a general election is looming in the UK.

Of course, let's be fair, most people in most places don't know much about the rest of the world. I mean to say, could you name the leaders of Denmark or The Netherlands or even Ireland? Of course you couldn't – and you are immensely intelligent and attentive. I can see that from here. No reason why you should. There is a lot of world out there to follow, and you have your hands full just keeping up with *EastEnders*. I understand.

But there is a difference. You are at least vaguely aware from reading the papers and watching or listening to the news that there is a world beyond the English Channel, and that people are doing things in that world (mostly blockading ports and making life jolly difficult for law-abiding lorry drivers from more civil nations, if memory serves).

It used to be like that here. *Time* magazine would be full of stories about tottering coalition governments in Italy and corruption scandals in South America, and the evening news would have at least a sprinkling of reports each showing a serious-looking correspondent in a Burberry standing with a microphone in front of a bourse or sampan or Congress of the People's Revolution – something in any case that was patently not in Nebraska. Even if you paid no attention to these dispatches, they at least reminded you that you existed in a wider world.

No longer. In the first three months of this year the US edition of *Time* did not have a single report from France, Italy, Spain or Japan, to name just a few of the countries that seem to have escaped its notice. Britain made it into the pages only because of Dolly the cloned sheep. Germany got in because of the Government's row there with Scientologists. Otherwise all has been darkness in Western Europe. The 'International' section of *Time* these days generally consists of a single story, almost never more than two. The amazing thing is that if you look at the masthead, *Time* has correspondents all over – in Paris, London, Rome, Vienna, you name it. Give me one of those jobs, please!

Television news is no better. Just to make sure I wasn't talking through my hat here (or indeed anything else round and inappropriate), I monitored the NBC evening news last night. This is one of the main national news programmes, the equivalent of the BBC's *Six O'clock News*, but with the addition of several minutes of advertising for denture fixatives, haemorrhoid creams and laxatives. (People who watch the evening news in America are evidently in a bad way.)

The NBC bulletin consisted of eleven items, of which ten were exclusively about the United States. Only one, concerning a visit by Vice-President Gore to China, acknowledged life beyond American shores, though in fact the report was really about American trade prospects and anyway lasted just twenty-two seconds. Still, it did include a two-second shot of flocks of people riding bicycles in front of a pagoda-like structure, so I guess it counts.

Later, I undertook a similar exercise with CNN's main evening bulletin. It lasted an hour, so it offered even more adverts for painkillers, salves and mentholated unguents (somebody really should get these viewers to a hospital), but also managed to squeeze in twenty-two snippets of news, of which all twenty-two were about the United States. This on a programme that calls itself *The World Today*.

Because there is so little exposure to non-American things, people here often get quite severely out of patience with anything that is not immediately recognizable to them. I have before me a review from the *New York Times* of a book by the British journalist Stephen Fay on Nick Leeson and the collapse of Barings, in which the reviewer complains, with really quite profound irritation, that the book is 'littered with needlessly confusing Britspeak'. Among the confounding expressions she cites are 'cock-up', 'just not on' and a reference to a trading floor being 'the size of a football pitch'. Well, imagine that – a book by a British writer about a British employee of a British bank containing some British expressions. That is, like, *so* inconsiderate. The next thing, they'll be expecting us to know who the prime minister is.

I find that sad. One of the things I liked about reading British books or watching British films when I was growing up was *not* knowing precisely what was going on – wondering what the characters meant when they said, 'I say, we jolly well knocked Jerry out of touch for six into a sticky wicket with those bouncing buzz bombs the boffins in G-section came up with at high tea yesterday fortnight, what?' and trying to deduce what Marmite could possibly be (never for a moment guessing that it's an edible lubricant). Americans don't want to do that now, I'm afraid.

I recently sat through a showing of *The English Patient* at our local cinema in which a woman behind me followed every line spoken by Juliette Binoche by turning to her partner and saying in a loud, pained, nasal voice, 'What's she *saying*?' It became so irksome that I finally had to smother the woman with my jacket.

In the same week, I read a newspaper review of a Jackie Chan movie in which the reviewer complained, again with deep exasperation, that Chan's dialogue was incomprehensible to him. (Hint to reviewer: the appeal of Jackie Chan movies does not lie in the quality of the discourse.) I have heard or read similar complaints about all or parts of *Secrets and Lies*, *My Left Foot*, *The Commitments*, *Shine*, *Shallow Grave* – indeed, almost any film to emerge from the non-American-speaking world.

I could go on and on, but alas I am out of space and I sense that you can't wait to get to the wireless to hear the outcome of those Belgian by-elections. Meanwhile, I shall be monitoring British affairs as closely as I can from here. But I would ask just one thing. If Mrs Thatcher is turned out of office, let me know at once. And please stop calling it a wireless.

THE CUPHOLDER REVOLUTION

I AM ASSURED THAT THIS IS A TRUE STORY.

A man calls up his computer helpline complaining that the cupholder on his personal computer has snapped off, and he wants to know how to get it fixed.

'Cupholder?' says the computer helpline person, puzzled. 'I'm sorry, sir, but I'm confused. Did you buy this cupholder at a computer show or receive it as a special promotion?'

'No, it came as part of the standard equipment on my computer.'

'But our computers don't come with cupholders.'

'Well, pardon me, friend, but they do,' says the man a little hotly. 'I'm looking at mine right now. You push a button on the base of the machine and it slides right out.'

The man, it transpired, had been using the CD drawer in his computer to hold his coffee cup.

I bring this up here by way of introducing our topic this week: cupholders. I don't know if cupholders exist in Britain yet, but if not, trust me, they are on their way. Cupholders are taking over the world.

If you are not familiar with them, cupholders are little trays, lids or other receptacles with holes for holding cups and other drinks containers, which are found in multiple locations throughout every modern American automobile. Often they are mounted on the backs of seats or built into armrests, but just as often they are ingeniously tucked away in places you would never think to look for a beverage stowage device. Generally, in my experience, if you push an unfamiliar button anywhere in an American car, either it will activate the back windscreen wiper, which will rub with a heavy dragging noise across the glass once every six seconds for the rest of eternity no matter what you do to try to stop it, or it will make a cupholder slide out, rise up, drop down or otherwise magically enter your life.

It would be almost impossible to exaggerate the importance of cupholders in American automotive circles these days. The *New York Times* recently ran a long article in which it tested a dozen family cars. It rated each of them for ten features, such as engine size, boot space, handling, quality of suspension, and, yes, number of cupholders. A car dealer acquaintance of ours tells us that they are one of the first things people remark on, ask about or play with when they come to look at a car. People buy cars on the basis of cupholders. Nearly all car advertisements note them prominently in the text.

Some cars, like the newest model of the Dodge Caravan, come with as many as seventeen cupholders. Seventeen! The largest Caravan holds seven passengers. You don't have to be a nuclear physicist, or even wide awake, to work out that that is 2.43 cupholders per passenger. Why, you may reasonably wonder, would each passenger in a vehicle need 2.43 cupholders? Good question.

Americans, it is true, consume positively staggering volumes of fluids. One of our local petrol stations, I am told, sells a flavoured confection called a Slurpee in containers up to sixty ounces in size. That is three English pints of sickly stuff that turns your tongue blue. But even if every member of the family had a Slurpee *and* a personal bottle of Milk of Magnesia for dealing with the after-effects, that would still leave three cupholders spare.

There is a long tradition of endowing the interiors of American cars with lots of gadgets and comforts, and I suppose a superfluity of cupholders is just an outgrowth of that tradition.

The reason Americans want a lot of comfort in their cars is because they live in them. Almost 94 per cent of all American trips from home involve the use of a car. (The figure in Britain is about 60 per cent, which is bad enough.) People in America don't just use their cars to get to the shops, but to get between shops. Most businesses in America have their own car parks, so someone running six errands will generally move the car six times on a single outing, even to get between two places on opposite sides of the same street.

There are 200 million cars in the United States – 40 per cent of the world's total, for about 5 per cent of its population – and an additional 2 million new ones hit the roads each month (though obviously many are also retired). Even so, there are about twice as many cars in America as there were twenty years ago, driving on twice as many roads, racking up about twice as many miles.

So, because Americans have a lot of cars and spend a lot of time in them, they like a lot of comforts. However, there is a limit to how many different features you can fit into a car interior. What better, then, than to festoon it with nifty cupholders, particularly when people seem to go for them in a big way? That's my theory.

What is certainly true is that not putting cupholders in a car is a serious mistake. I read a couple of years ago that Volvo had to redesign all its cars for the American market for this very reason. Volvo's engineers had foolishly thought that what buyers were looking for was a reliable engine, side-impact bars and heated seats, when in fact what they craved were little trays into which to insert their Slurpees. So a bunch of guys named Nils Nilsson and Lars Larsson were put to work designing cupholders into the system, and Volvo was thus saved from beverage ignominy, if not actual financial ruin.

Now from all the foregoing we can draw one important conclusion – that no matter how hard you try, it is not quite possible to fill a column space with a discussion just of cupholders.

So let me tell you how I happen to know that those fellows at Volvo were called Nils Nilsson and Lars Larsson.

Some years ago when I was in Stockholm and had nothing better to do one evening (it was after 7 p.m., you see, so the city had long since turned in for the night), I passed the hours before bedtime thumbing idly through the local phone directory and tallying various names. I had heard that there were only a handful of surnames in Sweden, and this was essentially so. I counted over 2,000 each for Eriksson, Svensson, Nilsson and Larsson. There were so few names (or, it has to be said, the Swedes were so cosmically dull) that many people used the same name twice. There were 212 people in Stockholm named Erik Eriksson, 117 named Sven Svensson, 126 named Nils Nilsson and 259 named Lars Larsson. I wrote these names and numbers down on a piece of paper, and have been wondering all these years when I would ever find a use for it.

From this, I believe, we can draw two further conclusions. Save all scraps of paper bearing useless information, for one day you may be glad you did, and if you go to Stockholm, take drink.

YOUR TAX FORM EXPLAINED

ENCLOSED IS YOUR 1997 UNITED STATES INTERNAL REVENUE SERVICE Tax Form 1040-ES OCR: 'Estimated Tax for Self-Employed Individuals'. You may use this form to estimate your 1997 fiscal year tax *if*:

1. You are the head of a household *and* the sum of the ages of your spouse and dependants, minus the ages of qualifying pets (see Schedule 12G), is divisible by a whole number. (Use Supplementary Schedule 142C if pets are deceased but buried on your property.)

2. Your Gross Adjusted Income does not exceed your Adjusted Gross Income (except where applicable) *and* you did not pay taxable interest on dividend income prior to 1903.

3. You are not claiming a foreign tax credit, except as a 'foreign' tax credit. (Warning: claiming a foreign tax credit for a foreign 'tax' credit, except where a foreign 'tax credit' is involved, may result in a fine of $125,000 and twenty-five years' imprisonment.)

4. You are one of the following: married and filing jointly; married and not filing jointly; not married and not filing jointly; jointed but not filing; other.

INSTRUCTIONS
Type all answers in ink with a number two lead pencil. Do not cross anything out. Do not use abbreviations or ditto marks. Do not misspell 'miscellaneous'. Write your name, address and social security number, and the name, address and social security numbers of your spouse and dependants, in full on each page twice. Do not put a

tick in a box marked 'cross' or a cross in a box marked 'tick' unless it is your wish to do the whole thing again. Do not write 'Search me' in any blank spaces. Do not make anything up.

Complete sections 47 to 52 first, then proceed to even-numbered sections and complete in reverse order. Do *not* use this form if your total pensions and annuities disbursements were greater than your advanced earned income credits *or* vice versa.

Under 'Income', list all wages, salaries, net foreign source taxable income, royalties, tips, gratuities, taxable interest, capital gains, air miles, pints paid on, and money found down the back of the sofa. If your earnings are derived wholly, or partially but not primarily, or wholly *and* partially but not primarily, from countries other than the United States (if uncertain, see USIA Leaflet 212W, 'Countries That Are Not the United States') *or* your rotated gross income from Schedule H was greater than your earned income credit on non-taxable net disbursements, you *must* include a Grantor/ Transferrer Waiver Voucher. Failure to do so may result in a fine of $1,500,000 and seizure of a child.

Under Section 890f, list total farm income (if none, give details). If you were born after 1 January 1897, and are *not* a widow(er), include excess casualty losses and provide carryover figures for depreciation on line 27iii. You must list number of turkeys slaughtered for export. Subtract, but do not deduct, net gross dividends from pro rata interest payments, multiply by the total number of steps in your home, and enter on line 356d.

On Schedule F1001, line c, list the contents of your garage. Include all electrical and non-electrical items on Schedule 295D, but do not include electrical or non-electrical items not listed on Supplementary Form 243d.

Under 'Personal Expenditures', itemize all cash expenditures of more than $1, and include verification. If you have had dental work *and* you are not claiming a refund on the federal oil spill allowance, enter your shoe sizes since birth and enclose specimen shoes. (Right foot only.) Multiply by 1.5 or 1,319, whichever is larger, and divide line 3f by 3d. Under Section 912g, enter federal income support grants for the production of alfalfa, barley (but not sorghum, unless for home consumption) and okra *whether or not* you received any. Failure to do so may result in a fine of $3,750,000 and death by lethal injection.

If your children are dependent but not living at home, or living at home but not dependent, or dependent and living at home but hardly ever there *and* you are not claiming exemption for leases of maritime vessels in excess of 12,000 tonnes deadweight (15,000 tonnes if you were born in Guam), you *must* complete and include a Maritime Vessel Exemption Form. Failure to do so may result in a fine of $111,000,000 and a nuclear attack on a small, neutral country.

On pages 924–926, Schedule D, enter the names of people you know personally who are Communist or use drugs. (Use extra pages if necessary.)

If you have interest earnings from savings accounts, securities, bearer bonds, certificates of deposit or other fiduciary instruments but *do not* know your hat size, complete Supplementary Schedules 112d and 112f and enclose with all relevant tables. (Do not send chairs at this time.) Include, but do not collate, ongoing losses from mining investments, commodities transactions and organ transplants, divide by the total number of motel visits you made in 1996, and enter in any remaining spaces. If you have unreimbursed employee expenses, tough.

To compute your estimated tax, add lines 27 through 964, deduct lines 45a and 699f from Schedule 2F (if greater or less than 2.2% of average alternative minimum estimated tax for last five years), multiply by the number of RPMs your car registers when stuck on ice, and add 2. If line 997 is smaller than line 998, start again. In the space marked 'Tax Due', write a very large figure.

Make your cheque payable to 'Internal Revenue Service of the United States of America and to the Republic for Which It Stands', and mark for the attention of Patty. On the back of your cheque write your social security number, Taxpayer Identification Number, IRS Tax Code Audit Number(s), IRS Regional Office Sub-Unit Zone Number (*unless* you are filing a T/45 Sub-Unit Zone Exclusion Notice), sexual orientation and smoking preference, and send to:

Internal Revenue Service of the United States of
   America
Tax Reception and Orientation Center
Building D/Annexe G78
Suite 900
Subduction Zone 12
Box 132677-02
Drawer 2, About Halfway Back
Federal City
Maryland 10001

If you have any questions about filing, or require assistance with your return, phone 1-800-BUSY SIGNAL. Thank you and have a prosperous 1998. Failure to do so may result in a fine of $125,000 and a long walk to the cooler.

WARNING: ANYONE HAVING FUN WILL BE REPORTED

ONE OF OUR BARS HERE IN THE SWEET AND ORDERLY LITTLE TOWN IN NEW Hampshire in which I live recently placed small printed notices in plastic holders on each of the tables – the sort of notices that normally invite you to order a jug of pina coladas at a special price or perhaps join mine hosts Chip and Tiffany for their convivial daily happy hour.

However, far from inviting anyone to engage in anything as hedonistic as that, what these notices said was this: 'We take our responsibility to the community seriously. Therefore we are introducing a policy of limiting each customer to a maximum of three drinks. We thank you for your understanding and cooperation.'

When a bar (and in a college town at that) starts telling you that you must leave after as little as three bottles of beer – that's about one and a half English pints – you know something is going on. The problem isn't that townsfolk here in Hanover have been disgracing themselves, you understand. The problem is that they might enjoy themselves more than the modest amount that is deemed socially acceptable in this challenging age in which we live.

H.L. Mencken once defined puritanism as 'the haunting fear that someone, somewhere, may be happy'. It was seventy years ago that he said it, but it is as true today as it was then. Everywhere you turn in America these days you encounter a strange and insistent kind of nannying, as in these preposterous new notices in our local bar.

The thing is, the notices are in any case completely unnecessary.

I have discovered to my dismay that when an American friend invites you out for a beer that is exactly what he means – a beer. You sip it delicately for about forty-five minutes until it is gone and then your companion says, 'Hey, that was fun. Let's do it again next year.' I don't know anybody – anybody – who would be so rakish as to consume three drinks at a sitting. All the people I know barely drink at all, never touch tobacco, watch their cholesterol as if it were HIV-positive, jog up to Canada and back about twice a day, and go to bed early. Now that is all very sensible and I know they will outlive me by decades, but it isn't much fun.

And Americans these days find the most extraordinary things to worry about. Newspaper reviews of movies, for instance, nearly always end with a paragraph noting what qualities the film contains that viewers may find disturbing – violence, sexual content, strong language, and so on. That seems unobjectionable enough in principle, but what is remarkable is the things the papers believe worthy of inclusion. The *New York Times* recently concluded a review of a new Chevy Chase movie with this sombre warning: '*Vegas Vacation* is rated PG (Parental Guidance suggested). Besides sexual suggestiveness, it shows rattlesnakes and gambling.'

Oh well, that's out, then.

The *Los Angeles Times*, meanwhile, warns its readers that *As Good as It Gets* contains 'strong language and thematic elements' (whatever they are), while *Mouse Hunt* has 'mayhem, comic sensuality and language'. Not strong language or suggestive language, but just 'language'. My God, think of it. Language in a movie! Not to mention mayhem. And to think I nearly took the children.

There is, in short, a huge and preposterous disquiet in the land about almost everything. The bookshops and bestseller lists are full of books like Robert Bork's *Slouching to Gomorrah*, suggesting that America is on the brink of some catastrophic moral collapse. Among the literally hundreds of things Bork is worried about are 'the angry activists of feminism, homosexuality, environmentalism [and] animal rights'. Oh, please.

Things that would raise barely a flicker in other countries are here looked upon as almost dangerously licentious. A woman in Hartford, Connecticut, recently was threatened with arrest when a security guard saw her breastfeeding her baby – discreetly, mind you, with a baby blanket over her shoulder and her back turned to the world – in her car in a remote corner of a restaurant car park. She had left the restaurant and gone to her car to feed the baby because it was more private – but not private enough. Someone with binoculars might have glimpsed what she was doing, and, well, you can imagine the consequences for a stable and orderly society.

Meanwhile, in Boulder, Colorado, which has one of the strictest anti-smoking ordinances in America (i.e., they shoot you), an actor in an amateur stage production was threatened with arrest, if you can believe it, for smoking a cigarette onstage during a performance, as his part required. Smoking is of course the great forbidden activity these days. Light up a cigarette almost anywhere in America now and you are looked upon as a pariah. Light up indoors in a public place and you will almost certainly be swept upon by a phalanx of security people.

Many states – Vermont and California to name two – have laws making it illegal to smoke virtually anywhere indoors, apart from private residences, and often even outdoors. Now I'm all for discouraging smoking, but increasingly this is getting carried to neurotic and even sinister extremes. A company here in New Hampshire recently instituted a policy that any employee who is suspected of having smoked a cigarette within forty-five minutes of coming to work faces dismissal, even if he was smoking within the privacy of his own home, on his own time, with government-approved smoking materials.

But the most amazing thing of all is that even young people are voluntarily relinquishing fun. One of the most astounding stories I have encountered lately was a report in the *Boston Globe* last month that two college fraternity organizations – live-in clubs for university students – are banning intoxicating beverages of all kinds from their chapters.

If any student is found on the premises with a single can of beer – no matter that he may be legally entitled by age to own it and drink it – he will be instantly dismissed, and if the fraternity house itself dares to organize a function involving so much as a thimble of sherry, it will be summarily shut down without appeal.

When I was young the whole apparent purpose of fraternities was to keep America's breweries humming. You could judge the quality of a fraternity by the number of bodies on the lawn on a Saturday night. Now I am not arguing for unbridled alcoholic consumption at universities (actually I am, but we'll pretend I'm not). But to suggest that a bunch of students can't knock back a few beers on graduation day or after a big football victory or upon the conclusion of final exams, or, what the hell, whenever they want seems to me ludicrously puritanical.

Astonishingly, all but one of the several students quoted in the article favoured the new proposal.

'It's about time we had a policy like this,' said one priggish young scholar from the Massachusetts Institute of Technology, who, in my view, wants a good sound slapping.

Call me heartless, but I hope the next movie he sees has scenes involving rattlesnakes, gambling, thematic elements and language, and that it disturbs the dickens out of him. Wouldn't that just serve him right?

THE STATES EXPLAINED

MY FATHER, WHO LIKE ALL DADS SOMETIMES SEEMED TO BE PRACTISING for a world's most boring man competition, used to have the habit, when I was a boy, of identifying and reporting the state of origin of all the other cars on any highway we happened to be travelling along.

In America, as I expect you know, each state issues its own number plates, so you can tell at a glance where another car is from, which enabled my father to make trenchant observations like, 'Hey, another car from Wyoming. That's three this morning.' Or: 'Mississippi. Wonder what he's doing way up here?' Then he would look around hopefully to see if anyone wanted to elaborate or offer speculation, but no-one ever did. He could go on like that all day, and often did.

I once wrote a book making good-natured fun of the old man for his many interesting and unusual talents when behind the wheel – the unerring ability to get lost in any city, to drive the wrong way down a one-way street so many times that people would eventually come and watch from their doorways, or spend an entire afternoon driving around within sight of an amusement park or other eagerly sought attraction without actually finding the entrance. One of my teenaged children recently read that book for the first time and came with it into the kitchen where my wife was cooking and said in a tone of amazed discovery, 'But this is *Dad*,' meaning of course me.

I have to admit it. I have become my father. I even read number plates, though my particular interest is the slogans. Many states,

you see, include a friendly message or nugget of information on
their plates, like 'Land of Lincoln' for Illinois, 'Vacationland' for
Maine, 'Sunshine State' for Florida, and the zippily inane 'Shore
Thing' for New Jersey.

I like to make quips and comments on these so when, for
instance, we see Pennsylvania's 'You've Got a Friend in
Pennsylvania', I turn to the passengers and say in an injured tone,
'Then why doesn't he call?' However, I am the only one who finds
this an amusing way to pass a long journey.

It's interesting – well, perhaps not interesting exactly, but
certainly a fact – that many states append slogans that are pretty
well meaningless. I have never understood what Ohio was thinking
when it called itself the 'Buckeye State' and I haven't the remotest
idea what New York means by dubbing itself the 'Empire State'. As
far as I am aware, New York's many undoubted glories do not
include overseas possessions.

Indiana, meanwhile, calls itself the 'Hoosier State' and has done
for 150 years. No-one has ever satisfactorily deduced (possibly
because who after all cares?) where the term comes from, though I
can tell you from experience that if you mention this in a book 250
people from Indiana will write to you with 250 different explan-
ations and the unanimous view that you are a dunce.

All this is by way of introducing our important lesson of the day,
namely that the United States isn't so much a country as a collection
of fifty small independent nations, and you forget this at your peril.
It all goes back to the setting up of a federal government after the
War of Independence when the former colonies didn't trust each
other. In order to keep them happy, the states were given an extraordinary range of powers. Even now each state controls all kinds of
matters to do with your personal life – where, when and at what
age you can legally drink; whether you may carry a concealed
weapon, own fireworks, or legally gamble; how old you have to be
to drive; whether you will be killed in the electric chair, by lethal
injection or not at all, and how bad you have to be to get yourself
in such a fix; and so on.

If I leave our town of Hanover, and drive over the Connecticut
River to Vermont, I will find myself suddenly subject to perhaps
500 completely different laws. I must, among much else, buckle my
seat belt, acquire a licence if I wish to practise dentistry, and give
up all hope of erecting roadside hoardings, since Vermont is one of
just two states to outlaw highway advertising. On the other hand,

I may carry a gun on my person with impunity and if I am arrested for drunken driving I may legally decline to give a blood sample.

Since I always buckle up anyway, don't own a gun, and haven't the faintest desire to stick my fingers in other people's mouths, even for very good money, these matters don't impinge on me. Elsewhere, however, differences between state laws can be dramatic, even alarming.

States decide what may or may not be taught in their schools, and in many places, particularly in the Deep South, curricula must accord with very narrow religious views. In Alabama, for instance, it is illegal to teach evolution as anything other than an 'unproven belief'. All biology textbooks must carry a disclaimer stating, 'This textbook discusses evolution, a controversial theory some scientists present as a scientific explanation for the origin of living things.' By law, teachers must give equal weight to the notion that Earth was created in seven days and everything on it – fossils, coal deposits, dinosaur bones – is no more than 7,500 years old. I don't know what slogan Alabama puts on its number plates, but 'Proud to Be Backward' sounds apt to me.

I shouldn't talk because New Hampshire has some pretty retrograde laws of its own. It is the only state that declines to observe Martin Luther King Day (he associated with Communists, you see) and one of only a couple not to guarantee at least a few basic rights to gay people. Worse, it has the most demented number-plate slogan, the strange and pugnacious 'Live Free or Die'. Perhaps I take these things too literally, but I really don't like driving around with an explicit vow to expire if things don't go right. I would much prefer something a bit more equivocal and less terminal – 'Live Free or Pout' perhaps, or 'Live Free If It's All the Same to You Thanks Very Much'.

On the other hand, New Hampshire is the only state to guarantee in its constitution the right of the people to rise up and overthrow the Government. I have no intention of exercising this option, you understand, but there is a certain comfort in having it in reserve, especially if they start messing with our schoolbooks.

THE WAR ON DRUGS

I RECENTLY LEARNED FROM AN OLD FRIEND IN IOWA THAT IF YOU ARE CAUGHT in possession of a single dose of LSD in my native state you face a mandatory sentence of seven years in prison without possibility of parole.

Never mind that you are, say, eighteen years old and of previous good character, that this will ruin your life, that it will cost the state $25,000 a year to keep you incarcerated. Never mind that perhaps you didn't even know you had the LSD – that a friend put it in the glovebox of your car without your knowledge or maybe saw police coming through the door at a party and shoved it into your hand before you could react. Never mind any extenuating circumstances whatever. This is America in the 1990s and there are no exceptions where drugs are concerned. Sorry, but that's the way it is. Next.

It would be nearly impossible to exaggerate the ferocity with which the United States now prosecutes drug offenders. In fifteen states you can be sentenced to life in prison for owning a single marijuana plant. Newt Gingrich, the House Speaker, recently proposed that anyone caught bringing as little as two ounces of marijuana into the United States should be imprisoned for life without possibility of parole. Anyone caught bringing more than two ounces would be executed. A law to this effect is currently working its way through Congress.

According to a 1990 study, 90 per cent of all first-time drug offenders in federal courts were sentenced to an average of five years in prison. Violent first-time offenders, by contrast, were imprisoned less often and received on average just four years in prison. You are, in short, less likely to go to prison for kicking an old lady down the stairs than you are for being caught in possession of a single dose of any illicit drug. Call me soft, but that seems to me a trifle disproportionate.

Please understand it is not remotely my intention here to speak in favour of drugs. I appreciate that drugs can mess you up in a big way. I have an old schoolmate who made one LSD voyage too many in about 1977 and since that time has sat on a rocker on his parents' porch examining the backs of his hands and grinning to himself. So I know what drugs can do. I just haven't reached the point where it seems to me appropriate to put to death someone for being foolish.

Not many of my fellow countrymen would agree with me. It is the clear and fervent wish of most Americans to put drug users behind bars, and they are prepared to pay almost any price to achieve this. The people of Texas recently voted down a $750 million bond proposal to build new schools, but overwhelmingly endorsed a $1 billion bond for new prisons, mostly to house people convicted of drug offences.

America's prison population has more than doubled since 1982. There are now 1,630,000 people in prison in the United States. That is more than the populations of all but the three largest cities in the country. Sixty per cent of federal prisoners are serving time for non-violent offences, mostly to do with drugs. America's prisons are crammed with non-violent petty criminals whose problem is a weakness for illegal substances.

Because most drug offences carry mandatory sentences and exclude the possibility of parole, other prisoners are having to be released early to make room for all the new drug offenders pouring into the system. In consequence, the average convicted murderer in the United States now serves less than six years, the average rapist just five. Moreover, once he is out, the murderer or rapist is immediately eligible for welfare, food stamps and other federal assistance. A convicted drug user, no matter how desperate his circumstances may become, is denied these benefits for the rest of his life.

The persecution doesn't end there. My friend in Iowa once spent four months in a state prison for a drug offence. That was almost twenty years ago. He did his time and since then has been completely clean. Recently, he applied for a temporary job with the Postal Service as a holiday relief mail sorter – part of an army of

casual workers taken on each year to deal with Christmas post. Not
only did he not get the job, but a week or so later he received by
recorded delivery an affidavit threatening him with prosecution for
failing to declare on his application that he had a felony conviction
involving drugs.

The Postal Service had taken the trouble to run a background
check for drug convictions on someone applying for a temporary
job sorting mail. Apparently it does this as a matter of routine – but
only with respect to drugs. Had he killed his grandmother and
raped his sister twenty-five years ago, he would in all likelihood
have got the job.

It gets more amazing. The Government can seize your property if
it was used in connection with a drug offence, even if you did not
know it. In Connecticut, according to a recent article in the *Atlantic
Monthly* magazine, a federal prosecutor named Leslie C. Ohta
made a name for herself by seizing the property of almost anyone
even tangentially connected with a drug offence – including a
couple in their eighties whose grandson was found to be selling
marijuana out of his bedroom. The couple had no idea that their
grandson had marijuana in the house (let me repeat: they were in
their eighties) and of course had nothing to do with it themselves.
They lost the house anyway.

(Soon after, Ohta's own eighteen-year-old son was arrested for
selling LSD out of his mother's car and was alleged also to have
sold drugs from her house. And did the adorable Ms Ohta lose her
house and car? Did she hell. She was merely transferred to another
assignment.)

The saddest part of this zealous vindictiveness is that it simply
does not work. America spends $50 billion a year fighting drugs,
and yet drug use goes on and on. Confounded and frustrated, the
Government enacts increasingly draconian laws until we find ourselves at the ludicrous point where the Speaker of the House can
seriously propose to execute people – strap them to a gurney and
snuff out their lives – for possessing the botanical equivalent of two
bottles of vodka, and no-one anywhere seems to question it.

My solution to the problem would be twofold. First, I would
make it a criminal offence to be Newt Gingrich. This wouldn't do
anything to reduce the drug problem, but it would make me feel
much better. Then I would take most of that $50 billion and spend
it on rehabilitation and prevention. Some of it could be used to take
coachloads of youngsters to look at that schoolmate of mine on his

Iowa porch. I am sure it would persuade most of them not to try drugs in the first place. It would certainly be less brutal and pointless than trying to lock them all up for the rest of their lives.

WHY NO-ONE WALKS

I'LL TELL YOU THIS, BUT YOU HAVE TO PROMISE THAT IT WILL GET NO further. Not long after we moved here we had the people next door round for dinner and – I swear this is true – they drove.

I was astounded (I recall asking them jokingly if they used a light aircraft to get to the supermarket, which simply drew blank looks and the mental scratching of my name from all future invitation lists), but I have since come to realize that there was nothing especially odd in their driving less than a couple of hundred feet to visit us. Nobody walks anywhere in America nowadays.

A researcher at the University of California at Berkeley recently made a study of the nation's walking habits and concluded that 85 per cent of people in the United States are 'essentially' sedentary and 35 per cent are 'totally' sedentary. The average American walks less than 75 miles a year – about 1.4 miles a week, barely 350 yards a day. I'm no stranger to sloth myself, but that's appallingly little. I rack up more mileage than that just looking for the channel changer.

One of the things we wanted when we moved to America was to live in a town within walking distance of shops. Hanover, where we settled, is a small, typical New England college town, pleasant, sedate and compact. It has a broad green, an old-fashioned Main Street, nice college buildings with big lawns, and leafy residential streets. It is, in short, an agreeable, easy place to stroll. Nearly everyone in town is within a level five-minute walk of the shops, and yet as far as I can tell virtually no-one does.

I walk to town nearly every day when I am at home. I go to the post office or library or the local bookshop, and sometimes, if I am feeling particularly debonair, I stop at Rosey Jekes Café for a cappuccino. Every few weeks or so I call in at the barbershop and let one of the guys there do something rash and lively with my hair. All this is a big part of my life and I wouldn't dream of doing it other than on foot. People have got used to this curious and eccentric behaviour now, but several times in the early days passing neighbours would slow by the kerb and ask if I wanted a lift.

'But I'm going your way,' they would insist when I politely declined. 'Really, it's no bother.'

'Honestly, I enjoy walking.'

'Well, if you're absolutely sure,' they would say and depart reluctantly, even guiltily, as if they felt they were leaving the scene of an accident.

People have become so habituated to using the car for everything that it would never occur to them to unfurl their legs and see what they can do. Sometimes it's almost ludicrous. The other day I was in a little nearby town called Etna waiting to bring home one of my children from a piano lesson when a car stopped outside the local post office and a man about my age popped out and dashed inside (and left the motor running – something else that exercises me inordinately). He was inside for about three or four minutes, then came out, got in the car and drove exactly sixteen feet (I had nothing better to do so I paced it off) to the general store next door, and popped in again, engine still running.

And the thing is this man looked really fit. I'm sure he jogs extravagant distances and plays squash and does all kinds of exuberantly healthful things, but I am just as sure that he drives to each of these undertakings. It's crazy. An acquaintance of ours was complaining the other day about the difficulty of finding a place to park outside the local gymnasium. She goes there several times a week to walk on a treadmill. The gymnasium is, at most, a six-minute walk from her front door. I asked her why she didn't walk to the gym and do six minutes less on the treadmill.

She looked at me as if I were tragically simple-minded and said, 'But I have a programme for the treadmill. It records my distance and speed, and I can adjust it for degree of difficulty.' It had not occurred to me how thoughtlessly deficient nature is in this regard.

According to a concerned and faintly horrified recent editorial in the *Boston Globe*, the United States spends less than 1 per cent of its $25 billion-a-year roads budget on facilities for pedestrians. Actually, I'm surprised it's that much. Go to almost any suburb developed in the last thirty years – and there are thousands to choose from – and you will not find a pavement anywhere. Often you won't find a single pedestrian-crossing. I am not exaggerating.

I had this brought home to me last summer when we were driving across Maine and stopped for coffee in one of those endless zones of shopping malls, motels, petrol stations and fast-food places that sprout everywhere in America these days. I noticed there was a bookshop across the street, so I decided to skip coffee and pop over. I needed a particular book and anyway I figured this would give my wife a chance to spend some important private quality time with four restive, overheated children.

Although the bookshop was no more than fifty or sixty feet away, I discovered that there was no way to get there on foot. There was a traffic crossing for cars, but no provision for pedestrians and no way to cross without dodging through three lanes of swiftly turning traffic. I had to get in the car and drive across. At the time it seemed ridiculous and exasperating, but afterwards I realized that I was probably the only person ever even to have entertained the notion of negotiating that intersection on foot.

The fact is, Americans not only don't walk anywhere, they *won't* walk anywhere, and woe to anyone who tries to make them, as a town here in New Hampshire called Laconia discovered to its cost. A few years ago Laconia spent $5 million pedestrianizing its town centre, to make it a pleasant shopping environment. Aesthetically it was a triumph – urban planners came from all over to coo and take photos – but commercially it was a disaster. Forced to walk one whole block from a car park, shoppers abandoned downtown Laconia for suburban malls.

In 1994 Laconia dug up its pretty brick paving, took away the benches and tubs of geraniums and decorative trees, and put the street back to the way it had been in the first place. Now people can park right in front of the shops again and downtown Laconia thrives anew. And if that isn't sad, I don't know what is.

GARDENING WITH MY WIFE

I'M GOING TO HAVE TO BE QUICK BECAUSE IT'S A SUNDAY AND THE weather is glorious and Mrs Bryson has outlined a big, ambitious programme of gardening. Worse, she's wearing what I nervously call her Nike expression – the one that says, 'Just do it.'

Now don't get me wrong. Mrs Bryson is a rare and delightful creature and goodness knows my life needs structure and super-vision, but when she gets out a pad and pen and writes the dread words 'Things To Do' (vigorously underscored several times) you know it's going to be a long time till Monday.

I love to garden – there is something about the combination of mindless activity and the constant unearthing of worms that suits me somehow – but frankly I am not crazy about gardening with my wife. The trouble, you see, is that she is English and thus can in-timidate me. She can say things like, 'Have you heeled in the nodes on the *Dianthus chinensis*?' and 'Did you remember to check the sequestrene levels on the *Phlox subulata*?'

All British people can do this, I find, and it's awful – terrifying. Even now I remember the astonishment of listening to *Gardeners' Question Time* for the first time many years ago and realizing with quiet horror that I was in a nation of people who not only knew and understood things like powdery mildew, peach leaf curl, optimum pH levels, and the difference between *Coreopsis verticillata* and *Coreopsis grandiflora*, but cared about them – indeed, found it gratifying to engage in long and lively discussions on such matters.

I come from a background where you are considered to have a

green thumb if you can grow a cactus on a window-sill, so my own approach to gardening has always been rather less scientific. My method, which actually works pretty well, is to treat as a weed anything that hasn't flowered by August and to sprinkle everything else with bone meal, slug pellets and whatever else I find lying around the potting shed. Once or twice a summer I tip everything with a skull and crossbones on the label into a spray canister and give everything a jolly good dousing. It's an unorthodox approach and occasionally, I admit, I have to leap out of the way of an abruptly falling tree that has failed to respond to ministrations, but generally it has been a success and I have achieved some interesting and novel mutational effects. I once got a fence post to fruit, for instance.

For years, especially when the children were small and capable of almost anything, my wife left me to the garden. Occasionally she would step out to ask what I was doing, and I would have to confess that I was dusting some weedy-looking things with an unknown powdery substance which I had found in the garage and which I was pretty confident was either nitrogen or cement mix. Usually at that moment one of the children would come out to announce that little Jimmy's hair was on fire, or something else similarly but usefully distracting, and she would fly off, leaving me to get on with my experiments in peace. It was a good arrangement and our marriage prospered.

Then the children grew large enough to attend to their own cranial blazes and we moved to America, and now I find Mrs B out there with me. Or rather I am there with her, for I seem to have acquired a subsidiary role which principally involves bringing or taking away the wheelbarrow at a trot. I used to be a keen gardener; now I'm a kind of rickshaw boy.

Anyway, gardening just isn't the same here. People don't even have gardens in America. They have yards. And they don't garden in those yards. They work in them. They actually call it 'yardwork'. Takes all the fun out of it somehow.

In Britain, nature is fecund and kindly. The whole country is a kind of garden, really. I mean to say, look at how wildflowers pop up along every roadside and dance across meadows. Farmers actually have to go out and exterminate them (well, they don't have to, but they sure like to). In America, the instinct of nature is to be a wilderness. What you get here are triffid-like weeds that come creeping in from every margin and must be continually hacked back with sabres and machetes. I am quite sure that if we left the property for a month we would come back to find that the weeds had captured the house and dragged it off to the woods to be slowly devoured.

American gardens are mostly lawn, and American lawns are mostly big. This means that you spend your life raking. In the autumn the leaves fall together with a single great *whoomp* – a sort of vegetative mass suicide – and you spend about two months dragging them into piles, while the wind does its best to put them all back where you found them. You rake and rake, and cart the leaves off to the woods, then hang up your rake and go inside for the next seven months.

But as soon as you turn your back, the leaves begin creeping back. I don't know how they do it, but when you come out in spring, there they all are again, spread ankle deep across your lawn, choking thorny shrubs, clogging drains. So you spend weeks and weeks raking them up and carting them back to the woods. Finally, just when you get the lawn pristine, there is a great *whoomp* sound and you realize it's autumn again. It's really quite dispiriting.

And now on top of all that my dear missus has suddenly taken a commanding interest in the whole business of domestic horti-culture. It's my own fault, I have to admit. Last year I filled the lawn spreader with a mixture of my own devising – essentially fertilizer, moss killer, rabbit food (initially by mistake, but then I thought, What the heck? and tossed in the rest) and a dash of something lively called buprimate and triforine. Two days later the front lawn erupted in vivid orange stripes of a sufficiently arresting and persistent nature to attract sightseers from as far as northern Massachusetts. So now I find myself on a kind of permanent probation.

Speaking of which, I've got to go. I've just heard the hard, clinical snap of gardening gloves going on and the ominous sound of metal tools being taken down from their perches. It's only a matter of time before I hear the cry of 'Boy! Bring the barrow – and look sharp!' But you know the part I really hate? It's having to wear this stupid coolie hat.

WHY EVERYONE IS WORRIED

HERE'S A FACT FOR YOU. IN 1995, ACCORDING TO THE *WASHINGTON Post,* computer hackers successfully breached the Pentagon's security systems 161,000 times. That works out at eighteen illicit entries every hour around the clock, one every 3.2 minutes.

Oh, I know what you are going to say. This sort of thing could happen to any monolithic defence establishment with the fate of the earth in its hands. After all, if you stockpile a massive nuclear arsenal, it's only natural that people are going to want to go in and have a look around, maybe see what all those buttons marked 'Detonate' and 'Code Red' mean. It's only human nature.

Besides, the Pentagon has got quite enough on its plate, thank you, with trying to find its missing logs from the Gulf War. I don't know if you've read about this, but the Pentagon has mislaid – irretrievably lost, actually – all but thirty-six of the 200 pages of official records of its brief but exciting desert adventure. Half of the missing files, it appears, were wiped out when an officer at Gulf War headquarters – I wish I was making this up, but I'm not – incorrectly downloaded some games into a military computer. The other missing files are, well, missing. All that is known is that two sets were dispatched to Central Command in Florida, but now nobody can find them (probably those cleaning ladies again), and a third set was somehow 'lost from a safe' at a base in Maryland, which sounds eminently plausible in the circumstances.

Now to be fair to the Pentagon, its mind has no doubt been distracted by the unsettling news that it has not been getting very good reports from the CIA. It has recently emerged, according to other news reports, that despite spending a decidedly whopping $2 billion a year monitoring developments in the Soviet Union, the CIA failed to foresee the break-up of the USSR – indeed, I understand, is still trying to confirm the rumour through its contacts at the McDonald's in Moscow – and understandably this has unnerved the Pentagon. I mean to say, you can't expect people to keep track of their wars if they're not getting reliable reports from the field, now can you?

The CIA, in its turn, was almost certainly distracted from its missions by the news – and again let me stress that I am not making any of this up – that the FBI had spent years filming one of its agents, Aldrich Ames, going into the Soviet embassy in Washington with bulging files and coming out empty-handed, but had not yet quite figured out what he was up to. The FBI knew Ames was a CIA employee, knew that he made regular visits to the Soviet embassy, and knew the CIA was looking for a mole in its midst, but had never managed to make the leap of thought necessary to pull these tantalizing strands together.

Ames was eventually caught and sentenced to a zillion years in prison for passing information, but no thanks to the FBI. But then, to be fair, the FBI has been absolutely snowed under with screwing up everything it comes in contact with.

First, there was its wrongful arrest of Richard Jewell, the security guard it suspected of last year's bombing in Atlanta's Olympic Park. Jewell, according to the FBI, planted the bomb and made a phone call alerting authorities, then raced a couple of miles in a minute or so in order to be back at the scene in time to be a hero. Even though there was not a shred of evidence to connect him with the bomb and it was conclusively demonstrated that he could not have made the call and returned to the park in the time alleged, it took the FBI months to realize it had the wrong man.

Then in April came news that FBI forensic labs had for years been botching, losing, spilling, contaminating, stepping in and tracking out to the car park most of the vital evidence that came its way. Occasionally they just made things up. In one incident, a lab scientist wrote an incriminating report based on microscopic findings without actually bothering to look through a microscope. Thanks to the labs' dogged and inventive work, at least 1,000 convictions, and perhaps many thousands more, have been placed at risk.

Among its continuing achievements, the FBI has still not found the perpetrator of the Atlanta bombing or a series of church bombings across the South, hasn't arrested anyone in a mysterious fatal derailment of a passenger train in Arizona in 1995, failed to catch the Unabomber (he was turned in by his brother), and still isn't able to say whether the crash of TWA flight 800 last year was a crime or an accident or what.

A lot of people conclude from this that the FBI and its agents are dangerously inept. Although this is indubitably so, there are extenuating circumstances for the bureau's low morale and poor performance – namely the discovery last year that there is a group of people even more astoundingly incompetent. I refer to America's sheriff's departments.

Space does not permit a comprehensive survey of the singular accomplishments of America's sheriff's departments, so I will cite just two. First, there was the news that the Los Angeles County Sheriff's Department set a record last year by incorrectly releasing twenty-three prisoners, some of them quite dangerous and cranky. After the release of prisoner number twenty-three, a supervisor explained to journalists that a clerk had received papers ordering that the prisoner be sent to Oregon to serve out a long sentence for burglary and rape, but had taken this to mean giving him back all his possessions, escorting him to the door and recommending a good pizza place around the corner.

Even better, in my view, were the sheriff's deputies in Milwaukee who were sent to the airport with a team of sniffer dogs to practise hunting out explosives. The deputies hid a five-pound packet of live explosives somewhere in the airport and then – I just love this – forgot where. Needless to say, the dogs couldn't find it. That was in February and they're still looking. It was the second time that the Milwaukee Sheriff's Department has managed to mislay explosives at the airport.

I could go on and on, but I'm going to break off here because I want to see if I can get into the Pentagon's computer. Call me a devil, but I've always had a hankering to blow up a minor country. It will be the perfect crime. The CIA won't notice it, the Pentagon will notice it but will lose the records, the FBI will spend eighteen months investigating and then arrest Mr Ed the Talking Horse, and the Los Angeles County Sheriff's Department will let him go. If nothing else, it will take people's minds off all these other things they have to worry about.

A FAILURE TO COMMUNICATE

OF ALL THE THINGS THAT HAVE BEEN PLACED ON EARTH TO TRY MY patience – and gosh aren't there a lot? – none has been more successful over the years than AT&T, the American telephone company.

Given a choice between, say, spilling a beaker of hydrochloric acid on my lap and dealing with AT&T, I would always choose the hydrochloric acid as less painful. AT&T has the world's most indestructible payphones. I know this for a fact because I have never had an experience with AT&T from a payphone that did not result in my giving their equipment a thorough workout.

As you are probably gathering, I don't much like AT&T. But that's OK because it doesn't like me. It doesn't like any of its customers, as far as I can tell. It dislikes them so much, in fact, that it won't even talk to them. It uses synthesized voices for everything now, which means that no matter how wrong things go – and you can be certain they will – you can never get through to a real person. All you get is a strange, metallic, curiously snotty robotic voice saying things like: 'The number you have dialled is not within a recognized dialling parameter.' It is immensely frustrating.

I was reminded of this the other day when I found myself stranded at Logan Airport in Boston because the mini-coach company that was supposed to pick me up and take me home forgot to. I knew that it had forgotten me, and not broken down or had an accident, because as I stood at the designated pick-up point the familiar Dartmouth Mini-Coach van approached and, as I bent to pick up my bags, sailed past and continued on to the airport exit road and disappeared into the distance, on a general heading for New Hampshire.

So I went off to find a payphone to ring the mini-coach company – just to say hello, you know, and let them know that I was there and ready to go if they would only throw open a door and slow down enough to let me jump on – and this meant calling AT&T. I gave a ruptured sigh at the prospect. I had just had a long flight. I was tired and hungry and stranded at a charmless airport. I knew it would be at least three hours before the next mini-coach was due. And now I had to deal with AT&T. I approached a bank of payphones outside the airport terminal with deep foreboding.

I didn't have the number for the mini-coach company on me, so I read the instructions for Directory Enquiries and rang the number. After a minute a synthetic voice came on and brusquely instructed me to deposit $1.05 in change. I was taken aback by this. Directory Enquiries always used to be free. I searched through my pockets, but I only had 67 cents. So I conducted a brief resiliency test with the receiver – yes, still indestructible – grabbed my bags and stalked off to the terminal to acquire change.

Of course none of the businesses would give change without a purchase, so I had to buy a copy of the *New York Times*, *Boston Globe* and *Washington Post* – each purchased separately, with a different note, as no other approach appeared to be allowable – until I had accumulated $1.05 in assorted silver coins.

Then I returned to the phone and repeated the process, but it was one of those phones that are very choosy about what coins they take, and it seemed to have a particular dislike for Roosevelt dimes. It's not easy to feed coins into a slot when you have a receiver pressed to your ear with a shoulder and three newspapers under your arm, and especially not when the phone is spitting back every third coin you feed it. After about fifteen seconds a robotic voice came on and started scolding me – I swear it, scolding me, in an irksome synthetic quaver – and telling me in effect that if I didn't get myself organized pronto it would cut me off. And then it cut me off. A moment later it regurgitated the coins I had deposited. But here's the thing. It didn't return all of them. Between what it had given back and what it wouldn't take, I now had just 90 cents.

So I conducted another, slightly more protracted resiliency test and trudged back into the terminal. I bought a *Providence Journal* and a *Philadelphia Inquirer* and returned to the phone. This time I got through to Directory Enquiries, announced the number I wanted and hastily pulled out a pen and notepad. I knew from experience that Directory Enquiries gives a number just once and then hangs up, so you have to get it down carefully. I listened intently and started to write. The pen was dry. I immediately forgot the number.

I returned to the terminal, bought a *Bangor Daily-News*, a *Poughkeepsie Journal* and a plastic biro, and returned. This time I got the number, carefully recorded it and dialled. Success at last.

A moment later a voice on the other end said brightly, 'Good morning! Dartmouth College!'

'Dartmouth College?' I stammered, aghast. 'I wanted the Dartmouth Mini-Coach Company.' I had used up all my remaining coins on this call and couldn't believe that I would have to go back into the terminal yet again to accumulate more. I suddenly wondered how many of those people in America who come up to you on corners and ask for spare change were once just people like me – respectable citizens who had led normal lives and ended up destitute, homeless and in need of constant small change for a pay-phone somewhere.

'I can give you the number if you'd like,' the lady offered.

'Really? Oh, yes please.'

She rattled off a number, clearly from memory. It was nothing like the number – not even remotely like the number – I had been given by AT&T. I thanked her profusely.

'No problem,' she said. 'It happens all the time.'

'What, they give your number when people ask for Dartmouth Mini-Coach?'

'All the time. Was it AT&T you used?'

'Yes.'

'Thought so,' she said simply. I thanked her again. 'It's been my pleasure. And hey – don't forget to give that phone a really good pounding before you leave.'

She didn't say that, of course. She didn't need to.

I had to wait four hours for the next mini-coach. But it could have been worse. At least I had plenty to read.

LOST AT THE MOVIES

EVERY YEAR ABOUT THIS TIME I DO A MILDLY FOOLISH THING. I GATHER up some of the smaller children and take them to one of the summer movies.

Summer movies are big business in America. This year between Memorial Day and Labor Day – our equivalents of the British May and August bank holidays – Americans will spend $2 billion on cinema tickets, plus half as much again on chewy things to stuff into their mouths while staring saucer-eyed at images of extremely costly mayhem.

Summer movies are nearly always bad, of course, but I believe this may be the worst summer ever. I base this entirely, but confidently, on a quotation I saw in the *New York Times* from Jan de Bont, director of *Speed 2: Cruise Control*, who boasted that the movie's biggest dramatic event – in which an out-of-control cruise ship carrying Sandra Bullock ploughs into a Caribbean village – came to him in a dream. 'The entire screenplay was written backward from that image,' he revealed proudly. There, I think, you have all you need to know about the intellectual quality of the average summer movie.

I always tell myself not to set my expectations too high, that summer movies are the cinematic equivalent of amusement park rides, and no-one ever expected a roller-coaster to provide a satisfying plot line. But the thing is, summer movies have become so dumb – so very, very dumb – that it is hard to abide them. No matter how much money has been spent on them – and it is worth noting that at least eight of this year's crop have budgets over $100 million –

there is always such a large measure of preposterous implausibility as to make you wonder whether the script was concocted over canapés the night before filming began.

This year we went to the new Jurassic Park movie, *Lost World*. Now never mind that it is largely identical to the last Jurassic Park movie – same booming footfalls and trembling puddles whenever T-rex comes into the vicinity, same mortified people backing away from a door against which velociraptors are hurling themselves (only to find another toothy creature looming over their shoulders), same scenes of vehicles dangling precariously from a jungly bluff while the heroes hold on for dear life. No matter. The dinosaurs are terrific and a dozen or so people get squashed or eaten in the first hour. This is what we've come for!

And then it all falls apart. In a culminating scene a tyrannosaurus escapes, in an improbable manner, from a ship, runs rampant through downtown San Diego, crushing buses and destroying petrol stations, and then – suddenly, inexplicably – is in the middle of a heavily slumbering suburban neighbourhood, alone and unobserved. Now does it strike you as remotely likely that a prehistoric, twenty-foot-high creature not seen on earth for 65 million years could cause mayhem in a city centre and then slip off into a residential zone without anyone's noticing? Does it not seem a trifle nagging and unsatisfactory that while downtown San Diego is full of people doing lively, mid-evening sorts of things – queueing up at cinemas, strolling round hand in hand – out in the residential area the streets are silent and every last soul is fast asleep?

And so it goes on from there. While police cars are dashing around bumping helplessly into each other, the hero and heroine manage to find the T-rex unaided and – undetected by anyone in this curiously unobservant city – lure him some miles back to the boat, so that he can be returned to his tropical island home, thus setting up the happy, inevitable and commercially gratifying possibility of a *Jurassic Park 3*. *Lost World* is slack and obvious and, for all its $100 million-plus budget, contains about $2.35 worth of actual thought, and so of course it is on its way to setting all kinds of records at the box office. In its first weekend alone it took in $92.7 million.

However, my problem is not really with *Lost World* or any of the other summer fare. I'm way past expecting Hollywood to provide me with a cerebral experience during the warmer months. My problem is with the Sony 6 Theatres of West Lebanon, New Hampshire, and the thousands of other suburban cinema complexes like it, which are doing to the American movie-going experience essentially what Steven Spielberg's tyrannosaurus rex did to San Diego.

Anyone who grew up in America in the 1960s or before will remember the days when going to the pictures meant visiting a single-screen institution, usually vast, usually downtown. In my hometown, Des Moines, the main cinema (imaginatively called The Des Moines) was a palatial extravaganza with spooky lighting and a decor that brought to mind an Egyptian crypt. By my era, it was something of a dump – I am sure from the smell that there was a dead horse in there somewhere, and certainly it hadn't been cleaned since Theda Bara was in her prime – but just being there, facing a vast screen in a cubic acre of darkness, was an entrancing experience.

Except in a few major cities, nearly all those great downtown cinemas are gone now. (The Des Moines went in about 1965.) Instead what you get nowadays are suburban multiplexes with an abundance of tiny screening rooms. Although *Lost World* is the hottest movie around, we saw it in a chamber of almost laughable minuteness, barely large enough to accommodate nine rows of seats, which were grudgingly padded and crammed so tight together that my knees ended up more or less hooked around my ears. The screen had the dimensions of a large beach towel and was so ill-placed that everyone in the first three rows had to look almost straight up, as if in a planetarium. The sound was bad and the picture frequently jerky. Before it started, we had to sit through thirty minutes of commercials. The popcorn and confections were outrageously expensive, and the salespeople had been programmed to try to sell you things you didn't want and hadn't asked for. In short, every feature of this cinema seemed carefully designed to make a visit a deeply regretted experience.

I'm not cataloguing all this to make you feel sorry for me, though sympathy is always welcome, but to point out that this is increasingly the standard experience for cinema-goers in America. I can handle a little audio-visual imbecility, but I can't bear to see the magic taken away.

I was talking about this to one of my older children the other day. She listened attentively, even sympathetically, then said a sad thing. 'Dad,' she told me, 'you need to understand that people don't want the smell of a dead horse when they go to the movies.'

She's right, of course. But if you ask me they don't know what they are missing.

THE RISK FACTOR

NOW HERE IS SOMETHING THAT SEEMS AWFULLY UNFAIR TO ME. BECAUSE I am an American and you, bless your heart, are not, it appears that I am twice as likely as you to suffer an untimely and accidental death.

I know this because I have just been reading something called *The Book of Risks: Fascinating Facts About the Chances We Take Every Day* by a statistical wonk (to use the engaging new American slang term for a boffin-type person) named Larry Laudan.

It is full of interesting and useful statistics, mostly to do with coming irremediably a cropper in the United States. Thus I know that if I happen to take up farm work this year I am three times more likely to lose a limb, and twice as likely to be fatally poisoned, than if I just sit here quietly. I now know that my chances of being murdered some time in the next twelve months are one in 11,000, of choking to death one in 150,000, of being killed by a dam failure one in 10 million, and of being fatally conked on the head by something falling from the sky about one in 250 million. Even if I stay indoors, away from the windows, it appears that there is a one in 450,000 chance that something will kill me before the day is out. I find that rather alarming.

However, nothing is more galling than the discovery that just by being an American, by standing to attention for the 'Star-Spangled Banner' and having a baseball cap as a central component of my wardrobe, I am twice as likely to die in a mangled heap as you are. This is not a just way to decide mortality, if you ask me.

Mr Laudan does not explain why Americans are twice as dangerous to themselves as Britons (too upset, I daresay), but I have been thinking about it a good deal, as you can imagine, and the answer – very obvious when you reflect for even a moment – is that America is an outstandingly dangerous place.

Consider this: every year in New Hampshire a dozen or more people are killed crashing their cars into moose. Now correct me if I am wrong, but this is not something that is likely to happen to you on the way home from Sainsbury's. Nor are you likely to be eaten by a grizzly bear or mountain lion, butted senseless by buffalo, or seized about the ankle by a seriously perturbed rattlesnake – all occurrences that knock off a few dozen hapless Americans every year. Then there are all the violent acts of nature – tornadoes, rock-slides, avalanches, flash floods, paralysing blizzards, the odd earthquake – that scarcely exist in your tranquil little island, but kill hundreds and hundreds of Americans every year.

Finally, and above all, there is the matter of guns. There are 200 million guns in the United States and we do rather like to pop them off. Each year, 40,000 Americans die from gunshot wounds, the great majority of them by accident. Just to put that in perspective for you, that's a rate of 6.8 gunshot deaths per 100,000 people in America, compared with a meagre 0.4 per 100,000 in the UK.

America is in short a pretty risky place. And yet, oddly, we get alarmed by all the wrong things in this country. Eavesdrop on almost any conversation at Lou's Diner here in Hanover and the talk will all be of cholesterol and sodium levels, mammograms and resting heart rates. Show most Americans an egg yolk and they will recoil in terror, but the most palpable and avoidable risks scarcely faze them.

Forty per cent of Americans still don't use a seatbelt, which I find simply amazing because it costs nothing to buckle up and clearly has the potential to save you from exiting through the windscreen like Superman. Even more remarkably, since a spate of recent news-paper reports about young children being killed by airbags in minor crashes, people have been rushing to get their airbags disconnected. Never mind that in every instance the children were killed because they were sitting on the front seat, where they should not have been in the first place, and in nearly all cases weren't wearing seatbelts. Airbags save thousands of lives, yet many people are having them disabled on the bizarre assumption that they present a danger.

Much the same sort of statistical illogic applies to guns. Forty per cent of Americans keep guns in their homes, typically in a drawer beside the bed. The odds that one of those guns will ever be used to

shoot a criminal are comfortably under one in a million. The odds
that it will be used to shoot a member of the household – generally
a child fooling around – are at least twenty times that figure. Yet
over 100 million people resolutely ignore this fact, even sometimes
threaten to pop you one themselves if you make too much noise
about it.

Nothing, however, better captures the manifest irrationality of
people towards risks as one of the liveliest issues of recent years:
passive smoking. Four years ago, the Environmental Protection
Agency released a report concluding that people who are over
thirty-five and don't smoke but are regularly exposed to the smoke
of others stand a one in 30,000 risk of contracting lung cancer in a
given year. The response was immediate and electrifying. All over
the country smoking was banned at work and in restaurants, shopping malls and other public places.

What was overlooked in all this was how microscopically small
the risk from passive smoking actually is. A rate of one in 30,000
sounds reasonably severe, but it doesn't actually amount to much.
Eating one pork chop a week is statistically more likely to give you
cancer than sitting routinely in a roomful of smokers. So, too, is con-
suming a carrot every seven days, a glass of orange juice once a
fortnight, or a head of lettuce every two years. You are five times
more likely to contract lung cancer from your pet budgie than you
are from secondary smoke.

Now I am all for banning smoking on the grounds that it is dirty
and offensive, unhealthy for the user and leaves unsightly burns in
the carpet. All I am saying is that it seems a trifle odd to ban it on
grounds of public safety when you are happy to let any old fool
own a gun or drive around unbuckled.

But then logic seldom comes into these things. I remember some
years ago watching my brother buy a lottery ticket (odds of
winning: about one in 12 million), then get in his car and fail to
buckle up (odds of having a serious accident in any year: one in
forty). When I pointed out the inconsistency of this, he looked at
me for a moment and said: 'And what are the odds, do you
suppose, that I will drop you four miles short of home?'

Since then, I have kept these thoughts pretty much to myself.
Much less risky, you see.

AH, SUMMER!

IN NEW ENGLAND, A FRIEND HERE RECENTLY EXPLAINED TO ME, THERE are three times of year. Either winter has just been, or winter is coming, or it's winter.

I know what he meant. Summers here are short – they start on the first of June and end on the last day of August, and the rest of the time you had better know where your mittens are – but for the whole of those three months the weather is agreeably warm and nearly always sunny. Best of all, the weather stays at a generally agreeable level, unlike Iowa, where I grew up and where the temperature and humidity climb steadily with every passing day of summer until by mid-August it is so hot and airless that even the flies lie down on their backs and just quietly gasp.

It's the mugginess that gets you. Step outside in Iowa in August and within twenty seconds you will experience a condition that might be called perspiration incontinence. It gets so hot that you will see department store mannequins with sweat circles under their arms. I have particularly vivid memories of Iowa summers because my father was the last person in the Midwest to buy an air-conditioner. He thought they were unnatural. (He thought anything that cost more than $30 was unnatural.)

The one place you could get a little relief was the screened porch. Up until the 1950s nearly every American home had one of these. A screened porch is a kind of summer room on the side of the house, with walls made of a fine but sturdy mesh to keep out insects. They give you all the advantages of being outdoors and indoors at the same time. They are wonderful and will always be associated in my mind with summer things – corn on the cob, watermelon, the nighttime chirr of crickets, the sound of my parents' neighbour Mr Piper arriving home late from one of his lodge meetings, parking his car with the aid of his dustbins, then serenading Mrs Piper with two choruses of 'Rose of Seville' before settling down for a nap on the lawn.

So when we came to the States, the one thing I asked for in a house was a screened porch, and we found one. I live out there in the summer. I am writing this on the screened porch now, staring out on a sunny garden, listening to twittering birds and the hum of a neighbour's lawnmower, caressed by a light breeze and feeling pretty darned chipper. We will have our dinner out here tonight (if Mrs B doesn't trip over a rucked carpet with the tray again, bless her) and then I will lounge around reading until bedtime, listening to the crickets and watching the cheery blink of fireflies. Summer wouldn't be summer without all this.

Soon after we moved into our house, I noticed that a corner of the mesh had come loose near the floor and that our cat was using it as a kind of cat flap to come in and sleep on an old sofa we kept out there, so I just left it. One night after we had been here about a month, I was reading unusually late when out of the corner of my eye I noticed the cat come in. Only here's the thing. The cat was with me already.

I looked again. It was a skunk. Moreover, it was between me and the only means of exit. It headed for the table and I realized it probably came in every night about this time to hoover up any dinner bits that had fallen on the floor. (And there very often are, on account of a little game the children and I play called 'Vegetable Olympics' when Mrs Bryson goes off to answer the phone or get more gravy.)

Being sprayed by a skunk is absolutely the worst thing that can happen to you that doesn't make you bleed or put you in the hospital. If you smell skunk odour from a distance, it doesn't smell too bad at all. It's rather strangely sweet and arresting – not attractive exactly, but not revolting. Everybody who has ever smelled a skunk from a distance for the first time thinks, 'Well, that's not so bad. I don't know what all the fuss is about.'

But get close – or, worse still, get sprayed – and believe me it will be a long, long time before anyone asks you to dance slow and close. The odour is not just strong and disagreeable, but virtually ineradicable. The most effective treatment, apparently, is to scrub yourself with tomato juice, but even with gallons of the stuff the best you can hope is to subdue the odour fractionally.

A schoolmate of my son's had a skunk get into her family's basement one night. It sprayed and the family lost virtually everything in their home. All their curtains, bedding, clothes, soft furnishings – everything, in short, that could absorb an odour – had to be thrown on a bonfire, and the rest of the house thoroughly scrubbed from top to bottom. The schoolmate of my son's never got near the skunk, left the house immediately and spent a weekend scouring herself with tomato juice, but it was weeks before anyone would walk down the same side of a street as her. So when I say you don't want to be sprayed by a skunk, believe me, you don't want to be sprayed by a skunk.

All of this went through my mind as I sat agog watching a skunk perhaps six feet away. The skunk spent about 30 seconds snuffling around under the table, then calmly padded out the way it had come. As it left, it turned and gave me a look that said: 'I knew you were there the whole time.' But it didn't spray me, for which I am grateful even now.

The next day I tacked the mesh back into place, but to show my appreciation I put a handful of dried cat food on the step, and at about midnight the skunk came and ate it. After that, for two summers, I put a little food out regularly and the skunk always came to collect it. This year it hasn't been back. There has been a rabies epidemic among small mammals which has seriously reduced the populations of skunks, raccoons and even squirrels. Apparently this happens every fifteen years or so as part of a natural cycle.

So I seem to have lost my skunk. In a year or so the populations will recover and I may be able to adopt another. I hope so because the one thing about being a skunk is that you don't have a lot of friends.

In the meantime, partly as a mark of respect and partly because Mrs B caught one in the eye at an inopportune moment, we have stopped playing food games even though, if I say it myself, I was comfortably in line for a gold.

HELP FOR THE
NONDESIGNATED INDIVIDUAL

THE OTHER DAY I HAD AN EXPERIENCE SO STARTLING AND UNEXPECTED that it made me spill a soft drink down my shirt. (Though, having said that, I don't actually need an unexpected event to achieve this. All I need is a soft drink.) What caused this fizzy outburst was that I called a government office – specifically, the US Social Security Admin-istration – and someone answered the phone.

There I was, all poised to have a recorded voice tell me: 'All our agents are busy, so please hold while we play you some irritating music interrupted at fifteen-second intervals by a recorded voice telling you all our agents are busy so please hold while we play you some irritating music' and so on until teatime.

So imagine my surprise when, after just 270 rings, a real person came on the line. He asked some of my personal details, and then said, 'Excuse me, Bill. I have to put you on hold a minute.'

Did you catch that? He called me Bill. Not Mr Bryson. Not sir. Not O mighty taxpayer. But Bill. Two years ago I would have regarded this as a gross impertinence, but now I find I've rather grown to like it.

There are certain times when the informality and familiarity of American life strains my patience – when a waiter tells me his name is Bob and that he'll be my server this evening, I still have to resist an impulse to say, 'I just want a cheeseburger, Bob. I'm not looking for a relationship' – but mostly I have come to like it. It's because it's symbolic of something more fundamental, I suppose.

There is no tugging of forelocks here, you see, but a genuine

universal assumption that no person is better than any other. I think
that's swell. My dustman calls me Bill. My doctor calls me Bill. My
children's headmaster calls me Bill. They don't tug for me. I don't
tug for them. I think that's as it should be.

In England, I used the same accountant for over a decade, and
our relations were always cordial but businesslike. She never called
me anything but Mr Bryson and I never called her anything but Mrs
Creswick. When I moved to America, I phoned an accountant for
an appointment. When I came to his office, his first words to me
were, 'Ah, Bill, I'm glad you could make it.' We were pals already.
Now when I see him I ask him about his kids.

It shows itself in other ways, too. Hanover, where we live, is a
college town. The local university, Dartmouth, is a private school
and quite exclusive – it's one of the Ivy League colleges, like
Harvard and Yale – but you would never guess it.

None of its grounds are off limits to us. Indeed, much of it is
open to the community. We can use the library, attend its concerts,
go to its commencement exercises if we want. One of my daughters
skates on the college ice rink. My son's high-school track team
practises in winter on the college's indoor track. The college film
society regularly puts on seasons of movies, which I often attend.
Just last night I saw *North by Northwest* on a big screen with one
of my teenagers, and afterwards we had coffee and cheesecake in
the student cafeteria. At none of these things do you ever have to
show ID or secure special permission, and never are you made
to feel as if you are intruding or unwelcome.

All this gives everyday encounters a sheen of openness and
egalitarianism which you may call shallow and artificial, or sometimes even inappropriate, but it also removes a lot of stuffiness
from life.

The one thing it won't do, however, is get you your wife's social
security number. Allow me to explain. A social security number is
approximately equivalent to a British national insurance number,
but far more important. It is essentially what identifies you as a
person. Failing to understand this, my wife had mislaid her card.
We needed the number fairly urgently for some tax form. I
explained this to the social security man when he came back on the
line. He had after all just called me Bill, so I had reason to hope that
we might get somewhere.

'We are only permitted to divulge that information to the designated individual,' he replied.

'The person named on the card you mean?'

'Correct.'

'But she's my wife,' I sputtered.

'We are only permitted to divulge that information to the designated individual.'

'Let me get this straight,' I said. 'If I were my wife, you would give me the number over the phone just like that?'

'Correct.'

'But what if it was somebody just pretending to be her?'

A hesitant pause. 'We would assume that the individual making the enquiry was the individual indicated as the designated individual.'

'Just a minute, please.' I thought for a minute. My wife was out, so I couldn't call on her, but I didn't want to have to go through all this again later. I came back on the phone and said in my normal voice: 'Hello, it's Cynthia Bryson here. Please could I have my card number?'

There was a nervous little chuckle. 'I know it's you, Bill,' the voice said.

'No, honestly. It's Cynthia Bryson. Please could I have my number?'

'I can't do that.'

'Would it make a difference if I spoke in a female voice?'

'I'm afraid not.'

'Let me ask you this – just out of curiosity. Is my wife's number on a computer screen in front of you right now?'

'Yes it is.'

'But you won't tell me it?'

'I'm afraid I can't do that, Bill,' he said and sounded as if he meant it.

I have learned from years of painful experience that there is not the tiniest chance – not the *tiniest* chance – that a US government employee will ever bend a rule to help you, so I didn't press the matter. Instead I asked him if he knew how to get strawberry pop stains out of a white T-shirt.

'Baking soda,' he replied without hesitation. 'Leave it to soak overnight and it will come right out.'

I thanked him and we parted.

I would have liked it, of course, if I had managed to get the information I needed, but at least I had made a friend and he was right about the baking soda. The T-shirt came up like new.

WHERE SCOTLAND IS,
AND OTHER USEFUL TIPS

RECENTLY I WAS ON AN AMERICAN AIRLINE FLIGHT WHEN I THUMBED through the in-flight magazine and came across a quiz entitled 'Your Cultural IQ'.

Interested to see whether I have one, I applied myself to the questions. The very first asked in which country it is in bad taste to enquire of a person 'Where do you live?' The answer, I learned to my surprise by turning to page 113, was England.

'One's home is a personal affair for the English,' the magazine solemnly informed me.

I am mortified to think of all the times over the years I have said to an English person, 'So where do you live, Clive?' (or whatever, because of course they weren't all named Clive), without for a moment suspecting that I was committing a serious social gaffe and that Clive (or whomever) was thinking: 'Nosy American git.' So of course I apologize now to all of you, especially Clive.

Then, a couple of days later, I came across an article on British politics in the *Washington Post*, which noted helpfully in passing that Scotland is 'to the north of England', a geographical distinction that I had always thought was common knowledge, and it dawned on me that perhaps it was not I who was under-informed, but – could this possibly be? – my entire nation.

I became curious to know just how much or little my fellow Americans know about the United Kingdom, but this is not easy. You can't just go up to a person, even someone you know quite well, and say, 'Do you have any idea what the Chancellor of the Exchequer does?' or 'Scotland is north of England. True or false?' any more than you could go up to an English person and say, 'Where do you live?' It would be impolite and impertinent, and possibly embarrassing for the interviewee.

Then it occurred to me that I might more discreetly get some idea by going to the library and looking at American guidebooks to Britain. These would tell me what sort of information Americans require before they embark on a visit to the UK.

So I went to the library and had a look at the travel section. There were four books exclusively on Britain, plus another eight or so on Europe generally, with chapters on Britain. My favourite, at a glance, was *Rick Steves' Europe 1996*. I had never heard of Rick, but according to the jacket blurb he spends several months each year 'feeling the fjords and caressing the castles', which sounds awfully diligent if a little pointless. I took all these books off to a table in the corner and spent the afternoon in fascinated study.

Well, I got my answer, which is that what Americans know about Britain is pretty nearly nothing, at least if these books are to be believed. According to the various texts, prospective American travellers to Britain require to be told that Glasgow 'doesn't rhyme with cow', that sterling is accepted in Scotland and Wales 'as freely as in England', that the country has 'well-trained doctors' and 'all the latest drugs', and, yes, that Scotland is north of England. (Quite far north, in fact, so better plan a full day there.)

American travellers, it appears, are a pretty helpless lot. The books tell them not just what to expect in Britain – rain and thatched cottages mostly – but how to pack their bags, find their way to the airport, even proceed through Customs.

'Be affable and cooperative, but don't be overly conversational,' advises Joseph Raff, author of *Fielding's Britain 1996*, on going through British immigration. 'Hold your passport casually in hand – don't flaunt it!' Perhaps it is none of my business, but if you need to be told how to clasp your passport, it seems to me you may not be quite ready to cross oceans.

My absolute favourite book was *The Best European Travel Tips* by one John Whitman. The book wasn't specifically about Britain, but it was so good that I read it almost cover to cover.

It was full of grave advice on pickpockets, avaricious waiters, even how to sue your airline if you are bumped from your flight. Mr Whitman clearly expects things to go wrong. His first tip for dealing with the idiosyncrasies of European hotels is 'Get the clerk's name when you check in.' With airline tickets he advises: 'Read all materials closely so you know your rights.'

Among his many useful suggestions, he advises that you bring 'a pen or two', hang a Do Not Disturb sign outside your hotel room door if you do not wish to be disturbed (I am not making this up; he even tells you to drape it over the knob) and notes sagely (for nothing gets past Mr Whitman's practised eye) that, with regard to lodging, Europe has 'a variety of places to stay'.

Elsewhere he warns: 'You'll find bidets in many European hotel rooms and WCs,' then adds warily, 'If you care to experiment with these toilet-shaped porcelain fixtures for your personal hygiene, do so.' Thanks for the permission, Mr Whitman, but to tell you the truth I've got my hands full with this Do Not Disturb sign!

Joseph Raff, meanwhile, provides a useful glossary for dealing with all those puzzling British terms like 'queue', 'flat', 'chips' and – here's one that's stumped me for years – 'motorcar'. Then he confidently asserts that a surname is one's first name and a Christian name is the last name, which would be useful information if it weren't completely wrong.

Errors rather abound in these books, I'm afraid. I learned that the beer you drink is called 'bitters', that the market in London is 'Covent Gardens', that when you go out you like to 'go to the cine', that the hill in the Lake District is 'Scarfell Pike', and – I particularly enjoyed this – that the Elizabethan architect was 'Indigo' Jones.

From *Let's Go Europe '96* I learned that Cardiff is 'the only urban centre' in Wales, which must come as something of a shock to the people of Swansea, and from the *Berkeley Budget Guide to Great Britain and Ireland* I discovered that 'nearly every city, town, village, hamlet or cluster of houses in the middle of nowhere has a post office – be it in a butcher shop, liquor store ("off-licence") or pharmacy ("chemist")'.

What I really learned is that what Americans need is new guidebooks. I'm thinking of producing one of my own, filled with advice like 'When dealing with a police officer, always call him "Mr Plod"', and 'To gain the attention of an elusive waiter, extend two fingers and wave your hand up and down vigorously several times. He will regard you as a native.' And finally, but obviously, 'Never ask a person named Clive where he lives.'

DYING ACCENTS

WE HAVE A MAN NAMED WALT WHO DOES A BIT OF CARPENTRY AROUND the house from time to time. He looks to be about 112 years old, but goodness me the man can saw and hammer. He has been doing handiwork around town for at least fifty years.

Walt lives in Vermont, just across the Connecticut River from our little town, and is a proper New Englander – honest, hardworking, congenitally disinclined to waste time, money or words. (He converses as if he has heard that someday he will be billed for it.) Above all, like all New Englanders, he is an early riser. Boy, do New Englanders like to get up early. We have some English friends who moved here from Surrey a few years ago. Soon after arriving, the woman called the dentist for an appointment and was told to come at six-thirty the next day. She showed up the following evening to find the dentist's office in darkness. They had meant 6.30 *a.m.* If Walt were told to come for a dental appointment at that hour I am positive he would ask if they had anything a little earlier.

Anyway, the other day he arrived at our house a few minutes before seven and apologized for being late because the traffic through Norwich had been 'fierce'. What was interesting about this was not the notion that traffic in Norwich could ever be fierce, but that he pronounced it 'Norritch', like the English city. This surprised me because everyone in Norwich and for miles around pronounces it 'Nor-wich' (i.e., with the 'w' sounded, as in 'sandwich').

I asked him about that.

'Ayuh,' he said, which is an all-purpose New England term,

spoken in a slow drawl and usually accompanied by the removal of a cap and a thoughtful scratching of the head. It means 'I may be about to say something, but then again I may not.' He explained to me that the village was pronounced 'Norritch' until the 1950s, when outsiders from places like New York and Boston began to move in and, for whatever reason, started to modify the pronunciation. Now virtually everyone who is younger than Walt, which is virtually everyone, pronounces it 'Nor-wich'. That seemed to me quite sad, the idea that a traditional local pronunciation could be lost simply because outsiders were too lazy or inattentive to preserve it, but it's only symptomatic of a much wider trend.

Thirty years ago, three-quarters of the people in Vermont were born there. Today the proportion has fallen to barely half, and in some places it is much lower. In consequence these days you are far less likely than you once were to hear locals pronouncing cow as 'kyow', saying 'so don't I' for 'so do I' or employing the colourful, if somewhat cryptic, expressions for which the state was once noted – 'heavier than a dead minister' and 'jeezum-jee-hassafrats' are two that spring to mind if not, alas, to many Vermont tongues any longer.

If you go to the remoter corners of the state and hang out at a general store you might just overhear a couple of old farmers (pronounced 'fahmuhs') asking for 'a frog skin more' of coffee, or saying 'well, wouldn't that just jar your mother's preserves', but more probably it will be urban refugees in Ralph Lauren attire asking the storekeeper if he has any guavas.

The same thing has been happening all over the country. I have just been reading an academic study on the dialect of Ocracoke Island off the coast of North Carolina. (The things I do for you, honestly.) Ocracoke is part of the Outer Banks, a chain of barrier islands where the inhabitants once spoke a hearty patois so rich and mysterious that visitors sometimes supposed they had stumbled on some half-lost outpost of Elizabethan England.

The locals – sometimes called 'Hoi-Toiders' for the way they pronounced 'high tide' – had an odd, lilting accent that incorporated many archaic terms, like 'quammish' (meaning to feel sick or uneasy), 'fladget' (for a piece of something) and 'mommuck' (meaning to bother) that hadn't been heard since Shakespeare put away his quill. Being a maritime people, they also used nautical terms in distinctive ways. For instance, 'scud', meaning to run before a gale with a small amount of sail, was employed for land-based movements, so that an Ocracoker might invite you to go for a scud in his car. Finally, just to make the bewilderment of outsiders complete, they absorbed a number of non-English words, like 'pizer' (apparently from the Italian 'piazza') for a porch, and pronounced the lot in a way that brought to mind George Formby doing a West Country accent. It was, in short, an interesting dialect.

All this scudded along, as you might say, in a dependable fashion until 1957, when the federal government built Ocracoke a bridge to the mainland. Almost at once tourists came in and the Ocracoke dialect began to go out.

This was scientifically monitored and recorded by linguists from North Carolina State University, who made periodic field trips to the island over half a century. Then, to everyone's surprise, the Ocracoke dialect began to undergo a revival. The researchers found that middle-aged people – those who had grown up in the 1950s and 1960s when tourism first became a dominant feature of island life – had more pronounced accents than even their parents had. The explanation, the researchers surmise, is that the islanders 'exaggerate their island dialect features, whether consciously or not, because they want there to be no mistake that they are "real" Ocracokers and not tourists or new residents recently relocated from the mainland'.

Much the same sort of phenomenon was found elsewhere. A study of the dialect on Martha's Vineyard, off the coast of Massachusetts, found that certain traditional pronunciations there, such as the flattening of the 'ou' sound in words like 'house' and 'mouse', making them something more like 'hawse' and 'mawse', staged an unexpected rally after nearly going extinct. The driving force, it turned out, was natives who returned to the island after living away and embraced the old speech forms as a way of distinguishing themselves from the mass of non-natives.

So does this mean that the rich and chewy Vermont accent will likewise recover and that once again we can expect to hear people say that something 'would give you a pain where you never had an ache' or that they 'felt rougher than a boar's rear end'? Sadly, it seems not.

From the evidence, it appears that these dialectal revivals happen only on islands or in communities that are in some way still comparatively isolated.

So it seems likely that when old Walt finally hangs up his saw and hammer whoever takes his place won't sound like an old-time Vermonter even if he was born and reared there. I only hope he's not such an early riser.

INEFFICIENCY REPORT

THE OTHER DAY SOMETHING IN OUR LOCAL NEWSPAPER CAUGHT MY EYE. It was an article reporting that the control tower and related facilities at our local airport are to be privatized. The airport loses money, so the Federal Aviation Administration is trying to cut costs by contracting out landing services to someone who can do it more cheaply. What especially caught my attention was a sentence deep in the article which said, 'A spokeswoman with the Federal Aviation Administration's regional office in New York City, Arlene Sarlac, could not provide the name of the company that will be taking over the tower.'

Well, that's really reassuring to hear. Now maybe I am hyper-touchy because I use the airport from time to time, and have a particular interest in its ability to bring planes down in an approximately normal fashion, so I would rather like to know that the tower hasn't been bought by, say, the New England Roller Towel Company or Crash Services (Panama) Ltd, and that the next time I come in to land the plane won't be guided in by some guy on a stepladder waving a broom. I would hope, at the very least, that the Federal Aviation Administration would have some idea of whom they were selling the tower to. Call me particular, but it seems to me that that's the sort of thing you ought to have on file somewhere.

The FAA, it must be said, is not the most efficient of enterprises. A government report in April noted that the agency had been plagued for years by power failures, malfunctioning and antiquated equipment, overworked and overstressed staff, inadequate training programmes, and mismanagement owing to a fragmented chain of command. With regard to equipment standards, the report found that '21 separate offices issued 71 orders, seven standards and 29 specifications'. The upshot was that the FAA didn't have any idea what equipment it owned, how it was being maintained, or even whose turn it was to make the coffee.

According to the *Los Angeles Times*: 'At least three airliner accidents may have been prevented had the FAA not fallen behind schedule in planned modernization of air traffic control equipment.'

I mention this because our subject this week is large-scale incompetence. Despite my best efforts there abounds a terrible myth, which I should like to lay to rest once and for all, that America is an efficient place. It is anything but.

Partly this is because it is a big country. Big countries spawn big bureaucracies. Those bureaucracies spawn lots of departments and each of those departments issues lots of rules and regulations.

An inevitable consequence is that with so many departments the left hand not only doesn't know what the right hand is doing, but doesn't seem to know that there is a right hand. This is interestingly illustrated by frozen pizza.

In the United States, frozen cheese pizza is regulated by the Food and Drug Administration. Frozen pepperoni pizza, on the other hand, is regulated by the Department of Agriculture. Each sets its own standards with regard to content, labelling and so on, has its own team of inspectors, and its own set of regulations which require licences, compliance certificates and all kinds of other costly paperwork. And that's just for frozen pizza. This kind of madness would not be possible in a small country like Britain. You need the European Union for that.

Altogether, it has been estimated, the cost to the nation of complying with the full whack of federal regulations is $668 billion a year, an average of $7,000 per household. That's a lot of compliance.

What gives American inefficiency its particular tang, however, is a peculiar insane cheapness. There is a kind of short-termism here that is simply mystifying. Consider an experience of the Internal Revenue Service, our equivalent of the Inland Revenue.

Every year in the United States an estimated $100 billion in taxes – a positively whopping sum, enough to wipe out the federal deficit at a stroke – goes unreported and uncollected. In 1995, as an experiment, the Government gave the IRS $100 million of extra funding to go looking for some of this extra money. At the end of the year it had found and collected $800 million – only a fraction of the missing money, but still $8 of extra government revenue for every $1 of additional collection costs.

The IRS confidently predicted that if the programme were extended it would net the Government at least $12 billion of missing tax revenues the following year, with more to come in succeeding years. Instead of expanding the programme, Congress chopped it as – wait for it – part of its federal deficit reduction programme. Do you begin to see what I mean?

Or take food inspection. All kinds of hi-tech gizmos exist to test meat for microbial infestations like salmonella and *E. coli*. But the Government is too cheap to invest in these, so federal food inspectors continue to inspect meat visually, as it rolls past on assembly lines. Now you can imagine how attentively a low-paid federal food inspector is going to be looking at each of 18,000 identical plucked chickens sliding past him on a conveyor belt every day of his working life. Call me a cynic, but I very much doubt that after a dozen years or so of this an inspector is likely to be thinking: Hey, here come some more chickens. These might be interesting. In any case – and here's a point that you would think might have occurred to somebody by now – micro-organisms are invisible.

As a result, by the Government's own admission, as much as 20 per cent of all chicken and 49 per cent of turkey is contaminated. What all this costs in illness is anybody's guess, but it is thought that as many as 80 million people may get sick each year from factory-contaminated food, costing the economy somewhere between $5 billion and $10 billion in additional healthcare costs, lost productivity and so on. Every year 9,000 people die of food poisoning in the United States.

All of which brings us back to the good old Federal Aviation Administration. (Actually it doesn't, but I had to get here somehow.) The FAA may or may not be the most inefficient bureaucracy in the United States, but it is indubitably the only one that has my life in its hands when I am 32,000 feet above the earth, so you may imagine my disquiet at learning that it is handing over our control tower to some people whose names it can't remember.

According to our newspaper, the handover will be complete by the end of the month. Three days after that, I am irrevocably committed to flying to Washington from that airport. I mention this merely in case you find a blank space here in a couple of weeks.

But it probably won't come to that. I just asked my wife what we are having for dinner.

Turkey burgers, she said.

A DAY AT THE SEASIDE

EVERY YEAR ABOUT THIS TIME, MY WIFE WAKES ME UP WITH A PLAYFUL slap and says: 'I've got an idea. Let's drive for three hours to the ocean, take off most of our clothes and sit on some sand for a whole day.'

'What for?' I will say warily.

'It will be fun,' she will insist.

'I don't think so,' I will reply. 'People find it disturbing when I take my shirt off in public. I find it disturbing.'

'No, it will be great. We'll get sand in our hair. We'll get sand in our shoes. We'll get sand in our sandwiches and then in our mouths. We'll get sunburned and windburned. And when we get tired of sitting, we can have a paddle in water so cold it actually hurts. At the end of the day we'll set off at the same time as 37,000 other people and get in such a traffic jam that we won't get home till midnight. I can make trenchant observations about your driving skills, and the children can pass the time sticking each other with sharp objects. It will be such fun.'

The tragic thing is that because my wife is English, and therefore beyond the reach of reason where salt water is concerned, she really will think it's fun. Frankly I have never understood the British attachment to the seaside.

Iowa, where I grew up, is a thousand miles from the nearest ocean, so to me (and I believe to most other Iowans, though I haven't had a chance to check with all of them yet) the word 'ocean' suggests alarming things like riptides and undertows. (I expect people in New York suffer similar terrors when you mention words like 'cornfields' and 'county fair'.) Lake Ahquabi, where I did all my formative swimming and sunburning, may not have the romance of Cape Cod or the grandeur of the rock-ribbed coast of Maine, but then neither did it grab you by the legs and carry you off helplessly to Newfoundland. No, you may keep the sea, as far as I am concerned, and every drop of water in it.

So when last weekend my wife suggested that we take a drive to the ocean, I put my foot down and said, 'Never – absolutely not,' which is of course why we ended up, three hours later, at Kennebunk Beach in Maine.

Now you may find this hard to believe, given the whirlwind of adventure that has been my life, but in all my years I had been to American ocean beaches just twice – once in California when I was twelve and managed to scrape all the skin from my nose (this is a true story) by mistiming a retreating wave as only someone from Iowa can and diving headlong into bare gritty sand, and once in Florida when I was a college student and far too intoxicated to notice a landscape feature as subtle as an ocean.

So I can't pretend to speak with authority here. All I can tell you is that if Kennebunk Beach is anything to go by, then American beaches are entirely unlike British ones. To begin with, there was no pier, promenade or arcades; no shops where everything is miraculously priced at £1; no places to buy saucy postcards or jaunty hats; no tearooms and fish and chip shops; no fortune tellers; no disembodied voice from a bingo parlour breathing out those strange, coded calls: '*Number 37 – the vicar's in the shrubs again*,' or whatever it is they say.

Indeed, there was nothing commercial at all – just a street lined with big summer homes, a vast sunny beach and an infinite and hostile sea beyond.

That isn't to say the people on the beach – of whom there were many hundreds – were going without, for they had brought everything they would ever need again in the way of food, beverages, beach umbrellas, windbreaks, folding chairs and sleek inflatables. Amundsen went to the South Pole with fewer provisions than most of these people had.

We were a pretty pathetic sight in contrast. Apart from being whiter than an old man's flanks, we had in the way of equipment just three beach towels and a raffia bag filled, in the English style, with a bottle of sunscreen, an inexhaustible supply of Wet Wipes, spare underpants for everyone (in case of vehicular accidents involving visits to an emergency room) and a modest packet of sandwiches.

Our youngest – whom I've taken to calling Jimmy in case he should one day become a libel lawyer – surveyed the scene and said: 'OK, Dad, here's the situation. I need an ice cream, a Lilo, a deluxe bucket and spade set, a hot dog, some candy floss, an inflatable dinghy, scuba equipment, my own water slide, a cheese pizza with extra cheese, and a toilet.'

'They don't have those things here, Jimmy,' I chuckled.

'I really need the toilet.'

I reported this to my wife. 'Then you'll have to take him to Kennebunkport,' she said serenely from beneath a preposterous sun hat.

Kennebunkport is an old town, at a crossroads, laid out long before anyone thought of the motorcar, and some miles from the beach. It was jammed with traffic from all directions. We parked an appallingly vast distance from the centre and searched all over for toilets. By the time we found a toilet (actually it was the back wall of the Rite-Aid Pharmacy – but please don't tell my wife), little Jimmy didn't need to go any longer.

So we returned to the beach. By the time we got there, some hours later, I discovered that everyone had gone off for a swim and there was only one half-eaten sandwich left. I sat on a towel and nibbled at the sandwich.

'Oh, look, Mummy,' said number two daughter gaily when they emerged from the surf a few minutes later, 'Daddy's eating the sandwich the dog had.'

'Tell me this isn't happening,' I whimpered.

'Don't worry, dear,' my wife said soothingly. 'It was an Irish setter. They're very clean.'

I don't remember much after that. I had a little nap and woke to find that Jimmy was burying me up to my chest in sand, which was fine except that he had started at my head, and I had managed to get so sunburned that a dermatologist invited me to a convention in Cleveland the following week as an exhibit.

We lost the car keys for two hours, the Irish setter came back and stole one of the beach towels, then nipped me on the hand for eating his sandwich, and number two daughter got tar in her hair. It was a typical day at the seaside, in other words. We got home about midnight after an inadvertent detour to the Canadian border –

though this at least gave us something to talk about on the long drive across Pennsylvania.

'Lovely,' said my wife. 'We must do that again soon.'

And the heartbreaking thing is she really meant it.

SPLENDID IRRELEVANCIES

NOW HERE'S A STORY I LIKE VERY MUCH.

Just before Christmas last year an American computer games company called Maxis Inc. released an adventure game called SimCopter in which players had to fly helicopters on rescue missions. When they successfully completed the tenth and final level, according to the *New York Times*, the winning players were supposed to be rewarded with some audio-visual hoopla involving 'a crowd, fireworks and a brass band'.

Instead, to their presumed surprise, the winners found images of men in swimsuits kissing each other.

The rogue images, it turned out, were the work of a mischievous thirty-three-year-old programmer named Jacques Servin. When contacted by the *Times*, Mr Servin said he had created the smooching fellows 'to call attention to the lack of gay characters in computer games'. The company hastily recalled 78,000 games, and invited Mr Servin to find employment elsewhere.

Here's another story I like.

In June of this year, while travelling alone across America by car, Mrs Rita Rupp of Tulsa, Oklahoma, got it in mind that she might be abducted by nefarious persons. So, just to be on the safe side, she prepared a note in advance, in appropriately desperate-looking handwriting, that said: 'Help, I've been kidnapped. Call the highway patrol.' The note then gave her name and address, and phone numbers for the appropriate armed authorities.

Now if you write a note like this, you want to make certain that either (a) you do get kidnapped or (b) you don't accidentally drop the note out of your handbag. Well, guess what happened? The hapless Mrs Rupp dropped the note, it was picked up and turned in by a conscientious citizen, and the next thing you know police in four states had set up roadblocks, issued all-points bulletins and generally got themselves pretty excited. Meanwhile, Mrs Rupp drove on to her destination sweetly unaware of the chaos she had left in her wake.

The trouble with these two stories, delightful though they are, is that I haven't figured out a way to get them into one of my columns. That's the trouble with this column-writing business, I find. I am forever coming across interesting and worthwhile titbits (or 'tidbits', as we insist on spelling it in the United States in order not to provoke anyone into an untimely sweat) and when I come across these diverting items I carefully cut them out or photocopy them and file them away under 'Computer Games (Men Kissing)' or 'Worst Highway Travel Tips', or whatever seems to suit.

Then, some time later – well, this afternoon to be precise – I come across them again and wonder what on earth I was thinking. I call this collecting of interesting but ultimately useless information the Ignaz Semmelweiss syndrome, after the Austro-Hungarian doctor Ignaz Semmelweiss, who in 1850 became the first person to realize that the spread of infection on hospital wards could be dramatically reduced by washing one's hands. Soon after making his breakthrough discovery Dr Semmelweiss died – from an infected cut on his hand.

You see what I mean? A splendid story, but I've got no place to put it. I might equally have called the phenomenon the Versalle syndrome, after the opera singer Richard Versalle, who in 1996, during the world première of the *The Makropulos Affair* at the Metropolitan Opera House in New York, sang the fateful words 'Too bad you can only live so long,' and then, poor man, fell down dead from a heart attack.

Then again I might have named it in honour of the great General John Sedgewick of the Union Army, whose last words, at the Battle of Fredericksburg during the American Civil War, were: 'I tell you, men, they could not hit a bull at this dis—'

What all these people have in common is that they don't have the slightest relevance to anything I have ever written about or probably ever will. The trouble is that I am never altogether sure what I am going to write about (I can't wait to find out where this is going, to tell you the truth), so I keep these things filed away just in case they may come in handy in a pinch.

In consequence, I have manila folders bulging with cuttings like – well, like this one here, from a newspaper in Portland, Maine, bearing the headline 'Man Found Chained to Tree Again'. It was the 'Again' that particularly caught my eye. If the headline had said 'Man Found Chained to Tree' I would probably have turned the page. After all, anyone can get himself chained to a tree once. But *twice* – well, now that's beginning to seem a tad careless.

The person concerned was one Larry Doyen of Mexico, Maine, who, it turns out, has the very interesting hobby of attaching himself to trees with a chain and padlock and throwing the key out of arm's reach. On this particular occasion, he had been out in the woods for two weeks and had very nearly expired.

A diverting story, and clearly a salutary lesson for any of us who were thinking of taking up alfresco bondage for a hobby, but it's hard to imagine at this remove what I was hoping to make of it *vis-à-vis* the estimable *Night & Day* magazine.

I am similarly at a loss to recall the presumed significance of a small story I saved from the *Seattle Times* concerning a group of army paratroopers who, as a public relations exercise, agreed to parachute onto a high-school football pitch in Kennewick, Washington, to present the game ball to the home team quarterback. With commendable precision they leapt from their aeroplane, trailing coloured smoke from special flares, executed several nifty and breathtaking aerobatic manoeuvres, and landed in an empty stadium on the other side of town.

I am equally unable to account fully for another story from the *New York Times*, about a couple who wrote down the gurgling sounds made by their infant daughter, presented it in the form of a poem (typical line: 'Bwah-bwah bwah-bwah bwah-bwah'), submitted it to something called the North American Open Poetry Contest, and won a semi-finalist prize.

Sometimes, alas, I don't save the whole article, but just a paragraph from it, so that all I am left with is a mystifying fragment. Here is a quotation from the March 1996 issue of the *Atlantic Monthly* magazine: 'It is perfectly legal for a dermatologist to do brain surgery in his garage if he can find a patient willing to get on the table and pay for it.' Here's another, from the *Washington Post*: 'Researchers at the University of Utah have discovered that most men breathe mainly through one nostril for three hours and mainly through the other for the following three.' Goodness knows what they do for the other eighteen hours of the day, because I didn't save the rest of the article.

I keep thinking that I will figure a way to work these oddments up into a column, but I haven't hit on it yet. However, the one thing I can confidently promise you is that when I do, you will read it here first.

ON LOSING A SON

THIS MAY GET A LITTLE SOPPY, AND I'M SORRY, BUT YESTERDAY EVENING I was working at my desk when my youngest child came up to me, a baseball bat perched on his shoulder, a cap on his head, and asked me if I felt like playing a little ball with him. I was trying to get some important work done before going away on a long trip, and I very nearly declined with regrets, but then it occurred to me that never again would he be seven years, one month and six days old, so we had better catch these moments while we can.

So we went out onto the front lawn and here is where it gets soppy. There was a kind of beauty about the experience so elemental and wonderful I cannot tell you – the way the evening sun fell across the lawn, the earnest eagerness of his young stance, the fact that we were doing this most quintessentially dad-and-son thing, the supreme contentment of just being together – and I couldn't believe that it would ever have occurred to me that finishing an article or writing a book or doing anything at all could be more important and rewarding than this.

Now what has brought on all this sudden sensitivity is that a week or so ago we took our eldest son off to a small university in Ohio. He was the first of our four to fly the coop, and now he is gone – grown up, independent, far away – and I am suddenly realizing how quickly they go.

'Once they leave for college they never really come back,' a neighbour who has lost two of her own in this way told us wistfully the other day.

This isn't what I wanted to hear. I wanted to hear that they come back a lot, only this time they hang up their clothes, admire you for your intelligence and wit, and no longer have a hankering to sink diamond studs into various odd holes in their heads. But the neighbour was right. He is gone. There is an emptiness in the house that proves it.

I hadn't expected it to be like this because for the past couple of years even when he was here he wasn't really here, if you see what I mean. Like most teenagers, he didn't live in our house in any meaningful sense – more just dropped by a couple of times a day to see what was in the refrigerator or to wander between rooms, a towel round his waist, calling out, 'Mum, where's my . . . ?' as in, 'Mum, where's my yellow shirt?' and 'Mum, where's my deodorant?' Occasionally I would see the top of his head in an easy chair in front of a television on which Oriental people were kicking each other in the head, but mostly he resided in a place called 'Out'.

My role in getting him off to college was simply to write cheques – lots and lots of them – and to look suitably pale and aghast as the sums mounted. You can't believe the cost of sending a child to university in the United States these days. Perhaps it is because we live in a community where these matters are treated gravely, but nearly every college-bound youth in our town goes off and looks at half a dozen or more prospective universities at enormous cost. Then there are fees for college entrance examinations and a separate fee for each university applied to.

But all this pales beside the cost of university itself. My son's tuition is $19,000 a year – that's nearly £12,000 in real money – which I am told is actually quite reasonable these days. Some schools charge as much as $28,000 for tuition. Then there is a fee of $3,000 a year for his room, $2,400 for food, $700 or so for books, $650 for health centre fees and insurance, and $710 for 'activities'. Don't ask me what that is. I just sign the cheques.

Still to come are the costs of flying him to and from Ohio at Thanksgiving, Christmas and Easter – holidays when every other college student in America is flying and so airfares are at their most stupefyingly extreme – plus all the other incidental expenses like spending money and long-distance phone bills. Already my wife is calling him every other day to ask if he has enough money, when in fact, as I point out, it should be the other way round. Oh, and this goes on for four years here, rather than three as in Britain. And here's one more thing. Next year I have a daughter who goes off to university, so I get to do this twice.

So you will excuse me, I hope, when I tell you that the emotional side of this event was rather overshadowed by the ongoing financial shock. It wasn't until we dropped him at his university dormitory and left him there looking touchingly lost and bewildered amid an assortment of cardboard boxes and suitcases in a spartan room not unlike a prison cell that it really hit home that he was vanishing out of our lives and into his own.

Now that we are home it is even worse. There is no kickboxing on the TV, no astounding clutter of trainers in the back hallway, no calls of 'Mum, where's my . . . ?' from the top of the stairs, no-one my size to call me a 'doofus' or to say, 'Nice shirt, Dad. Did you mug a boat person?' In fact, I see now, I had it exactly wrong. Even when he wasn't here, he was here, if you see what I mean. And now he is not here at all.

It takes only the simplest things – a wadded-up sweatshirt found behind the back seat of the car, some used chewing gum left in a patently inappropriate place – to make me want to blubber help-lessly. Mrs Bryson, meanwhile, doesn't need any kind of prod. She just blubbers helplessly – at the sink, while hoovering, in the bath. 'My baby,' she wails in dismay and blows her nose with an alarm-ing honk on any convenient piece of fabric, then whimpers some more.

For the past week I have found myself spending a lot of time wandering aimlessly through the house looking at the oddest things – a basketball, his running trophies, an old holiday snapshot – and thinking about all the carelessly discarded yesterdays they repre-sent. The hard and unexpected part is the realization not just that my son is not here, but that the boy he was is gone for ever. I would give anything to have them both back. But of course that cannot be. Life moves on. Kids grow up and move away, and, if you don't know this already, believe me it happens faster than you can imagine.

Which is why I am going to finish here and go off and play a little baseball on the front lawn while the chance is still there.

HIGHWAY DIVERSIONS

IF YOU HAVE BEEN FOLLOWING THIS SPACE CLOSELY (AND IF NOT, WHY not?) you will recall that last week I discussed how we recently drove from New Hampshire to Ohio in order to deliver my eldest son to a university which had offered to house and educate him for the next four years in return for a sum of money not unadjacent to the cost of a moon launch.

What I didn't tell you then, because I didn't want to upset you on my first week back from holiday, is what a nightmare experience it was. Now please understand, I am as fond of my wife and children as the next man, no matter how much they cost me per annum in footwear and Nintendo games (which is frankly a lot), but that isn't to say that I wish to pass a week with them ever again in a sealed metal chamber on an American highway.

The trouble is not my family, I hasten to add, but the American highway. Oh, is the American highway dull. As a Briton, you really cannot imagine boredom on this scale (unless perhaps you are from Stevenage). Part of the problem with American highways is that they are so very long – it is 850 miles from New Hampshire to central Ohio and, I can now personally attest, just as far back – but mostly it is because there is nothing to get excited about along the way.

It didn't used to be like this. When I was a boy, the highways of the United States were scattered with diversions. They weren't very good diversions, but that didn't matter at all.

At some point on every day, you could count on seeing a hoarding that would say something like: 'Visit World-Famous

Atomic Rock – It Really Glows!' A few miles later there would be another hoarding saying: 'See the Rock That Has Baffled Science! Only 162 Miles!' This one would have a picture of a grave-looking scientist with a cartoon bubble beside his mouth confiding: 'It Is Truly a Marvel of Nature!' or 'I Am Quite Baffled!'

A few miles beyond that would be: 'Experience the Atomic Rock Force Field . . . *If You Dare*! Just 147 Miles!' This one would show a man, interestingly not unlike one's own father, being violently flung back by some strange radiant force. In smaller letters would be the warning: 'Caution: May Not Be Suitable for Small Children.'

Well, that would be it. My big brother and sister, squeezed onto the backseat with me and having exhausted all the possibilities for diversion that came with holding me down and drawing vivid geometric patterns on my face, arms and stomach with a biro, would set up a clamour to see this world-famous attraction, and I would weakly chime in.

The people who put up these hoardings were brilliant, among the greatest marketing geniuses of our age. They knew precisely – to the mile, I would guess – how long it would take a carful of children to wear down their father's profound and inevitable opposition to visiting something that was going to waste time and cost money. The upshot, in any case, is that we always went.

The world-famous Atomic Rock would of course be nothing like the advertised attraction. It would be almost comically smaller than illustrated and wouldn't glow at all. It would be fenced off, ostensibly for the safety of onlookers, and the fence would be covered with warnings saying: 'Caution: Dangerous Force Field! Approach No Further!' But there would always be some kid who would crawl under the fence and go up and touch it, indeed clamber all over it, without being flung aside or suffering any other evident consequences. As a rule, my extravagant biro tattoos would draw more interest from the crowd.

So in disgust my father would pile us all back into the car vowing never to be duped like this again and we would drive on until, some hours later, we would pass a hoarding that said: 'Visit World-Famous Singing Sands! Only 214 Miles!' and the cycle would start again.

Out west, in really boring states like Nebraska and Kansas, people could put up signs saying pretty much anything – 'See the Dead Cow! Hours of Fun for the Whole Family!' or 'Plank of Wood! Just 132 Miles!' Over the years, I well recall, we visited a dinosaur footprint, a painted desert, a petrified frog, a hole in the ground that claimed to be the world's deepest well, and a house made entirely of beer bottles. In fact, from some of our holidays that is all I can remember.

These things were always disappointing, but that wasn't the point. You weren't paying 75 cents for the experience. You were paying 75 cents as a kind of tribute, a thanks to the imaginative person who had helped you to pass 127 miles of uneventful highway in a state of genuine excitement, and, in my case, without being drawn on. My father never understood this.

Now, I regret to say, my children don't understand it either. On this trip as we drove across Pennsylvania, a state so ludicrously vast that it takes a whole day to traverse, we passed a sign that said: 'Visit World-Famous Roadside America! Just 79 Miles!'

I had no idea what Roadside America was, and it wasn't even on our route, but I insisted that we go there anyway. These things simply don't exist any longer. Nowadays the most exciting thing you can hope to get along the American highway is a McDonald's Happy Meal. So something like Roadside America, whatever it might be, is to be devoutly cherished. The great irony is that I was the only one in the car, and by a considerable margin, who wanted to see it.

Roadside America turned out to be a large model railway, with little towns and tunnels, farms with miniature cows and sheep, and lots of trains going round in endless circles. It was a little dusty and ill-lit, but charming in a not-touched-since-1957 sort of way. We were the only customers that day, possibly the only customers for many days. I loved it.

'Isn't this great?' I said to my youngest daughter.

'Dad, you are like so pathetic,' she said sadly and went out.

I turned hopefully to her little brother, but he just shook his head and followed.

I was disappointed, naturally, but I think I know what to do next time. I'll hold them down for two hours beforehand and draw all over them with a biro. Then they'll appreciate any kind of highway diversion. Of that I am certain.

SNOOPERS AT WORK

NOW HERE IS SOMETHING TO BEAR IN MIND SHOULD YOU EVER FIND yourself using a changing cubicle in an American department store or other retail establishment. It is perfectly legal – indeed, it is evidently routine – for the store or shop to spy on you while you are trying on their clothes.

I know this because I have just been reading a book by Ellen Alderman and Caroline Kennedy called *The Right to Privacy*, which is full of alarming tales of ways that businesses and employers can – and enthusiastically do – intrude into what would normally be considered private affairs.

The business of changing-cubicle spying came to light in 1983 when a customer trying on clothes in a department store in Michigan discovered that a store employee had climbed a stepladder and was watching him through a metal vent. (Is this tacky or what?) The customer was sufficiently outraged that he sued the store for invasion of privacy. He lost. A state court held that it was reasonable for retailers to defend against shoplifting by engaging in such surveillance.

He shouldn't have been surprised. Nearly everyone is being spied on in some way in America these days. A combination of technological advances, employer paranoia and commercial avarice means that many millions of Americans are having their lives delved into in ways that would not have been possible, or even thinkable, a dozen years ago.

Log on to the Internet and nearly every website you go to will make a record of what you looked at and how long you lingered there. This information can, and generally will, then be sold on to mail order and marketing companies, or otherwise used to bombard you with blandishments to spend.

Worse still, there are now scores of information brokers – electronic private investigators – who make a living going through the Internet digging out personal information on people for a fee. If you are an American resident and have ever registered to vote they can get your address and date of birth, since voter registration forms are a matter of public record in most states. With these two pieces of information they can (and for as little as $8 or $10 will) provide almost any personal information about any person you might wish to know: court records, medical records, driving records, credit history, hobbies, buying habits, annual income, phone numbers (including ex-directory numbers), you name it.

Most of this was possible before, but it would take days of enquiries and visits to various government offices. Now it can be done in minutes, in complete anonymity, through the Internet.

Many companies are taking advantage of these technological possibilities to make their businesses more ruthlessly productive. In Maryland, according to *Time* magazine, a bank searched through the medical records of its borrowers – apparently quite legally – to find out which of them had life-threatening illnesses, and used this information to cancel their loans. Other companies have focused not on customers but on their own employees – for instance to check what prescription drugs the employees are taking. One large, well-known company teamed up with a pharmaceutical firm to comb through the health records of employees to see who might benefit from a dose of anti-depressants. The idea was that the company would get more serene workers; the drug company would get more customers.

According to the American Management Association two-thirds of companies in the United States spy on their employees in some way. Thirty-five per cent track phone calls and 10 per cent actually tape phone conversations to review at leisure later. About a quarter of companies admit to going through their employees' computer files and reading their e-mail.

Still other companies are secretly watching their employees at work. A secretary at a college in Massachusetts discovered that a hidden video camera was filming her office twenty-four hours a day. Goodness knows what the school authorities were hoping to find with their surveillance. What they got were images of the woman changing out of her work clothes and into a tracksuit each night in order to jog home from work. She is suing and will probably get a pot of money. But elsewhere courts have upheld companies' rights to spy on their workers.

In 1989, when an employee of a large Japanese-owned computer products company discovered that the company was routinely reading employees' e-mail, even though it had assured the employees that it was not, she blew the whistle and was promptly fired. She sued for unfair dismissal and lost the case. A court upheld the right of companies not only to review employees' private communications but to lie to them about doing it. Whoa.

And to return to a well-aired theme, there is a particular paranoia about drugs. I have a friend who got a job with a large manufacturing company in Iowa a year or so ago. Across the street from the company was a tavern that was the company after-hours hangout. One night my friend was having a beer after work with his colleagues when he was approached by a fellow employee who asked if he knew where she could get some marijuana. He said he didn't use the stuff himself, but to get rid of her – for she was very persistent – he gave her the phone number of an acquaintance who sometimes sold it.

The next day he was sacked. The woman, it turned out, was a company spy employed solely to weed out drug use in the company. He hadn't supplied her with marijuana, you understand, hadn't encouraged her to use marijuana, and had stressed that he didn't use marijuana himself. None the less he was fired for 'encouraging and abetting the use of an illegal substance'.

Already, 91 per cent of large companies – I find this almost unbelievable – now test some of their workers for drugs. Scores of companies have introduced what are called TAD rules – TAD being short for 'tobacco, alcohol and drugs' – which prohibit employees from using any of these substances at any time, including at home. There are companies, if you can believe it, that forbid their employees to drink or smoke at any time – even one beer, even on a Saturday night – and enforce the rules by making their workers give urine samples. That is outrageous, but there you are.

But it gets even more sinister than that. Two leading electronics companies working together have invented something called an 'active badge', which tracks the movements of any worker compelled to wear one. The badge sends out an infrared signal every fifteen seconds. This signal is received by a central computer, which is thus able to keep a record of where every employee is and has been, whom they have associated with, how many times they have been to the toilet or water cooler – in short, to log every single action of their working day. If that isn't ominous, I don't know what is.

However, there is one development, I am pleased to report, which makes all of this worthwhile. A company in New Jersey has patented a device for determining whether restaurant employees have washed their hands after using the lavatory. Now *that* I can go for.

HOW TO HIRE A CAR

WE'VE BEEN BACK IN THE STATES FOR NEARLY TWO AND A HALF YEARS now, if you can believe it (and even, come to that, if you can't), so you would think I would be getting the hang of things by now, but alas no. The intricacies of modern American life still often leave me muddled. Things are so awfully complicated here, you see.

I had occasion to reflect on this the other week when I went to pick up a hire car at the airport in Boston, and the clerk, after logging every number that has ever been associated with me and taking imprints from several credit cards, said: 'Do you want Third Party Liability Waiver Damage Exclusion Cover?'

'I don't know,' I said uncertainly. 'What is it?'

'It provides cover in the event of a Second Party Waiver Indemnification Claim being made against you, or a First or Second Party Exclusion Claim being made by you on behalf of a fourth party twice removed.'

'Unless you're claiming a First Party Residual Cross-Over Exemption,' added a man in the queue behind me, causing me to spin my head.

'No, that's only in New York,' corrected the hire car man. 'In Massachusetts you can't claim cross-over exemption unless you have only one leg and are not normally resident in North America for tax purposes.'

'You're thinking of Second Party Disallowance Invalidity Cover,' said a second man in the queue to the first. 'Are you from Rhode Island?'

'Why, yes, I am,' said the first man.

'Then that explains it. You have Variable Double-Negative Split-Weighting down there.'

'I don't understand any of this,' I cried, wretchedly.

'Look,' said the car hire man a little impatiently, 'suppose you crash into a person who has Second Party Disallowance Invalidity Cover but not First and Third Party Accident Indemnification. If you've got Third Party Waiver Damage Exclusion Cover you don't have to claim on your own policy under the Single Digit Reverse Liability Waiver. How much Personal Loss Rollover do you carry?'

'I don't know,' I said.

He stared at me. 'You don't know?' he said in a tone of level incredulity. Out of the corner of my eye I could see the other people in the queue exchanging amused glances.

'Mrs Bryson deals with these things,' I explained a trifle inadequately.

'Well, what's your Baseline Double Footfault Level?'

I gave a small, helpless, please-don't-hit-me look. 'I don't know.'

He drew in breath in a way that suggested that perhaps I should consider walking. 'It sounds to me like you need the Universal Full-Cover Double Top-Loaded Comprehensive Switchback Plan.'

'With Graduated Death Benefit,' suggested the second man in the queue.

'What's all that?' I asked unhappily.

'It's all here in the leaflet,' said the clerk. He passed me a leaflet. 'Basically, it gives you a hundred million dollars of coverage for theft, fire, accident, earthquake, nuclear war, swamp gas explosions, meteor impact, derailment leading to hair loss and intentional death – so long as they occur simultaneously and providing you give twenty-four hours' notice in writing and file an Incident Intention Report.'

'How much is it?'

'One hundred and seventy-two dollars a day. But it comes with a set of steak knives.'

I looked to the other men in the queue. They nodded.

'OK, I'll take it,' I said in exhausted resignation.

'Now do you want the Worry-Free Fuel Top-Up Option,' the clerk went on, 'or the Fill-It-Yourself Cheap Person's Option?'

'What's that?' I asked, dismayed to realize that this hell wasn't yet over.

'Well, with the Worry-Free Fuel Top-Up Option you can bring

the car back on empty and we will refill the tank for a one-time charge of $32.95. Under the other plan, you fill the tank yourself before returning the car and we put the $32.95 elsewhere on the bill under "Miscellaneous Unexplained Charges".'

I consulted with my advisers and took the Worry-Free plan.

The clerk ticked the appropriate box. 'And do you want the Car Locator Option Arrangement?'

'What's that?'

'We tell you where the car is.'

'Take it,' urged the man nearest me with feeling. 'I didn't take it once in Chicago, and spent two and a half days wandering around the airport looking for the damned thing. Turned out it was under a tarpaulin in a cornfield near Peoria.'

And so it went. Eventually, when we had worked our way through 200 or so pages of complexly tiered options, the clerk passed the contract to me.

'Just sign here, here and here,' he said. 'And initial here, here, here and here – and over here. And here, here and here.'

'What am I initialling?' I asked warily.

'Well, this one gives us the right to come to your home and seize one of your children or a nice piece of electronic equipment if you don't bring the car back on time. This one is your agreement to take a truth serum in the event of a dispute. This one waives your right to sue. This one avows that any damage to the car now or at any time in the future is your responsibility. And this one is a twenty-five-dollar donation to Bernice Kowalski's leaving do.'

Before I could respond, he whipped away the contract and replaced it on the counter with a map of the airport.

'Now to get to the car,' he continued, drawing on the map as if doing one of those maze puzzles that you find in children's colouring books, 'you follow the red signs through Terminal A to Terminal D2, then you follow the yellow signs – including the green ones – through the parking garage to the Sector R escalators. Take the down escalator up to Passenger Assembly Point Q, get on the shuttle marked "Satellite Parking/Mississippi Valley" and take it to Parking Lot A427-West. Get off there, follow the white arrows under the harbour tunnel, through the quarantine exclusion zone and past the water filtration plant. Cross runway 22-Left, climb the fence at the far side, go down the embankment, and you'll find your car parked in bay number 12,604. It's a red Flymo. You can't miss it.'

He passed me my keys and a large box filled with documents, insurance policies and other related items.

'And good luck to you,' he called after me.

I never did find the car, of course, and I was hours late for my appointment, but in fairness I have to say that we have had a lot of pleasure from the steak knives.

FALL IN NEW ENGLAND

AH, AUTUMN! Every year about this time, for a tantalizingly short while – a week or two at most – an amazing thing happens here. The whole of New England explodes in colour. All those trees that for months have formed a sombre green backdrop suddenly burst into a million glowing tints and the countryside, as Frances Trollope put it, 'goes to glory'.

Yesterday, under the pretence of doing vital research, I drove over to Vermont and treated my startled feet to a hike up Killington Peak, 4,235 feet of sturdy splendour in the heart of the Green Mountains. It was one of those sumptuous days when the world is full of autumn muskiness and tangy, crisp perfection, and the air so clean and clear that you feel as if you could reach out and ping it with a finger, as you would a polished wineglass. Even the colours were crisp: vivid blue sky, deep green fields, leaves in a thousand luminous hues. It is a truly astounding sight when every tree in a landscape becomes individual, when each winding back highway and plump hillside is suddenly and infinitely splashed with every sharp shade that nature can bestow – flaming scarlet, lustrous gold, throbbing vermilion, fiery orange.

Forgive me if I seem a tad effusive, but it is impossible to describe a spectacle this grand without babbling. Even the great naturalist Donald Culross Peattie, a man whose prose is so dry you could use it to mop spills, totally lost his head when he tried to convey the wonder of a New England autumn.

In his classic *Natural History of Trees of Eastern and Central*

North America, Peattie drones on for 434 pages in language that can most generously be called workmanlike (typical passage: 'Oaks are usually ponderous and heavy-wooded trees, with scaly or furrowed bark, and more or less five-angled twigs and, consequently, five-ranked leaves . . .'), but when at last he turns his attention to the New England sugar maple and its vivid autumnal regalia, it is as if someone has spiked his cocoa. In a tumble of breathless metaphors he describes the maple's colours as 'like the shout of a great army . . . like tongues of flame . . . like the mighty, marching melody that rides upon the crest of some symphonic weltering sea and, with its crying song, gives meaning to all the calculated dissonance of the orchestra'.

'Yes, Donald,' you can just about hear his wife saying, 'now take your tablets, dear.'

For two fevered paragraphs he goes on like this and then abruptly returns to talking about drooping leaf axils, scaly buds and pendulous branchlets. I understand completely. When I reached the preternaturally clear air of Killington's summit, with views to every horizon soaked in autumn lustre, I found it was all I could do not to fling open my arms and burst forth with a medley of John Denver tunes. (For this reason it is a good idea to hike with an experienced companion and to carry a well-stocked first-aid kit.)

Occasionally you read about some academic who has gone out with the scientific equivalent of a paint chart and announced with a grave air of discovery that the maples of Michigan or the oaks of the Ozarks achieve even deeper tints, but this is to completely miss the special qualities that make New England's fall display unique.

For one thing, the New England landscape provides a setting that no other area of North America can rival. Its sunny white churches, covered bridges, tidy farms and clustered villages are an ideal complement to the rich earthy colours of nature. Moreover, there is a variety in its trees that few other areas achieve: oaks, beeches, aspens, sumacs, four varieties of maples, and others almost beyond counting provide a contrast that dazzles the senses. Finally, and above all, there is the brief, perfect balance of its climate in fall, with crisp, chilly nights and warm, sunny days, which help to bring all the deciduous trees to a coordinated climax. So make no mistake. For a few glorious days each October, New England is unquestionably the loveliest place on earth.

What is all the more remarkable about this is that no-one knows quite why it happens.

In autumn, as you will recall from your school biology lessons (or, failing that, from *Tomorrow's World*), trees prepare for their long winter's slumber by ceasing to manufacture chlorophyll, the chemical that makes their leaves green. The absence of chlorophyll allows other pigments, called carotenoids, which have been present in the leaves all along, to show off a bit. The carotenoids are what account for the yellow and gold of birches, hickories, beeches and some oaks, among others. Now here is where it gets interesting. To allow these golden colours to thrive, the trees must continue to feed the leaves even though the leaves are not actually doing anything useful except hanging there looking pretty. Just at a time when a tree ought to be storing up all its energy for use the following spring, it is instead expending a great deal of effort feeding a pigment that brings joy to the hearts of simple folk like me but doesn't do anything for the tree.

What is even more mysterious is that some species of trees go a step further and, at considerable cost to themselves, manufacture another type of chemical called anthocyanins, which result in the spectacular oranges and scarlets that are so characteristic of New England. It isn't that the trees of New England manufacture more of these anthocyanins, but rather that the New England climate and soil provide exactly the right conditions for these colours to bloom in style. In climates that are wetter or warmer, the trees still go to all this trouble – have done for years – but it doesn't come to anything. No-one knows why the trees make this immense effort when they get nothing evident in return.

But here is the greatest mystery of all. Every year literally millions of people, genially and collectively known to locals as 'leaf peepers', get in their cars, drive great distances to New England and spend a succession of weekends shuffling round craft shops and places with names like 'Norm's Antiques and Collectibles'.

I would estimate that no more than 0.05 per cent of them stray more than 150 feet from their cars. What a strange, inexplicable misfortune that is, to come to the edge of perfection and then turn your back on it.

They miss not only the bosky joys of the out of doors – the fresh air, the rich, organic smells, the ineffable delight of strolling through drifts of dry leaves – but the singular pleasure of hearing the hills ringing with 'Take Me Home, Country Road' sung in a loud voice in a pleasingly distinctive Anglo-Iowa twang. And that, if I say so myself, is definitely worth getting out of your car for.

A SLIGHT INCONVENIENCE

OUR SUBJECT TODAY IS CONVENIENCE IN AMERICA, AND HOW THE MORE convenient things supposedly get the more inconvenient they actually become.

I was thinking about this the other day (I'm always thinking, you know – it's amazing) when I took my younger children to a Burger King for lunch, and there was a line of about a dozen cars at the drive-through window. Now a drive-through window is not, despite its promising name, a window you drive through, but a window you drive up to and collect your food from, having placed your order over a speakerphone along the way. The idea is to provide quick takeaway food for those in a hurry.

We parked, went in, ordered and ate, and came out again all in about ten minutes. As we departed, I noticed that a white pickup truck that had been last in the queue when we arrived was still four or five cars back from collecting its food. It would have been much quicker if the driver had parked like us, and gone in and got his food himself, but he would never have thought that way because the drive-through window is *supposed* to be speedier and more convenient.

You see my point, of course. Americans have become so attached to the idea of convenience that they will put up with almost any inconvenience to achieve it. It's crazy, I know, but there you are. The things that are supposed to speed up and simplify our lives more often than not actually have the opposite effect, and this set me to thinking (see, there I go again) why this should be.

Americans have always had a strange devotion to the idea of

assisted ease. It is an interesting fact that nearly all the everyday inventions that take the struggle out of life – escalators, automatic doors, passenger lifts, refrigerators, washing machines, frozen food, fast food – were invented in America, or at least first widely embraced here. Americans grew so used to a steady stream of labour-saving advances, in fact, that by the 1960s they had come to expect machines to do pretty much everything for them.

I remember the moment I first realized that this was not necessarily a good idea was at Christmas of 1961 or '62 when my father was given an electric carving knife. It was an early model and rather formidable. Perhaps my memory is playing tricks on me, but I have a clear impression of him donning goggles and heavy rubber gloves before plugging it in. What is certainly true is that when he sank it into the turkey it didn't so much carve the bird as send pieces of it flying everywhere in a kind of fleshy white spray, before the blade struck the plate with a shower of blue sparks, and the whole thing flew out of his hands and skittered across the table and out of the room, like a creature from a Gremlins movie. I don't believe we ever saw it again, though we used to sometimes hear it thumping against table legs late at night.

Like most patriotic Americans, my father was forever buying gizmos that proved to be disastrous – clothes steamers that failed to take the wrinkles out of suits but had wallpaper falling off the walls in whole sheets, an electric pencil sharpener that could consume an entire pencil (including the metal ferrule and the tips of your fingers if you weren't real quick) in less than a second, a water pick (which is, for those of you who don't know, a water-jet device which 'blast-cleans' your teeth) that was so lively it required two people to hold and left the bathroom looking like the inside of a car wash, and much else.

But all of this was as nothing compared with the situation today. Americans are now surrounded with items that do things for them to an almost absurd degree – automatic cat-food dispensers, electric juicers and tin openers, refrigerators that make their own ice cubes, automatic car windows, disposable toothbrushes that come with the toothpaste already loaded. People are so addicted to convenience that they have become trapped in a vicious circle: the more labour-saving appliances they buy, the harder they need to work; the harder they work, the more labour-saving appliances they feel they need.

There is nothing, no matter how ridiculous, that won't find a receptive audience in America so long as it promises to provide some kind of relief from effort. I recently saw advertised, for $39.95, a 'lighted, revolving tie rack'. You push a button and it parades each of your ties before you, saving you the exhausting ordeal of making your selection by hand.

Our house in New Hampshire came replete with contraptions installed by earlier owners, all of them designed to make life that little bit easier. Up to a point, a few actually do (my favourite, of course, being the garbage disposal unit), but most are just kind of wondrously useless. One of our rooms, for instance, came equipped with automatic curtains. You flick a switch on the wall and four pairs of curtains effortlessly open or close. That, at any rate, is the idea. In practice what happens is that one opens, one closes, one opens and closes repeatedly, and one does nothing at all for five minutes and then starts to emit smoke. We haven't gone anywhere near them since the first week.

Something else we inherited was an automatic garage door opener. In theory this sounds wonderful and even rather classy. You sweep into the driveway, push a button on a remote control unit and then, depending on your sense of timing, pull into the garage smoothly or take the bottom panel off the door. Then you flick the button again and the door shuts behind you, and anyone walking past thinks: Wow! Classy guy!

In reality, I have found, our garage door will close only when it is certain of crushing a tricycle or mangling a rake, and, once closed, will not open again until I get up on a chair and do something temperamental to the control box with a screwdriver and hammer, and eventually call in the garage door repairman, a fellow named Jake who has been taking his holidays in the Maldives since we became his clients. I have given Jake more money than I earned in my first four years out of college, and still I don't have a garage door I can count on.

You see my point again. Automatic curtains and garage doors, electric cat-food dispensers and revolving tie racks only *seem* to make life easier. In fact, all they do is add expense and complication to your existence.

And therein lie our two important lessons of the day. First, never forget that the first syllable of convenience is *con*. And second, send your children to garage door repair school.

SO SUE ME

I HAVE A FRIEND IN BRITAIN, AN ACADEMIC, WHO WAS RECENTLY approached by lawyers working for an American company to be an expert witness for a case they were handling. They told him they wanted to fly the lead attorney and two assistants to London to meet him.

'Wouldn't it be simpler and cheaper if I flew to New York instead?' my friend suggested.

'Yes,' he was told without hesitation, 'but this way we can bill the client for the cost of three trips.'

And there you have the American legal mind at work.

Now I have no doubt that a large number of American lawyers – well, two anyway – do wonderfully worthwhile things that fully justify charging their clients $150 an hour, which I gather is the going rate here. But the trouble is that there are too many of them. In fact – and here is a truly sobering statistic – the United States has more lawyers than all the rest of the world put together: almost 800,000 of them, up from an already abundant 260,000 in 1960. We now boast 300 lawyers for every 100,000 citizens. Britain, by contrast, has eighty-two, Japan a mere eleven.

And of course all those lawyers need work. Most states now allow lawyers to advertise, and many of them most enthusiastically do. You cannot watch TV for half an hour without encountering at least one commercial showing a sincere-looking lawyer saying: 'Hi, I'm Vinny Slick of Bent and Oily Law Associates. If you've suffered an injury at work, or been in a vehicular accident, or just feel like having some extra money, come to me and we'll find someone to sue.'

Americans, as is well known, will sue at the drop of a hat. In fact, I daresay someone somewhere has sued over a dropped hat, and won $20 million for the pain and suffering it caused. There really is a sense that if something goes wrong for whatever reason and you are anywhere in the vicinity, then you ought to collect a pot of money.

This was neatly illustrated a couple of years ago when a chemical plant in Richmond, California, suffered an explosion which spewed fumes over the town. Within hours, 200 lawyers and their representatives had descended on the excited community, handing out business cards and advising people to present themselves at the local hospital. Twenty thousand residents eagerly did so.

News footage of the event makes it look like some kind of open-air party. Of the 20,000 happy, smiling, seemingly very healthy people who lined up for examination at the hospital's emergency room, just twenty were actually admitted. Although the number of proven injuries was slight, to say the least, 70,000 townspeople – virtually all of them – filed claims. The company agreed to a $180 million settlement. Of this, the lawyers got $40 million.

Every year over 90 million lawsuits are filed in this extravagantly litigious country – that's one for every two and a half people – and many of these are what might charitably be called ambitious. As I write, two parents in Texas are suing a high-school baseball coach for benching their son during a game, claiming humiliation and extreme mental anguish. In Washington state, meanwhile, a man with heart problems is suing the local dairies 'because their milk cartons did not warn him about cholesterol'. I am sure you read about the woman in California who sued the Walt Disney Company after she and her family were mugged in a car park at Disneyland. A central part of the suit was that her grandchildren suffered shock and trauma when they were taken behind the scenes to be comforted and they saw Disney characters taking off their costumes. The discovery that Mickey Mouse and Goofy were in fact real people inside costumes was apparently too much for the poor tykes.

That case was dismissed, but elsewhere people have won fortunes out of all proportion to any pain or loss they might actually have suffered. Recently there was a much-publicized case in which an executive at a Milwaukee brewery recounted the racy plot of a

Seinfeld television show to a female colleague, who took offence and reported him for sexual harassment. The brewery responded by sacking the fellow, and he responded by suing the brewery. Now I don't know who deserved what in this case – it sounds to me, frankly, like they all wanted a good sound spanking – but the upshot is that the sacked executive was awarded $26.6 million, roughly 400,000 times his annual salary, by a sympathetic (i.e., demented) jury.

Allied with the idea that lawsuits are a quick way to a fortune is the interesting and uniquely American notion that no matter what happens, someone else must be responsible. So if, say, you smoke eighty cigarettes a day for fifty years and eventually get cancer, then it must be everyone else's fault but your own, and you sue not only the manufacturer of your cigarettes, but the wholesaler, the retailers, the haulage firm that delivered the cigarettes to the retailer, and so on. One of the most extraordinary features of the American legal system is that it allows plaintiffs to sue people and companies only tangentially connected to the alleged complaint.

Because of the way the system works (or more accurately doesn't work) it is often less expensive for a company or institution to settle out of court than to let the matter proceed to trial. I know a woman who slipped and fell while entering a department store on a rainy day and, to her astonishment and gratification, was offered a more or less instant settlement of $2,500 if she would sign a piece of paper agreeing not to sue. She signed.

The cost of all this to society is enormous – several billion dollars a year at least. New York City alone spends $200 million a year settling 'slip and fall' claims – people tripping over kerbs and the like. According to a recent ABC television documentary on America's runaway legal system, because of inflated product liability costs consumers in the United States pay $500 more than they need to for every car they buy, $100 more for football helmets, and $3,000 more for heart pacemakers. According to the documentary, they even pay a little on top (as it were) for haircuts because one or two distressed customers successfully sued their barbers after being given the sort of embarrassing trims that I receive as a matter of routine.

All of which, naturally, has given me an idea. I am going to go and smoke eighty cigarettes, then slip and fall while drinking high-cholesterol milk and relating the plot of a *Seinfeld* show to a passing female in the Disneyland car park, and then I'll call Vinny Slick and see if we can strike a deal. I don't expect to settle for less than $2.5 billion – and that's before we've even started talking about my latest haircut.

THE GREAT INDOORS

I WAS OUT FOR A WALK THE OTHER DAY AND I WAS STRUCK BY AN ODD thing. It was a glorious day – as good as a day can get, and very probably the last of its type that we shall see for many a long wintry month around here – yet almost every car that passed had its windows up.

All these drivers had adjusted their temperature controls to create a climate inside their sealed vehicles that was identical to the climate already existing in the larger world outside, and it occurred to me that where fresh air is concerned Americans have rather lost their minds, or sense of proportion, or something.

Oh, occasionally they will go out for the novel experience of being out of doors – they will go on a picnic, say, or for a day at the beach or to a big amusement park – but these are exceptional events. By and large most Americans have grown so reflexively habituated to the idea of passing the bulk of their lives in a series of climate-controlled environments that the possibility of an alternative no longer occurs to them.

So they shop in enclosed malls, and drive to those malls with the car windows up and the air-conditioning on, even when the weather is flawless, as it was on this day. They work in offices where they could not open the windows even if they wanted to – not, of course, that anyone would want to. When they go on holiday, it is often in an outsized motor-home that allows them to experience the great outdoors without actually exposing themselves to it. Increasingly, when they go to a sporting event it will be in an indoor stadium. Walk through almost any American

..ood now in summer and you won't see children on bikes or playing ball, for they are all inside. All you will hear is the uniform hum of air-conditioning units.

Cities across the nation have taken to building what are called skywalks – enclosed pedestrian flyovers, climate-controlled of course – connecting all the buildings in their centres. In my home-town of Des Moines, Iowa, the first skywalk was erected between a hotel and department store about twenty-five years ago and was such a hit that soon other developers were getting in on the act. Now it is possible to walk for half a mile or more downtown in any direction without ever setting foot outdoors. All the shops that used to be at street level have moved up to the first floor, where the pedestrian traffic now is. Now the only people you ever see at street level in Des Moines are winos and office workers standing around having a smoke. The outdoors, you see, has become a kind of purgatory, a place to which you are banished.

There are even clubs composed of office workers who change into sweatsuits and spend their lunch hours taking brisk, healthful hikes along a measured course through the skywalks. It would never occur to them to step outside to do this. Similar clubs, typically composed of retired people, can be found at nearly every shopping mall in the nation. These are people, you understand, who meet at malls not to shop but to get their daily exercise.

The last time I was in Des Moines, I ran into an old friend of the family. He was dressed in a sweatsuit and told me that he had just come from a session with the Valley West Mall Hiking Club. It was a splendid April day, and I asked him why the club didn't use any of the city's several large and handsome parks.

'No rain, no cold, no hills, no muggers,' he replied without hesitation.

'But there are no muggers in Des Moines,' I pointed out.

'That's right,' he agreed at once, 'and do you know why? Because there's nobody outside to mug.' He nodded his head emphatically, as if I hadn't thought of that, as indeed I had not.

The apotheosis of this strange movement may be the Opryland Hotel in Nashville, Tennessee, where I went a year or so ago on a magazine assignment. The Opryland Hotel is an extraordinary institution. To begin with, it is immense and almost gorgeously ugly – a sort of *Gone with the Wind* meets Graceland meets Mall of America.

But what really sets the Opryland apart is that it is a Total Indoor

Environment. At its heart are three enormous glass-ro
five or six storeys high and extending to nine acres overall that offer
all the benefits of the out of doors without any of the in-
conveniences. These 'interiorscapes', as the hotel calls them, are
replete with tropical foliage, full-sized trees, waterfalls, streams,
'open-air' restaurants and cafés and multi-level walkways. The
effect is strikingly reminiscent of those illustrations you used to get
in 1950s science-fiction magazines showing what life would be
like in a space colony on Venus (or at least what it would be like if
all the space colonists were overweight middle-aged Americans in
Reeboks and baseball caps who spent their lives walking around
eating hand-held food).

It is, in short, a flawless, aseptic, self-contained world, with a
perfect unvarying climate and an absence of messy birds, annoying
insects, rain, wind or indeed any kind of reality.

On my first evening, anxious to escape the hordes of shuffling
grazers and curious to see what the weather was like back on Planet
Earth, I stepped outside with a view to having a stroll through the
grounds. And guess what? There were no grounds – just acres and
acres of car park, rolling across the landscape for as far as the eye
could see in nearly every direction. Across the way, only a couple of
hundred yards distant, was the Opryland Amusement Park, but
there was no way to gain entrance to it on foot. The only means of
access, I discovered by enquiring, was to purchase a $3 ticket and
board an air-conditioned bus for a forty-five-second ride to the
front gate.

Unless you wanted to walk around among thousands of parked
cars, there was no place to take the air or stretch your legs. At
Opryland, the outdoors is indoors, and that, I realized with a
shiver, is precisely the way many millions of Americans would have
the whole country if it were possible.

As I stood there, a bird dropped onto the toe of my left shoe the
sort of thing you don't normally appreciate a bird dropping (to coin
a phrase). I looked from the sky to my shoe and back to the sky
again.

'Thank you,' I said, and I believe I really meant it.

A VISIT TO THE BARBERSHOP

YOU HAVE TO UNDERSTAND THAT I HAVE VERY HAPPY HAIR. NO MATTER how serene and composed the rest of me is, no matter how grave and formal the situation, my hair is always having a party. In any group photograph you can spot me at once because I am the person at the back whose hair seems to be listening, in some private way, to a disco album called *Dance Craze '97*.

Every so often, with a sense of foreboding, I take this hair of mine uptown to the barbershop and allow one of the men there to amuse himself with it for a bit. I don't know why, but going to the barber brings out the wimp in me. There is something about being enshrouded in a cape and having my glasses taken away, then being set about the head with sharp cutting tools that leaves me feeling helpless and insecure.

I mean there you are, armless and squinting, and some guy you don't know is doing serious, almost certainly regrettable, things to the top of your head. I must have had 250 haircuts in my life by now, and if there is one thing I have learned it is that a barber will give you the haircut he wants to give you and there is nothing you can do about it.

So the whole experience is filled with trauma for me. This is particularly so as I always get the barber I was hoping not to get – usually the new guy they call 'Thumbs'. I especially dread the moment when he sits you in the chair and the two of you stare together at the hopeless catastrophe that is the top of your head, and he says, in a worryingly eager way, 'So what would you like me to do with this?'

'Just a simple tidy-up,' I say, looking at him with touching hope-fulness, but knowing that already he is thinking in terms of extravagant bouffants and mousse-stiffened swirls, possibly a fringe of bouncy ringlets. 'You know, something anonymous and respectable – like a banker or an accountant.'

'See any styles up there you like?' he says and indicates a wall of old black and white photographs of smiling men whose hairstyles seem to have been modelled on *Thunderbirds* characters.

'Actually, I was hoping for something a bit less emphatic.'

'A more natural look, in other words?'

'Exactly.'

'Like mine, for instance?'

I glance at the barber. His hairstyle brings to mind an aircraft carrier advancing through choppy seas, or perhaps an extravagant piece of topiary.

'Even more subdued than that,' I suggest nervously.

He nods thoughtfully, in a way that makes me realize we are not even in the same universe taste-in-hairwise, and says in a sudden, decisive tone: 'I know just what you want. We call it the Wayne Newton.'

'That's really not quite what I had in mind,' I start to protest, but already he is pushing my chin into my chest and seizing up his shears.

'It's a very popular look – everyone on the bowling team has it,' he adds, and with a buzz of motors starts taking hair off my head as if stripping wallpaper.

'I really don't want the Wayne Newton look,' I murmur with feeling, but my chin is buried in my chest and in any case my voice is drowned in the hum of his dancing clippers.

And so I sit for a small, tortured eternity, staring at my lap, under strict instructions not to move, listening to terrifying cutting machinery trundling across my scalp. Out of the corner of my eyes I can see large quantities of shorn hair tumbling onto my shoulders.

'Not too much off,' I bleat from time to time, but he is engaged in a lively conversation with the barber and customer at the next chair about the prospects for the Chicago Bulls basketball team, and only occasionally turns his attention to me and my head, generally to mutter, 'Oh, dang,' or 'Whoopsie.'

Eventually he jerks my head up and says: 'How's that for length?'

I squint at the mirror, but without my glasses all I can see is what looks like a pink balloon in the distance. 'I don't know,' I say. 'It looks awfully short.'

I notice he is looking unhappily at everything above my eyebrows. 'Did we decide on a Paul Anka or a Wayne Newton?' he asks.

'Well, neither, as a matter of fact,' I say, pleased to have an opportunity to get this sorted out at last. 'I just wanted a modest tidy-up.'

'Let me ask you this,' he says. 'How fast does your hair grow?'

'Not very,' I say and squint harder at the mirror, but I still can't see a thing. 'Why, is there a problem?'

'Oh, no,' he says, but in that way that means 'Oh, yes.' 'No, it's fine,' he goes on. 'It's just that I seem to have done the left side of your head in a Paul Anka and the right in a Wayne Newton. Let me ask you this, then: do you have a big hat?'

'What have you done?' I ask in a rising tone of alarm, but he has gone off to his colleagues for a consultation. They look at me the way you might look at a road accident victim, and talk in whispers.

'I think it must be these antihistamines I'm taking,' I hear Thumbs say to them sadly.

One of the colleagues comes up for a closer look, and decides it's not as disastrous as it looks. 'If you take some of this hair here from behind the left ear,' he says, 'and take it around the back of his head and hook it over the other ear, and maybe reattach some of this from here, then you can make it into a modified Barney Rubble.' He turns to me. 'Will you be going out much over the next few weeks, sir?'

'Did you say "Barney Rubble"?' I whimper in dismay.

'Unless you go for a Hercules Poirot,' suggests the other barber.

'Hercules Poirot?' I whimper anew.

They leave Thumbs to do what he can. After another ten minutes he hands me my glasses and lets me raise my head. In the mirror I am confronted with an image that brings to mind a lemon meringue pie with ears. Over my shoulder, Thumbs is smiling proudly.

'Turned out pretty good after all, eh?' he says.

I am unable to speak. I hand him a large sum of money and stumble from the shop. I walk home with my collar up and my head sunk into my shoulders.

At the house my wife takes one look at me. 'Did you say something to upset them?' she asks in sincere wonder.

I shrug helplessly. 'I told him I wanted to look like a banker.'

She gives one of those sighs that come to all wives eventually. 'Well, at least you rhyme,' she mutters in that odd, enigmatic way of hers, and goes off to get the big hat.

BOOK TOURS

TEN YEARS AGO THIS MONTH I GOT A PHONE CALL FROM AN AMERICAN publisher telling me that they had just bought one of my books and were going to send me on a three-week, sixteen-city publicity tour.

'We're going to make you a media star,' he said brightly.

'But I've never been on TV,' I protested in mild panic.

'Oh, it's easy. You'll love it,' he said with the blithe assurance of someone who doesn't have to do it himself.

'No, I'll be terrible,' I insisted. 'I have no personality.'

'Don't worry, we'll *give* you a personality. We're going to fly you to New York for a course of media training.'

My heart sank. All this had a bad feeling about it. For the first time since I accidentally set fire to a neighbour's garage in 1961, I began to think seriously about the possibility of plastic surgery and a new life in Central America.

So I flew to New York and, as it turned out, the media training was less of an ordeal than I had feared. I was put in the hands of a kindly, patient man named Bill Parkhurst, who sat with me for two days in a windowless studio somewhere in Manhattan and put me through an endless series of mock interviews.

He would say things like: 'OK, now we're going to do a three-minute interview with a guy who hasn't looked at your book until ten seconds ago and doesn't know whether it's a cookery book or a book on prison reform. Also, this guy is a tad stupid and will interrupt you frequently. OK, let's go.'

He would click his stopwatch and we would do a three-minute interview. Then we would do it again. And again. And so it went for two days. By the afternoon of the second day I was having to push my tongue back in my mouth with my fingers. 'Now you know what you'll feel like by the second day of your tour,' Parkhurst observed cheerfully.

'What's it like after twenty-one days?' I asked.

Parkhurst smiled. 'You'll love it.'

Amazingly he was nearly right. Book tours are actually kind of fun. You get to stay in nice hotels, you are driven everywhere in big silver cars, you are treated as if you are much more important than you are, you can eat steak three times a day at someone else's expense, and you get to talk endlessly about yourself for weeks at a stretch. Is this a dream come true or what?

It was an entirely new world for me. As you will recall if you have been committing these columns to memory, when I was growing up my father always took us to the cheapest motels imaginable – the sort of places that made the Bates Motel in *Psycho* look sophisticated and well appointed – so this was a gratifyingly novel experience. I had never before stayed in a really fancy hotel, never ordered from room service, never called on the services of a concierge or valet, never tipped a doorman. (Still haven't, come to that!)

The great revelation to me was room service. I grew up thinking that ordering from the room service menu was the pinnacle of graciousness – something that happened in Cary Grant movies, but not in the world I knew – so when a publicity person suggested I make free use of it, I jumped at the chance. In doing so I discovered something you doubtless knew already: room service is *terrible*.

I ordered room service meals at least a dozen times in hotels all over the United States, and it was always dire. The food would take hours to arrive and it was invariably cold and leathery. I was always fascinated by how much effort went into the presentation – the white tablecloth, the vase with a rose in it, the ostentatious removal of a domed silver lid from each plate – and how little went into keeping the food warm and tasty.

At the Huntington Hotel in San Francisco, I particularly remember, the waiter whipped away a silver lid to reveal a bowl of white goo.

'What's that?' I asked.

'Vanilla ice cream, I believe, sir,' he replied.

'But it's melted,' I said.

'Yes, it has,' he agreed. 'Enjoy,' he added with a bow, pocketing my tip and withdrawing.

Of course, it's not all lounging around in swank hotel rooms, watching TV and eating melted ice cream. You also have to give interviews – lots and lots of them, more than you can imagine, often from before dawn till after midnight – and do a positively ludicrous amount of travelling in between. Because there are so many authors out there flogging books – as many as 200 at busy periods, I was told – and only so many radio and TV programmes to appear on, you tend to be dispatched to wherever there is an available slot.

In one five-day period, I flew from San Francisco to Atlanta to Chicago to Boston and back to San Francisco. I once flew from Denver to Colorado Springs in order to do a thirty-second interview which – I swear – went like this:

Interviewer: 'Our guest today is Bill Bryson. So you've got a new book out, have you, Bill?'

Me: 'That's right.'

Interviewer: 'Well, that's wonderful. Thanks so much for coming. Our guest tomorrow is Dr Milton Greenberg, who has written a book about bedwetting called *Tears at Bedtime*.'

In three weeks I gave over 250 interviews of one type or another and never once met anyone who had read my book or had the faintest idea who I was. At one radio station the interviewer covered the microphone with his hand just before we went on and said: 'Now tell me, are you the guy who was abducted by aliens or are you the travel writer?'

The whole point, as Bill Parkhurst taught me, is to sell yourself shamelessly, and believe me you soon learn to do it.

I suppose all this is on my mind because by the time you read this I will be in the middle of a three-week promotional tour in Britain. Now I don't want you to think I am sucking up, but touring in Britain is a dream compared with America. Distances are shorter, which helps a lot, and you find on the whole that the interviewers have read the book, or at least read a book. Bookshop managers and staff are invariably dedicated and kindly, and the reading public are, without exception, intelligent, discerning, enormously good-looking and generous in their purchasing habits. Why, I have even known people to throw down a Sunday newspaper and say, 'I think I'll go out and buy that book of old Bill's *right now*. I might even buy several copies as Christmas presents.'

It's a crazy way to make a living, but it's one of those things you've got to do. I just thank God it hasn't affected my sincerity.

DEATH WATCH

THE LAST TIME IT OCCURRED TO ME, IN A SERIOUS WAY, THAT DEATH IS out there – you know, really out there, just hovering – and that my name is in his book, was on a short flight from Boston to Lebanon, New Hampshire, when we got in a little trouble.

The flight is only fifty minutes, over the old industrial towns of northern Massachusetts and southern New Hampshire, and on towards the Connecticut River, where the plump hills of the Green and White Mountains lazily merge. It was a late October afternoon, just after the clocks changed for winter, and I had hoped I might enjoy the last russety blush of autumn colour on the hills before the daylight went, but within five minutes of take-off our little plane – a sixteen-seater De Havilland – was enveloped in bouncy cloud, and it was obvious that there would be no spectacular panoramas this day.

So I read a book and tried not to notice the turbulence or to let my thoughts preoccupy themselves with unhappy fantasies involving splintering wings and a long, shrill plunge to earth.

I hate little planes. I don't like most planes much, but little planes I dread because they are cold and bouncy and make odd noises, and they carry too few passengers to attract more than passing attention when they crash, as they seem to do quite regularly. Almost every day in any American newspaper you will see an article like this:

> Dribbleville, Indiana – All nine passengers and crew died today when a sixteen-seat commuter plane operated by

Bounce Airlines crashed in a ball of flames shortly after take-off from Dribbleville Regional Airport. Witnesses said the plane fell for, oh gosh, ages before slamming into the ground at 1,892 miles an hour. It was the eleventh little-noted crash by a commuter airline since Sunday.

These things really do go down all the time. Earlier this year a commuter plane crashed on a flight from Cincinnati to Detroit. One of the passengers who died was on her way to a memorial service for her brother, who had been killed in a crash in West Virginia two weeks before.

So I tried to read my book, but I kept glancing out of the window into the impenetrable murk. Something over an hour into the flight – later than usual – we descended through the bumpy clouds and popped out into clear air. We were only a few hundred feet over a dusky landscape. There were one or two farmhouses visible in the last traces of daylight, but no towns. Mountains – severe and muscular – loomed up around us on all sides.

We rose back up into the clouds, flew around for a few minutes and dropped down again. There was still no sign of Lebanon or any other community, which was perplexing because the Connecticut River Valley is full of little towns. Here there was nothing but darkening forest stretching to every horizon.

We rose again, and repeated the exercise twice more. After a few minutes the pilot came on and in a calm, laid-back voice said: 'I don't know if you folks have noticed, but we're having a little trouble eyeballing the airport on account of the, ah, inclement weather. There's no radar at Lebanon, so we have to do all of this visually, which makes it a little, ah, tricky. The whole of the eastern seaboard is socked in with fog, so there's no point in trying another airport. Anyway, we're gonna keep trying because if there is one thing for certain it's that this plane is going to have to come down *somewhere*!'

Actually, I just made that last line up, but that was the gist of it. We were blundering around in cloud and dying light looking for an airport tucked among mountains. We had been in the air for almost ninety minutes by now. I didn't know how long these things could fly, but at some point clearly we would run out of fuel. Meanwhile, at any moment we could slam into the side of a mountain.

This didn't seem fair. I was on my way home from a long trip. Scrubbed little children, smelling of soap and fresh towels, would be waiting. There was steak for dinner, possibly with onion rings. Extra wine had been laid in. I had gifts to disburse. This was not a convenient time to be flying into mountains. So I shut my eyes and said in a very quiet voice: 'Please please please oh please get this thing down safely and I promise I will be good for ever, and I really mean it. Thank you.'

Miraculously it worked. On about the sixth occasion that we dropped from the clouds there below us were the flat roofs, illuminated signs and gorgeously tubby customers of the Lebanon Shopping Plaza, and just across the road from it was the perimeter fence of the airport. We were aimed slightly the wrong way, but the pilot banked sharply and brought the plane in on a glidepath that would, in any other circumstance, have had me shrieking.

We landed with a lovely smooth squeal. I have never been so happy.

My wife was waiting for me in the car outside the airport entrance, and on the way home I told her all about my gripping moment in the air. The trouble with believing you are going to die in a crash, as opposed to actually dying in a crash, is that it doesn't make nearly as good a story.

'You poor sweetie,' my wife said soothingly, but just a little distractedly, and patted my leg. 'Well, you'll be home in a minute and there's a lovely cauliflower supreme in the oven for you.'

I looked at her. 'Cauliflower supreme? What the—' I cleared my throat and put on a new voice. 'And what is cauliflower supreme exactly, dear? I understood we were having steak.'

'We were, but this is much healthier for you. Maggie Higgins gave me the recipe.'

I sighed. Maggie Higgins was an irksomely health-conscious busybody whose strong views on diet were forever being translated into dishes like cauliflower supreme for me. She was fast becoming the bane of my life, or at least of my stomach.

Life's a funny thing, isn't it? One minute you're praying to be allowed to live, vowing to face any hardship without complaint, and the next you are mentally banging your head on the dashboard and thinking: I wanted steak, I wanted steak, I wanted steak.

'Did I tell you, by the way,' my wife went on, 'that Maggie fell asleep with hair colouring on the other day and her hair turned bright green?'

'Really?' I said, perking up a little. This was good news indeed. 'Bright green, you say?'

'Well, everyone told her it was kind of lemony, but really, you know, it looked like Astroturf.'

'Amazing,' I said – and it was. I mean to say, two prayers answered in the same evening.

THE BEST AMERICAN HOLIDAY

IF I AM LOOKING A LITTLE BLOATED AND SLUGGISH TODAY, IT IS BECAUSE it was Thanksgiving here on Thursday, and I haven't quite recovered yet.

I have a special fondness for Thanksgiving because, apart from anything else, when I was growing up it was the one time of year we ate in our house. All the other days of the year we just kind of put food into our mouths. My mother was not a great cook, you see.

Now please don't misunderstand me. My mother is a kindly, cheerful, saintly soul, and when she dies she will go straight to heaven, but believe me no-one is going to say, 'Oh, thank goodness you're here, Mrs Bryson. Can you fix us something to eat?'

To be perfectly fair to her, my mother had several strikes against her in the kitchen department. To begin with she couldn't cook – always a bit of a handicap where the culinary arts are concerned. Mind you, she didn't especially want to be able to cook, and anyway she couldn't have even if she had wanted to. She had a career, you see, which meant that she was always flying in the door two minutes before it was time to put dinner on the table.

On top of this, she was a trifle absent-minded. She tended to confuse similarly coloured ingredients like sugar and salt, pepper and cinnamon, vinegar and maple syrup, cornflour and plaster of Paris, which often lent her dishes an unexpected dimension. Her particular speciality was to cook things while they were still in the packaging. I was almost full-grown before I realized that clingfilm wasn't a sort of chewy glaze. A combination of haste, forgetfulness and a charming incompetence where household appliances were concerned meant that most of her cooking experiences were punctuated with billows of smoke and occasional small explosions. In our house, as a rule of thumb, it was time to eat when the firemen departed.

Strangely, all this suited my father. My father had what you might call rudimentary tastes in food. His palate really only responded to three flavours – salt, ketchup and burnt. His idea of an outstanding meal was a plate that contained something brown and unidentifiable, something green and unidentifiable, and something charred. I am quite sure that if you slow-baked, say, a loofah and covered it sufficiently with ketchup, he would have said, 'Hey, this is very tasty.' Good food, in short, was something that was wasted on him, and my mother worked hard for years to see that he was never disappointed.

But on Thanksgiving, by some kind of miracle, she pulled out all the stops and outdid herself. She would call us to the table and there we would find, awaiting our unaccustomed delectation, a sumptuous spread of food – an enormous and glistening turkey, baskets of cornbread and warm rolls, vegetables that you could actually recognize, a tureen of cranberry sauce, a bowl of exquisitely fluffed mashed potatoes, a salver of plump sausages, and much else.

We would eat as if we had not eaten for a year (as, in effect, we had not) and then she would present the *pièce de résistance* – a golden, flaky-crusted pumpkin pie surmounted by a Matterhorn of whipped cream. It was perfect. It was heaven.

And it has left me with the profoundest joy and gratitude for this most wonderful of holidays – for Thanksgiving is the most splendid of occasions, and make no mistake.

Most Americans, I believe, think that Thanksgiving has always been held on the last Thursday of November and that it has been going on for ever – or at least as near for ever as anything gets in America.

In fact, although the *Mayflower* pilgrims did indeed hold a famous feast in 1621 to thank the local Indians for their help in getting them through their first difficult year and showing them how to make popcorn and so on (for which I am grateful even yet), there is no record of when that feast was held. Given the climate of New England, it was unlikely to have been late November. In any case, for the next 242 years Thanksgiving as an event was hardly noted.

The first official celebration wasn't held until 1863 – and then in August, of all months. The next year President Abraham Lincoln moved it arbitrarily to the last Thursday in November – no-one seems to recall now why a Thursday, or why so late in the year – and there it has stayed ever since.

Thanksgiving is wonderful and for all kinds of reasons. To begin with, it has the commendable effect of staving off Christmas. Whereas in Britain the Christmas shopping season seems nowadays to kick off round about the August bank holiday, Christmas mania doesn't traditionally begin in America until the last weekend in November.

Moreover, Thanksgiving remains a pure holiday, largely unsullied by commercialization. It involves no greetings cards, no trees to trim, no perplexed hunt through drawers and cupboards for decorations. At Thanksgiving all you do is sit at a table and try to get your stomach into the shape of a beach ball, and then go and watch a game of American football on the TV. This is my kind of holiday.

But perhaps the nicest, and certainly the noblest, aspect of Thanksgiving is that it gives you a formal, official occasion to give thanks for all those things for which you should be grateful. Speaking personally, I have a great deal to be thankful for. I have a wife and children I am crazy about. I have my health and retain full command of most of my faculties (albeit not always simultaneously). I live in a time of peace and prosperity. Ronald Reagan will never be president again. These are all things for which I am grateful, and I am pleased to let the record show it.

The only downside is that the passage of Thanksgiving marks the inescapable onset of Christmas. Any day now – any moment – my dear wife will appear beside me and announce that the time has come to shift my distended stomach and get out the festive decorations. This is a dread moment for me and with good reason, since it involves physical exertion, wobbly ladders, live electricity, wriggling ascents through a loft hatch, and the collaborative direction of said dear missus – all things with the power to do me a serious and permanent injury. I have a terrible feeling that today may be that day.

Still, it hasn't happened yet – and for that, of course, I give my sincerest thanks of all.

DECK THE HALLS

WHEN I LEFT YOU LAST WEEK I WAS EXPRESSING A CERTAIN QUEASY foreboding at the thought that at any moment my wife would step into the room and announce that the time had come to get out the Christmas decorations.

Well, here we are, another week gone and just eighteen fleeting days till Christmas, and still not a peep from her. I don't know how much more of this I can take.

I hate doing the Christmas decorations because, for a start, it means going up into the loft. Lofts are dirty, dark, disagreeable places. You always find things up there you don't want to find – lengths of gnawed wiring, gaps in the slates through which you can see daylight and sometimes even pop your head, and crates full of useless oddments that you must have been out of your mind ever to have hauled up there. Three things alone are certain when you venture into a loft: that you will crack your head on a beam at least twice, that you will get cobwebs draped over your face, and that you will not find what you went looking for.

The worst part about going into a loft is knowing that when the time comes to climb down you will find that the stepladder has mysteriously moved three feet towards the bathroom door. I don't know how this happens, but it always does.

So you lower your legs through the hatch and blindly grope for the ladder with your feet. If you stretch your right leg to its furthest extremity, you can just about get a toe to it, which is not much good, of course. Eventually, you discover that if you swing your legs back and forth, like a gymnast on parallel bars, you can get one foot on top of the ladder and then both feet on. This, however, does not represent a great breakthrough because you are now lying at an angle of about sixty degrees and unable to make any further progress. Grunting softly, you try to drag the ladder nearer with your feet, but succeed only in knocking it over, with a crash.

Now you really are stuck. You try to wriggle back up into the loft, but haven't the strength, so you hang by your armpits. You call to your wife, but she doesn't hear you. This is both discouraging and strange. Normally, your wife can hear things that no-one else on earth can hear. She can hear a dab of jam fall onto a carpet two rooms away. She can hear spilled coffee being furtively mopped up with a good bathtowel. She can hear dirt being tracked across a clean floor. She can hear you just *thinking* about doing something you shouldn't do. But get yourself stuck in a loft hatch and suddenly it is as if she has been placed in a soundproof chamber.

So when eventually, an hour or so later, she passes through the upstairs hallway and sees your legs dangling there, it takes her by surprise. 'What are you doing?' she says at length.

You squint down at her. 'Loft hatch aerobics,' you reply with just a hint of sarcasm.

'Do you want the ladder?'

'Oh, now there's an idea. Do you know, I've been hanging here for ages trying to think what it is that's missing, and here you've cracked it straight off.'

You hear the sound of the ladder being righted and feel your feet being guided down the steps. The hanging has evidently done you good because suddenly you remember that the Christmas decorations are not in the loft – never were in the loft – but in the basement, in a cardboard box. Of course! How silly not to have recalled! Off you dash.

Two hours later you find the decorations hidden behind some old tyres and a broken pram. You lug the box upstairs and devote two hours more to untangling strings of lights. When you plug the lights in, naturally they do not work, except for one string that hurls you backwards into a wall with a lively jolt and a shower of sparks, and then does not work.

You decide to leave the lights and get the tree in from the garage. The tree is immense and prickly. Clutching it in a clumsy bearhug, you gruntingly manhandle it to the back door, fall into the house, get up and press on. As branches poke your eyes, needles puncture your cheeks and gums, and sap manages somehow to run backwards up your nose, you blunder through rooms, knocking pictures from walls, clearing tabletops, upsetting chairs. Your wife, so recently missing and unaccounted for, now seems to be everywhere, shouting confused and lively instructions – 'Mind the thingy! Don't go that way – go that way! To the left! Not *your* left – *my* left!' and eventually, in a softer voice, 'Oooh, are you all right, honey? Didn't you see those steps?' By the time you reach the living room the tree looks as if it has been defoliated by acid rain, and so do you.

It is at this point that you realize that you have no idea where the Christmas tree stand is. So, sighing, you hike up to town to the hardware store to buy another, knowing that for the next three weeks all the Christmas tree stands you have ever purchased – twenty-three in all – will spontaneously reappear in your life, mostly by dropping onto your head from a high shelf when you are rooting in the bottom of a cupboard, but occasionally in the middle of darkened rooms or lurking near the top of the hall stairs. If you don't know it already, know it now: Christmas tree stands are the work of the devil and they want you dead. While you are at the hardware store you buy two additional strings of lights. These will not work either.

Eventually, exhausted in both mind and body, you manage to get the tree up, lit and covered with baubles. You stand in the posture of Quasimodo regarding it with a kind of weak loathing.

'Oh, it's *lovely*!' your wife cries, clasping her hands ecstatically beneath her chin. 'Now let's do the outside decorations,' she announces suddenly. 'I bought a special treat this year – a life-sized Father Christmas that goes on the chimney. You fetch the forty-foot ladder and I'll open the crate. Oh, isn't this such fun!' And off she skips.

Now you might reasonably say to me: 'Why put yourself through all this? Why go up to the loft when you know the decorations won't be there? Why untangle the lights when you know they haven't a chance of working?' And my answer to you is that this is part of the ritual. Christmas wouldn't be Christmas without it.

Which is why I've decided to make a start now even though Mrs Bryson hasn't ordered me to. There are some things you just have to do in life, whether you want to or not.

If you need me for anything, I'll be hanging from the loft.

THE WASTE GENERATION

ONE OF THE MOST ARRESTING STATISTICS THAT I HAVE SEEN IN A GOOD while is that 5 per cent of all the energy used in the United States is consumed by computers that have been left on all night.

I can't confirm this personally, but I can certainly tell you that on numerous occasions I have glanced out of hotel room windows late at night, in a variety of American cities, and been struck by the fact that every light in every neighbouring office building is still on, and that computer screens are indeed flickering.

Why don't Americans turn these things off? For the same reason, I suppose, that so many people here let their car motors run when they pop into a shop, or leave lights blazing all over their house, or keep the central heating cranked up to a level that would scandalize a Finnish sauna housekeeper – because, in short, electricity, petrol and other energy sources are so relatively cheap, and have been for so long, that it doesn't occur to them to behave otherwise.

Why, after all, go through the irksome annoyance of waiting twenty seconds for your computer to warm up each morning when you can have it at your immediate beck by leaving it on all night?

We are terribly – no, we are ludicrously – wasteful of resources in this country. The average American uses twice as much energy to get through life as the average European. With just 5 per cent of the world's population, we consume 20 per cent of its resources. These are not statistics to be proud of.

In 1992 at the Earth Summit in Rio de Janeiro, the United States, along with other developed nations, agreed to reduce the emission of greenhouse gases to 1990 levels by 2000. This wasn't a promise to think about it. It was a promise to do it.

In the event, greenhouse emissions by the United States have continued relentlessly to rise – by 8 per cent overall since the Rio summit, by 3.4 per cent in 1996 alone. In short, we haven't done what we promised. We haven't tried to do it. We haven't even pretended to try to do it, which is the way we usually deal with these problems. All that the Clinton administration has done is introduce a set of voluntary standards which industries are free to ignore if they wish, and mostly of course they so wish.

There are almost no incentives to conserve here. Alternative energy sources like windpower are not only very low, but actually falling. In 1987 they accounted for about four-tenths of one per cent of the total energy production in the country; today just two-tenths of a per cent.

Now, as you will have read, President Clinton wants another fifteen or sixteen years before rolling back greenhouse gas emissions to 1990 levels. It is hard to find anyone here who is actually much bothered about this. Increasingly there is even a kind of antagonism to the idea of conservation, particularly if there is a cost attached. A recent survey of 27,000 people around the globe by a Canadian group called Environics International found that in virtually every advanced nation people were willing to sacrifice at least a small measure of economic growth if it meant cleaner air and a healthier environment. The only exception was the United States. It seems madness to think that people would rate a growing economy above an inhabitable earth, but there you are.

Even President Clinton's inventively cautious proposals to transfer the problem to a successor four terms down the road have met with fervent opposition. A coalition of industrialists and other interested parties called the Global Climate Information Project has raised $13 million to fight pretty much any initiative that gets in the way of their smokestacks. It has been running national radio ads grimly warning that if the president's new energy plans are implemented petrol prices could go up by 50 cents a gallon.

Never mind that that figure is probably inflated. Never mind that even if it were true Americans would still be paying but a fraction for petrol what people in other rich nations pay. Never mind that it would bring benefits that everyone could enjoy. Never mind any of that. Mention an increase in petrol prices for any purpose at all and – however small the amount, however good the reason – most people in America will instinctively recoil in horror.

What is saddest about all this is that a good part of these goals to cut greenhouse emissions could be met without any cost at all if Americans merely modified their extravagance. It has been estimated that the nation as a whole wastes about $300 billion of energy a year. We are not talking here about energy that could be saved by investing in new technologies. We are talking about energy that could be saved just by switching things off or turning things down. According to *US News & World Report*, a weekly news magazine, the United States must maintain the equivalent of five nuclear power plants just to power equipment and appliances that are on but not being used – video recorders left in permanent standby mode, computers left on when people go to lunch or home for the night, all those mute, wall-mounted TVs that flicker unwatched in the corners of bars.

I don't know how worrying global warming is. No-one does. I don't know how much we are imperilling our futures by being so singularly casual in our consumption. But I can tell you this. Last year I spent a good deal of time hiking the Appalachian Trail, a long-distance footpath. In Virginia, where the trail runs through Shenandoah National Park, it was still possible when I was a teenager – not so very long ago – to see Washington, DC, seventy-five miles away, on clear days. Now, in even the most favourable conditions, visibility is less than half that. In hot, smoggy weather, it can be as little as two miles.

The Appalachian Mountains are one of the oldest mountain chains in the world and the forest that covers them is one of the richest and loveliest. A single valley in the Great Smoky Mountains National Park can contain more species of native trees than the whole of Western Europe. A lot of those trees are in trouble. The stress of dealing with acid rain and other airborne pollutants leaves them helplessly vulnerable to diseases and pests. Oaks, hickories and maples are dying in unsettling numbers. The flowering dogwood – one of the most beautiful trees in the American South, and once one of the most abundant – is on the brink of extinction. The American hemlock seems poised to follow.

This may be only a modest prelude. If global temperatures rise by 4 degrees Centigrade over the next half-century, as some scientists confidently predict, then all of the trees of Shenandoah National Park and the Smokies, and for hundreds of miles beyond, will die. In two generations one of the last great forests of the temperate world will turn into featureless grassland.

I think that's worth turning off a few computers for, don't you?

SHOPPING MADNESS

I WENT INTO A TOYS Я US THE OTHER DAY WITH MY YOUNGEST SO THAT he could spend some loot he had come into. (He had gone short on Anaconda Copper against his broker's advice, the little scamp.) And entirely by the way, isn't Toys Я Us the most mystifying name of a commercial concern you have ever heard of? What does it mean? I have never understood it. Are they saying they believe themselves to be toys? Do their executives carry business cards saying 'Dick Я Me'? And why is the R backwards in the title? Surely not in the hope or expectation that it will enhance our admiration? Why, above all, is it that even though there are thirty-seven checkout lanes at every Toys Я Us in the world, only one of them is ever open?

These are important questions, but sadly this is not our theme today, at least not specifically. No, our theme today, as we stand on the brink of the busiest retail week of the year, is shopping. To say that shopping is an important part of American life is like saying that fish appreciate water.

Apart from working, sleeping, watching TV and accumulating fatty tissue, Americans devote more time to shopping than to any other pastime. Indeed, according to the Travel Industry Association of America, shopping is now the number one holiday activity of Americans. People actually plan their vacations around shopping trips. Hundreds of thousands of people a year travel to Niagara Falls, it transpires, not to see the falls but to wander through its two mega-malls. Soon, if developers in Arizona get their way, holiday-makers will be able to travel to the Grand Canyon and not see it either, for there are plans, if you can believe it, to build a 450,000-square-foot shopping centre by its main entrance.

Shopping these days is not so much a business as a science. There is now even an academic discipline called retail anthropology whose proponents can tell you exactly where, how and why people shop the way they do. They know which proportion of customers will turn right upon entering a store (87 per cent) and how long on average those people will browse before wandering out again (2 minutes and 36 seconds). They know the best ways to lure shoppers into the magic, high-margin depths of the shop (an area known in the trade as 'Zone 4') and the layouts, colour schemes and background music that will most effectively hypnotize the unassuming browser into becoming a helpless purchaser. They know everything.

So here is my question. Why, then, is it that I cannot go shopping in America without wanting either to burst into tears or kill someone? For all its science, you see, shopping in this country is no longer a fun experience, if it ever was.

A big part of the problem is the stores. They come in three types, all disagreeable.

First, there are the stores where you can never find anyone to help you. Then there are the stores where you don't want any help, but you are pestered to the brink of madness by a persistent sales assistant, probably working on commission. Finally, there are the stores where, when you ask where anything is, the answer is always 'Aisle seven.' I don't know why, but that is what they always tell you.

'Where's women's lingerie?' you ask.

'Aisle seven.'

'Where's pet food?'

'Aisle seven.'

'Where's aisle six?'

'Aisle seven.'

My least favourite of all store types is the one where you can't get rid of the sales assistant. Usually these are department stores at big malls. The sales assistant is always a white-haired lady working in the menswear department.

'Can I help you find anything?' she says.

'No thank you, I'm just browsing,' you tell her.

'OK,' she replies, and gives you a smarmy smile that says: 'I don't really like you; I'm just required to smile at everyone.'

So you wander round the department and at some point you idly finger a sweater. You don't know why because you don't like it, but you touch it anyway.

In an instant, the sales assistant is with you. 'That's one of our most popular lines,' she says. 'Would you like to try it on?'

'No, thank you.'

'Go ahead, try it on. It's you.'

'No, I really don't think so.'

'The changing rooms are just there.'

'I really don't want to try it on.'

'What's your size?'

'Please understand, I don't want to try it on. I'm just browsing.'

She gives you another smile – her withdrawing smile – but thirty seconds later she is back, bearing another sweater. 'We have it in peach,' she announces.

'I don't want that sweater. In any colour.'

'How about a nice tie, then?'

'I don't want a tie. I don't want a sweater. I don't want anything. My wife is having her legs waxed and told me to wait for her here. I wish she hadn't, but she did. She could be hours and I still won't want anything, so please don't ask me any more questions. Please.'

'Then how are you off for pants?'

Do you see what I mean? It becomes a choice between tears and manslaughter. The irony is that when you actually require assistance there is never anyone around.

At Toys Я Us my son wanted a Star Troopers Intergalactic Cosmic Death Blaster, or some such piece of plastic mayhem. We couldn't find one anywhere, nor could we find anyone to guide us. The store appeared to be in the sole charge of a sixteen-year-old boy at the single active checkout till. He had a queue of about two dozen people, which he was processing very slowly and methodically.

Patient queueing is not one of my advanced social skills, particularly when I am queueing simply to acquire information. The line moved with painful slowness. At one point the young man took ten minutes to change a till roll, and I nearly killed him then.

At last my turn came. 'Where's the Star Troopers Intergalactic Cosmic Death Blasters?' I said.

'Aisle seven,' he replied without looking up.

I stared at the top of his head. 'Don't trifle with me,' I said.

He looked up. 'Excuse me?'

'You people always say, "Aisle seven."'

There must have been something in my look because his answer came out as a kind of whimper. 'But, mister, it *is* aisle seven – Toys of Violence and Aggression.'

'It'd better be,' I said darkly and departed.

Ninety minutes later we found the Death Blasters in aisle two, but by the time I got back to the till the young man had gone off duty.

The Death Blaster is wonderful, by the way. It fires those rubber-cupped darts that stick to the victim's forehead – not painful, but certainly startling. My son was disappointed, of course, that I wouldn't let him have it, but you see I need it for when I go shopping.

OF MISSING PLANES
AND MISSING FINGERS

GOODNESS ME, CAN YOU BELIEVE IT, ANOTHER YEAR GONE ALREADY. I don't know where the time goes. Same place as my hair, I guess.

I was going to write this week about my New Year's resolutions, but unfortunately the first resolution I made this year was not to make any resolutions I couldn't keep (I'm not even sure I can keep that one, to tell you the truth), and that rather put an end to it. So I thought we might instead have a little review of the year.

As always when one is working on the leading edge of investigative journalism (or, in the case of this column, just blathering on week after week) there are loose ends to be tied up, and what better time to do it than when we stand on the brink of a new year?

One of the more dismaying aspects of writing for print, I have found, is that as soon as you make a statement – almost any statement at all – it will generally be contradicted by developments. Last March, for instance, I filed a glowing report about what a safe and delightfully crime-free community our little New Hampshire town is. Well, wouldn't you know it, but not four days after that article appeared a pair of masked men burst into a jeweller's shop on Main Street and, waving handguns in a lively manner, took away a large but undisclosed amount of cash and baubles. A day or so later, a woman was politely mugged as she strolled beside the college campus. Neither of these things had happened here before – nor, I might add, since – but it did seem a trifle uncanny that there should be a sudden eruption of malfeasance in the very week that I suggested it was unknown in these parts.

I don't mean to suggest that there is anything mystical in this; more that there is a kind of sod's law of public discourse that anything you write or say will instantly be undone by events – what you might call the Michael Fish Hurricane Prediction syndrome.

Still, if you are of a paranoid bent, as I am, you begin to feel an uneasy sense of responsibility. In October I made some passing quip about the music of John Denver. The next day he fatally crashed his plane into the sea, poor man.

On the other hand, I did have a couple of proud and prescient moments. In July I wrote about how alarmingly slack America is concerning food safety and hygiene, and not three weeks later, as if on cue, a huge Hudson's Food processing plant in Nebraska was shut down after it was found that it was, well, alarmingly slack about food safety and hygiene. Over 22 million pounds of beef had to be tracked down and destroyed – the biggest food recall in history.

At about the same time, the US Senate held hearings at which the head of the Internal Revenue Service, America's tax-collecting agency, was roundly criticized and delightfully humiliated for overseeing a department that was inefficient, heartless, vindictive and incompetent. I don't wish to boast, but the record will show that I had made all this manifestly clear in these pages as far back as last April.

The biggest story of the year was the mysterious disappearance of a jet aircraft in the woods near here. A year ago Christmas Eve, as you may dimly recall from my column of last February, a Lear jet carrying two men was circling around to make a routine landing at the airport when it abruptly lost radio contact and disappeared from the control tower's radar screen.

Over the next few weeks the biggest ground and air search in the state's history was undertaken, but the plane was not found. A year later, it still has not been found and the mystery of what became of it has only deepened.

A big element of the mystery is that an exceptionally large number of people – 275 at last count – claim to have seen the jet just before it crashed. Some said they were close enough to see the two men peering out of the windows. The trouble is that these witnesses were widely scattered across two states, in locations up to 175 miles apart. Clearly they can't all have seen the plane in the moments before it crashed, so what *did* they see?

A good deal of other news about that fateful flight has emerged since I wrote about the plane's disappearance. The most startling news to me was that a plane vanishing in the New Hampshire woods is not that exceptional an event. In 1959, according to our local paper, two professors from the university here went down in the woods in a light plane during a winter storm. Notes they left behind showed that they survived for at least four days. Unfortunately, their plane was not found for two and a half months. Two years later, another light plane disappeared in the woods and wasn't found for six months. A third plane crashed in 1966 and wasn't found until 1972, long after most people had forgotten about it. The woods, it seems, can swallow a lot of wreckage and not give much away.

Even so, the utter disappearance of a Lear jet seems inexplicable. To begin with a Lear jet is a big plane, with a wingspan of forty feet. You wouldn't think that something that large could vanish without trace, but evidently it can. Then there was all the technology that could now be brought to bear – heat sensors, infrared viewers, long-range metal detectors and the like. The Air Force even lent the use of a re-connaissance satellite. All to no avail. The fate of the doomed plane is as much a mystery now as it was a year ago. I will keep you posted.

To my surprise, the column that generated more post than any other during the year was my account last spring of our preposterously exasperating, two-year-long struggle to get the US immigration authorities to recognize that my wife has a right to live with me in my own country. It appears that many of you have also experienced the mind-numbing obtuseness and inflexibility of the US Immigration and Naturalization Service.

Just after that column appeared, I came across a story in the paper of a man named Raul Blanco, whose application for citizenship had been repeatedly turned down because he had failed to provide a full set of fingerprints. As Blanco patiently explained in letter after letter, he couldn't supply a full set because he had only seven fingers, having lost three in an industrial accident years earlier in his native Cuba. At last report, Blanco was still trying to get someone at the Immigration and Naturalization Service to understand his problem. He would be better off trying to find the missing fingers.

My wife, I am pleased to tell you, received her documentation six weeks after my column ran and still has all her fingers, so all things considered it has been a pretty good year. And on that note may I just wish you all a very happy, prosperous and fully digited 1998.

YOUR NEW COMPUTER

CONGRATULATIONS. YOU HAVE PURCHASED AN ANTHRAX/2000 Multimedia 615X Personal Computer with Digital Doo-Dah Enhancer. It will give years of faithful service, if you ever get it up and running. Also included with your PC is a bonus pack of pre-installed software – 'Lawn Mowing Planner', 'Mr Arty-Farty', 'Blank Screen Saver', and 'East Africa Route Finder' – which will provide hours of pointless diversion while using up most of your computer's spare memory.

So turn the page and let's get started!

Getting Ready: Congratulations. You have successfully turned the page and are ready to proceed.

Important meaningless note: The Anthrax/2000 is configured to use 80386, 214J10 or higher processors running at 2,472 hertz on variable speed spin cycle. Check your electrical installations and insurance policies before proceeding. Do not tumble dry.

To prevent internal heat build-up, select a cool, dry environment for your computer. The bottom shelf of a refrigerator is ideal.

Unpack the box and examine its contents. (Warning: Do not open box if contents are missing or faulty as this will invalidate your warranty. Return all missing contents in their original packaging with a note explaining where they have gone and a replacement will be sent within twelve working months.)

The contents of the box should include some of the following: monitor with mysterious De Gauss button; keyboard with 2½ inches of flex; computer unit; miscellaneous wires and cables not necessarily designed for this model; 2,000-page *Owner's Manual*; *Short Guide to the Owner's Manual*; *Quick Guide to the Short Guide to the Owner's Manual*; *Laminated Super-Kwik Set-Up Guide for People Who Are Exceptionally Impatient or Stupid*; 1,167 pages of warranties, vouchers, notices in Spanish, and other loose pieces of paper; 292 cubic feet of styrofoam packing material.

Something They Didn't Tell You in the Shop: Because of the additional power needs of the pre-installed bonus software, you will need to acquire an Anthrax/2000 auxiliary software upgrade pack, a 900-volt memory capacitator for the auxiliary software pack, a 50-megaherz oscillator unit for the memory capacitator, 2,500 mega-gigabytes of additional memory for the oscillator, and an electrical substation.

Setting Up: Congratulations. You are ready to set up. If you have not yet acquired a degree in electrical engineering, now is the time to do so.

Connect the monitor cable (A) to the portside outlet unit (D); attach power offload unit sub-orbiter (Xii) to the co-axial AC/DC servo channel (G); plug three-pin mouse cable into keyboard housing unit (make extra hole if necessary); connect modem (B2) to offside parallel audio/video lineout jack. Alternatively, plug the cables into the most likely looking holes, switch on and see what happens.

Additional important meaningless note: The wires in the ampule modulator unit are marked as follows according to international convention: blue = neutral or live; yellow = live or blue; blue and live = neutral and green; black = instant death. (Except where prohibited by law.)

Switch the computer on. Your hard drive will automatically download. (Allow three to five days.) When downloading is complete, your screen will say: 'Yeah, what?'

Now it is time to install your software. Insert Disc A (marked 'Disc D' or 'Disc G') into Drive Slot B or J, and type: 'Hello! Anybody home?' At the DOS command prompt, enter your Licence Verification Number. Your Licence Verification Number can be found by entering your Certified User Number, which can be found by entering your Licence Verification Number. If you are unable to find your Licence Verification or Certified User numbers, call the Software Support Line for assistance. (Please have your Licence

Verification and Certified User numbers handy as the support staff cannot otherwise assist you.)

If you have not yet committed suicide, then insert Installation Diskette 1 in Drive Slot 2 (or vice versa) and follow the instructions on your screen. (Note: Owing to a software modification, some instructions will appear in Romanian.) At each prompt, reconfigure the specified file path, double click on the button launch icon, select a single equation default file from the macro selection register, insert the VGA graphics card in the rear aerofoil, and type 'C:\>' followed by the birthdates of all the people you have ever known.

Your screen will now say: 'Invalid file path. Whoa! Abort or continue?' Warning: selecting 'Continue' may result in irreversible file compression, permanent loss of memory and a default overload in the hard drive. On the other hand, selecting 'Abort' will require you to start the whole tedious, maddening installation process all over again. Your choice.

When the smoke has cleared, insert Disc A2 (marked 'Disc A1') and repeat as directed with each of the 187 other discs.

When installation is complete, return to file path, and type your name, address and credit card numbers and press 'SEND'. This will automatically register you for our free software prize, 'Blank Screensaver IV: Nighttime in Deep Space', and allow us to pass your name to lots and lots of computer magazines, online services and other commercial enterprises, who will be getting in touch shortly.

Congratulations. You are now ready to use your computer. Here are some simple exercises to get you off to a flying start.

Writing a letter: Type 'Dear—' and follow it with the name of someone you know. Write a few lines about yourself, and then write, 'Sincerely yours' followed by your own name. Congratulations.

Saving a file: To save your letter, select File Menu. Choose Retrieve from Sub-Directory A, enter a backup file number and place an insertion point beside the macro dialogue button. Select secondary text box from the merge menu, and double click on the supplementary cleared document window. Assign the tile cascade to a merge file and insert in a text equation box. Alternatively, write the letter out longhand and put it in a drawer.

Advice on Using the Spreadsheet Facility: Don't.

Troubleshooting Section: You will have many, many problems with your computer. Here are some common problems and their solutions.

Problem: My computer won't turn on.

Solution: Check to make sure the computer is plugged in; check to make sure the power button is in the ON position; check the cables for damage; dig up underground cables in your garden and check for damage; drive out into country and check electricity pylons for signs of fallen wires; call hotline.

Problem: My keyboard doesn't seem to have any keys.

Solution: Turn the keyboard the right way up.

Problem: My mouse won't drink its water or go on the spinning wheel.

Solution: Try a high-protein diet or call your petshop support line.

Problem: I keep getting a message saying: 'Non-System General Protection Fault'.

Solution: This is probably because you are trying to use the computer. Switch the computer to OFF mode and any annoying messages will disappear.

Problem: My computer is a piece of useless junk.

Correct – and congratulations. You are now ready to upgrade to an Anthrax/3000 Turbo model, or to go back to pen and paper.

IN PRAISE OF DINERS

A COUPLE OF YEARS AGO, WHEN I WAS SENT AHEAD OF THE REST OF THE family to scout out a place for us to live in the States, I included the town of Adams, Massachusetts, as a possibility because it had a wonderful old-fashioned diner on Main Street.

Unfortunately, I was compelled to remove Adams from the short-list when I was unable to recall a single other virtue in the town, possibly because it didn't have any. Still, I believe I would have been happy there. Diners tend to take you like that.

Diners were once immensely popular, but like so much else they have become increasingly rare. Their heyday was the years just after the First World War, when Prohibition shut the taverns and people needed some place else to go for lunch. From a business point of view, diners were an appealing proposition. They were cheap to buy and maintain and, because they were factory built, they came virtually complete. Having acquired one, all you had to do was set it on a level piece of ground, hook up water and electricity and you were in business. If trade didn't materialize, you simply loaded it on to a flatbed truck and tried your luck elsewhere. By the late 1920s, about a score of companies were mass-producing diners, nearly all in a streamlined art deco style known as *moderne*, with gleaming stainless-steel exteriors, and insides of polished dark wood and more shiny metal.

Diner enthusiasts are a bit like train-spotters. They can tell you whether a particular diner is a 1947 Kullman Blue Comet or a 1932 Worcester Semi-Streamliner. They appreciate the design details that mark out a Ralph Musi from a Starlite or an O'Mahoney, and will drive long distances to visit a rare and well-preserved Sterling, of which only seventy-three were made, between 1935 and 1941.

The one thing they don't talk about much is food. This is because diner food is generally much the same wherever you go – which is to say, not very good. My wife and children refuse to accompany me to diners for this very reason. What they fail to appreciate is that going to diners is not about eating; it's about saving a crucial part of America's heritage.

We didn't have diners in Iowa when I was growing up. They were mostly an east coast phenomenon, just as restaurants built in the shape of things (pigs, doughnuts, bowler hats) were a west coast phenomenon. The closest thing we had to a diner was a place down by the river called Ernie's Grill. Everything about it was squalid and greasy, including Ernie, and the food was appalling, but it did have many of the features of a diner, notably a long counter with twirly stools, a wall of booths, patrons who looked as if they had just come in from killing big animals in the woods (possibly with their teeth), and a fondness for diner-style lingo. When you ordered, the waitress would call out to the kitchen in some indecipherable code, 'Two spots on a dot, easy on the Brylcreem, dribble on the griddle and cough twice in a bucket,' or something similarly alarming and mystifying.

But Ernie's was in a square, squat, anonymous brick building, which patently lacked the streamlined glamour of a classic diner. So when, decades later, I was sent to look for a livable community in New England, a diner was one of the things high on my shopping list. Alas, they are getting harder and harder to find.

Hanover, where we eventually settled, does have a venerable eating establishment called Lou's, which celebrated its fiftieth anniversary last year. It has the superficial ambience of a diner, but the menu features items like quiches and fajitas, and it prides itself on the freshness of its lettuce. The customers are all well heeled and yuppie-ish. You can't imagine any of them climbing into a car with a deer lashed to the bonnet.

So you may conceive my joy when, about six months after we moved to Hanover, I was driving one day through the nearby community of White River Junction, and passed an establishment called the Four Aces. Impulsively, I went in and found an early post-war Worcester in nearly mint condition. It was wonderful. Even the food was pretty good, which was a bit disappointing, but I have learned to live with it.

No-one knows how many diners like this remain. Partly it is a problem of definition. A diner is essentially any place that serves food and calls itself a diner. Under the broadest definition, there are about 2,500 diners in the United States. But no more than a thousand of these, at the outside, are what could be called 'classic' diners, and the number of those diminishes yearly. Only a couple of months ago Phil's, the oldest diner in California, closed. It had been in business in north Los Angeles since 1926, making it, by Californian standards, as venerable as Stonehenge, but its passing was hardly noted.

Most diners can't compete with the big fast food chains. A traditional diner is small, with perhaps eight booths and a dozen or so counter spaces, and because they provide waitress service and individually cooked meals their operating costs are higher. Most diners are also old, and in America it is almost always much cheaper to replace than to preserve. An enthusiast who bought an old diner in Jersey City, New Jersey, discovered to his horror that it would cost $900,000 – perhaps twenty years' worth of potential profits – to bring it back to its original condition. Much cheaper to tear it down and turn the site over to a Kentucky Fried Chicken or McDonald's.

What you get a lot of instead these days are ersatz diners. The last time I was in Chicago I was taken to a place called Ed Debevic's, where the waitresses wore badges giving their names as Bubbles and Blondie and where the walls were lined with Ed's bowling trophies. But there never was an Ed Debevic. He was just the creative figment of a marketing man. No matter. Ed's was humming. A dining public that had disdained genuine diners when they stood on every corner was now queueing to get into a make-believe one. It mystifies me beyond measure, but this is a common phenomenon in America.

You find it at Disneyland, where people flock to stroll up and down a Main Street just like the ones they abandoned wholesale in the 1950s for shopping malls. It happens at restored colonial villages like Williamsburg, Virginia, or Mystic, Connecticut, where visitors pay good money to savour the sort of tranquil village atmosphere that they long ago fled for the happy sprawl of suburbs. I can't begin to account for it, but it appears, to coin a phrase, that Americans really only want something when it isn't really real.

But that is another column. We shall return to this subject next time. Meanwhile, I am off to the Four Aces while the chance is still there. There aren't any waitresses called Bubbles, but the bowling trophies are real.

Just under three months after this article appeared, in early April 1998, the Four Aces closed.

UNIFORMLY AWFUL

I REMEMBER THE FIRST TIME I TASTED EUROPEAN CHOCOLATE. IT WAS IN the central railway station in Antwerp, on 21 March 1972, my second day in Europe as a young backpacker. While waiting for a train I bought a bar of Belgian chocolate from a station kiosk, tore off a bite and, after a moment of startled delight, began to emit a series of involuntary rapturous noises of an intensity sufficient to draw stares from twenty yards away.

You know how a baby eats a bowl of pudding – with noise and gusto and an alarming amount of gurgly drool? Well, that was me. I couldn't help myself. I didn't know that chocolate could be this good. I didn't know that *anything* could be this good.

American chocolate bars, as you are perhaps aware, are mysteriously bland affairs. I have been told that it wasn't always so. Many times I have heard from people of my parents' generation that when they were young American chocolate bars packed a proper wallop – that they were fatter, creamier, more lusciously endowed with nuts and nougat and gustatory ecstasy. My father reminisced fondly about candy bars of the 1920s so chewy that they would take most of the day to eat and a couple of weeks to digest. The same bars now are pallid little nothings.

The popular explanation is that these products have been constantly reformulated – perhaps I should say deformulated – over the years to hold down costs and to broaden their appeal to people with less intensive palates. It is certainly true that an awful lot of American foodstuffs – white bread, most domestic cheeses, nearly all convenience foods, the bulk of beers, a good deal of the coffee –

are nothing like as robust and flavourful and varied as their counterparts almost anywhere in Europe, Britain included. It's an odd thing in a country that loves to eat, but there you are.

I put it down to two things. The first is cost. Everything in America is predicated on cost, far more than in other countries. If price is a factor between competing businesses (and it always is), then the cheaper will inevitably drive out the costlier, and this seldom leads to improved quality. (Actually, it never leads to improved quality.)

There used to be a good fast food Mexican restaurant in the next town from where I live. Then about a year ago, Taco Bell, part of a national chain, opened up across the road. I don't believe there is a person alive who would argue that Taco Bell offers really good Mexican food. But it is cheap – at least 25 per cent cheaper than the restaurant it was competing with across the road. Within a year the old restaurant was gone. So now if you want Mexican fast food in our neck of the woods, you have to settle for the cheap but carefully uninspired offerings of Taco Bell.

Because Taco Bell is so vigorously competitive on price, its dominance is well nigh universal. Almost wherever you go along the American highway these days, if you want a taco you must settle for Taco Bell. The stupefying thing is that this seems to be the way most people want it. And here we come to the second of our factors – the strange, unshakeable attachment of American consumers to predictable uniformity. Americans, in a word, like things to be the same wherever they go. This is the part that mystifies me.

Take Starbucks, a chain of coffee shops for which I have a mild and possibly irrational dislike, if only because they are becoming ubiquitous. Starbucks started quietly in Seattle some years ago, but in the last five years the number of its outlets has grown tenfold, to 1,270, and the number is intended to double roughly in the next two years. Already in many cities if you are looking for a coffee bar, the choice is pretty well Starbucks or nothing.

Now there is nothing wrong with Starbucks, but nothing all that special either. It offers a decent cup of coffee. Big deal. I can give you a decent cup of coffee. The impression you get is that Starbucks' principal motivating force is not to produce the finest coffees but rather to produce more Starbucks. If the American coffee-drinking public demands truly excellent coffee, then Starbucks will have to provide it if it wants to stay pre-eminent, but the American public won't demand that, so there won't be any particular pressure on Starbucks to provide exceptional quality. It may, but there won't be any commercial necessity for it, especially because in most places (a) it will be the only coffee bar around and (b) its customers will be completely habituated to the Starbucks brand.

We have two very congenial coffee bars in Hanover, but I am certain that if Starbucks were to open here people would be excited. (You should have seen the delirium when The Gap moved in.) Starbucks would be seen as a kind of affirmation for the town from the outside world. Visitors, on whom the town depends, would almost certainly favour it overwhelmingly because they know it and are comfortable with it.

People have grown so used to uniformity that they have become, as it were, hypnotized by it. About five miles from where I live, there was until recently a nice, old-fashioned, family-owned restaurant. A couple of years ago, a McDonald's opened opposite it. Almost at once the bulk of passing trade transferred from one side of the road to the other. Last summer, the family-owned restaurant closed. Shortly afterwards I mentioned to a neighbour how disappointing I found it that people would forsake a local establishment for the universal appeal of McDonald's.

'Yeah,' my neighbour said in that thoughtful, drawn-out way that indicates a proposition not entirely agreed with. 'But at least you know where you are with McDonald's, don't you?'

'Exactly!' I cried with feeling. 'Don't you see, that's the whole *problem*!'

I wanted to grab him by the lapels and explain to him that it was because of this kind of thinking that chocolate in America has no kick, white bread tastes like wadding, and cheese has a hundred names (colby, Monterey jack, cheddar, American, provolone) but just one flavour, one texture and one vivid yellow hue.

But I could see there was no point. He was like one of the pod people in *Invasion of the Body Snatchers*. The forces of blandness had captured his spirit and there was no getting it back. He had become a McPerson.

He looked at me uneasily – people don't usually get excited in our street – and I could see he was thinking: Whoa! Emotional fellow!

Maybe he was right. I have to admit I have been a little out of sorts in recent months. I put it down to severe chocolate deprivation.

THE FAT OF THE LAND

I HAVE BEEN THINKING A LOT ABOUT FOOD LATELY. THIS IS BECAUSE I AM not getting any. My wife, you see, recently put me on a diet after suggesting (a little unkindly, if you ask me) that I was beginning to look like something Richard Branson would try to get airborne.

It is an interesting diet of her own devising, which essentially allows me to eat anything I want so long as it contains no fat, cholesterol, sodium or calories, and isn't tasty. In order to keep me from starving altogether, she went to the supermarket and bought everything that had 'bran' in its title. I am not sure, but I believe I had bran cutlets for dinner last night. I am very depressed.

Obesity is a serious problem in America. (Well, serious for fat people anyway.) Half of all adult Americans are overweight and more than a third are defined as obese (i.e., big enough to make you think twice before getting in a lift with them).

Now that hardly anyone smokes, it has taken over as the number one health fret in the country. About 300,000 Americans die every year from diseases related to obesity, and the nation spends $100 billion treating illnesses arising from overeating – diabetes, heart disease, high blood pressure, cancer, and so on. (I hadn't realized it, but being overweight can increase your chance of getting colon cancer – and this is a disease you really don't want to have – by as much as 50 per cent. Ever since I read that, I keep imagining a proctologist examining me and saying: 'Wow. Just how many cheeseburgers have you had in your life, Mr Bryson?') Being overweight also substantially reduces your chances of surviving surgery, not to mention getting a decent date.

Above all, it means that people who are theoretically dear to you will call you 'Mr Blimpy' and ask you what you think you are doing every time you open a cupboard door and, entirely by accident, remove a large bag of Cheez Doodles.

The wonder to me is how anyone can be thin in this country. We went to a restaurant the other night where they were promoting something called 'Skillet Sensations'. Here (and every word of this is true) is the menu's description of the Chilli Cheese Tater Skillet:

> 'We start this incredible combination with crispy, crunchy waffle fries. On top of those we generously ladle spicy chilli, melted Monterey jack and cheddar cheeses, and pile high with tomatoes, green onions, and sour cream.'

You see what I am up against? And this was one of the more modest offerings. The most depressing thing is that my wife and children can eat this stuff and not put on an ounce. When the waitress came, my wife said: 'The children and I will have the De Luxe Supreme Goo Skillet Feast, with extra cheese and sour cream, and a side order of onion rings with hot fudge sauce and biscuit gravy.'

'And for Mr Blimpy here?'

'Just bring him some dried bran and a glass of water.'

When, the following morning over a breakfast of oat flakes and chaff, I expressed to my wife the opinion that this was, with all respect, the most stupid diet I had ever come across, she told me to find a better one, so I went to the library. There were at least 150 books on diet and nutrition – *Dr Berger's Immune Power Diet, Straight Talk About Weight Control, The Rotation Diet* – but they were all a little earnest and bran-obsessed for my tastes. Then I saw one that was precisely of the type I was looking for. By Dale M. Atrens, Ph.D., it was called *Don't Diet*. Now here was a title I could work with.

Relaxing my customary aversion to consulting a book by anyone so immensely pratty as to put 'Ph.D.' after his name (I don't put Ph.D. after my name on my books, after all – and not just because I don't have one), I took the book to that reading area that libraries put aside for people who are strange and have nowhere to go in the afternoons but none the less are not quite ready to be institutionalized, and devoted myself to an hour's reflective study.

The premise of the book, if I understood it correctly (and forgive me if I am a little sketchy on some details, but I was distracted by the man next to me, who was having a quiet chat with a person from the next dimension), is that the human body has been programmed by aeons of evolution to pack on adipose tissue for insulating warmth in periods of cold, padding for comfort, and energy reserves in times of crop failures.

The human body – mine in particular, evidently – is extremely good at doing this. Tree shrews can't do it at all. They must spend every waking moment eating. 'This may be why tree shrews have produced so little great art or music,' Atrens quips. Ha! Ha! Ha! Then again, it may be because the tree shrew eats leaves, whereas I eat Ben and Jerry's double chocolate fudge ice cream.

The other interesting thing Atrens points out is that fat is exceedingly stubborn. Even when you starve yourself half to death, the body shows the greatest reluctance to relinquish its fat reserves.

Consider that each pound of fat represents 5,000 calories – about what the average person eats in total in two days. That means that if you starved yourself for a week – ate nothing at all – you would lose no more than 3½ pounds of fat, and, let's face it, still wouldn't look a picture in your swimming costume.

Having tortured yourself in this way for seven days, naturally you would slip into the pantry when no-one was looking and eat everything in there but a bag of chickpeas, and gain back all the loss, *plus* – and here's the crux – a little something extra because now your body knows that you have been trying to starve it and are not to be trusted, so it had better lay in a little extra wobble in case you get any more foolish notions.

This is why dieting is so frustrating and hard. The more you try to get rid of your fat, the more ferociously your body holds on to it.

So I have come up with an ingenious alternative diet. I call it the Fool-Your-Body-Twenty-Hours-a-Day Diet. The idea is that for twenty hours in each twenty-four you ruthlessly starve yourself, but at four selected intervals during the day – for convenience we'll call them breakfast, lunch, dinner and midnight snack – you feed your body something like a plate of sausage, chips and beans, or a large bowl of double chocolate fudge ice cream, so that it doesn't *realize* that you are starving it. Brilliant, eh?

I don't know why I didn't think of this years ago. I think it may be that all this bran has cleared my head. Or something.

THE SPORTING LIFE

WE HAVE A FRIEND, A SINGLE MUM, WHOSE SIX-YEAR-OLD SON RECENTLY signed up to play ice hockey, a sport taken very seriously here.

At the first team meeting, one of the other parents announced that he had devised a formula for determining how much each child would play. Essentially the best seven players would play 80 per cent of each game, and the remaining, more hopeless kids would divide up whatever time was left – so long, of course, as victory was not in doubt.

'I think that's the most fair way of doing it,' he said to solemn nods from the other dads.

Failing to understand the role of testosterone in these matters, our friend stood up and suggested that a more fair approach might be to let all the children play equally.

'But then they wouldn't win,' said the father, looking half aghast.

'Yes,' agreed our friend. 'So?'

'But what's the point in playing if you don't win?'

These were, let me remind you, six-year-olds. There isn't space here – there isn't space in this newspaper – to discuss all the things that have gone wrong with sport in America, at nearly every level, so let me just cite a few specimen examples to give you an idea of how America approaches competitive pursuits these days.

Item: In an effort to spur them on and plump up our standings in the medals tables (which is, of course, the most important thing in the universe), US swimmers were paid up to $65,000 from official sources for every medal they won at the last Olympics. Apparently, representing one's nation and doing one's best are no longer sufficient incentives.

Item: To delight the home fans and enhance their positions in the national rankings, the largest college football teams now regularly schedule matches against hopelessly inadequate opponents. In one especially proud moment for sport last season, the University of Florida, ranked number two in the nation, took on the unsung might of little Central Michigan University, and won by a score of 82 to 6.

Item: In order to watch sixty minutes of football on this year's Super Bowl on television, it was necessary to sit through 113 commercials, programme trailers or product plugs. (I counted.)

Item: The average cost for a family of four to go to a Major League baseball game now is over $200.

I mention all this not to make the point that commercial overkill and blunted sportsmanship have taken much of the joy out of sport in this country, though they have, but to explain why I love Dartmouth College basketball games so much.

Dartmouth is the local university and it is in the Ivy League, a confederation of eight venerable and brainy institutions – Harvard, Yale, Princeton, Brown, Columbia, Penn, Cornell and Dartmouth. These kids go to Ivy League schools because they are going to become rocket scientists and professors, not because they are going to make $12 million a year playing professional basketball. They play for the love of the game, the camaraderie, the thrill of taking part – all those things that we have mostly lost in this country.

I first went to a game three winters ago, when I saw a schedule in a shop window in town and noticed that the season opener was that night. I hadn't been to a basketball game in twenty years.

'Hey, Dartmouth's got a game tonight,' I announced in excitement when I got home. 'Who's coming?'

Five faces looked at me with an expression I hadn't seen since I suggested we go camping in Slovenia for our next holiday. 'OK, I'll go on my own,' I sniffed, though in the end my youngest daughter, then eleven, took pity and accompanied me.

Well, we had a wonderful time. Dartmouth won a nail-biter, and my daughter and I came home gabbling. A few nights later Dartmouth won another squeaker with a basket at the buzzer, and we came home gabbling again.

Now everyone wanted to come. But here's the thing. We wouldn't let them. This was our little thing.

Since then, for three seasons, going to Dartmouth games has become a ritual for my daughter and me. Everything about it is splendid. The arena where the team plays is an easy walk from our house. Tickets are cheap, and the crowds are small, friendly and loyal. An endearingly nerdy band plays perky tunes like the theme from *Hawaii Five-0*, to get us bouncing. Afterwards we emerge into the wintry night air and walk home chatting. It is because of these walks that I know the identities of the Spice Girls, that *Scream 2* was way cool, and that Matthew Perry is so cute it's like almost not real. When there is not the slightest chance that a living person might see, she sometimes takes my hand. It's perfect.

But at the heart of it is the game. For two hours we shout and wince and rend our hair, and become wholly absorbed with the hope that our boys can put a ball through a hoop more times than their boys. If Dartmouth win, we are elated. If they don't – well, no matter. It's just a game. This is the way sport should be.

One of the Dartmouth players last year was a seven-foot giant named Chris, who had all the attributes of greatness except, alas, an ability to play basketball. In consequence he spent nearly the whole of his career on the low end of the bench. Very occasionally, he would be put in for the last fifteen or twenty seconds of a game. Invariably on these occasions someone would pass him the ball and someone smaller would come and take it away. He would shake his head regretfully, then lope giraffe-like to the other end of the court. He was our favourite player.

By tradition, the last game of the season is parents' night, when parents fly in from all over to watch their sons play. Also by tradition, on the last home game the graduating seniors are put in to start.

This particular game was of no consequence, but news of that seemed not to have reached our lanky hero. He came onto the court with an intense psyched-up look. This was his first and last chance to shine and he wasn't going to blow it.

The referee blew the whistle to start the game. Our Chris ran up and down the court four or five times and then, to our dismay and his, was taken out and returned to the bench. He had played no more than a minute or so. He hadn't done a thing wrong – hadn't had a chance to do a thing wrong. He took his customary seat, cast his parents an apologetic look and watched the rest of the game through eyes welled with tears. Someone had forgotten to tell the coach that winning isn't everything.

This week Dartmouth has its last home game of the season. This year, I believe, there are two players who will be allowed to run gamely up and down the court for a token minute or two, and will then be replaced by abler hands.

My daughter and I have decided to skip this one. When perfection is so difficult to find, it's hard to see it spoiled.

LAST NIGHT ON THE TITANIC

'On the night of the wreck our dinner tables were a picture! The huge bunches of grapes which topped the fruit baskets on every table were thrilling. The menus were wonderfully varied and tempting. I stayed at table from soup to nuts.'

Titanic passenger Kate Buss, quoted in
Last Dinner on the Titanic:
Menus and Recipes from the Great Liner

'Good lord, Buss, what's all the commotion?'

'Oh, hello, Smythe. Not like you to be up at this hour. Smoke?'

'Thank you, don't mind if I do. So what's the kerfuffle? I saw the captain as I came by and he looked in a dreadful stew.'

'It appears we're sinking, old boy.'

'Never!'

'Do you recall that iceberg we saw at dinner?'

'The one that was as big as a twenty-storey building?'

'That's the one. Well, it seems we struck the deuced thing.'

'Rotten luck.'

'Rather.'

'I suppose that explains why my cabin door was underneath the bed when I woke up. I thought it a bit odd. I say, is this a Monte Cristo?'

'H. Upmann, actually. I have a man in Gerrard Street who gets them specially.'

'Awfully nice.'

'Yes . . . Pity, really.'

'What's that?'

'Well, I just ordered a dozen bo... suppose young Bertie will be glad to get...

'So you don't think we're going to make it?'

'Doesn't look good. Mrs Buss asked Croaker, the quarterdeck steward, when he brought her nightcap and he said we had less than two hours. How's Mrs Smythe, by the way? Is her stomach better?'

'Couldn't say. She's drowned, you see.'

'Oh, rotten luck.'

'Went out the starboard porthole when we started to list. It was her shout that woke me, as a matter of fact. Shame she's missed all the excitement. She always enjoyed a good sinking.'

'Mrs Buss is just the same.'

'She didn't go over as well, did she?'

'Oh, no. She's gone to see the purser. Wanted to cable Fortnum's and cancel the order for the garden fête. Not much point now, you see.'

'Quite. Still, all in all it's not been a bad voyage, wouldn't you say?'

'Couldn't agree more. The food's been top-notch. Young Kate was particularly taken with the place-settings. She thought the dinner tables a picture and the grapes thrilling. She stayed from soup to nuts. You haven't seen her, by any chance?'

'No, why do you ask?'

'It's just that she rushed off in a rather odd way. Said there was something she had to do with young Lord D'Arcy before we went under. Something to do with flags, I gather.'

'Flags? How odd.'

'Well, she made some reference to needing a jolly roger, if I heard her right. I can't pretend I understand half the things she goes on about. And in any case I was somewhat distracted. Mrs Buss had just spilled her nightcap down her peignoir – in consequence of the impact, you see – and was in a terrible temper because Croaker wouldn't bring her another. He told her to get it herself.'

'What extraordinary insolence.'

'I suppose he was a bit out of sorts because he won't be getting his tips now, will he? Can't say I blame him really.'

'Still.'

'I reported him, of course. One has to remember one's station even in a crisis or we should be in a terrible mess, don't you agree? The quartermaster assured me he won't get another posting on this ship.'

'I should think not.'

'Bit of a technicality, I suppose, but at least it's been noted in the book.'

'It's been a funny old night, when you think about it. I mean to say, wife drowns, ship sinks, and there was no Montrachet '07 at dinner. I had to settle for a very middling '05.'

'You think that's disappointing? Have a look at these.'

'Sorry, old boy, I can't see in this light. What are they?'

'Return tickets.'

'Oh, that is bad luck.'

'Outside port cabin on the Promenade Deck.'

'Very bad luck . . . I say, what's that noise?'

'That will be the steerage passengers drowning, I expect.'

'No, it sounded like a band.'

'I believe you're right. Yes, you are quite right. A bit mournful, don't you think? I shouldn't want to try to dance to that.'

' "Nearer My God to Thee", isn't it? They might have chosen something a bit more festive for our last night at sea.'

'Still, I think I'll wander down and see if they've put out supper yet. Coming?'

'No, I think I'll turn in with a brandy. It's going to be a short night as it is. How long have we got, do you suppose?'

'About forty minutes, I'd say.'

'Oh dear. Perhaps I'll skip the brandy then. I don't suppose I'll be seeing you again?'

'Not in this life, old sport.'

'Oh, I say, that's very good. I must remember that. Well, good-night, then.'

'Goodnight.'

'By the by, just a thought. The captain didn't say anything about getting into lifeboats, did he?'

'Not that I recall. Shall I wake you if he makes an announce-ment?'

'That would be very good of you, if you're sure it's no trouble.'

'No trouble at all.'

'Well, goodnight, then. Give my regards to Mrs Buss and young Kate.'

'With the greatest pleasure. I'm sorry about Mrs Smythe.'

'Well, worse things happen at sea, as they say. I expect she'll bob up somewhere. She was awfully buoyant. Well, goodnight.'
'Goodnight, old sport. Sleep well.'

FUN IN THE SNOW

FOR REASONS I CANNOT BEGIN TO UNDERSTAND, WHEN I WAS ABOUT eight years old my parents gave me a pair of skis for Christmas. I went outside, strapped them on, and stood in a racing crouch, but nothing happened. This is because there are no hills in Iowa.

Casting around for something with a slope, I decided to ski down our back porch steps. There were only five steps, but on skis the angle of descent was surprisingly steep. I went down the steps at about, I would guess, 110 miles an hour, and hit the bottom with such force that the skis jammed solid, whereas I continued onward and outward across the patio in a graceful rising arc. About twelve feet away loomed the back wall of our garage. Instinctively adopting a spreadeagled posture for maximum impact, I smacked into it somewhere near the roof and slid down its vertical face in the manner of food flung against a wall.

It was at this point I decided that winter sports were not for me. I put away the skis and for the next thirty-five years thought no more about the matter. Then we moved to New England, where people actually look forward to winter. At the first fall of snow they cry out with joy and root in cupboards for sledges and ski poles. They become suffused with a strange vitality – an eagerness to get out into all that white stuff and schuss about on something fast and reckless.

With so many active people about, including every member of my own family, I began to feel left out. So a few weeks ago, in an attempt to find a winter pastime, I borrowed some ice skates and went with my two youngest to Occum Pond, a popular local spot for skating.

'Are you sure you know how to skate?' my daughter asked uneasily.

'Of course I do, my petal,' I assured her. 'I have been mistaken many times for Jayne Torvill, on the ice and off.'

And I do know how to skate, honestly. It's just that my legs, after years of inactivity, got a little overexcited to be confronted with so much slipperiness. As soon as I stepped onto the ice they decided they wanted to visit every corner of Occum Pond at once, from lots of different directions. They went this way and that, scissoring and splaying, sometimes getting as much as twelve feet apart, but constantly gathering momentum, until at last they flew out from under me and I landed on my butt with such a wallop that my coccyx hit the roof of my mouth and I had to push my oesophagus back in with my fingers.

'*Wow!*' said my startled butt as I clambered heavily back to my feet. 'That ice is *hard.*'

'Hey, let *me* see,' cried my head and instantly down I went again.

And so it went for the next thirty minutes, with various extremities of my body – shoulders, chin, nose, one or two of the more adventurous internal organs – hurling themselves at the ice in a spirit of investigation. From a distance I suppose I must have looked like someone being worked over by an invisible gladiator. Eventually, when I had nothing left to bruise, I crawled to shore and asked to be covered with a blanket. And that was it for my attempt at ice skating.

Next I tried sledging, which I don't even want to talk about, except to say that the man was very understanding about his dog, all things considered, and that that lady across the road would have saved us all a lot of trouble if she had just left her garage door open.

It was at about this juncture that my friend Prof. Danny Blanchflower stepped into the picture. Danny – his real name is David, but he is English, so when he was growing up everyone naturally called him Danny, and the name stuck – is a professor of economics at Dartmouth and a very brainy fellow. He writes books with sentences like 'When entered contemporaneously in the full specifications of column 5.7, profit-per-employee has a coefficient of 0.00022 with a t-statistic of 2.3,' and isn't even joking. For all I know, it may even mean something. As I say, he's a real smart guy, except for one thing. He is mad on snowmobiling.

Now a snowmobile, I should perhaps explain, is a rocket ship designed by Satan to run on snow. It travels at speeds up to 70 mph, which – call me chicken, I don't care – seems to me a trifle fleet on narrow, winding paths through boulder-strewn woods.

For weeks Danny pestered me to join him in a bout of this alfresco madness. I tried to explain that I had certain problems with outdoor activities *vis-à-vis* the snowy season, and that somehow I didn't think a powerful, dangerous machine was likely to provide a solution.

'Nonsense!' he cried. Well, to cut a long story short, the next thing I knew I was on the edge of the New Hampshire woods, wearing a snug, heavy helmet that robbed me of all my senses except terror, and sitting nervously astride a sleek beastlike conveyance, its engine throbbing in anticipation of all the trees against which it might soon dash me. Danny gave me a rundown on the machine's operation, which for all I understood might have been a passage from one of his books, and jumped onto his own machine.

'Ready?' he shouted over the roar of his engine.

'No.'

'Great!' he called and took off with a flare of after-burners. Within two seconds he was a noisy dot in the distance.

Sighing, I gently engaged the throttle and, with a startled cry and a brief wheelie, took off with a velocity seldom seen outside a Road Runner cartoon. Shrieking hysterically and jettisoning weight via my bladder with every lively bump, I flew through the woods as if on an Exocet missile. Branches slapped my helmet. Moose reared and fled. The landscape flashed past as if in some hallucinogen-induced delirium.

Eventually, Danny stopped at a crossroads, beaming all over, engine purring. 'So what do you think?'

I moved my lips but no sound emerged. Danny took this as assent.

'Well, now that you've got the hang of it, shall we bang up the pace a bit?'

I formed the words 'Please, Danny, I want to go home. I want to see my mom,' but again no sound emerged.

And off he went. For hours we raced at lunatic speeds through the endless woods, bouncing through streams, swerving past boulders, launching into flight over fallen logs. When at length this waking nightmare concluded, I stepped from my machine on legs made of water.

Afterwards, to celebrate our miraculous intactness, we repaired to Murphy's Tavern for a pint. When the barmaid put the glasses down in front of us it occurred to me, with a flash of inspiration, that here at last was something I could do: winter drinking.

I had found my calling. I'm not as good at it yet as I hope to be – my legs still tend to go after about three hours – but I'm doing a lot of stamina training and am looking for a very good season in 1998–9.

THE FLYING NIGHTMARE

MY FATHER WAS A SPORTSWRITER WHO FLEW A LOT FOR HIS WORK IN THE days before it was common to do so, and occasionally he would take me on one of his trips with him. It was exciting, of course, just to go away for a weekend with my dad, but at the heart of the experience was the thrill of getting on a plane and going somewhere.

Everything about the process felt special and privileged. Checking in, you would be one of a small group of well-dressed people (for in those days people actually dressed up to fly). When the flight was called, you would stroll across a broad tarmac to a gleaming silver plane, and up one of those wheeled staircases. Entering the plane was like being admitted to some special club. Just stepping aboard, you became a little more stylish and sophisticated. The seats were comfy and, for a small boy, commodious. A smiling stewardess would come and give you a little winged badge that said 'Assistant Pilot' or something similarly responsible-sounding.

All that romance has long since vanished. Today in America commercial planes are little more than winged buses, and the airlines, without detectable exception, regard passengers as irksome pieces of bulk freight that they consented, at some time in the remote past, to carry from place to place and now wish they hadn't.

I cannot begin to describe in a space this modest all the spirit-sapping features of modern American air travel – the routinely overbooked flights, the endless queueing, the delays, the discovery that your 'direct' flight to Miami actually stops in Pittsburgh and involves a layover of ninety minutes and a change of planes, the near-impossibility of finding a friendly face among the ground staff, the being treated like an idiot and a cypher.

Yet in the oddest ways airlines continue to act as if it is still 1955. Take the safety demonstration. Why after all these years do the flight attendants still put a life vest over their heads and show you how to pull the little cord that inflates it? In the history of commercial aviation no life has been saved by the provision of life vests. I am especially fascinated by the way they include a little plastic whistle on each vest. I always imagine myself plunging vertically towards the ocean at 1,200 miles an hour and thinking: Well, thank gosh I've got this whistle.

It is no good asking what they are thinking because they are not thinking anything. I recently boarded a flight from Boston to Denver. When I opened the overhead storage compartment I found an inflated dinghy entirely filling the space.

'There's a boat in here,' I breathed in amazement to a passing flight attendant.

'Yes, sir,' said the flight attendant snappily. 'This plane meets FAA specifications for overwater flights.'

I stared at him in small wonder. 'And which ocean do we cross between Boston and Denver?'

'The plane meets FAA specifications for overwater flights whether or not overwater flights are scheduledly anticipated,' was his crisp reply, or something similarly inane and mangled.

'Are you telling me that if we go down in water, one hundred and fifty passengers are supposed to get into a two-man dinghy?'

'No, sir, there's another flotation craft in here.' He indicated the bin on the opposite side.

'So two boats for one hundred and fifty people? Does that strike you as just a little absurd?'

'Sir, I don't make the rules, and you are blocking the aisle.'

He talked to me like this because all airline employees eventually talk to you like this if you press them a little bit, and sometimes even if you don't. I feel safe in saying that there is not an industry anywhere in the United States where the notions of service and customer satisfaction are less regarded. All too often the most innocuous move – stepping up to a counter before the check-in clerk is ready to receive you, enquiring why a flight is delayed, ending up with no place to stow your coat because your overhead locker contains an inflated boat – can lead to snappishness and rebuke.

Mind you, with the notable exception of me and a few other meek souls who believe in orderliness, most passengers in America these days deserve what they get. This is because they take on jumbo suitbags and wheeled carry-ons that are at least twice the officially permitted size, so that the overhead bins fill up long before the flight is fully boarded. To make sure they get a bin to themselves, they board before their row is called. On any flight in America now you will find at least 20 per cent of the seats filled by people whose row numbers have not been called. I have watched this process with weary exasperation for some years, and I can tell you that it takes roughly twice as long for an American plane to get boarded and airborne as it does elsewhere.

The result of this is a kind of war between airline employees and passengers, which all too often redounds on the innocent in a way that cries out for justice.

I particularly recall an experience of a few years ago when my wife, children and I boarded a flight in Minneapolis to fly to London and discovered that we had been allocated seats in six different parts of the aircraft, up to twenty rows apart. Bemused, my wife pointed this out to a passing stewardess.

'And what do you expect me to do about it?' the stewardess replied in a tone that suggested an urgent need for a refresher course in customer relations.

'Well, we'd like some seats together, please.'

The stewardess gave a hollow laugh. 'There's nothing I can do now. We're boarding. Didn't you check your boarding passes?'

'Only the top one. The check-in clerk' – who was, let me interject here, a disagreeable specimen herself – 'didn't tell us she was scattering us all over the plane.'

'Well, there's nothing I can do now.'

'But we have small children.'

'Sorry.'

'Are you telling me to put a two-year-old and a four-year-old off by themselves for an eight-hour flight across the Atlantic?' my wife asked. (This was an idea that I believed I could warm to, but I made a grave face, in solidarity.)

The stewardess gave an elaborate sigh and, with an undisguised show of resentment, asked a kindly but timid white-haired couple to swap seats, which allowed my wife and the two youngest to sit together. The rest of us would remain separated.

'Next time look at your boarding passes before you leave

the terminal,' the attendant snapped at my wife in parting.

'No, next time we will fly with someone else,' my wife replied, and indeed ever since we have.

'And one day, I'll have a column in a newspaper and I'll write about this,' I called after her in a haughty voice. Of course, I didn't say any such thing, and it would be a terrible abuse of my position to tell you that it was Northwest Airlines that treated us in this shabby way, so I won't.

LOST IN CYBER LAND

WHEN WE MOVED TO AMERICA, THE CHANGE IN ELECTRICAL SYSTEMS meant I needed all new stuff for my office – computer, fax machine, answering machine and so on. I am not good at shopping or parting with large sums of money at the best of times, and the prospect of trailing around a succession of shops listening to sales assistants touting the wonders of various office products filled me with foreboding.

So imagine my delight when in the first computer store I went to I found a machine that had everything built into it – fax, answering machine, electronic address book, Internet capability, you name it. Advertised as 'the Complete Home Office Solution', this computer promised to do everything but make the coffee.

So I took it home and set it up, flexed my fingers, and wrote a perky fax to a friend in London. I typed his fax number in the appropriate box as directed and pushed 'Send'. Almost at once, noises of international dialling came out of the computer's built-in speakers. Then there was a ringing tone, and finally an unfamiliar voice that said: '*Allo? Allo?*'

'Hello?' I said in return, and realized that there was no way I could talk to this person, whoever he was.

My computer began to make shrill fax noises. '*Allo? Allo?*' the voice said again, with a touch of puzzlement and alarm. After a moment, he hung up. Instantly, my computer redialled his number.

And so it went for much of the morning, with my computer repeatedly pestering some unknown person in an unknown place while I searched furiously through the manual for a way to abort the operation. Eventually, in desperation, I unplugged the computer, which shut down with a series of Big Mistake! and Crisis in the Hard Drive! noises.

Three weeks later – this is true – we received a phone bill with $68 in charges for calls to Algiers. Subsequent enquiries revealed that the people who had written the software for the fax program had not considered the possibility of overseas transmissions. The program was designed to read American phone numbers only. Confronted with anything else, it went into nervous breakdown mode.

I also discovered that the electronic address book had a similar quirky aversion to non-American addresses, rendering it useless, and that the answering machine function had a habit of coming on in the middle of conversations.

For a long time it puzzled me how something so expensive, so leading edge, could be so useless, and then it occurred to me that a computer is a stupid machine with the ability to do incredibly smart things, while computer programmers are smart people with the ability to do incredibly stupid things. They are, in short, a dangerously perfect match.

You will have read about the millennium bug, I am sure. You know, then, that at the stroke of midnight on 1 January 2000, all the computers in the world will for some reason go through a thought process something like this: 'Well, here we are in a new year that ends in '00. I bet it's 1900. But if it's 1900, computers haven't been invented yet. Therefore I don't exist. Guess I had better shut down and wipe my memory clean.' The estimated cost to put this right is $200 trillion gazillion or some such preposterous sum. A computer, you see, can calculate pi to 20,000 places but it can't work out that time always moves forward. Programmers, meanwhile, can write 80,000 lines of complex code, but fail to note that every hundred years you get a new century. It's a disastrous combination.

When I first read that the computer industry had created a problem for itself so basic, so immense and so foolish, I suddenly understood why my fax facility and other digital toys are worthless. But this still doesn't adequately explain the wondrous – the towering – uselessness of my computer's spelling checker.

Like nearly everything else to do with computers, a spelling checker is marvellous in principle. When you have done a piece of work, you activate it and it goes through the text looking for words that are misspelled. Actually, since a computer doesn't understand what words are, it looks for letter clusters it isn't familiar with, and here is where the disappointment begins.

First, it doesn't recognize any proper nouns – names of people, places, corporations, and so on – or non-American spellings like *kerb* and *colour*. Nor does it recognize many plurals or variant forms (like *steps* or *stepped*), or abbreviations or acronyms. Nor, evidently, any word coined since Eisenhower was president. Thus, it recognizes *sputnik* and *beatnik*, but not *Internet*, *fax*, *cyberspace* or *butthead*, among many others.

But the really distinctive feature of my spelling checker – and here is the part that can provide hours of entertainment for anyone who doesn't have anything approaching a real life – is that it has been programmed to suggest alternatives. These are seldom less than memorable. For this column, for instance, for *Internet* it suggested *internat* (a word that I cannot find in any dictionary, British or American), *internode*, *interknit* and *underneath*. *Fax* prompted no fewer than thirty-three suggested alternatives, including *fab*, *fays*, *feats*, *fuzz*, *feaze*, *phase* and at least two more that are unknown to lexicography: *falx* and *phose*. *Cyberspace* drew a blank, but for *cyber* it came up with *chubbier* and *scabbier*.

I have tried without success to discern the logic by which a computer and programmer working in tandem could decide that someone who typed *f-a-x* would really have intended to write *p-h-a-s-e*, or why *cyber* might suggest *chubbier* and *scabbier*, but not, say, *watermelon* or *full-service petrol station*, to name two equally random alternatives. Still less can I explain how non-existent words like *phose* and *internat* would get into the program. Call me exacting, but I would submit that a computer program that wants to discard a real word in favour of one that does not exist is not ready to be offered for public use.

Not only does the system suggest imbecilic alternatives, it positively aches to put them in. You have to all but order the program not to insert the wrong word. If you accidentally accept its prompt, it automatically changes that word throughout the text. Thus, to my weary despair, I have in recent months produced work in which 'woollens' was changed throughout to 'wesleyans', 'Minneapolis' to 'monopolists' and – this is a particular favourite – 'Renoir' to 'rainware'. If there is a simple way to unpick these involuntary transformations, then I have not found it.

Now I read in *US News & World Report* that the same computer industry that failed to notice the coming of a new millennium has equally failed for years to realize that the materials on which it stores information – magnetic tapes and so forth – swiftly degrade. NASA scientists who recently tried to access material on the 1976 Viking mission to Mars discovered that 20 per cent of it has simply vanished and that the rest is going fast.

So it looks as if computer programmers will be putting in some late nights over the next couple of years. To which, frankly, I say hooray. Or *haywire*, *heroin* and *hoopskirt*, as my computer would prefer it.

HOTEL CALIFORNIA

IT WOULD BE HARD TO IMAGINE A MORE EVIL PIECE OF WORK THAN Robert Alton Harris. After a lifetime of vicious, random crime, in 1979 in California he murdered two teenaged boys in cold blood for their car. As he drove away, he finished off the cheeseburgers they had been eating.

He was arrested within hours, and confessed his guilt freely. Even so, it took the state of California thirteen years of complex and costly trials and retrials to exhaust all the legal possibilities necessary to put Harris to death.

There are almost 500 other people like Harris on death row in California. Altogether the state spends an estimated $90 million a year pursuing death penalty cases. Since 1967 it has spent $1 billion (over £600 million) on capital cases and executed exactly two people (Harris being one of them).

Now it seems to me evident from this, if nothing else, that the death penalty in America is madness. Think what California could have done with that $1 billion if it had spent it on, say, education.

Nearly everyone agrees that such a convoluted legal process is crazy, but the problem is that Americans love the death penalty. Polls consistently show that about three-quarters of them support capital punishment. Moreover, they want it – indeed, insist on it – for a very wide range of offences. Roughly half of Americans, for instance, would make it a capital offence to sell drugs to children. Already in the United States you can be put to death for more than fifty types of crime.

Quite apart from moral issues, there are, it seems to me, several practical considerations that make it difficult to defend. One is that it is inconsistently applied. Those sentenced to death are almost without exception male – only one woman has been put to death since 1962, though another is scheduled to die in Texas this month – and disproportionately poor and black, and their victims are overwhelmingly white. Of the approximately 360 people executed in the United States since 1977, 83 per cent had been convicted of killing a white person, even though white people represent only about half of all murder victims. Depending on the state, criminals are anywhere from four to eleven times more likely to be sentenced to death for killing a white person than a black person – hardly a ringing endorsement of the principle that justice is blind.

There is also a striking geographical disparity. Thirty-nine US states have the death penalty, but in only seventeen of them – mostly in the South – were people put to death last year. If you are going to murder someone in a state with the death penalty, you are much better off doing it in New Hampshire, where they have not executed anyone for decades, than in Texas or Florida, where people are dispatched with comparative enthusiasm. Texas alone last year executed thirty-seven people, as much as all the rest of the country put together.

Altogether in the United States there are about 3,000 people on death row. In 1997, seventy-four of them were executed, the highest number in forty years. Even so, the number added to death row each year outstrips by about four to one the number eliminated. (The leading cause of death on death row is actually natural causes.) To clear the backlog and deal with the rising number of new inmates, America would have to execute one person a day for twenty-five years. Because of the legal process, that is never going to happen.

The question is why they bother. On average, it takes ten years and five months to exhaust all the appeals processes necessary for execution. As a result, according to a study at Duke University, it costs $2 million more to execute a prisoner than to incarcerate him for life.

Of course, you could argue that convicted murderers shouldn't be allowed to appeal endlessly on frivolous technicalities. Congress, accepting this view with all its heart, in 1995 voted to abolish the $20 million of federal money that was being spent on assisting death row inmates with appeals. Almost overnight the average length of time from conviction to execution fell by eleven months.

This would be good news if you were confident that everyone put to death deserved it, but in fact this is not so. Consider the case of Dennis Williams of Chicago, who spent seventeen years on death row for a murder he vociferously claimed not to have committed for the very good reason that he hadn't. He was saved only because a journalism professor at the University of Chicago assigned his students to look into the case as a class project. They found, among other things, that the police had suppressed evidence, witnesses had lied, and that another man was prepared to confess to the crime if only someone would listen to him.

Like most death row inmates, Williams had been defended by a court-appointed lawyer. Illinois pays public defenders $40 an hour. The going rate for lawyers in private practice is $150 an hour. You don't have to be a genius to work out that the best lawyers are unlikely to be doing public work. Typically they are granted just $800 to prepare and present their defence in capital cases, so even the most dedicated lawyer will hardly be able to secure expert witnesses, independent forensic tests, or anything else that might prove his client's innocence.

Thanks to the students' school project, Williams was released last September. This is less unusual than you might expect. Since 1977, when Illinois reintroduced the death penalty, the state has executed eight people, but freed nine. Nationally in the last twenty-five years sixty-nine people convicted of murder have later been found to be innocent and freed. With federal funds for appeals curtailed, few of those people could expect such happy outcomes now.

It is one thing for a citizen to murder an innocent person, quite another for the state to do it. Yet amazingly even this is a minority view. According to a 1995 Gallup poll, 57 per cent of people in the United States would remain in favour of the death penalty even if it were found that one person in every hundred was wrongly executed.

I don't believe there is a politician in America – certainly none of any stature – who would stand up to such a weight of feeling. There used to be a time when politicians tried to change public opinion. Now they just respond to it, which is unfortunate because these things are not immutable.

Writing in the *New Yorker* in 1992, Richard L. Nygaard noted that West Germany outlawed the death penalty in 1949 even though 74 per cent of people approved of it. By 1980, the proportion in favour had slumped to 26 per cent. As Nygaard observes: 'Among people who don't grow up with it, capital punishment comes to be seen as a barbaric relic, like slavery or branding.'

Would that it were so here.

ENOUGH ALREADY

I HAVE FINALLY FIGURED OUT WHAT IS WRONG WITH EVERYTHING. THERE
is too much of it. I mean by that that there is too much of every
single thing that one could possibly want or need, except time,
money, good plumbers and people who say thank you when you
hold open a door for them. (And, entirely by the way, I would like
to put it on the record here that the next person who goes through
a door that I've held open and doesn't say 'Thank you' is going to
get it in the kidneys.)

America is of course a land of bounteous variety, and for a long
time after we first moved here I was dazzled and gratified by the
wealth of choice everywhere. I remember going to the supermarket
for the first time and being genuinely impressed to find that it
stocked no fewer than eighteen varieties of incontinence nappy.
Two or three I could understand. Half a dozen would seem to
cover every possible incontinence contingency. But eighteen –
gosh! This *was* a land of plenty. Some were scented, some were
dimpled for extra comfort, and they came in a whole range of
strengths from, as it were, 'Oops, bit of a dribble' to 'Whoa!
Dambusters!' Those weren't the labels they actually used,
of course, but that was the gist of it. They even came in a choice of
colours.

For nearly every other type of product – frozen pizzas, dog food,
ice creams, biscuits, crisps – the choices were often literally in the
hundreds. Every new flavour seemed to have pupped another flavour.
When I was a boy shredded wheat was shredded wheat and that was
it. Now you could have it coated in sugar, in bite-sized morsels, with

slices of genuine banana-like material, and goodness knows what else. I couldn't have been more impressed.

Lately, however, I have come to realize that you can get too much choice. I had this brought home to me the other week when I was at an airport in Portland, Oregon, standing in a queue of about fifteen people at a coffee stand. It was 5.45 a.m., not my best time of day, and I had just twenty minutes till my flight was to be called, but I really, really needed to get some caffeine into my system. You know how it is.

It used to be if you wanted a cup of coffee that's what you asked for and that's what you got. But this place, being a 1990s coffee stand, offered twenty choices – espresso, latte, caramel latte, breve, macchiato, mocha, espresso mocha, Black Forest mocha, Americano, and goodness knows what else – in four different sizes. There was also a galaxy of muffins, croissants, bagels and pastries. All of these could be had in any number of variations, so that every order went something like this:

'I'll have a caramel latte combo with decaf mocha and a cinnamon twist, and a low-fat cream cheese sourdough bagel, but I'd like the pimiento grated and on the side. Are your poppyseeds roasted in polyunsaturated vegetable oil?'

'No, we use double-extra-lite canola extract.'

'Oh, that's no good for me. In that case, I'll have a New York three-cheese pumpernickel fudge croissant. What kind of emulsifiers do you use in that?'

In my mind's eye, I saw myself taking hold of each customer by the ears, shaking his or her head thirty or forty times and saying: 'You're just trying to get a cup of coffee and a bread product before your flight. Now ask for something simple and clear off.'

Fortunately for all these people, until I have had my first cup of coffee in the morning (and this is particularly true during hours in single figures) all I can do is rise, dress myself (a bit) and ask for a cup of coffee. Anything else is beyond me. So I just stood and waited stoically while fifteen people placed complex, time-consuming and preposterously individualized orders.

When at last my turn came, I stepped up and said: 'I'd like a large cup of coffee.'

'What kind?'

'Hot and in a cup and very large.'

'Yeah, but what kind – mocha, macchiato, what?'

'I want whichever one is a normal cup of coffee.'

'You want Americano?'

'If that means a normal cup of coffee, then yes.'

'Well, they're all coffees.'

'I want a normal cup of coffee like millions of people drink every day.'

'So you want an Americano?'

'Evidently.'

'Do you want low-cal whipped cream or regular with that?'

'I don't want whipped cream.'

'But it comes with whipped cream.'

'Look,' I said in a low voice, 'it is 6.10 a.m. I have been standing for twenty-five minutes behind fifteen seriously indecisive people, and my flight is being called. If I don't get some coffee right now, I am going to murder someone, and I think you should know that you are extremely high on my list.' (I am not, as you will gather, a morning person.)

'So does that mean you want low-cal whipped cream or regular?'

And so it went.

This abundance of choice not only makes every transaction take ten times as long as it ought to, but in a strange way actually breeds dissatisfaction. The more there is, the more people crave, and the more they crave, the more they, well, crave more. You have a sense in America of being among millions and millions of people needing more and more of everything, constantly, infinitely, unquenchably. We appear to have created a society in which the principal activity is grazing through retail establishments looking for things – textures, shapes, flavours – not before encountered.

And it applies to everything. You can now choose, apparently, among thirty-five varieties of Crest toothpaste. According to *The Economist*, 'the average supermarket in America devotes 20 feet of shelving to medicine for coughs and colds'. Yet of the 25,500 'new' consumer products launched in the United States last year, 93 per cent were merely modified versions of existing products.

The last time I went for breakfast, I had to choose among nine options for my eggs (poached, scrambled, sunny side up, over easy, and so on), sixteen types of pancake, six varieties of juice, two shapes of sausage, four kinds of potato and eight varieties of toast or muffin. I have taken out mortgages that involved less decision-making than that. I thought I had finished when the waitress said: 'Do you want whipped butter, pat butter, margarine, butter–margarine blend or butter substitute?'

'You're joking,' I said.

'I don't joke about butter.'

'Then pat butter,' I said weakly.

'Low-sodium, no-sodium or regular?'

'Surprise me,' I answered in a whisper.

To my astonishment, my wife and children love all this. They love going into an ice cream parlour and being able to choose among seventy-five flavours of ice cream, and then seventy-five types of topping to put on that ice cream.

I can't tell you how I long to go to England and just have a nice cup of tea and a simple bun, but I'm afraid I am the only person in the house who feels that way. I trust that my wife and kids will eventually grow sated by all this, but there is no sign of it happening yet.

Still, looking on the bright side, at least I am well fixed for incontinence nappies.

STUPIDITY NEWS

I WOULD LIKE TO SAY A FEW WORDS ABOUT STUPIDITY IN AMERICA.
Now before I go a single word further, let me make it categoric-
ally clear that Americans are not inherently more simple than other
people. America has the largest economy, the most comfortably off
people, the best research facilities, many of the finest universities
and think-tanks, and more Nobel Prize winners than the rest of the
world put together. You don't get all that by being stupid.

Even so, you do sometimes wonder. Consider this. According to
an opinion poll, 13 per cent of women in the United States cannot
say whether they wear their tights under their knickers or over
them. That's something like 12 million women walking around in
a state of chronic foundation garment uncertainty. Perhaps because
I so seldom wear ladies' clothing I don't fully appreciate the
challenges involved, but I am almost certain that if I did wear tights
with knickers I would know which was on top. More to the point,
if a stranger with a clipboard came up to me in the street and asked
how my underwear was configured, I don't believe that I would tell
him that I didn't know.

Which raises another interesting point: why were they asking?
How did anyone think up such a question, and what were they
hoping to do with the data? You see, all this points to a much larger
kind of dumbness, not just among the 13 per cent of women who
are underwear underaware, to coin a nifty phrase, but among those
who set and disseminate public opinion polls.

One thing is certain, and that is that there is an awful lot of
dumbness about. I know this for a fact because a friend in New

York recently sent me a collection of stupid quotes made by notable Americans in 1997. Here, for instance, is the actress Brooke Shields, without any help from grown-ups, explaining to an interviewer why you shouldn't smoke: 'Smoking kills. If you're killed, you've lost a very important part of your life.'

Well said, Brooke. And here is the singer Mariah Carey getting to the heart of Third World troubles: 'Whenever I watch TV and see those poor starving kids all over the world, I can't help but cry. I mean I'd love to be skinny like that, but not with all those flies and death and stuff.'

Whatever is the stage beyond the mind boggling is the stage I reach each time I read that quotation. My favourite, however, was the answer Miss Alabama gave in a Miss Universe contest when asked if she would choose to live for ever: 'I would not live for ever, because we should not live for ever, because if we were supposed to live for ever then we would live for ever, but we cannot live for ever, which is why I would not live for ever.'

Call me unkind, but I would bet good money that Miss Alabama not only would not know whether her tights were under or over her pants, but would not be entirely certain which limbs to insert in the holes.

So where does all this dumbness come from? I have no idea, but I am certain – quite seriously certain – that there is something in modern American life that is acting to suppress thought, even among more or less normal people. I was reminded of this yesterday while waiting behind a man who was speaking on a payphone. The man – middle-aged, well dressed, probably a lawyer or accountant by the look of him – was obviously talking to a colleague's or client's small child, and he said: 'So when do you expect your mommy to be out of the shower, honey?'

Now think about that for a minute. When you find yourself asking a three-year-old how long an adult will take to complete an activity, it is time to invest in a new brain. And anyway, how long does *anybody* spend in the shower?

America has no monopoly on imbecility, goodness knows, but there is at least one factor that seems to exist here in greater measure than elsewhere, to wit the habit among newspapers, periodicals and broadcasters of always stating the extremely obvious. We have already seen in this space how the *Washington Post* will inform its readers without embarrassment that Scotland 'is north of England' or how columnists will tell a joke and then explain the punchline. The idea – well intentioned, I'm sure – is to spare readers having to grapple with challenging or unfamiliar notions (like just where the heck Scotland is), but it has the powerful and insidious effect of lobotomizing the audience.

The unfortunate side of all this is that it is relatively easy to prey on people who have lost the power of thought. Once or twice a week, like nearly every household in the nation, we receive a letter from a magazine subscription company saying something like 'Congratulations, Mr W. Bryson. You Have Won $5 Million!' Just above this promising statement, in much smaller letters, it says: 'If your sweepstakes number matches the prize draw number, then we will say to you . . .' You don't have to be terribly on the ball to work out that you haven't actually won $5 million. Unfortunately, lots of people are not terribly on the ball.

The papers carried a story recently about a man called Richard Lusk who flew from California to Florida clutching a prize letter telling him, as he understood it, that he had won $11 million and had just five days to claim his prize. The company showed him the fine print and sent him home. Three months later Mr Lusk received another, essentially identical letter, and flew to Florida again, just as happy and expectant as he had been the first time. According to the Associated Press, at least twenty other people have flown to Florida in the past four years in the same ecstatic but mistaken belief.

That's a rather depressing thought, so let's finish with the story of my favourite dumb person of the moment – namely, a would-be robber in Texas who covered his face with a balaclava in order to rob a grocery store, but forgot to remove from his breast pocket the clip-on badge that bore his photograph, name and place of employment, which were duly noted by something like twelve witnesses.

I am sure there is a moral in this somewhere, and I will let you know as soon as it occurs to me. Now if you will excuse me, I am going to go and check my underwear in case anyone starts asking questions.

SPINNING THE TRUTH

ONE OF THE THINGS YOU GRADUALLY GET USED TO IN AMERICA IS THE extent to which corporations and other big businesses lie to you. Actually, I was lying myself just then. You never get used to it.

A couple of years ago, when we were still new to the country, we were driving across Michigan looking for a place to stay when we passed a big hoarding for a national motel chain advertising a very attractive special offer. I don't recall the details, but it included free lodging for the children and breakfast vouchers for all the family for a deeply gratifying all-in price of something like $35.

Naturally, by the time I had read all this I had sailed past the exit, and had to drive fifteen miles on, then fifteen miles back, then hunt around on slip roads for half an hour while everyone in the car pointed out vastly more accessible motels with better facilities. So the exasperation was considerable. But never mind. For $35 and a free cooked breakfast, you can exasperate me all you want.

So imagine my countenance, then, when I checked us in and the clerk slid me a bill that came to something like $149.95.

'What about the special offer?' I whinnied.

'Ah,' he said suavely, 'that only applies to a selected number of rooms.'

'How many rooms?'

'Two.'

'And how many rooms are there in the motel?'

'One hundred and five.'

'But that's fraud,' I said.

'No, sir, that's America.'

Actually, in truth I don't believe he said that, but he might as well
have. And this was a large, well-known corporation whose
executive officers, I am sure, would be hurt and dismayed to find
themselves described as scoundrels and cheats. They were simply
following the fluid moral rules of commerce in the United States.

I have just been reading a book called *Tainted Truth: The
Manipulation of Fact in America*, which is full of arresting stories
of misleading claims by advertisers, distorted scientific studies,
skewed opinion polls and so on – what, anywhere else, would be
called fraud.

Nearly all car advertisements, for instance, boast safety features,
such as side-impact bars, which are required by law anyway.
Chevrolet once advertised a car with '109 advantages designed to
keep it from becoming old before its time'. When looked into by an
automotive journalist, these special advantages turned out to
include rear-view mirrors, reversing lights, balanced wheels and
other such features that were in fact standard on all cars.

What is astonishing to me is not that commercial enterprises try
to spin the truth in their favour, but the extent to which they are
allowed to get away with it. Food manufacturers can place nothing
or next to nothing of a particular ingredient in a product and still
pretend that it is there in abundance. One large and well-known
food company, to take a nearly random example, sells 'blueberry
waffles' which have never seen a blueberry. The blueberry-like
chunks it contains are really just clumps of flavoured chemicals,
entirely artificial, though you could spend half a day studying the
packet without realizing it.

If it isn't possible to cheat on the contents, then the manufacturers often distort the serving sizes. A popular type of low-fat
chocolate cake boasts a modest 70 calories per portion. But the
suggested portion is one ounce – a size that is physically almost
impossible to cut.

The most irksome of deceits to me, because the most inescapable,
is junk mail. Every person in America receives on average 34
pounds – 500 pieces – of unsolicited mail each year. Because there
is so much of it, senders resort to the basest tricks to get you to look
inside. They design the envelopes to look as if they contain a prize
cheque or vital government documents, or have been delivered by
special courier, or could even get you in trouble if you don't give
them your serious attention. Today, for instance, I received an
envelope marked 'Documents Enclosed For Addressee Only . . .

$2,000 Fine or 5 Years Imprisonment for Any Person Who Tampers or Obstructs Delivery; US Code Title 18, Sec. 1702.' This was something important, clearly. In fact, it contained an invitation to test drive a car in the next town.

To my despair, even quite worthwhile organizations have taken to these ruses. I recently received an official-looking envelope bearing the message 'Cheque Enclosed'. It turned out to be a letter from the Cystic Fibrosis Foundation, a leading charity, asking for a donation. There wasn't any cheque enclosed – just a piece of paper in the form of a facsimile cheque showing what a $10 donation made by me to the foundation would look like. When even decent, well-meaning charities feel compelled to lie to you to get your attention, you know there is something wrong with the system.

It begins to feel as if you can trust no-one. Cynthia Crossen, author of the aforementioned *Tainted Truth*, points out in her book just how many supposedly scientific studies are in fact shams. She notes one study, widely reported in the nation's press, which claimed that eating white bread helps promote weight loss. The 'study' on which this claim was based involved 118 subjects for two months and actually found no evidence to support the claim, but the researchers said they believed the assertions would have been corroborated 'if the study had continued'. The work was funded by the nation's largest manufacturer of white bread. Another study – again faithfully and unquestioningly reported in newspapers – asserted that eating chocolate actually reduces tooth decay. That study, you won't be surprised to hear, was deeply dubious and paid for by a leading maker of chocolate.

Even reports in the most respected medical journals may be suspect, it seems. Last year, according to the *Boston Globe*, two universities, Tufts and UCLA, looked into the financial interests of the authors of 789 articles in leading medical journals, and found that in 34 per cent of cases at least one of the authors had an undeclared financial interest in the success of the report. In one typical case a researcher who had tested the efficacy of a new cold treatment owned several thousand shares in the company that manufactured it. Upon publication of the report, the shares soared and he sold them at a profit of $145,000. I'm not saying that the man performed bad science, but it must have crept through his mind that a negative report would have rendered the shares worthless.

The most striking example of this sort of thing came in 1986 when the *New England Journal of Medicine* simultaneously received two reports on a new type of antibiotic. One report claimed that the drug was effective, the other that it was not. The positive report, it turned out, came from a researcher whose lab had received $1.6 million from the pharmaceutical industry, and who had personally received $75,000 a year from the companies involved. The negative report came from an independent researcher who had not been funded by the pharmaceutical companies.

So who can you trust and believe? Only me, I'm afraid, and then only up to a point.

FOR YOUR CONVENIENCE

OUR TOPIC THIS WEEK IS A FEATURE OF MODERN LIFE THAT REALLY GETS up my nasal passages, namely the way corporations do things to make life easy for themselves and then pretend it's for your benefit. You can usually tell this is happening when the phrase 'for your convenience' or 'in order to provide a better service for our customers' appears somewhere in writing.

For example, I was recently in a big hotel when I went to get ice, and I traipsed around miles of corridors (possibly, I see now, in a large continuous circle) without finding any. It used to be that there was an ice machine on every floor of every hotel in America. I think it was guaranteed in the Constitution, just above the right to bear arms and below the right to shop till we drop. But there was nothing on the eighteenth floor of this hotel. Finally, I found an alcove where an ice machine clearly had once stood, and on the wall was a sign that said: 'For your convenience, ice machines are now located on floors 2 and 27.' You see my point, of course.

My objection isn't to the removal of ice machines *per se*, but to the pretence that it was done with my happiness in mind. If the sign had said something honest like 'What do you want ice for anyway? Your beverage is already chilled. Go back to your room and stop wandering around semi-public areas in inappropriate attire,' I would have no problem with the situation.

Of course, this is not a strictly American phenomenon. Residents of Skipton, North Yorkshire, may recall the morning a couple of years back when an anonymous and unassuming American-born journalist, in a hurry to catch a train, was to be seen hurling himself bodily at the door of the High Street branch of a leading bank and shouting vivid sentiments through the letter slot with regard to a notice in the window that said: 'In order to provide a better service, the bank will open forty-five minutes later on Mondays for staff training.' (The same bank later made thousands of employees redundant and claimed without evident irony that it was 'to provide a better service to our customers'. One awaits the day when it sacks everyone and stops handling money altogether, at which point its service should be impeccable.)

Still, like most things, good and bad, corporate hypocrisy exists in greater measure here than in most other places. I was in another hotel, in New York City, when I noticed that the room service menu said: 'For your convenience, a charge of 17½ per cent will be added to all orders.'

Curiosity aroused, I called room service and asked in what way it would be convenient to me to have 17½ per cent added to my room service charge.

There was a long silence. 'Because it guarantees that you will get your food before next Thursday.' That may not be the precise form of words the man used, but that was clearly the drift of his sentiment.

There is a simple explanation for why this happens. Most big companies don't like you very much, except for hotels, airlines and Microsoft, which don't like you at all.

I think – though this is a very tough call – hotels may be the worst. (Actually, Microsoft is the worst, but if I started on them I would never finish.) A couple of years ago, I arrived at about 2 p.m. at a large hotel in Kansas City, of all places, having flown in from Fiji, of all other places. Fiji, as you will appreciate, is a long way from Kansas City and I was tired and keenly eager for a shower and a little lie-down.

'Check-in time is four p.m.,' the clerk informed me serenely.

I looked at him with that pained, helpless expression I often wear at check-in desks. 'Four p.m.? Why?'

'It's company policy.'

'Why?'

'Because it is.' He realized this was a trifle inadequate. 'The cleaners need time to clean the rooms.'

'Are you saying that they don't finish cleaning any of the rooms until four p.m.?'

'No, I am saying the rooms are not available until four p.m.'

'Why?'

'Because it's company policy.'

At this point I poked him in the eyes with two forked fingers and stalked off to pass a delightful two hours at a shopping mall food court across the road.

Another place to seek out this sort of thing, if you are looking to torment yourself, is airline magazines. Airline magazines nearly always carry a column from a smiling chief executive explaining how something that cannot possibly be considered an improvement – making you change planes in Cleveland when flying from New York to Miami, say – has been done to provide a better service. My favourite in this vein was a chairman's letter explaining, quite earnestly, that overbooking (which happens on nearly every flight here) was actually a good thing. The logic, as he explained it, was that by making sure all flights were full the airline would maximize its earnings, which would allow it to thrive, which in turn would enable it to offer more and better services. He really appeared to believe this.

I have long suspected that the people who run America's airlines have completely lost touch with reality, and I believe I have now had this confirmed. It was in a report in the *New York Times* investigating how infrequently airlines serve food on domestic flights these days and how much paltrier that food is compared with yore. In the course of the article, an official of Delta Airlines, one Cindy Reeds, is quoted as saying: 'The public asked us to eliminate the food.'

Excuse me? The customers *asked* not to be fed? Frankly, I find that a little hard to, uh, swallow.

A little further on in the article, Ms Reeds explains the airline's interesting line of reasoning: 'About a year and a half ago,' she says, 'we took a survey of a thousand passengers . . . and they said they wanted lower fares, so we got rid of the meals.'

Well, hold on a minute, Cindy. If you say to passengers, 'Would you like lower fares?' and they reply, 'Yes, we certainly would' (which is pretty much what you would expect them to say, is it not?) that is not actually the same as their saying: 'Yes, we certainly would, and please stop serving us food while you are at it.'

But try explaining this, or anything else, to an airline. At least she did not claim that the airline had stopped serving food as a convenience to customers – though perhaps on reflection she should have.

Anyway, in an attempt to provide a better service, I'm stopping here.

OLD NEWS

'SCIENCE FINDS THE SECRET OF AGEING,' ANNOUNCED A HEADLINE IN our paper the other day, which surprised me because I've never thought of it as a secret. It just happens. No secret in that.

As far as I am concerned, there are three good things about getting older. I can sleep sitting up, I can watch *Morse* repeats over and over without knowing how they are going to finish, and I can't remember the third thing. That's the problem with getting older, of course – you can't remember anything.

For me, it's getting worse. Increasingly I have telephone conversations with my wife that go like this:

'Hello, dear. I'm in town. Why am I here?'

'You've gone to get your hair cut.'

'Thank you.'

You would think that as I get older this would get better because there is less of my mind to grow absent, but it doesn't seem to work that way. You know how as the years tick by you find yourself more and more standing in some part of the house you don't often visit – the laundry area, perhaps – looking around with pursed lips and a thoughtful gaze, trying to remember why you are there? It used to be with me that if I retraced my steps to where I began, the purpose of my exploration would come back to me. No more. Now I can't remember where I began. No idea at all.

So I wander through the house for twenty minutes looking for some sign of recent activity – a lifted floorboard, perhaps, or a burst pipe, or maybe a telephone receiver on its side and a curious little voice squawking: '*Bill? You still there?*' – something that might have prompted me to get up and go off in search of a notepad or stopcock or goodness knows what. Usually in the course of these wanderings I find some other thing that needs attending to – a lightbulb that's burned out, say – so I go off to the kitchen cupboard where the lightbulbs are kept and open the door and . . . yes, that's right, have no idea why I am there. So the process starts again.

Time is my particular downfall. Once something moves into the past tense, I lose all track of it. My sincerest dread in life is to be arrested and asked: 'Where were you between the hours of 8.50 a.m. and 11.02 a.m. on the morning of December the eleventh?' When this happens, I will just hold out my wrists for the handcuffs and let them take me away because there isn't the remotest chance of my recalling. It has been like this for me for as long as I can remember, which of course is not very long.

My wife does not have this problem. She can remember everything that ever happened and when. I mean every little detail. Out of the blue she will say things to me like: 'It was sixteen years ago Sunday your grandmother died.'

'Really?' I reply, amazed. 'I had a grandmother?'

The other thing that happens a lot these days is that when I am out with my wife somebody I would swear I have never seen before comes up and chats with us in a friendly and familiar fashion.

'Who was that?' I will ask when he has departed.

'That was Lottie Rhubarb's husband.'

I think for a moment, but nothing comes.

'Who's Lottie Rhubarb?'

'You met her at the Talmadges' barbecue at Big Bear Lake.'

'I've never been to Big Bear Lake.'

'Yes, you have. For the Talmadges' barbecue.'

I think again for a minute. 'So who are the Talmadges?'

'The people on Park Street who had the barbecue for the Skowolskis.'

By now I am beginning to feel desperate. 'Who are the Skowolskis?'

'The Polish couple you met at the barbecue at Big Bear Lake.'

'I didn't go to a barbecue at Big Bear Lake.'

'Of course you did. You sat on a skewer.'

'I sat on a *skewer*?'

We have had conversations like this that have gone on for three days, and I have still been none the wiser at the end.

I have always been absent-minded, I'm afraid. When I was a boy

I had an afternoon newspaper round in the wealthiest neighbourhood in town, which sounds like a plum assignment but was not
because, in the first place, wealthy people are the biggest skinflints
at Christmas (especially, let the record show, Mr and Mrs Arthur J.
Niedermeyer of 27 St John's Road, Dr and Mrs Richard Gumbel in
the big brick house on Lincoln Place and Mr and Mrs Samuel
Drinkwater of the Drinkwater banking fortune; I hope you are all
in nursing homes now) and because every house was set back a
quarter of a mile from the street at the end of a long, curving drive.

Even in hypothetically ideal circumstances, it would take hours
to complete such a round, but I never got to such a point. My problem was that while my legs did the round, my mind would be in
that state of total vacant reverie that characterizes all absent-
minded people.

Without fail, at the end of the round I would look into my bag
and, with a sigh, find half a dozen papers left over, each representing a house I had visited – a long drive I had trudged up, a porch I
had crossed, a screened door I had opened – without actually
leaving a newspaper behind. Needless to say, I would have no
recollection of which of the eighty properties on my route these
were, so I would sigh again and walk the route a second time. By
such means did I pass my childhood. I wonder whether the
Niedermeyers, Gumbels and Drinkwaters, had they known what
hell I went through every day to get them their stupid *Des Moines
Tribune*, would have been quite so happy to stiff me at Christmas.
Probably.

Anyway, you are probably wondering about this secret of ageing
I alluded to in the opening paragraph. According to the newspaper
account, it appears that a Dr Gerard Schellenberg at the Seattle
Veterans Administration Medical Research Center has isolated the
genetic culprit behind ageing. It seems that embedded in each gene
is something called a helicase, which is part of a family of enzymes,
and that this helicase, for no good reason that I can see, peels apart
the two strands of chromosomes that make up your DNA, and the
next thing you know you are standing at the kitchen cupboard trying to remember what the dickens brought you there. I can't give
you any more details because naturally I have mislaid the article,
and anyhow it hardly matters because in a week or two somebody
else will come along and uncover some other secret of ageing, and
everyone will forget about Dr Schellenberg and his findings – which
is, of course, precisely what I have begun to do already.

So in conclusion we can see that forgetfulness is probably not such a bad thing after all. I believe that's the point I was trying to make, but to tell you the truth I don't remember now.

SENSE OF HUMOUR FAILURE

HERE'S MY TIP OF THE WEEK. DON'T MAKE JOKES IN AMERICA. EVEN IN experienced hands – and I believe I speak with some authority here – a joke can be a dangerous thing.

I came to this conclusion recently while passing through Customs and Immigration at Logan Airport in Boston. As I approached the last immigration official, he said to me: 'Any fruit or vegetables?'

I considered for a moment. 'Sure, why not,' I said. 'I'll have four pounds of potatoes and some mangoes if they're fresh.'

Instantly, I could see that I had misjudged my audience and that this was not a man who ached for banter. He looked at me with one of those slow, dark, cerebrally challenged expressions that you never want to see in a uniformed official, but especially in a US Customs and Immigration officer because, believe me, these people have powers you really do not want to put to the test. If I just mention the words 'strip search' and 'rubber gloves' I think you will latch on to my meaning. When I say they have the legal right to interrupt your passage I mean it in every possible sense.

Luckily, this man appeared to conclude that I was just incredibly thick. 'Sir,' he enquired more specifically, 'are you carrying any items of a fruit or vegetable nature?'

'No, sir, I am not,' I answered at once and fed him the most respectful and grovelling look I believe I have ever mustered.

'Then keep moving, please,' he said.

I left him shaking his head. I am sure that for the rest of his career he will be telling people about the knucklehead who thought he was a greengrocer.

So take it from me, never joke with an authority in America, and when you fill in your landing card, under the question 'Have you ever been a member of the Communist Party or employed irony in a public situation?' tick 'No'.

Irony is, of course, the key word here. Americans don't use it much. (I'm being ironic; they don't use it at all.) In most circumstances this is actually rather a nice thing. Irony is cousin to cynicism, and cynicism is not a virtuous emotion. Americans – not all of them, but a significant proportion – have no need for either one. Their approach to everyday encounters is trusting, straightforward, almost touchingly literal. They don't expect any verbal sleight of hand in conversations, so it tends to throw them when you employ it.

We have a neighbour on whom I tested this hypothesis for the first two years we were here. It began innocently enough. Soon after we moved in, he had a tree come down in his front garden. I passed his house one morning to see that he was cutting the tree into smaller pieces and loading them onto the roof of his car to take away to the tip. It was a bushy tree and the branches were hanging over the sides in an extravagant manner.

'Ah, I see you're camouflaging your car,' I remarked drily.

He looked at me for a moment. 'No,' he said emphatically. 'I had a tree come down in the storm the other night and now I'm taking it away for disposal.'

After that, I couldn't stop myself from making little jokes with him. The crunch, so to speak, came when I was telling him one day about some disastrous airline trip I'd had, which had left me stranded overnight in Denver.

'Who did you fly with?' he asked.

'I don't know,' I replied. 'They were all strangers.'

He looked at me with an expression that betrayed a kind of panic. 'No, I meant which airline did you fly with.'

It was just after this that my wife ordered me to cease making jokes with him because apparently our chats were leaving him with migraine.

The easy conclusion to draw from this, and one to which even the most astute outside observers are all too often tempted, is that Americans are constitutionally incapable of getting a joke. I have just been reading *In the Land of Oz* by your own Howard Jacobson, a man of intelligence and discernment, who notes in passing that 'Americans don't have a sense of humour.' It would be but an afternoon's work to find thirty or forty comments in a similar vein in modern works.

I can understand the sentiment, but it is actually quite wrong. As even a moment's reflection should remind us, many of the very funniest people who have ever lived – the Marx Brothers, W.C. Fields, S.J. Perelman, Robert Benchley, Woody Allen, Dorothy Parker, James Thurber, Mark Twain – were or are Americans. Moreover, and just as obviously, they could not have achieved their fame if they had not found a large and appreciative following in their own land. So it's not as if we can't generate or relish a droll jape over here.

But it is certainly true that wit is not as venerated a quality here as it is in Britain. John Cleese once said: 'An Englishman would rather be told he was a bad lover than that he had no sense of humour.' (Which is probably just as well, all things considered.) I don't think there are many Americans who would subscribe to that view. Humour here is like good driving skills or having a nose for wine or being able to pronounce *feuilleton* correctly – commendable, worthy of admiration, but not actually vital.

It isn't that there are no people with an active sense of humour in America, just far fewer. When you encounter one it's a little as I imagine it must be when two Masons recognize each other across a crowded room. The last time I experienced this was a few weeks ago when I arrived at our local airport and approached a cab for a ride home.

'Are you free?' I innocently asked the driver.

He looked at me with an expression I recognized at once – the look of someone who knows a good straight line when it's handed to him.

'No,' he said with mock sincerity, 'I charge just like everyone else.'

I could almost have hugged him, but that, of course, would have been taking the joke too far.

THE ACCIDENTAL TOURIST

OF ALL THE THINGS I AM NOT VERY GOOD AT, LIVING IN THE REAL WORLD is perhaps the most outstanding. I am constantly filled with wonder at the number of things that other people do without any evident difficulty that are pretty much beyond me. I cannot tell you the number of times that I have gone looking for the lavatory in a cinema, for instance, and ended up standing in an alley on the wrong side of a self-locking door. My particular speciality now is returning to hotel desks two or three times a day and asking what my room number is. I am, in short, easily confused.

I was thinking about this the last time we went *en famille* on a big trip. It was at Easter, and we were flying to England for a week. When we arrived at Logan Airport in Boston and were checking in, I suddenly remembered that I had recently joined British Airways' frequent flyer programme. I also remembered that I had put the card in the carry-on bag that was hanging around my neck. And here's where the trouble started.

The zip on the bag was jammed. So I pulled on it and yanked at it, with grunts and frowns and increasing consternation. I kept this up for some minutes but it wouldn't budge, so I pulled harder and harder, with more grunts. Well, you can guess what happened. Abruptly the zip gave way. The side of the bag flew open and every-thing within – newspaper cuttings and other loose papers, a fourteen-ounce tin of pipe tobacco, magazines, passport, English money, film – was extravagantly ejected over an area about the size of a tennis court.

I watched dumbstruck as a hundred carefully sorted documents

came raining down in a fluttery cascade, coins bounced to a variety of
noisy oblivions and the now-lidless tin of tobacco rolled crazily across
the concourse disgorging its contents as it went.

'My tobacco!' I cried in horror, thinking what I would have to
pay for that much tobacco in England now that another Budget had
come and gone, and then changed the cry to 'My finger! My finger!'
as I discovered that I had gashed my finger on the zip and was
shedding blood in a lavish manner. (I am not very good around
flowing blood generally, but when it's my own – well, I think
hysterics are fully justified.) Confused and unable to help, my hair
went into panic mode.

It was at this point that my wife looked at me with an expression
of wonder – not anger or exasperation, but just simple wonder –
and said: 'I can't believe you do this for a living.'

But I'm afraid it's so. I always have catastrophes when I travel.
Once on an aeroplane, I leaned over to tie a shoelace just at the
moment someone in the seat ahead of me threw his seat back into full
recline, and found myself pinned helplessly in the crash position. It
was only by clawing the leg of the man sitting next to me that I
managed to get myself freed.

On another occasion, I knocked a soft drink onto the lap of a
sweet little lady sitting beside me. The flight attendant came and
cleaned her up, and brought me a replacement drink, and instantly
I knocked it onto the woman again. To this day, I don't know how
I did it. I just remember reaching out for the new drink and watching helplessly as my arm, like some cheap prop in one of those
1950s horror movies with a name like *The Undead Limb*, violently
swept the drink from its perch and onto her lap.

The lady looked at me with the stupefied expression you would
expect to receive from someone whom you have repeatedly
drenched, and uttered an oath that started with 'Oh', finished with
'sake' and in between had some words that I have never heard
uttered in public before, certainly not by a nun.

This, however, was not my worst experience on a plane flight.
My worst experience was when I was writing important thoughts
in a notebook ('Buy socks', 'clutch drinks carefully', etc.), sucking
thoughtfully on the end of my pen as you do, and fell into conversation with an attractive young lady in the next seat. I amused
her for perhaps twenty minutes with a scattering of urbane *bons
mots*, then retired to the lavatory where I discovered that the pen
had leaked and that my mouth, chin, tongue, teeth and gums were

now a striking, scrub-resistant navy blue, and would remain so for several days.

So you will understand, I trust, when I tell you how much I ache to be suave. I would love just once in my life to rise from a dinner table without looking as if I have just experienced an extremely localized seismic event, get in a car and close the door without leaving fourteen inches of coat outside, wear light-coloured trousers without discovering at the end of the day that I have at various times sat in chewing gum, ice cream, cough syrup and motor oil. But it is not to be.

Now on planes when the food is delivered, my wife says: 'Take the lids off the food for Daddy' or 'Put your hoods up, children. Daddy's about to cut his meat.' Of course, this is only when I am flying with my family. When I am on my own, I don't eat, drink or lean over to tie my shoelaces, and never put a pen anywhere near my mouth. I just sit very, very quietly, sometimes on my hands to keep them from flying out unexpectedly and causing liquid mischief. It's not much fun, but it does at least cut down on the laundry bills.

I never did get my frequent flyer miles, by the way. I never do. I couldn't find the card in time. This has become a real frustration for me. Everyone I know – everyone – is forever flying off to Bali first class with their air miles. I never get to collect anything. I must fly 100,000 miles a year, yet I have accumulated only about 212 air miles divided between twenty-three airlines.

This is because either I forget to ask for the air miles when I check in, or I remember to ask for them but the airline then manages not to record them, or the check-in clerk informs me that I am not entitled to them. In January, on a flight to Australia for this esteemed publication – a flight for which I was going to get about a zillion air miles – the clerk shook her head when I presented my card and told me I was not entitled to any.

'Why?'

'The ticket is in the name of B. Bryson and the card is in the name of W. Bryson.'

I explained to her the close and venerable relationship between Bill and William, but she wouldn't have it.

So I didn't get my air miles, and I won't be flying to Bali first class just yet. Perhaps just as well, really. I could never go that long without eating.

WHAT MAKES AN ENGLISHMAN

I SEEM TO HAVE BEEN A LITTLE HARD ON MY FELLOW AMERICANS LATELY. In recent weeks I have accused them of lying in their adverts, not knowing whether their tights were on top of their knickers or underneath them, and being unable to recognize a joke if you put it in a sheep's bladder and hit them over the head with it. All true, of course, but a little harsh none the less.

So I thought it might be a good time to point out some nice things about my dear old nation. I have a timely reason for this, too, for today marks the third anniversary of our move to the States.

It occurs to me that I have never explained in this space why we took this momentous step and that you might wonder how we decided on it. Me, too.

What I mean by that is that I honestly don't recall how or when we decided to transfer countries. What I can tell you is that we were living in a fairly out-of-the-way village in the Yorkshire Dales and, beautiful though it was and much as I enjoyed having conversations in the pub that I couldn't begin to understand ('Been tupping sheep up on Windy Poop and it were that mucky at sinkhole I couldn't cross beck. Haven't known it this barmish since last back end o' wittering, and mine's a Tetley's if you're thinking of offering'), it was becoming increasingly impractical, as the children grew and my work took me further afield, for us to live in an isolated spot.

So we took the decision to move somewhere a little more urban and built-up. And then – this is the part that gets hazy – somehow this simple concept evolved into the notion of settling in America for a time.

Everything seemed to move very swiftly. Some people came and bought the house, I signed a lot of papers and a corps of removal men came and took our stuff away. I can't pretend that I didn't know what was happening, but I can clearly recall, exactly three years ago today, waking up in a strange house in New Hampshire, looking out of the window and thinking: What on earth am I doing here?

I really didn't want to be there. I had nothing against America, you understand. It's a perfectly splendid country. But this felt uncomfortably like a backward step – like moving in with one's parents in middle age. They may be perfectly lovely people, but you just don't want to live with them any longer. Your life has moved on. I felt like that about a country.

As I stood there in a state of unfolding dismay, my wife came in from an exploratory stroll around the neighbourhood. 'It's wonderful,' she cooed. 'The people are friendly, the weather is glorious, and you can walk anywhere without having to look out for cowpats.'

'Everything you could want in a country,' I remarked queasily.

'Yes,' she said and meant it.

She was smitten, and remains so, and I can understand that. There is a great deal about America that is deeply appealing. There are all the obvious things that everyone always remarks on – the ease and convenience of life, the friendliness of the people, the astoundingly abundant portions, the intoxicating notion that almost any desire or whim can be simply and instantly gratified.

My problem was that I had grown up with all this, so it didn't fill me with quite the same sense of novelty and wonder. I failed to be enchanted, for instance, when people urged me to have a nice day.

'They don't actually care what kind of day you have,' I would explain to my wife. 'It's just a reflex.'

'I know,' she would say, 'but it's still nice.'

And of course she was right. It may be an essentially empty gesture, but at least it springs from the right impulse.

As time has passed, much of this has grown on me as well. As one of nature's cheapskates, I am much taken with all the free stuff in America – free parking, free bookmatches, free refills of coffee and soft drinks, free basket of sweets by the till in restaurants and cafés. Buy a dinner at one of the local restaurants and you get a free ticket to the cinema. At our photocopying shop there is a table along one wall that is cluttered with free things to which you can help yourself – pots of glue, stapler, sticky tape, a guillotine for neatening edges, boxes of elastic bands and paper clips. You don't have to pay an extra fee for any of this, or even be a customer. It's just there for anyone who wants to wander in and use it. In Yorkshire we sometimes went to a baker's where you had to pay an extra penny – a penny! – if you wanted your bread sliced. It's hard not to be charmed by the contrast.

Much the same could be said of the American attitude to life, which, generally speaking, is remarkably upbeat and lacking in negativity – a characteristic, I regret to say, that I tend to take for granted here, but am reminded of from time to time in Britain. The last time I arrived at Heathrow, the official who checked my passport looked me over and asked if I was 'that writer chap'.

I was chuffed, as you can imagine, to be recognized. 'Yes, I am,' I said proudly.

'Come over to make some more money, have you?' he said with disdain and handed me back my passport.

You don't get much of that in the States. By and large, people have an almost instinctively positive attitude to life and its possibilities. If you informed an American that a massive asteroid was hurtling towards Earth at 125,000 miles an hour and that in twelve weeks the planet would be blown to smithereens, he would say: 'Really? In that case, I suppose I'd better sign up for that Mediterranean cookery course now.'

If you informed a Briton of the same thing, he would say: 'Bloody typical, isn't it? And have you seen the weather forecast for the weekend?'

To be sure, America's relentless optimism can seem a touch simplistic at times – I'm thinking, for instance, of the evident conviction among nearly all Americans that if you watch your cholesterol levels, exercise regularly and drink bottled water you will live for ever – and I can't pretend that I want to spend the rest of my life around it, but it has a certain refreshing aspect that I am pleased to enjoy for the time being.

I asked my wife the other day if she would ever be ready to go back to England.

'Oh, yes,' she said without hesitation.

'When?'

'One day.'

I nodded, and I must say I wasn't as filled with despair as I once would have been. It's not a bad place, all in all, and she was certainly right about one thing. It is nice not to have to watch out for cowpats.

Now please – and I really mean this – have a nice day.